AF646725

ESSENTIALS OF PRACTICAL JOURNALISM

By the same Author

—*Hand Book of Journalism and Mass Communication*
—*Media and Society: Challenges and Opportunities*
—*Media Policy and Nation Building—Select Issues and Themes*
—*Translation of Two AMIC Publications (in Hindi)*
—*Press Systems in SAARC and Role of Media in National Crisis*

About the Author

Dr. Vir Bala Aggarwal is a senior researcher and academic, had a brilliant and scholastic career in Master of Journalism and Mass Communication and B.Tech. (Printing Technology). She has also acquired post-graduation in Economics with a brilliant record. Her doctoral thesis was in the area of Mass Media.

She started her career at Panjabi University, Patiala and then went to *Punjab State University Text Book Board,* Chandigarh as a Publication Officer. In 1986, she joined Himachal Pradesh University Shimla and established the deptt. of Journalism and Mass Communication where she is presently the chairperson of the department. She has co-authored a text book titled *Handbook of Journalism and Mass Communication* with Prof. V.S. Gupta.

Earlier she brought out five books. She worked on the translation project of *Toyota Foundation, Japan.* In 2001 she organised a National Seminar and brought out a book on the seminar papers titled: *Media and Society: Challenges and Opportunities.*

Dr. Aggarwal has participated and presented papers in national and international seminars and has published about 30 research papers in journals of repute, some of which have been included as articles/chapters in various books.

She has been a visiting fellow to many universities in the country. She is also associated with University Grants Commission for multifarious educational activities. Dr. Aggarwal is also a member of national and international organizations.

ESSENTIALS OF PRACTICAL JOURNALISM

Dr. Vir Bala Aggarwal

*Chairperson, Department of Journalism and Mass Communication,
Himachal Pradesh University, Shimla*

CONCEPT PUBLISHING COMPANY, NEW DELHI-110059

Cataloging in Publication Data—DK
Courtesy: D.K. Agencies (P) Ltd. <docinfo@dkagencies.com>

Aggarwal, Vir Bala, 1956-
Essentials of practical journalism / Vir Bala Aggarwal.
p. cm.
Includes bibliographical references (p.)
Includes index.
ISBN 8180692515

1. Journalism—India. I. Title.

DDC 079.54 21

All rights reserved. No part of this work may be reproduced, stored in a retrieval system, or transmitted in any form or by any means electronic, mechanical, photocopying, micro-filming recording or otherwise, without the prior written permission of the copyright owner and the publisher.

ISBN 81-8069-252-3 (PB)

First Published 2006

© Author

Published and Printed by
Ashok Kumar Mittal
Concept Publishing Company
A/15-16, Commercial Block, Mohan Garden
New Delhi (INDIA)

Phones : 25351460, 25351794
Fax : 091-11-25357103
Email : publishing@conceptpub.com

PREFACE

When I authored my first text book *Handbook of Journalism and Mass Communication* with Prof. V.S. Gupta, I received a overwhelming response throughout the country. The result was that within three years three reprints came out. A well known journalist and media academic remarked, "This is one of the best books as it covers almost all the aspects on Mass Communication". Another senior academic, unfortunately no more, told me that during his teaching assignment at Tezpur University (Assam) he taught entire advertising from my book. The postive response that I got from a wide readership across the country has encouraged me to write its companion volume *Essentials of Practical Journalism* which was not included in my previous book.

This book has been written so as to conform to the course contents of Journalism and Mass Communication of Indian Universities and is designed to fill a gap due to the lack of an appropriate text book on the subject.

Efforts have been made to acquaint the readers with the nuances of the changing trends in journalism. Most of the examples given are from a large number of newspapers and magazines, mostly Indian so that the reader/student gets a complete picture of the practical exercises.

Written in a clear, simple language, this book, I hope, would be useful to those who want to take up journalism as a career. The book takes care of the varied aspects of journalism ranging from writing to editing, from ethics to laws, from print to broadcast, and much more.

The book has been divided into eight sections. Section One: *Introduction to Newsroom* includes chapters on *nature of news, newspaper—its organization and working,* and *newspaper designing, layout and make-up.*

Section two is on *Basic Skills* and includes chapters on *editing news, structure of news story, elements of good writing, interviewing,* and *finding sources* for writing news story.

Section three deals with *Basic Journalism* and has chapters on *how to report speeches, press conferences and meetings.* This section also explains *how to cover stories related to accidents, disasters and obituaries.* Likewise it also discusses *service and civic journalism.*

Fourth Section is on *Specialized reporting* and has been designed to include chapters on *investigative reporting, development reporting* besides *sports, business* and *online reporting.*

Feature writing, editorial writing, book review and art appreciation are given in section five of the book.

A journalist/student must be conversant with *ethics and press laws* which form the subject matter of section six.

Section seven deals with writing for *broadcast news* and section eight with *news agencies* and *feature syndicates.*

A significant feature of the book is the compilation of *Annexures* painstakingly undertaken for supplementing the information included in the text. The *Glossary* which appears at the end of the book has been compiled to include terms related to the subject. Exercises/questions given at the end of each chapter will help the students in evaluating themselves about their understanding of the given topic.

While writing this book, I have tried to consult all the relevant material that I could lay my hands on. I have tried to illustrate various points with the latest examples from newspapers and magazines. My debt of gratitude is therefore so large that it is impossible to acknowledge all cases of direct and indirect influence. The ideas of leading scholars and researchers who have been active in a number of academic fields have been incorporated so as to enrich the contents of the book.

Though every effort has been made to acquaint the readers with practical journalism, yet hands on practice is must for joining this field.

I hope that the book would be a step forward in the better understanding on the subject.

Suggestions for improvement of the book are welcome and shall be incorporated in the forthcoming edition/s.

Vir Bala Aggarwal
email: virbala.aggarwal@rediff.com

ACKNOWLEDGEMENTS

This book has grown out of my numerous visit to many universities in India as a visiting fellow. My interaction with students and teachers gave me insight to the requirements of the students of Journalism and Mass Communication. This helped me a lot in writing the book in a way so as to be useful to the students and teachers of journalism. I wish, therefore, to gratefully acknowledge my deep gratitude to:

— Prof. L.R. Verma, Vice-Chancellor, Himachal Pradesh University, Shimla for his encouragement and insipiration to write this book.

— All the media professionals, faculty members and students of my department who supported me at every step.

— All the research fellows working under me for their timely help.

— Mr. Ashok Mittal, the publisher for his keen co-operation and interest in bringing out this publication.

— My children—Kunal and Medhavi who are always a source of inspiration.

— My husband Mr. A.B. Aggarwal whose creative and emancipated thinking provided much of the content of the book.

Vir Bala Aggarwal

CONTENTS

Section VI
Ethics and Press Laws

Section VII
Broadcast News

Section VIII
Wire Style

SECTION I

INTRODUCTION TO NEWSROOM

1

NATURE OF NEWS

News

The Chamber's Dictionary defines news as; information on recent event, and current affairs, a report of recent event, newly received information something and had not heard before. Likewise William L.Rivers in his book. *The Mass Media* says : News is the timely report of events, facts and opinions that interests a significant number of people. The key words are: "timely" and "interest a significant number". It is not enough that a report be only timely; if it does not interest at least a large majority of its potential audience, it is not news. Similarly, information that is only interesting cannot be considered news; it must have some element of timelines.

"When a dog bites a man, that's not news. But when a man bites a dog this is a news." It was John B.Bogart, city editor of the *NewYork Sun*, who uttered this famous dictum more than a century ago. To some extent it still stands true because news is often the account of something rare or out of the ordinary.

"News is what will make people talk." Charles Dana, editor of the *New York Sun* made that point, which certainly is true today. If you walked past ten houses of a street, and found number seven engulfed in a roaring fire, which one would you talk about when you go home? To a large extent, news is guided by human nature. You will not talk about house three or five where all is calm, when house seven is on fire. And it is human nature to wonder about the occupants. Did they get out safely? Will their house be saved? How much loss will they suffer? Do they have insurance? It's the kind of curiosity that produces good reporters.

In his book, *Professional Journalism,* M.V. Kamath has put together a number of definitions of News, some of which are:

"News is any event, idea or opinion that is timely, that interests or affects a large number of people in a community and that is capable of being understood by them."

"News is anything and everything interesting about life and materials in all their manifestation."

"What is new is news."

News has no geographic boundaries. News is always revealing. News is what interests people. News is news.

Spencer Crump describes news in his book *'Fundamentals of Journalism* as "News is the breakdown of human relationship and the occurrence of events which are unexpected and even surprising .

One text book describes the news as: The very 'new' element is inherent in news. All these exercises bring forth one definition which is very much functional, that is, Now is New is News.

"One big trouble with news is that nobody knows what it is. The other trouble is that nobody knows what it means." That remark came not from an editor but from a political scientist, Leon V. Sigal. He took an insightful excursion into the world of the working journalist and reached that conclusion in his book *Reporters and Officials,* published in 1973.

Today's definitions of news are no less bewildering. In 1982 the American Society of Newspaper Editors published a pamphlet entitled "What is news? Who decides? And how?" The definitions of news from some 500 journalists who responded to a survey ranged from "News is what raises eyebrows" to "News is what I want to write about."

The variety of definitions, the uncertainty, may sound ominous to the aspiring journalist, though it need not be. News is a recounting of the events, situations and ideas that human nature prompts us—as reasonably intelligent, alert, and interested people—to take note of. Or we would take note of them if we knew about them. The journalist's job is to anticipate the elements that audience will find interesting, important, and useful.

There are basically two types of news: *Spot news* and *diary news. Spot news* is the unexpected or unpredictable; disasters, plane crashes, train accidents, earthquakes, fires, inflation, drought etc. *Diary news* is news which can be anticipated : a speech by the Prime Minister, the visit of a foreign dignitary, the opening of a bank, inauguration of a bridge, etc.

Elements of News

Generations of journalists have used similar criteria in deciding the news value of each day's happenings and in deciding which news stories are more important than others. All such decisions take into account the audience for which the news is intended because no audiences are identical. Most of them probably differ substantially from you in background, interests, age, education and outlook on the world. Therefore what seems interesting or important to you may not be viewed that way by your readers. People are more concerned about things that affect their lives directly. A big part of the journalist's job is figuring out what these things are and what the effects may be.

Newspapers and broadcasters study their audiences regularly for guidance. The most common tool used in such studies is the survey, which can reveal not only the characteristics of the people in the audience—including age, sex, background, education and income—but also what kinds of news these people need and want. Another research tool being used with growing frequency is the 'focus group'. This differs from the survey in that small groups of people are engaged in detailed discussion rather than having many people answer brief questionnaires. The two approaches can be used together to information that is both broad and deep. Knowing your audience is essential in making news judgements.

Some of the important criterion for judging news value are:-

Timeliness

One of the significant elements of news is timeliness. News has to be new. The event itself may not be new but the discovery of it may be. News, like fish, can go stale quickly. Therefore, with news, the fresher the better. Reporters and editors, newspapers and broadcast stations, compete to be first with a big story.

Timeliness is not everything, though no print reporter can hope to compete with broadcast colleagues in sheer speed. If an event is important enough, the broadcaster can be on the area with in minutes. Tomorrow's newspaper won't be until tomorrow.

So newspaper and magazine journalists have come to concentrate less on the 'when' of a story and more on the 'why' and 'how.' Though they still want to cover the story in the next day's or next week's issue, these reporters and editors look less at the clock and more at the content. Often, both reporters cover as many details of an event as possible under the pressures of the clock, and then—a few hours or days later- return with a backgrounder, analysis that puts those details in context and explains what they mean.

Proximity

The geographic nearness or distance of an event can make a story more or less attractive to the reader. People like to read about what is near to them. Proximity means news happens close by readers and viewers want to learn about their neighbourhood, town, or country. All other things being equal, news from close to home is more newsworthy than news from a foreign country.

A train derailment in England for example, is less likely to be reported than a similar derailment in your country. Similarly a tragic auto accident in your local area will receive attention because people are familiar with the terrain and may even know the injured.

In a weekly or regional newspaper the factor of proximity may narrow the scope of stories holding readership attention. Editors may emphasize articles regarding nearby schools, universities, colleges, hospitals, police stations and political events, knowing they are meaningful to readers, while occurrences a few miles away are meaningless.

Prominence

"Names makes news," goes the cliche, still, happening that involve well-known people on institutions are likely to be interesting even if not important. Stories about well-known people have a higher readership than those about persons in the lower rank. The more important a person, the more valuable, he or she is as a news source. Thus, activities of the Prime Minister, President and other heads of the country attract tremendous media attention. In addition to political leaders, the activities of sports and entertainment figures are also deemed newsworthy. Even the prominence of infamous has news value. The past lives and recent exploits of many criminals are frequently given media coverage.

Impact

Another important criterion for determining news value is impact: how many people an event or idea affects and how seriously it affects them determine its importance as news. So does the extent to which the information may be useful. For example, if a university announces that tuition fees will be doubled due to curtailment of funds by UGC (University Grants Commission), there are consequences for prospective students, society, the faculty, and a community whose economy may be geared to the education. A bus strike may affect not only the students and commuters but also the supply and prices of vital goods.

The weather report, for example, snow in Shimla, will affect the supply of essential commodities, fuel consumption, environment and leisure activities. News of medical or scientific achievements is of great consequence because of the hope they offer.

News of nuclear war will create impact on its readers throughout the world. Similarly terrorist activities in a country will have its consequences in that particular country.

Conflict

Most reporters spend most of their time covering conflict—whether wars, politics, crime or sports. Conflict is both a contributing and a complicating factor in news. Usually present, it is often hard to understand and harder to describe.

Nearly every story on each of our front pages is a story of conflict. The murders and manhunt are the most graphic. Conflict is a central feature of most news. Sometimes it is physical, as in war or sports. Sometimes it is more subtle or sophisticated, political conflict falls into this category, though it may lead to physical struggle, social and economic conflict may also produce bloodshed, though most often they too are fought with words.

Mankind's relationships seem to be bound with conflict and competition. These elements are found in court cases, winning scholarships, awards for pictures, prizes for outstanding journalists, and a host of other daily activities.

One of the important functions of journalists in a democratic society is to make complex events understandable. Reporters must translate jargon into standard English and try to get at real causes and real effects. The pursuit of this unquestionably worthy goal can, however, produce questionable results.

Often some of the important stories of conflict are also the most complex. Sometimes, it is difficult to know even what the real questions are. The answers usually are far from simple. Sometimes there are no answers, or none we can discover.

It is therefore, important that you seek to understand the nature of the conflict you are covering. It almost certainly is more complicated than is apparent at first glance. It is vital, too, that you avoid oversimplification while seeking clarity. Clarity leads to understanding; oversimplification makes understanding impossible.

Disaster and Progress

Two important news values, disaster and progress, are at opposite ends of the scale. With human psychology as it is, disaster or bad news usually triumphs over progress or good news. When an earthquake rocks a place, for example, as was in Gujarat, newspapers devoted pages to stories and pictures describing the loss of lives and property. An explosion rips a building, and readers eagerly consume the news stories detailing the tragedy. By contrast, plans to build an over-bridge or flood control project rates relatively small space and only passing reader interest. One factor, of course, in many 'good news' stories is the lack of human elements that help develop emotional involvement.

The 'bad' news, unfortunately usually outdraws the positive in exciting reader interest. While the public complains that editors overemphasize news with negative or violent overtones, few people would bother to read the publication that failed to print the news of society's efforts and failures in minority relations, war and peace, fighting poverty, or slowing the crime rate. Few people will read the article on how the community welfare organization uses contributions to help the needy, but virtually all readers will eagerly consume details of how the agency's trusted executive embezzled funds. The article reporting how someone provided parties for disabled children will rate little space or readership compared to the story situation involving a person in sex crimes.

Readers expect the news of tragedies, disasters, violence, and breakdowns in human relationships.

Journalists, too, wish the world was filled with good news and their audiences wanted to hear about it.

Human interest

These are stories that arouse some emotion in the audience's stories that are ironic, bizarre, uplifting or dramatic. Typically, these items concern ordinary people who find themselves in circumstances with which the audience can identify. For example, the story may involve a child's unusual pet or a senior citizen's success in a field usually reserved for younger people. Journalists classify such situations as 'human interest' stories, even though all stories presumably are of interest to people.

The 'human interest' category covers several subjects that may lack story elements such as prominence, real consequences, disaster, or conflict. The story situations are worthy because they deal with such elements or youth or senior citizen's, pets, adventure, attractive girls or women, the problems of disease or poverty, overcoming handicaps, romance, strange places or merely unusual people. Another term which can be used for these stories is 'feature' stories.

These stories often are timeless and can be held with the photographs that usually accompany them until the newspaper has the space to display them properly.

In addition to these seven traditional elements of news value, there are other things that influence what information gets published or broadcast. Most journalists agree that economics plays a large role. First, some stories cast more to cover than others. It is cheaper to send a reporter or a camera crew to cover Municipal Corporation meeting team than to assign a team of reporters to investigate Municipal Corporation corruption. The latter would require a long time, extra resources, extra personnel and patience. All of which costs money. Some news operations might not be willing to pay the price for such a story or conversely, after spending a large sum of money pursuing a story, the news organizations might run it, even if it had little traditional news value, simply to justify its cost to management. By the same token, the cost of new technology is reflected in the types of stories that are covered. When TV stations went to Electronic News Gathering (ENG), stories that could be covered live became more important. In fact, many organizations, conscious of the scheduling of TV news programmes, planned their meetings and/or demonstrations during the newscast to enhance their chances for live TV coverage.

These traditional criteria for judging what is news and what is not continue to be applied by print and broadcast journalists alike, but the range of issues and events to which the criteria are applied is broadening significantly. Creed Black, then President of the American Society of Newspaper Editors, wrote in 1988.

If we can believe what we tell each other at our seminars and conventions, most American editors now agree that 'news' is no longer just an account of what has happened since yesterday's paper was published. Underlying trends, particularly in the area of social changes, also claim and deserve our attention. Most of us would also agree, however, that we don't do as well as we should in identifying and reporting these trends. The traditional patterns of covering and editing the news are strong and old habits take time to break.

Categories of News

Generally, news can be categorised into two broad categories:

1. Hard news
2. Soft news

Hard News

These stories make up the bulk of news reporting. Hard news consists of basic facts: Who, What, Where, When, How. It is news of important public events, such as government actions, international happenings, social conditions, the economy, crime, environment and science. Hard news has significance for large number of people. The front sections of a newspaper or magazine and the lead stories of a radio or TV newscast are usually filled with hard news.

There is a standard technique used to report hard news. In the print media, it is the traditional inverted pyramid form. The main facts of the story are delivered in the first sentence (called the lead) in a unvarnished style. Less important facts come next, with the least important at the end. This structure aids the reporter (who uses it to compose facts quickly), the editor (who can delete the last few paragraphs of a story to make it fit the page without doing wholesale damage to the sense of the story) and the reader (who can tell at a glance if he or she is interested in all, some, or none of the story). This format has been criticized for being predictable and old-fashioned. More literary writing styles have been suggested as alternatives, but the inverted pyramid has survived and will probably be around far into the future.

In the broadcast media, with the added considerations of limited time, sound, and idea, the inverted pyramid format is not used. Instead, broadcast reporting follows a square format. The information level stays about the same throughout the story. There is usually no time for the less important facts that would come in the last paragraphs of a newspaper story. TV and radio news stories use either a 'hard' or a 'soft' lead. A hard lead contains the most important information, the basic facts of the story. For example, "The state Govt. has rejected a plan to build over bridge." A soft lead is used to get the viewers attention; it may not convey much information. For example, "That proposed over bridge is in the news again." The lead is then supported by the body of the story, which introduces new information and amplifies what was mentioned in the lead. The final few sentences in the report, can be used to personalize the main point, introduce another fact, or discuss future developments.

Of course, the writing style of broadcast news is completely different. The writing is more informal, conversational and simple.

Soft News

Soft or feature news covers a wide territory. Features may not be timely or have much importance to the lives of the audience. The one thing that all soft news has in common is that it interests the audience. Features typically rely on human interest for their news value. They appeal to people's curiosity, sympathy, skepticism, or amazement. They can be about places, people, animals, topics, events, or products. Some stories that would be classified as soft or feature news might include the birth of a kangaroo at the local zoo, a personality sketch of a vice-chancellor of the university.

Features are entertaining and the audience like them. The techniques for reporting features are as varied as the features themselves. In the print media, features seldom follow the inverted pyramid pattern. The main point of the feature is often withheld to the end. Other features might be written in chronological order, others might start with a shocking statement such as, "your secrets just might kill you" and then go on with an explanation, "If you have a medical problem, you should wear a Medic-Alert bracelet". Still other features can be structures on the question and answer format. In short reporters are free to adopt whatever structures they think is suitable.

TV features are more common than radio features. In some large TV markets, one or more reporters may be assigned to cover nothing but features. Almost all stations have a feature file where story ideas are catalogued. If a local station does not have the resources to produce local features, there are syndication companies that will provide general-interest features for a fee. Broadcast features also use a variety of formats. Humorous leads and delaying the main point until the end sometimes work well. Other times a simple narrative structure, used in everyday story telling will be quite effective. The interview format is also popular, particularly when the feature is about a well-known personality (More in the feature chapter).

Exercises

1. Locate a 'human interest' story in the paper.
2. Using your regional newspaper, select examples of stories evidently used because of the following news elements; (a)Prominence (b) Conflict (c) Disaster (d) Proximity.
3. Identify the news elements in a day's news items.
4. Collect material for as many fresh human-interest stories as you can. Select the best among them and prepare them, as they should appear in a newspaper.
5. Are there any reports, which carry obvious contradictions? Cut them out and paste them. Write down against each the errors that it carries.

2

NEWSPAPER

Its Organization and Working

Daily newspaper, particularly a big daily, is a complex team-work. Although the hierarchy is well coded and the reporting authorities are well-defined. Since the actual challenge before them is to bring out the newspaper in time, one has to work in close cooperation with the others, at times even cutting across the lines of hierarchy.

No two newspapers are organized exactly alike. Large dailies with large staffs obviously operate differently from small ones with small staffs. There are enough similarities. They generally have a publisher who presides over the entire newspaper operation but usually concentrates on financial matters. He or she sets the paper's editorial policy and is responsible for the tone and overall personality of the newspaper. The *four main departments* at most newspapers are:-

(a) Editorial
(b) Advertising
(c) Circulation
(d) Printing

Figures 1, 2 and 3 are simplified departmental charts for a typical newspaper. The figures reflect the historical fact that news and opinions are kept separate. The editorial columns contain opinion, while the news columns contain objective reporting. Now we will discuss the working of all these four departments separately.

Editorial Department

The role and responsibilities of the members of a newspaper editorial department depend on its administrative structure. This, in turn, is determined by the number of staff members employed. Newspapers and

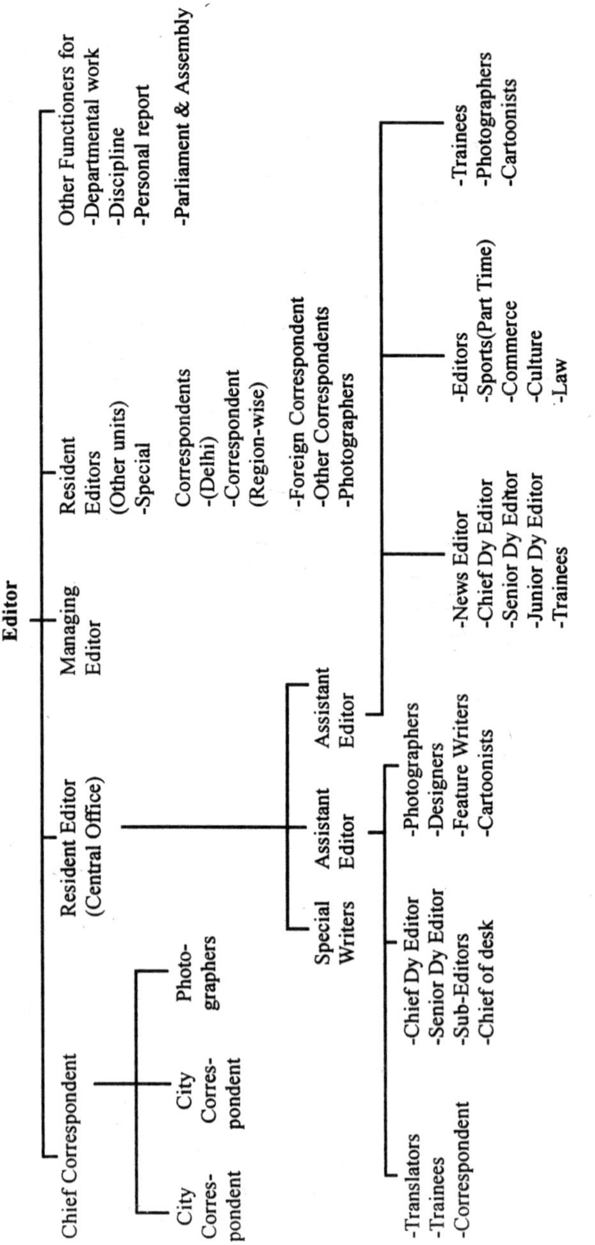

Fig. 1: Organisational structure in editorial department.

Source : Kothari, Gulab, *Newspaper Management in India.* Netherlands : Intercultural Open University, 1995

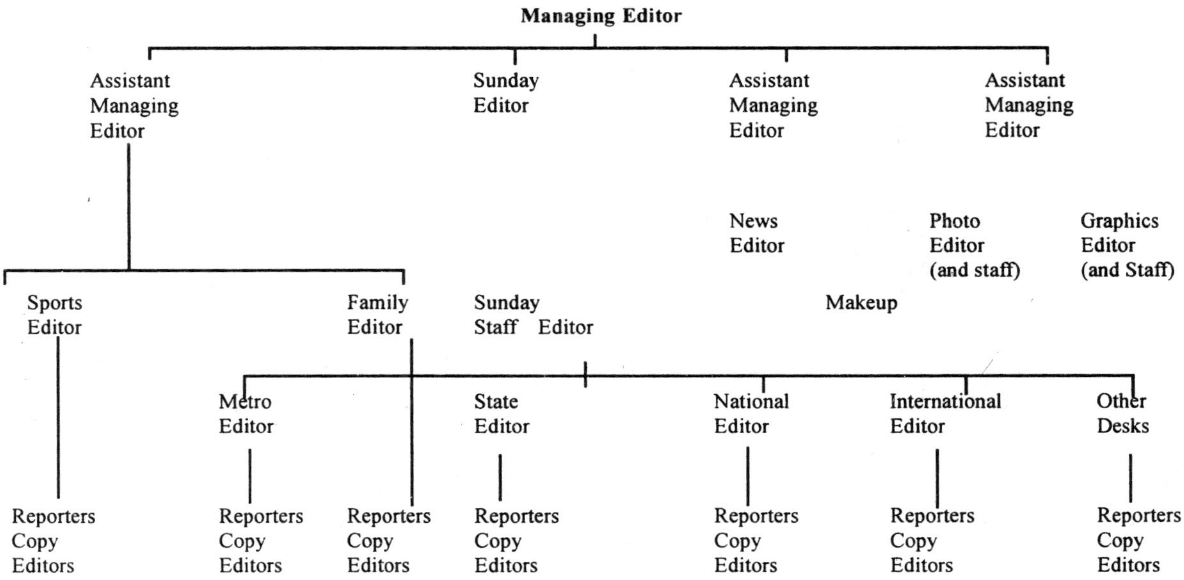

Fig. 2: Typical news room organization of the metropolitan daily newspaper.
Source : Brooks, Brian, S. *et al.*, *'News Reporting and Writing*, New York : St. Martin's Press 1988.

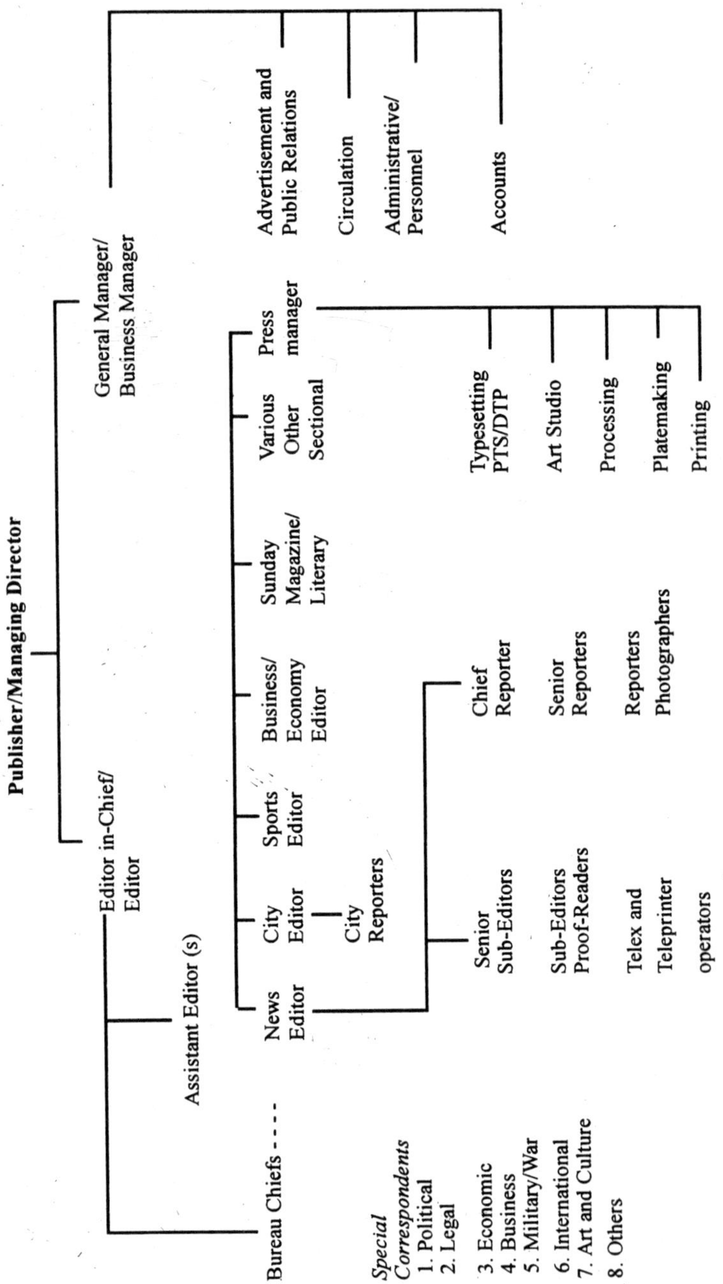

Fig. 3: Publishing/Managing Organisation of metropolitan daily newspaper

magazines have different structures. Since a newspaper has to be produced every day, it calls for speedy work with more persons working in it than in a magazine which may be weekly, fortnightly or monthly. In publication houses which bring out a group of newspapers and magazines, the chief editor is the one who is responsible for the total policy of the publishing house. Though individual editors are free to express their opinions and to adopt attitudes, the chief editor has to bring in a community of approach to avoid direct personal criticism by editors of one another. He is the link between the management and editorial departments. The term Chief Editor has come into vogue only recently in India. In west, Editor-in-Chief is often known simply as the editor. In cases where newspapers are published from different centres, the chief editor is one who has a number of resident editors each incharge of the edition coming out from that particular city. *The Indian Express, The Times of India, The Statesman, The Hindustan Times* all are chain newspapers with resident editors for particular editions.

The main functions of the editorial department are:

— Gathering of news
— Macro and micro selection of news and features
— Editing of news and features
— Interpretation of news
— Selection of lead articles
— Editorial writings

Working of Editorial Department

Editor

The editor holds the key position in the newspaper organization. He is responsible for the editorial content of the newspaper including everything from comics to news stories to editorials. *Basket and Sissors* have succinctly remarked that *"the editor is a diamond cutter who refines and polishes, removes the flaws and shapes a stone into a gem. He searches for ills in copy and meticulously scans the product for flaws and inaccuracy, even searching for the maximum power of words."** Unless somebody works as a reporter, he will have little contact with the editor. The editor's influence is exerted through those who report directly to the editor, usually the managing editor and the editorial page editor.

* Floyed K. Baskette and Jack Z. Sissors, *The Art of Editing*, New York; MacMillan Publishing Co. Inc, 1977. p. 4

The editor of a newspaper alone cannot handle the editing work. He is therefore, assisted by a number of persons such as: special correspondents, principal correspondents, resident editors, managing editors, assistant editors, news editors, reporters, sub-editors, and other functionaries like photographers, cartoonists and feature writers etc. In fact, the editor is the captain of the team. He guides those working under him and is aware of their talents and makes the best use of their abilities. His main concern is to get material from the assistant editors in order to fill up the editorial page. A good editor of a newspaper is aware of the scope and interpretation of news. He takes keen interest in the presentation of news and is aware of the details of important happenings. He keeps track of the readers' requirements. He influences people to strive willingly for mutual objectives. The editor gauges the public mind to give his ideas and opinions on current issues to maintain cordial public relations.

He is also responsible for day-to-day review of the newspaper. Such a review is done in meeting which is held every day by the editor. It is during these meetings that a decision is taken on editorials, comments, standard of news, its presentation and placement, news in competing papers, allotment of work, arrangement of photographs, correction and denial of news, etc.

In a modern newspaper organization, the editors have to work in accordance with the views and established preferences of newspaper management. His views on particular subjects or issues, and his policies are also reflected in the editorials. *Denis* states, "Reporters may then deliberately or unwittingly slant their stories to fit those policies. Failure to do so might slow promotion, or even put a journalist on the unemployment line. The extent to which formal and informal controls can influence the individual's work varies with the structure of the organization. Often the debate between news and business values hinges on the belief that when news organizations worry too much about profits, they court consensus in their communities and avoid controversy, which is the essence of news". *Bailey* bristled at "the growing tendency to encourage, in fact, to require, editors to become businessmen to be part of a 'management team' to concentrate on things that involve business rather than journalism".*

---

* Charles W. Bailey, Exit Lines from a Minnesota Editor, *Washington Journalism Review*, February 1983, p. 14-15.

News Editor

The news editor in many ways is next to the editor. Although the editor has assistant editors working under him, the most important work in the newspaper is done under the guidance of the news editor. If the editor represents the conscience of a newspaper, the news editor is its eyes and the ears. The manner of news coverage is directly linked with the philosophy or the policy of a newspaper. This is where a news editor becomes a partner with the editor.

The news editor is not only responsible for all the news that appears, but also has to deal with other aspects of obtaining news and use of news. This job is not just that of a senior journalist guiding other journalists. It involves a great deal of administration, for he has to arrange duties, leave and assignments for the staff under his control.

The news editor decides the timings of the newspaper's 'city' edition, which is intended for the city in which it is printed and the other the 'dak' edition, meant for distant places. In order to ensure that everything goes according to schedule, the news editor also keeps in touch with the printing section.

He lays down, precise instructions for the chief sub-editor in charge of an edition, giving details of what the important reports are, what items are likely to come and what possible use to make of them. Of course, the chief sub-editor is the ultimate arbiter, of the actual shape the edition will take. He has to ensure that the pages are finished in time and there is no delay on night shift, every minute is precious, since modern machinery prints at a fast pace. Even a delay of five minutes can mean a delay in printing thousands of copies.

The news editor is aware of what is happening. He remains in touch with the office from home, during the night. When he hears anything of importance over the radio or through other source, he checks up whether the chief sub-editor has received it or not, and what use is being made of it. Although the chief sub-editor and the sub-editors are actually engaged in bringing out an edition, it is the news editor who is the captain of the team and the ultimate responsibility is his.

Bureau Chief

The Bureau Chief is stationed at the head-quarters. Working with him is a team of reporters, many of whom are veterans in the field. He decides on their regular duties and the special areas to be covered by them. The Bureau Chief ensures that nothing is missed. He decides which of the many happenings in the city should be reported. His office is flooded with invitations for press conferences, public addresses, agitations and strikes. Government handouts, press notes from publicity agencies are received by him. The Bureau Chief judges all these and decides which are important for his publication. At the same time, he is expected to pitch in as a reporter when something important is taking place, or when work is heavy.

He has to retain contact with various sources of information, cultivate new contacts and yet keep his distance. Many temptations in the form of facilities, gifts, even money can come his way. He has to remain aloof from all these. He has to keep himself abreast of all happenings by constant reading, and be fully aware of what rival newspapers are doing.

Special Correspondents

These are regular employees of a newspaper or an agency, sent to their places for full time reporting work. They cover special areas in the capital of the country. They attend Parliament sessions, remain in touch with government sources or cover other special areas. The most glamorous job is that of the *Foreign Correspondents* who are stationed in different parts of the world.

Reporters

The newsroom staff member with whom the public is most familiar is the reporter, who indeed is the backbone of editorial operations. Several types of reporters, or writers, serve on a typical staff. They include :

(i) The beat reporter, assigned to cover a particular 'beat' or place such as a police station, courts, hospitals, secretariat, educational institution or other regular source of news.

(ii) The general assignment reporter, who waits in the newspaper office for news breaks such as speeches, interviews with visiting celebrities, a development relayed by a beat reporter.

(iii) Special assignment reporters who may be given a specific assignment to conduct an investigation or develop a series of articles.

(iv) The rewrite reporter, whose duties include (a) taking notes from another reporter over the phone and writing a story, (b) rewriting another reporter's poorly written story, or (c) writing news stories based on material brought or sent to the office by a public relations department.

Let us take an analogy. If a newspaper is a building, then the editor is the architect. The reporter is the supplier of building material and the sub-editor is the building contractor. On the materials supplied depends the ultimate strength and durability of the structure.

The primary duty of a reporter is to remain objective in his reports, this reporting is not opinion writing. He has to avoid bias because he is only a recorder of events usually seen at first hand.

Though a by-line is given to special reports, it is still a good practice to avoid the use of the word 'I'. A reporter must have a detached view of things. He is reporting as a newspaperman and not as an individual. Sometimes he has to present other's opinions. In adding this, he must identify them clearly and use only those which are relevant to his report. When enough details are not available, there is the temptation to bring in unimportant information. This does not really help because accuracy is the keyword to whatever appears in a newspaper.

Liner

Liner lives in a small town, and is not a full-time journalist. While he pursues some other profession, he also sends reports to a newspaper which pays him on the basis of the lines of the news item published in the paper.

Stringer

The 'stringer' title comes from the old time custom of measuring a correspondent's total inches of stories with a string of a given length to determine his pay. Sometimes the term 'liner' and 'stringer' are used synonymously. He too is not a full-time journalist, but pursues the profession in addition to whatever else he is doing. Such a correspondent is given a retainer, a fixed amount to retain him for the newspaper.

The Columnist and Freelancer

The columnist and the free-lance writers are alike, in that they are not necessarily regular staff members of the publication. They retain their independent identity, and their writing is accepted on the basis of its suitability and quality. At times, their own personality counts. Often, a newspaper wants an article from a known individual without really being concerned about the quality of his writing. The fact that he is writing gives it importance enough to be published.

Almost every good newspaper has a column on the same subject written regularly by a single writer. It may be on sociological, political, and sports subjects, or from any other field. Such regular contributions are called 'columnists' because, in many cases, they occupy a set space in a column. The writer's style is known, the field of writing is predetermined and the author is a popular person. Kuldip Nayar became popular for his column 'Between the Lines' and Kushwant Singh for 'This Above All' in *The Tribune* and 'The Malice Towards All' in the *Hindustan Times*.

Columns have a by-line or a pseudonym and are written with a personal approach. The use of the 'I' is not taboo. Stylistically, a column is fast-paced and easy to understand. It can only be described as alive and gossipy. The writing is free and the outlook light. No restrictions are imposed and the statements are relatively free of editorial restraint.

A column can entertain, inform, enthuse and cajole. Since the author is identified, it is naturally opinionated. There is an unabashed exposure of ideas and points of view.

Working at the Desk

Sub-Editor

The Sub-editor is at the centre of all journalist activity. On him depends the ultimate quality and style a publication achieves. He polishes the story (sent by a reporter) for maximum readability. He deals with copy by eliminating errors and improving it without harm to the original matter or style of presentation. In cases of poorly-structured material, reshaping and rewriting has to be done.

He also writes headlines and carries out the policy of his newspaper or publication with regard to the material it contains. Reporters, half-joking and half-serious, often accuse sub-editors of a 'Wrecking' their stories. Sub-editors, in turn, with a mixture of humour and seriousness, frequently claim that they 'save the reporter's job' by making the proper additions or deletions on a story.

Both sub-editors and reporters can be alternatively right and wrong, and they must remember that they are working on a team to produce readable stories. Most reporter-sub-editor conflicts can be resolved by friendly discussions and a mutual understanding of the problems each job involves. If a real dispute should develop, it usually would be settled by an editor. Taking a correct decision would include the fact that journalists must accumulate considerable skill and experience before becoming sub-editors, and once in such a position they must retain the authority to make decisions to be effective.

A sub-editor must have following qualities:

- Acquaintance with important happenings, particularly in the areas where his publication is read, is important for the sub-editor.
- Awareness of all events elsewhere, people's way of thinking and their attitudes are also essential.
- He should have 'jack of all trades.' He should know geography, history, human nature and life styles and possess an uncommon degree of common sense. In the numerous stories that he has to scrutinize, there is every possibility of factually incorrect information creeping in. Therefore, he has to be alert about it.
- He should also know the basic structure of the Constitution, the major laws in the country and the laws applicable to the press.
- His other qualities also include awareness of literary trends, books, magazines and their critical appreciation, and familiarity with public tastes, particularly in comparison with the newspaper's attitude towards them.
- He must be willing to work at odd hours, because night duty is an important part of his functioning.

The ***duties of a Sub-editor*** *are as under:*

1. The primary function of the sub-editor is to check errors of grammar, capitalization, punctuation, abbreviations, spellings and style. These are adjusted to the style observed by an individual newspaper or publication particularly those regarding capitalizing, spelling, punctuation and abbreviation in which consistency has to be maintained. The desk man has to bear these in mind when he is editing the copy. Errors of fact can creep in because either the reporter or the writer has made a genuine mistake, or is careless. Well-trained reporters keep

errors to the minimum. If the reporter continually makes the same errors, sub-editor must gently advise him. He can refer to books like who's who, encyclopaedias, telephone directory, dictionaries, historical studies, government list, or almanacs.

2. He checks the article for facts and logic. While the sub-editor relies on the reporter's ability and skill, he also uses his own memory to ascertain whether familiar names are used correctly and draws on his knowledge of many subject areas to determine credibility.
3. Having taken care of this, he runs his eye through the copy again to improve its structure. It is not necessary to bring in construction changes always. The style of the newspaper plays no part in this; but if there is some confusion or fogginess to convey, the sub-editor has to remove it.
4. He has to take care of verbose phrases, substitute appropriate words with reference to the context of the material, he is dealing with and give it a direct approach. Sometimes, however, doubts seize him with regard to the intention or the motivation of the author. He is not sure what the writer is trying to convey pertinent facts are missing in the story, or if important information is 'hidden' toward the end of the article when it should be near the lead. At this stage, it becomes necessary for the sub-editor to refer the copy back, and if necessary he can be asked to rewrite his copy.
5. Sub-editor must note any parts of stories that may contain libel, and query the reporter or chief sub-editor to determine whether consideration has been given to these points. When material is obviously libelous, sub-editor deletes the references immediately.
6. When the story is roughly grasped, its important points understood, suitable headline is given. Suitability is determined by the importance of the story, the newspaper's policy with regard to the stress that it can permit on certain types of stories.
7. After deciding the headline, he indicates the size of the type to be used and whether the headline will be one, two, three, or more columns wide. While this information is frequently given by the chief-sub-editor, the decision may be made in situations where sub-editors design specific pages.
8. The sub-editor must be on guard against items which are patently absurd, irresponsible, improper, cheap and stall. Publicists and press agents in the performance of their normal duties try to

> sneak in propaganda material. The sub-editor should be almost above them. It is his job to keep free publicity and suspicious material out.

In the ultimate analysis whatever appears in the newspaper is the responsibility of the sub-editor. The blame or credit should go to him.

Advertising Department

Newspapers derive their revenue from two sources: advertising and circulation. Advertising provides 75-80 per cent of the total revenue while circulation accounts for about 20-25 per cent. Hence advertising department is the most important department. As such, the work of collection and publication of advertisements becomes crucial in a newspaper organization. This department must constantly strive to improve the advertising service and increase the advertising volume because rising costs of newsprint, competition among newspapers and the threat from satellite television have greatly affected the financial status of the newspaper industry.

Advertising revenue comes mainly from three sources:

(i) Display advertising
(ii) Local or causal advertising
(iii) Classified advertising

Display advertising

Display advertisements may have few words, much blank space and often an illustration of the product.

They draw strong attention value and high legibility because of the conspicuous arrangement of contents—large or bold face type, attractive illustrations, colour and other devices. Display advertisements are charged is terms of column centimeter on page. Extra rates are charged for the use of colour. While an open rate is charged for single insertion, usually lower rates are offered to advertisers who plan to run a series of advertisements in the newspaper over a period on contract basis.

Newspaper advertising is usually sold by the publisher on a *run of paper* (ROP) basis, ROP means the advertisement will be placed in the position in the paper that is most suitable and satisfactory to the publisher. Thus the newspaper does not make a commitment as to the exact placement of the advertisement. However, certain advertisers prefer 'special position' of the advertisements in the newspaper. Newspapers charge extra for preferred positions. Newspapers also charge extra for *split-run* service. The split run is the process by which alternate copies of the same newspaper are printed with different advertisements for the same product.

Local or Casual Advertising

Local advertising originates from local or regional advertisers on an irregular basis to announce some special event such as a sale, opening a branch, starting a new business or introducing a new service or product in the area. Casual advertising may also come in response to special supplements a newspaper or some other organisations initiate.

Newspaper advertising departments often help causal advertisers in writing or preparing copy and designing advertisements. These advertisers are often charged on individual basis.

Classified Advertising

Classified advertisements are published without any conspicuous display on specific pages of newspapers. With the passage of time, it becomes a convention for each newspaper to publish classified advertisements in a particular section. Classified advertisements are grouped by contents and contain diverse elements. They are set in small point size type. Headings and sub heads are set slightly in larger type sizes. They come from many sources and cover an extreme range of products and services. As the name implies, classified advertisements are categorised under small heads. For instance, advertisements such as 'Public appointments, Tender notices', 'Plot for sale', 'Accommodation wanted', 'Accommodation available', 'Lost and found', 'Tuition', 'Matrimonial', and many more. These advertisements are small and often require editing or rewriting since people who provide the advertisement matter are sometimes unable to state their requirements clearly.

The rates of these advertisements are quoted per word, per column, per line, or per column centimeter. The newspapers normally require such advertisements to be paid for in advance. Public notices, tenders and other statutory publicity by Government departments are usually published in the classified section to conserve space and minimise cost. Public notices and legal advertising are legally required to be published in newspapers and other media. They convey information to the public which is essential for the democratic functioning of Government and sound conduct of its business.

Functions of Advertising Department

Designing and Production

The general purpose of advertising is to attract attention, create an interest in the product or service advertised. It should create desirability to use among the users. Advertisements obtained from agencies cause no problem to the advertising department. However, for local and directly released advertisements, the department offers its services and expertise in preparing copy and layouts to produce the desired impact. In case advertisements do not produce the results advertisers expect, the newspaper will be blamed for lacking advertising potential and the advertisements released in it will be considered a waste.

Billing and Collection

Preparation of bills and collection of payments from advertisers is an important function of the advertising department. Payments for classified advertisements are usually received in advance. Payments for those released by agencies accredited to INS become due only after 75 days. In some newspapers, billing and collection may be an integral function of the department, while in others this may be left to the accounts department. In either case the advertising department should be aware of the credit worthiness of its clients.

Dummy Preparation

To prepare a dummy edition means to plan a blueprint of an advertising and/or editorial contents of a publication. Elements are only sketched or miniature layouts are prepared. No proofs or pasting are involved. Dummy preparation, which finally ends in giving the ratio between editorial contents and advertising space also begins with the determination of approximate space to be allocated to the two elements. While a newspaper is supposed to be the first of all a vehicle for conveying news, how much news and the number of pages to be published in an edition are normally decided by the volume of advertisements rather than the amount of news available. After the advertising department has made its claim, the editorial department is notified of the number of pages planned and the size of the newsreel available to it.

For advertising department, dummy preparation provides a way by which it can blueprint the exact location of every advertisement instead of the leaving that important function to the composing department. By doing this work itself, the department is able to rotate the page positioning of advertisers in a planned way. It guarantees that advertisements of competing advertisers will not appear on facing pages. The dummy system places responsibility on the editorial department for the choice and positioning of all reading matter directly in the hands of editorial staff. Hence dummy system provides a means of planning an edition in a controlled and orderly fashion.

Circulation Department

Circulation means the number of newspaper copies sold and paid for. It is the foundation of a newspaper's success: it is the basis of all revenue. It is true that newspaper sales account for less revenue than advertising, but circulation is the force that makes the advertising pay. More the circulation more will be the advertising. Without it, there would be no advertising. Circulation also is a measure of the newspaper's service. Greater circulation gives the evidence that the newspaper is fulfilling its obligations to the community. Frank Thayer has rightly stated, *"Circulation is a channel through which the results of essential newspaper objectives are tested. Circulation is a gauge to measure newspaper effectiveness. When circulation is impaired, publishing hazards tend to be multiplied and intensified".*

Role of the Circulation Manager

The accomplishments of the circulation department depend greatly upon the energy, far-sightedness and ingenuity of the manager. Because there are so many details to be handled in developing circulation, it might possible for the circulation manager to create an unnecessarily expensive and cumbersome operation but if his horizon is wide, he can organize the circulation department to maximum capability. To some degree at least he should assume the following roles :

- He should be top executive, concerned with overall results of a highly specialized business.
- A sales manager, capable of directing a large sales crew.
- An auditor with a sound knowledge of bookkeeping and billing.

- A credit manager who will watch all accounts closely to determine the amounts of credit to be extended and when dealers should be changed and accounts closed.
- A traffic manager who knows the schedules and rates of all type of transportation because newspapers employ every means possible to provide prompt delivery to their readers.
- A public relations person capable of adjusting complaints and handling difficult situations.
- An all around advertising and sales promotion expert.
- A social service worker who could understand the community.
- A practical newspaper person who knows the problems faced in the mechanical, editorial, news, advertising as well as in the circulation department.
- Efficient, experienced enlightened, sincere, hard-working and intelligent personnel.

Variable Factors in Determining Circulation

No department of a newspaper runs more risk of getting off balance in its workflow than the circulation department. The paper must be delivered at homes at regular hours each day and it must be in good order. Circulation volume must rise continually or at least remain stabilized at a profitable level.

The following factors have a great bearing on circulation:

Population

No doubt more the population more will be the circulation, but the size of the population does not always determine the volume of circulation. Some communities with small population have newspapers with large circulation, and some communities with large populations prove to be poor newspaper receivers. This can only mean that internal population conditions as well as population numbers have a strong bearing on circulation.

Education

The enrolment of students in institutions of higher learning has increased. The opening of new fields of learning, rapid advances in all phases of science, better methods of teaching, and greater expenditure on education have all contributed to greater eagerness for information and wider and more intensive reading of newspapers.

Social Conditions

Shifting tides of urban renewal, population mobility, sub-urban flight and other sociological factors directly affect circulation. Whether such conditions are localized or national in scope, newspaper management is obviously challenged to cope in ways that call for resourceful and innovative approaches to the problem at hand.

Functions of Circulation Department

Circulation department of a newspaper establishment is akin to the marketing department of a business or industrial establishment. Its activities may be classified as follows:

Packing and Dispatch

As the newspaper comes out of the press, arrangements must be made to pack them as quickly as possible in packets for dispatch to sales agents. In packing care has to be taken that they reach the agents without damage or delay. Mistakes in counting papers or addressing packets would result in inconvenience to both agents and readers and also mean some extra costs for the organization.

Transportation and Distribution

Since the newspaper has a very short life, the speed with which it can be distributed become critically important. The circulation manager has to co-ordinate various modes of transportation so that the daily could reach the readers in the shortest possible time. Public transportation system is not dependable. Depending on the geographical area to be covered, and the number of agents to be served, each newspaper has to work out its own transportation network in determining the distribution in the minimum possible time.

Relationship with Agents

The agents are the most important persons for circulation department because they come in direct contact with the readers and are aware of the likes and dislikes of the readers. They also know about the position of other competing newspapers because they are in direct touch with the readers. They can be extremely helpful to know the response of the readers about contents of the newspapers, price of paper, timely supply of newspaper etc. Gulab Kothari suggested it, therefore, becomes important to motivate the agents and hawkers through higher commission, conveyance facilities and many more.

Subscription

This section usually deals with the distribution of newspapers sent by mail. Some subscription copies may also be distributed through agents. The subscription section receives advance payment for a newspaper for a definite period. Posts and telegraphs department provides concessional rates for dispatching the newspapers to any part of the country or to a destination beyond its borders. Trilok Sindhwani states, *"The cost of distribution of newspapers rises progressively because of increased cost of freight and incidentals. Sometimes it is only through a subscription service that a newspaper can be supplied economically to readers far from the centre of publication."*

Collection of Sales

The main responsibilities of the circulation department are selling newspaper, delivering it timely and collecting its revenue. Although these functions are distinct and separate, they are closely related. Efficient collection is one of the key factors in building a list of permanent subscribers. If the paper is delivered by independent contractor, its proceed is collected on dual system. The contractor collects it from the customers and the newspaper collects it from the contractor. Circulation revenue therefore, forms a vital component of the cash flow and total revenue recoveries.

Print Order

The number of copies to be printed of each edition is usually determined by the circulation department. This department prepares print order for each edition on the basis of supply requirements of agents, hawkers, subscribers, advertising voucher copies, complimentary copies and other requirements. This is a time bound operation and to a large extent establishes deadlines for other departments.

Supply of Information to RNI and ABC

To supply information to the Registrar of Newspapers of India (RNI) and to the Audit Bureau of Circulation (ABC) is a statutory obligation. These are the accounting organisations which audits and accredits circulation of daily and periodical newspapers.

Promoting Circulation

Building, maintaining and promoting circulation are the primary functions of the circulation department. Without it, advertising would suffer, thus loss of revenue. Circulation can be promoted by giving inducements to the new subscribers, distributing free supplements, reducing advertising rates and by prize winning contests, etc. Quick and timely supply of the paper at the desired place also help in building circulation.

Production Department

The Production department as its name implies, is responsible for transforming the creative work of reporters, editors and advertising sales people into the finished product—the newspaper. Mainly, press manager heads this department. Since most dailies use cold type methods (where molten metal at the temperature of 750° F is not used) the arrangement of this department has changed markedly over the last few years. The major sub-divisions of the production department are the composing room, where types and pages are assembled or set either by old methods—like hand composing, linotype, monotype, ludlow or through computer and photo type setters. The plate making department where plates or surfaces are prepared to be mounted on the machines to reproduce the printed pages, and the press room itself where ink actually meets paper on letterpress, offset and on graver machines.

Large newspapers may subdivide these departments further: Regardless of the newspaper's organization, all the functions mentioned are vital on producing a newspaper from the weekly to the largest daily. At the outset, we will discuss how the matter is composed what are the various techniques of typesetting—traditional and latest and then how the printing is done from the composed matter. What are the various methods of printing? Plate making will be taken up along with each printing process.

Typesetting Techniques—Traditional

Barring a few illustrations photograph line drawing and so on, newspapers, magazines and books primarily provide text or reading matter and this text is arranged in headings, sentences, paragraphs, news stories, articles and chapters etc. For the purpose of printing this text is to be composed or set correctly by assembling type characters or slugs of type characters in proper order. The technique of assembling type characters for the purpose of printing process is called 'typesetting' or 'composing.'

Before the invention of printing calligraphy was the conventional method of writing or preparing books and other documents by hand. After the invention of printing the art of calligraphy has been used for preparing master plates for lithography offset process of printing particularly for Urdu, Persian and Arabic publications. Readable and legible types for these languages are not forthcoming. Accordingly the whole reading matter is written down by hand either on a sheet of paper or on a plate. Urdu newspapers and magazines accordingly use calligraphy as the standard type-setting technique.

Methods of Composition

There are two general basic classifications or methods of composition hot and cold type. It is significant that the development of these methods paralleled the development of what has come to be called the 'information explosion.' For more than four hundred years after Gutenberg, all composition was done by hand. Hot metal composition was introduced late in the nineteenth century. But in this era of 'information technology' man's knowledge has multiplied many times. Computerization has made composing an exciting process that offers considerable scope for 'playing around' creatively. This is a giant leap forward from the days of hand composing when individual type characters were picked up from pigeon-hole cases, assembled into words and justified into columns, used for printing and then laboriously redistributed into the case for later re-use.

Hot-metal Composition

Hot metal composition is the setting type characters cast in metal. Such type may be pre-cast metal and assembled by hand called 'Hand Composing.' More commonly such composition is done by machines which manufacture type as they are operated either as a line of words called 'slug' or as single letter. Like hand-set or foundry type, the faces of the letters cast on these machines stand in relief.

There are four kinds of hot metal composition machines: 1. The Linotype, 2. Inter type (together called line casting machines), 3. The Monotype, and 4. The Ludlow

Among all these machines, 'Monotype' is still used, the rest of other machines are rarely used.

The Line casters—Linotype and Intertype

Linotype machine was invented by *Ottmar Mergenthaler,* a German by birth, in America in 1885 and the *Inter type* was produced by *Herman Ridder,* publisher of the *New York Staats Zeitung,* and was put into operation at the New York Journal of Commerce in 1913. The *'Linotype'* and its substantially identical competitor the *Intertype* are mechanical type setting machines that cast lines of type characters as solid metal slugs. These machines were universally used for setting newspapers. The range of type sizes available on slug casting machine varied according to their models. The normal range was 4½ pt. to 48 pt. The maximum width of slug which could be cast was 36 pica ems.

Functioning

This machine had 91 keys. The operator of a Linotype machine used to sit at a keyboard somewhat like a typewriter. Above the keyboard was magazine (means store) with narrow channels each containing a number of matrices (moulds) for each letter. When he touched the key a matrix dropped into an assembler. When the matrices for one line were assembled, the line was automatically justified and the metal was forced against the matrices casting a Linotype slug ready for assembly into columns and pages for the purpose of printing.

Uniform spacing in between the words and justification or alignment of lines on both sides could be achieved with the use of 'space bands' wedge -shaped strips of metal which were dropped in between the words. Just before a line was cast, these wedges were pushed up mechanically to fill up the left over space of the line by redistributing it in between the words. Above the magazine there was 'distributor' which used to send back the matrices in their own channel of magazine. The used slugs were remelted and the metal was re-circulated.

Merits

- It was fast and mechanical method of composing at that time. An average compositor could compose 1000 words per hour or fourteen newspaper lines per minute.
- It ensured optimum printing quality as fresh cast slug of type was used. The slug being a solid metal strip could withstand heavy printing pressures conveniently.
- It offered wide range of type sizes, faces and families.
- With special attachments headlines could also be composed in various sizes of types.
- It was cheap and needed one operator only.

Demerits

- Corrections were not only expensive but time consuming also as a line having even one correction had to be reset on the machine once again.
- These machines are now outdated, hazardous and unhygienic.
- Many occupational diseases (due to lead) used to occur.
- Lot of space was required to install these machines.

The Monotype

This machine was invented by Tolbert Lanston in 1886 in America. This machine is still used in some of the presses. It casts single type characters. The types are automatically assembled in lines which are duly justified both sides. The assembled lines are transferred, to a tray called galley one by one, forming a whole column of lines.

Functioning

In reality the Monotype has two machines, a keyboard and a caster. The keyboard operator perforates a paper tape, which is then fed into the caster. Holes in the tape represent the characters of the type font and the spacing required. The keyboard unit signals the operator when a line is ready for justifying and hyphenation. He codes the needed information into the tape. As the tape is fed to the caster it activates levers to move a matrix case backward, forward and side to side. When the proper character matrix is over the mould, molten metal is injected into the mat to form the character. Casting is done at a rate of 150 per minute, as each character is cast, it is pushed into position until a full line is formed. Then another is started.

The normal range of type sizes available on this machine is 4½ pt. to 16 pt. and the length of line is 60 Pica ems. or 10 inches. Larger type sizes can also be cast with special attachments.

The following advantages and disadvantages are worthy of attention:

Advantages

- The monotype offers greater precision in spacing between words so that composition is more eye-pleasing.
- Although cost of composition on an hourly basis exceeds that of line casters, it can prove less costly for complicated materials.
- Corrections are easy than in the case of line caster since the casting is not done by lines but individually, character by character.
- It ensures, fast rate printing quality because of new types cast for every job. These types after use are melted and type metal is re-circulated.
- It also offers a wide range of type sizes, faces and families for different types of newspapers.

Disadvantages

- Monotype is somewhat more expensive than the Linotype for routine work particularly in respect of its recurring cost. It requires two machines and two operators.
- It is hazardous process. Many occupational diseases may occur due to use of lead.
- Co-ordination between two machines also creates problem.
- Again, this is unhygienic method of typesetting.
- Lot of space is also required to install these machines.

Ludlow

This machine was introduced by *Washington I, Ludlow* in 1909 and later developed by *Willam A. Reade.* It is a semi-automatic machine. A compositor sets the matrices of type characters in a special 'stick'. The 'stick' is then fed into the machine which casts the slugs, trims it and delivers the same after cooling it. Spacing and justification are manual processes. It was widely used for casting display lines in sizes as large as

144 pt. The maximum length of the line is 27 Pica ems. or 4½ inches. For longer lines two slugs can be aligned in continuation. Although it is akin to hand composition it makes possible the use of fresh metal for each job printed.

Direct Impression / Strike on Composition

Special typewriters as *Varityper, Justowriter* and the *IBM Selectric* are available for this technique. The main characteristics of these typewriters are that justification of the lines on both sides is possible. They can produce composition that looks like type, provide different type designs and have proportional spacing.

Differences between Varityper, Justowriter and IBM Selectric Composer

Varityper: It requires two typings to achieve justification. Faces can be mixed, and a wide range of type styles is available.

The Justowriter: It consists of two units: recorder and re-producer. The former produces a perforated tape and hard copy-that is it also types on paper. The reproducer accepts the tape and automatically types justified copy in a type face. The reproducer has only one face in one size.

The IBM Selectric Composer: It requires two typings for justified copy. Different type faces are available, however, mixing is not feasible. An alternative use of the *selectric* is possible. Typing can be done on a recorder, which places the message on coded magnetic tape and produces hard copy. The tape is processed in a console which has been given type format instructions—line width, leading, and so on. The tape drives a modified *Selectric Composer;* If errors are found in the first typing, corrections are recorded on a second tape. Together with the original tape it is fed into the console, which merges them to drive the composer. The system is known as the MT/SC (Magnetic Tape Selectric Composer).

Type Setting Technique—Latest

Assembling the letters either by hand or by machines has become obsolete process of typesetting. Though some of the small printing presses still use it but in the modern newspaper houses all typesetting is done on computers. Even compositors who use to join the letters are not required. Stories are typeset by reporters themselves on VDT (Video Display Terminal).

VDTs are keyboards with attached television like screens that display information as it is typed. They are similar to the home computers. Indeed, many small newspapers have begun to use personal computers with specially designed software, or computer programs, to produce their daily and weekly editions. The terminal screen substitutes for the paper copy produced by a typewriter. Corrections, deletions and insertions can be made easily and quickly, and the writer has the advantage of working with clean copy at all times. There are no strikeovers or handwritten insertions.

As you strike a key, the character appears on the VDT screen, it is stored on disk by a computer, called a controller, to which the VDT is attached by cable. The controller allows you to store your story for later retrieval or to send it to your editor.

Learning to operate a VDT is more complicated than learning to use a typewriter because there are more keys with which to contend. In addition to the standard typewriter keyboard layout, there are keys to control *the cursor*, a rectangle of light that indicates your position in the text. Still other keys control computer functions such as routing the story from desk to desk. Despite the extra keys, VDTs usually can be mastered in a half a day. Newspapers often provide training for newcomers when they join the staff.

Once you master the keyboard and become accustomed to seeing your story on a VDT screen rather than on paper, the rest is simple. Mistakes can be corrected as you write simply by moving the cursor backward and striking over the incorrect letters. By striking the insert key, you can insert characters, words, sentences, paragraphs and even larger blocks of type at any point in the text. Sentences and paragraphs can be moved with similar ease.

Each terminal screen displays about 14 lines of text. As more space is needed, lines disappear from the screen but are stored in the memory of the computer. You simply depress a key to move forward or backward to any part of the story.

Once you are satisfied with your article, you can make a paper printout of it by depressing another key. The printout replaces the carbon copy produced in the traditional process and can be used for later reference.

With yet another key you transmit your article to the controller and assign it to the editor's queue. The editor can instruct the VDT to provide a *directory,* or index, of stories awaiting attention. When it is time to process your story, the editor simply strikes another key and the story appears on the screen for editing. The article moves from editor to editor in this way until finally it is sent electronically to the typesetter, much as a voice travels over telephone lines.

At some large newspapers, a copy of the story is filed in an electronic *morgue* or reference library. When newspapers have such a system, reporters may be able to call to their VDT screens background information from earlier stories. That eliminates the need to go to the morgue for a search through old clippings.

Printing Processes

Printing is the means of reproducing the written message for mass communication. It is an art or science producing large number of copies from an original. There are mainly three processes, which are used for printing of newspaper and magazines. These are as follows:

1. Letterpress process (Relief Printing)
2. Gravure (Intaglio)
3. Offset process (Planography)

Letterpress

Letterpress, also known as relief printing, is the oldest of the printing methods and probably the easiest to understand. When we print a woodblock or use a rubber stamp, we are printing by letterpress. The area to be printed is raised; when the surface is inked, the surrounding area, being lower, receives no ink and therefore does not print. The ink is transferred from the printing plate directly to the paper by means of pressure.

Because letterpress plates involve photography and engraving, they are called photoengraved printing plates (more often referred to as engravings, cuts, or zincs), and the platemaker is called an engraver. Letterpress plates are usually made of zinc, magnesium, or copper. Zinc is primarily used for line copy and coarse screen work, while magnesium is used where detail and wearability are important. Copper, which is easier to etch and work, is used for high-quality line work.

Plate Making

To make a letterpress plate, a photographic negative is brought into contact with a light-sensitive metal plate. The plate and negative are exposed to a light that passes through the clear part of the negative and strikes the plate. The exposed areas are light-hardened. The plate is then dipped into an acid bath. The hardened image area of the plate is impervious to the acid, while the remaining areas are etched to the desired depth. This leaves the image area raised and ready to be inked.

The plate is then "blocked", that is, mounted on a piece of wood or metal to make it type-high (.918"). After the plate is blocked, it is inked and a proof is pulled. A copy of the proof is sent to the client and the plate is sent to the printer.

Not all letterpress printing requires a printing plate. Type that is handset or cast can simply be inked and printed. If an illustration or halftone is to be combined with the type, then an engraving is made for that piece of art only. Most letterpress jobs are an assortment of type and engravings all "locked up" together on the press. An advantage of this system is that elements can be changed without the expense of having to make an entirely new plate.

There are times when the printer may wish to convert from one printing method to another. This is particularly common in cases where a job that was originally printed by letterpress is to be printed by offset lithography. In this case, the printing plates are converted to film from which a new plate is made.

In recent years a great number of jobs, especially newspapers, have been converted from letterpress to offset. This is not because of a lack of quality in letterpress printing but because of the time involved in plate-engraving. To counteract the flow of business away from letterpress to offset, the letterpress industry has developed the photo polymer direct relief (PPDR) printing plate. This is a photosensitive plastic plate which when mounted on metal can be used as a regular letterpress plate. The photo polymer plate drastically reduces the time required to make a letterpress plate, which is one of the major advantages of offset printing, while at the same time retaining the letterpress advantages of being able to use cheaper paper and ink.

Characteristics of Letterpress

* Capable of high-speed, high-quality printing of jobs of a variety of sizes in black and white and in colour.
* Consistent quality throughout run.
* Printing plates are generally more expensive than offset, but considerably less expensive than gravure.

* Capable of printing from handset or machine-set type as well as from original or duplicate printing plates.
* Duplicate plates are relatively expensive. The most commonly used duplicate plates are electrotypes, plastic plates, rubber plates, and stereotypes.
* Prints best on book papers. If half-tones are to be printed, the paper must be calendered or coated. Also, accepts papers of any thickness, from the very thinnest to cardboard, depending on the type of press.
* When printing from original metal type or engravings, any part of the job can be changed without the expense of having to make entirely new plates. This does not apply when printing from one-piece duplicate plates or from curved plates (rotary).
* Among the uses of letter press are short-run printing from type and engravings, jobs requiring numbering (tickets, forms, etc.); and imprinting, imprint changes, on-press die-cutting, slotting, perforating, embossing, debossing etc. Also used for fine long-run publication work where the cost of the press plates can be economically amortized over a number of printings.
* Proofing is relatively inexpensive.
* Lays down an ink film thicker than offset but not as thick as gravure.
* Requires a lot of make-ready time to compensate for the varying thicknesses of materials used: type, plates, engraving, etc.

Presses

There are three basic types of letterpress printing presses: platen, flatbed cylinder, and rotary.

Platen

A press in which two flat surfaces come together to make an impression: one surface holds the printing plate; the other, called the platen, provides the pressure necessary to make the impression on the paper. There are two kinds of platen presses: the platen *flat-bed* (which was the press used by Gutenberg) and the platen *clamshell* (also called a *jobbing platen*). The clamshell is still in use today, mainly in commercial shops for short-run jobs of stationery, business cards, etc.

Flat-bed Cylinder

As the name implies, this press consists of a flat bed, which supports the printing plate or type form, and a cylinder which replaces the platen in providing the necessary pressure. These presses are usually larger and faster than platen presses. Excellent for booklets, catalogues, etc.

Rotary

Unlike the platen and the flat-bed cylinder press, in which the type or engravings to be printed are flat, the rotary press has a curved printing plate that either fits on a cylinder or wraps completely around it. This permits printing at high speeds and is ideally suited to long runs of high-quality work. A rotary press can print from individual sheets of paper (sheet-fed) or from a continuous roll (web-fed). Other rotary presses, called *perfecting presses*, can print both sides of the paper at the same time.

Gravure

Gravure is the commercial form of intaglio printing. Intaglio is the second oldest printing process, dating back to 15th century Germany. The original process is very simple: the image to be printed is cut or etched into the surface of the plate; the plate is then inked and wiped clean, leaving ink only in the incised areas. When printed under pressure, the paper draws the ink out of the etched areas, transferring the image onto the paper.

Plate Making

Gravure is printed from either curved plates, designed to wrap around a plate cylinder, or directly from etched cylinders. Like letterpress plates, gravure plates are photoengraved; however, unlike letterpress plates, the area to be printed is lowered, not raised. To print, the entire surface of the plate is inked and then wiped clean with a flexible steel scraper called a "doctor blade, " leaving ink only in the etched areas.

The unique aspect of gravure printing is that all copy, continuous-tone and line, must be screened. *This includes type.* The screening process is much more complicated than that used for either letterpress or offset lithography. However, the purpose is the same: to break the image up into thousands of microscopic dots which when etched in acid become tiny cells, varying in depth and diameter. The tonal gradations of the printed image are determined by the depth of the cells: the deep cells hold more ink and therefore print darker tones; the shallow cells hold less ink and print lighter tones.

Presses

Gravure printing is done on a rotary press that is either *sheet-fed* or *web-fed* (rotogravure). *Sheet-fed gravure* is used most often for short runs and to reproduce works of art. The *rotogravure* press is designed to run at tremendous speeds and is ideally suited to long-run jobs such as mass-circulation catalogues, newspaper inserts, cigarette packages, postage stamps, etc. *Reader's Digest and National Geographic* are but two of the many national magazines that are printed with *gravure.*

Characteristics of Gravure

- High-quality, high-speed printing of black and white and of colour.
- Consistent quality throughout run.
- Richest blacks and widest tonal range of all the printing processes.
- Most economical for long runs at high speed (web-fed). However, with careful preparation and attention to detail, short-run jobs can be printed at a cost competitive with that of quality letter-press or offset.
- Plates or cylinders are more expensive than either letterpress or offset plates, but they last longer.
- Duplicate plates or cylinders are expensive.
- Capable of printing on a wide range of surfaces. Although the highest quality is attained on smooth or coated stock, gravure can also produce high-quality work on inexpensive uncoated papers. An example of this is the Sunday supplements printed by rotogravure (web-fed gravure).
- Corrections are expensive because a new printing plate must be made.
- Proofing is much more expensive than for either letterpress or offset.
- Gravure printing recognizable by the fact that the entire image areas is screened, including the type. For this reason, gravure printing is better suited to reproducing continuous-tone images

than to reproducing type (especially type with fine serifs or strokes and in sizes of less than 8 point).

- Able to most closely simulate the continuous-tone effect.

Offset Lithography

Of the three major printing processes, offset lithography is the most recent. It is a highly refined form of lithography invented in 1799 by a German named *Aloys Senefelder. Lithography,* which means "stone-writing," is based on the principle that water and grease do not mix but they repel each other. The image to be printed is drawn with a special grease crayon on a slab of highly polished limestone. The stone is then sponged with a solution of water, gum arabic, and acid. This solution is rejected by the greasy image areas and absorbed by the non-image area. When the stone is inked, the opposite happens: the ink, which is greasy, is accepted by the image area and rejected by the non-image area. To print the image, a sheet of paper is placed over the stone, pressure is applied, and the image is transferred to the paper. Properly prepared, a lithograph stone can produce hundreds of high-quality prints.

The commercial form of lithography is *offset lithography,* more commonly known simply as "offset." (method of transferring the image from the plate to the paper.) In offset lithography the flat stone is replaced by a thin, flexible metal printing plate designed to wrap around a printing cylinder.

Plate Making

The fist step in making an offset plate is to "strip" both the line and half-tone film negatives into their proper positions according to the mechanical. This makes up what is called a "flat." Before the actual offset plates are made, a photographic paper proof is made from the flat that shows the client the exact position of the elements. These proofs are called by various names, reflecting their general colour: Van Dykes, browns, silvers, blues, or salts. After the proof has been approved, the plate is made and the job printed.

Offset plates are made photographically. The plate, which may be aluminum, stainless steel, or a specially processed paper, is coated with a light-sensitive chemical similar to that used on photographic paper. The flat is brought into contact with the plate and exposed to a high-intensity light. The plate is then either processed by hand or put through an automatic processor where it is developed and made press-ready. (That is, the plate is chemically treated so that the image area will reject the water solution and accept ink and the non-image area will accept the water and reject ink.)

As the platemaking process for offset is much simpler than for either gravure or letterpress, the printer will very often make his own plates rather than depend on the services of an outside platemaker or engraver.

Characteristics of Offset

- Capable of printing jobs of a variety sizes in black and white and in colour at a relatively low cost.
- Requires more attention than letterpress or gravure to maintain image consistency throughout run.
- Printing plates are relatively inexpensive and require only a short time to make as compared with letterpress and gravure plates.
- Duplicate plates are inexpensive.
- Printing plates can be either negative-working or positive-working (deep etch); that is, made from either film positives or film negatives.
- Although the quality is highest on smooth or coated papers, offset can print effectively on rough-surface papers as well.
- Corrections require making a new plate, but plates are inexpensive.
- Proofing can be done either on the production press or special proofing presses. Proofing on the production press is expensive.

Presses

There is wide variety of offset presses available, ranging in size from small office duplicators to huge web-fed perfecting presses capable of printing an entire book in a single run.

All offset presses are of the rotary type and have three cylinders: a *plate cylinder,* around which the printing plate is wrapped; a *blanket cylinder,* onto which the image is offset; and an *impression cylinder,* which presses the paper against the blanket cylinder.

In operation, the printing plate first comes into contact with dampening rollers. These wet the plate with a solution of water, gum arabic, and acid. This water solution is accepted by the non-image area and rejected by the image area. Next, the plate is inked. The ink, repelled by the water solution in the non-image area, is accepted only by the image area.. The inked image is then transferred, or "offset," onto the blanket cylinder, which in turn transfers the image to the paper.

The reason the image is offset onto the rubber blanket rather than printed directly on the paper is because the offset plate is very delicate and the abrasiveness of the paper's surface would cause damage. In addition to extending the life of the plate, the rubber blanket, because it is compressible and conforms to the slightest degree of texture on the paper's surface, makes it possible to print on rough papers.

Digital Printing

Digital printing has revolutionized the printing industry. It has changed the production cycle and drastically shortened the turn-around time of a job. There are two basic approaches to digital printing: *Direct imaging or hybrid presses and digital toner-based printing.*

Direct Imaging Presses

Direct imaging presses are presses with a digital front end and a conventional ink based printing unit. Plates are imaged on press from digital data received by networking, essentially incorporating a computer-to-plate (C-T-P) unit within the press. There are several advantages to this type of press over a conventional press.

Advantages

- Because the plate cassette is mounted on the press prior to imaging, there are almost no registration problems.
- The system significantly reduces press make-ready time.
- The plate often uses waterless technology, which is more stable and allows greater ink densities than water based lithography.
- Material costs are competitive with traditional system, but the process saves as much as 60 percent in labour costs.

The main limitations of a direct imaging press is that duplex printing can be done only by the operator running the sheets through again with new plates and that once a plate is etched it cannot be altered. Although this technology does not allow for true variable data printing (VDP), certain types of versioning can be done by printing colour shells that can then run through a digital printer for personalization. Direct imaging presses are gaining in acceptance due to the fact that the back end is truly an offset press and provides quality output measurable against completely conventional presses, yet with a far faster turn-around time and less manual labour. There are predictions that by the year 2005 purchase of direct imaging presses may outnumber those of conventional presses.

Digital Toner Based Printing

Digital toner-based printing has truly caused a revolution in printing. Originally introduced in 1993, it has allowed "full-colour pages to be printed directly or remotely from digital page data with the ability to vary the information at every cylinder revolution."* (Landa-Indigo) Four-colour jobs can now be turned around in hours rather than days or weeks, and print runs of one are now possible.

Press Configuration

Different vendors have different solutions, but the two basic digital print imaging technologies used are **laser electrophotographic** and **LED electrophotographic**. Digital printers from companies such as Xerox and Canon use a digitally driven laser beam that reflects off a rotating prism to charge parts of the imaging drum. Toner powder is then attracted to the charged parts and subsequently transferred to the paper. Indigo, a manufacturer of digital printing presses, uses a liquid ink called ElectroInk rather than a dry toner. Charged ink is injected at the plate, adhering to any area with an opposite charge. This plate transfers the image to a blanket, which in turn transfers it to the substrate. When the ElectroInk contacts the substrate, it hardens instantly and peels from the blanket completely. This offers two major *advantages*. First, because the ink dries upon contact with the paper, dimensional stability is guaranteed. Most offset inks dry on the paper by absorption or **aerial oxidation**, which introduces moisture into the sheet or leaves a wet ink layer. When dimensional stability is assured, more accurate colour is possible.

The second primary advantage, which is also true for LED (light-emitting diode) electrophotographic imaging, is that no residual ink remains on the blanket after each rotation. In contrast, conventional ink splits between the paper and blanket and leaves a residue. The lack of

* Mr. Benny Landa, Chairman and Chief Executive Officer of Indigo Group.

residual ink also helps eliminate dot gain. Because unused ink does not build up on the blanket, halftone dot size is assured.

Implications of Direct Digital Presses

Before Gutenberg, there was **demand-based publishing**. In demand-based publishing, if people wanted and could afford books they looked for ones to purchase or paid scribes to copy them. Gutenberg created **market-based publishing**. Gutenberg's invention created a situation where the printer decided what to print, prepared many copies, and then sought to convince the market it wanted the product.

For the past 500 years there have been few opportunities for individuals to participate in a demand-based information environment. Someone else decided what to reproduce and distribute.

The introduction of DTP in 1984 was the first step toward individual control and access to focused information. The reality of a true digital press in 1993 took the next step toward these goals, and will continue to transform both the graphic arts industry and our daily lives.

Digital presses can be used to personalize every publication that comes to your home. Advertisers that sell products in your interest areas can purchase advertising space in your exclusive magazine or newspaper.

In the office community database management can be used to create one-of-a-kind reports, reference manuals, and information books for every employee.

Elimination of Traditional Bookstores

Bookstores sell books. They are everywhere when you walk in the door. Book lovers revel in the environment. However, even the most ardent book lover does not need 200 copies of the same book-one copy suffices.

Large bookstores are large because they need to shelve many copies of every title. If you do not come in and make a purchase then that storage space is wasted. Bookstores of the future may shelve only one sample copy of a work and print a fresh copy on a digital press when you have made your decision to purchase. Personalized information can be included in the copy in the process.

No Out -of -Print Books

Publishers only print and promote books that they can sell. If after the first year of publication, the buying population of a book dwindles, then the publisher stops printing and promoting that book. The book then becomes out of print and is only available through libraries, used bookstores, or from a friend.

With digital presses a book will never go out of print. Computer archives can store digital information and anyone can order one or many copies of any book, no matter its current status.

Mass Marketing Replaced by Personalized Marketing

Mass marketing involves sending millions of pieces of mail to millions of individuals with the hope of selling an idea, service or product to one or two percent of those individuals. With a direct digital press, every consumer can receive a different catalogue. It is now possible to deliver custom catalogues containing items the seller knows matches each buyer's personal interest.

In this example, the customer could program the digital press to deliver custom catalogues containing items it knows match your personal interests.

Virtual Elimination of Warehousing

Traditional printing relies upon economics of scale Companies order tens of thousands of copies of books, brochures, technical booklets, reference sheets, promotional items, and training manuals and store them for future use. The cost of warehouse space can be considerable, however.

All print storage space can be replaced by a digital press, computer memory, and a lot of blank paper. When a document is needed it can be simply ordered, printed, and delivered. Demand printing becomes a reality in this way.

Low Cost access to Quality Colour

Anyone with a computer and the right software can afford to prepare and create professional looking documents for personal use with digital printers. Small to medium business can print a variety of short-run promotional pieces at competitive prices and not have to store excess inventory. The ability to personalize a document with every revolution of the drum is already changing the face of advertising today.

Digital printing will have a significant impact on your life and career in printing.

Plate Making

After the copy has been shot and the film developed, you get a film negative. It is from this film negative that the printing plate is made. (Although printing plates can also be made from film positives we shall base our discussions only on those made with film negatives.)

All printing plates have one thing in common: the area to be printed must stand apart from the non-printing area. There are three basic ways to separate the printing area from the non-printing area: (1) raise the printing area. (2) lower the printing area, or (3) leave both areas on the same level and treat the plate chemically so that the printing area accepts ink while the non-printing area rejects it. These three ways form the bases of our three major printing processes: *letterpress, gravure, and offset lithography.*

Although there is a great deal of difference between letterpress, gravure, and offset plates, they are made in much the same way. In all cases the plates are made photographically by using a film negative, a light-sensitive metal plate, and chemicals.

Modern Technology Section

Newspaper technology is now almost all computer driven, and most publishers continue to automate their operations as new technology becomes available. Electronic pagination and page make-up of display advertisements with graphics have become a reality. Eventually, electronic make-up has eliminated typesetting on photosensitive paper and paste-up of mechanicals. This new system has made newspaper composition more flexible and cheaper. After making-up the pages, offset plates are prepared out of negatives of made-up pages.

As the plates are being readied, huge rolls of newsprint are threaded into the presses. The plates are then attached to the press, and the printing process begins. Finished and folded papers emerge from the press and are sent by conveyor belt to the distribution area. The distribution staff counts and bundles the newspapers and then hands them over to the circulation truck drivers, who then deliver them to newsstands and carriers.

Newspaper technology has also been at work on another messy problem for newspaper publishers ink-rub off. The tendency of newspaper ink to come off on hand and clothing is one of the principal reasons subscribers cancel. To attack this problem, many companies are experimenting with treated oil inks that adhere strongly to the paper and are less likely to darken fingers.

On the printing side, flexographic printing, a system that uses a plastic plate and has a device that controls excess ink, has been adopted by several papers. 'Flexo', as it is called, has the advantages of better printing quality, less paper waste and use of a water based ink that helps the rub off problem.

On another front, newspaper photography has been replaced by filmless electronic photography. Now the news photographers record pictures on videotape or with electronic cameras and transmit them via-modem to newspaper computers. An editor views the picture on a computer monitor crop it to fit available space, and adds a caption. The new system means no more silver-based film, darkroom and traditional photo morgue. Sony and Canon have developed the prototype for such a system. The Sony still video camera, for example, uses a floppy disk instead of film. Each disk can hold upto 25 images. The resolution is not yet as good as film but the pictures can be sent by phone lines or by satellite from the field to the paper where they are stored until needed. The whole process takes between two and three minutes compared with the hours previously necessary to physically transport the film back to the paper develop and print it. Wire services are also starting to use digital technology to transmit photos to their subscribers via satellite. Since each element of a picture is stored using a string of 0s and 1s, it becomes fairly easy to use the computer to edit, change or modify the photo.

Exercises

1. Invite an editor from a national newspaper to give a brief talk on the organization of his news staff.
2. Develop a news staff organization chart designed to make a regional or local newspaper operate with more efficiency.
3. Visit any national daily newspaper. Talk with staff members about how the staff is organized. Once you understand the system, draw an organizational chart for the news department.
4. Draw a copy flow chart that shows how copy moves from the reporter to the typesetter at the newspaper you visited.
5. Discuss with a newspaper librarian about the resources available in his or her library. If the newspaper does data base searches for reporters, describe how one reporter's news story was improved by using a search engine.
6. Discuss the characteristics of different kinds of advertising.

7. How does an advertising department function?
8. Circulation is the basis of all revenue. Comment.
9. What are the variable factors which have a great bearing on circulation? Elaborate.
10. Explain the various activities of the circulation department.
11. Explain the traditional methods of composition.
12. List the advantages of modern typesetting over the traditional typesetting.
13. How does relief printing process differ from offset printing process?
14. Explain the offset principle.
15. What are the main characteristics of rotogravure printing?
16. What advantages does a digital press have over traditional printing methods?
17. How does a platen press differ from a flat-bed cylinder press?
18. Why is the rotary press design efficient for printing?
19. List four characteristics of gravure that make it ideal for high-quality, long-run jobs.
20. What is the purpose of a doctor blade on a gravure press?

3

DESIGNING, PAGE-MAKING AND PICTURE-EDITING

Designing, layout and make-up of a publication are becoming increasingly important. Designers, in some newspapers, are highly paid professionals. Several magazines have picture editors at a very senior level. Photo-journalism is coming in its own. Since competition is very stiff, particularly in metropolitan towns, (Examples, Newspapers—*Hindustan Times* and *The Times of India;* Newsmagazines—*India Today, Frontline* and *Outlook*) lot of attention is paid to see that the product is attractive. Some publications have an art department, where experts and artists make-up special pages with the help of sub-editors.

Newspapers have started developing a personality of their own. In these days when a newspaper is considered a product, 'packaging' is becoming quite important so the importance of designing and lay-out cannot be ignored. Laying out pictures is in itself an art which calls for a high degree of aesthetics. Selection of a picture, its cropping, and size; placement within a page—all this is meant to get the maximum impact from the material available for the particular edition of the newspaper or a magazine. A picture should never be used as a filler. Some magazines like *Frontline* publish a number of pictures for each article. Sometimes picture features are brought out with a single theme; which serves to focus on a particular subject in depth. Several newspapers and magazines brought out picture features in their special issues on the 50th Anniversary of the Independence day of India, Kargil war, Godhra issue recently, Gujarat carnage, and now on tsunami waves.

DESIGN AND ITS IMPORTANCE

Design is not just the pattern or the style of a newspaper. It is the architecture on the basis of which the whole structure is built. If nobody had any preferences, any newspaper would have been good enough. But this is not so, every publication is designed, has a pattern of display which is followed almost religiously. Although contents go a long way towards creating a paper's reputation, its appearance cannot be ignored.

When we are enticed into buying a particular brand of perfume, it is not just because of the material inside. The shape and size of the bottle, smell, style and wording on the label are equally important, manufactures spend huge amounts to obtain the effect that will sell their product.

Design plays an important part in our routine life. We cannot conceive of any period in our life which has not been influenced by design in some form or the other. When you buy a TV or refrigerator, design is important, so also with other innumerable items of daily consumption.

A publication is not free from this. Deliberate attention is paid to planning a newspaper, deciding which item will appear in which position on which page and whether it will carry a figure or an illustration. Fitting all items into the limited space available for matter other than advertisements is not easy. All this is called the make-up design of a newspaper. Make-up is the sum or total of layout and designing of newspaper pages.

As a general practice in India, the chief sub-editor does this job. He plans the front page and sometimes under his guidance, the others do it. Since he is bringing out the edition, he ascertains how much space is available, allocates pages for sports, national , international, business and local news. He decides on the stories that are to be displayed prominently on each page, and selects the lead for the front page. Therefore the pages are designed. As the stories keep flowing in, they are given headlines according to the basic plan.

In the magazines, the sub-editors do not necessarily design all the pages, the help of experts is obtained because of large number of photographs and larger variations in heading styles. Moreover, magazines have more time at their disposal. Therefore, pages can be designed with greater artistic attention.

It is often debatable whether design is important or matter is important. Pendulum is always towards contents of a newspaper. Reports, editorials and the other material make only the soul of the newspaper and not the body, it is only the design which makes it. It must be stressed here that design is not the language itself. It is only a medium for journalism. News comes first, design follows to present it well, to make it acceptable. No matter how good a product is, if it is not made acceptable and attractive it cannot do much good, because few people will buy it.

Morning Versus Evening Newspapers

In general, morning newspapers have a greater depth of appeal than do afternoon newspapers. The more favourable deadlines and delivery times, along with their more affluent readers, help make morning newspapers more penetrating. Afternoon papers usually are designed to appeal to the newsstand customer. They emphasize stories expected to attract the casual buyer to a greater degree than do most morning newspapers. This emphasis is carried to the front-page make-up which is designed to 'stop' the prospective buyer.

More newspapers are sold from newsstands in the afternoons and evenings than during the mornings because commuters have more time to read, combining travel time with an evening at home. Afternoon newspapers or tabloids therefore employ more sensation both in material used as well as in make-up. They use large headlines which are meant to draw the attention of an onlooker even from a distance. They use darker and thicker types and the limited number of stories on page one, primarily because of display.

Designing a Page

Each page in a newspaper deserves consideration so that it will be artistic and pleasing to the reader. The ingredients for designing a page are basically photographs and type, all in varying sizes so that the make-up will create eye-appeal.

The use of photographs today is a highly important factor since readers are accustomed to visuals in magazines and on television. A good photograph, therefore, should dominate a page, particularly when the page contains no advertisements.

The Choice Areas

Surveys indicate that right-hand pages attract higher readership than left-hand pages because the public almost automatically look first at the former. The top of a page, whether it is on the right or left, commands more attention than the bottom. Editors regard the upper right-hand corner of the right page as the most choice, or the place where readers will look first.

Right Versus left pages

For artistic balance and for maximum use of the areas where eyes look first, editors often 'weight', or place the emphasis in the upper right hand half of the right page or in the upper left hand half of left hand pages.

Bottom of the page

On pages without advertisements, editors regard the bottom area as a place where considerable interest can be created. An editor frequently will balance the bottom with a good photograph or a large head stretching over a story covering several columns. This picture is usually placed in different columns at the top. This tends to prevent monotony for the casual reader, who subconsciously finds variety pleasing.

Principles of design and layout

Professor Roy Paul Nelson puts it, *'design principles serve the same purpose for the designer that grammar rules serve for the copywriter. These principles provide the guidelines for assembling the design elements in ways that are both pleasing to the eye and effective as advertising'.*

The basic principle of newspaper design, apart from making the product an attractive, saleable proposition, is to give the paper an identity; what kind of newspaper is to be produced and even what kind of readership is being sought.

In countries where there is wide selection of different newspapers, the person buying the newspaper can look at the shop counter where they are all displayed and take his pick according to the impression they make upon him, first appearances are very important. Though this consideration barely applies in many developing countries where there may be only one or perhaps two newspapers, the basic principle is still sound.

It is important for the newspaper to have a typographical identity. First it must be immediately recognizable for what it is, so that the reader comes to look upon it almost as an old friend. But it must also be flexible enough not to become a boring old friend. Almost as much as the quality of the contents of the paper is concerned it is this familiar identity which is an enormous aid to encouraging regular newspaper readers.

A newspaper must look like a newspaper and not like a train time table or a poster advertising of a cricket match. A properly designed newspaper will aim to draw the reader's eye from one part of the page to another in an orderly intelligent fashion. Readers should not expect to battle their way through a maze. The trick is to be attractive without being garnish.

The following principles of design and layout should be kept in mind while making-up the page.

Page Proportion

Page proportion is very important to all two dimensional graphic materials. One of the first decisions a designer makes is in selecting the most functional and attractive plan for the page. The basis for this selection depends on the amount of copy to be placed on the page and also upon the intended use of the material being prepared. Several page proportions are being used for example 3x5, 4x6 and 5x8 inches. Photographic enlargements are usually 5x7 or 8x10 inches.

The page proportion selected for the particular graphic layout can be reduced or enlarged by the diagonal line method. When the diagonal line is drawn through the intersection of the horizontal and vertical axes and extended through the opposite corner, one can select any width of page desired either smaller or larger than the original proportion measurement. The new width is selected and a perpendicular line is drawn from the horizontal axis to the diagonal line. A horizontal line is extended from the point of intersection to the vertical axis.

The 3x5 inch page proportion was used by the ancient Greek architects. They followed this ratio in designing the magnificent structures that have endured through the ages.

The square page is not usually used for two dimensional graphic materials. It is uninteresting to their eye because it does not suggest movement or change.

Balance

Balance is important in designing pages because, consciously or subconsciously, our sense of balance affects our reactions and judgements. Balance gives the page an equilibrium that is as reassuring to the reader as it is fundamental to the designer. An unbalanced page is an unstable page; the reader will have difficulty coping with it. A balanced page, on the other hand, is a harmonious page with which the reader can and will like to identify himself.

To achieve formal or symmetrical balance the elements of the page are centered horizontally and an equal amount of each major unit is placed on either side of the imaginary centre line. In perfect symmetrical balance left side of the page is balanced exactly with the right side of the page. For example, a two column 3.6 pt heading in columns one and two would be balanced by a two column 3.6 pt. heading in columns 7 and 8 and so on all the way through. Even pictures and boxes would be sized precisely and placed in symmetrical patterns.

Formal balance based on symmetry has virtually gone out of newspaper pages for one excellent reason: news cannot be manufactured to fit pre-determined pattern. The excitement of news comes from its unpredictability. To work out a symmetrical pattern and then look for news to fill it out will be like building a great dam and then searching for a river suitable to its size and scope. Make-up should fit news, not the other way round. The symmetrical route to balance is very simple. But it is abhorred by seasoned journalists because news never flows according to a formula.

To achieve informal balance, you do not have to mirror the pieces in size and shape from side to side and top to bottom. Instead you make sure that the sum of the optical weights are equal. Weight is nothing but the thickness or blackness of an element. In an informal balance elements are arranged according to the optical centre which is the imaginary centre line slightly 1/10 above the geometrical line.

The larger an element is, the more optical weight it has, but colour and shape affect optical weight as well. Colours weigh more than black or white space, black space weighs more than gray, and unusual shapes weigh more than ordinary shapes. Also, the farther an element is from the centre, the more weight it has.

There is no way these factors can be converted into mathematical calculations to yield a make-up pattern. There is no need either. What the page designer needs is to understand the logic of weights so that he may develop his aesthetic judgement regarding their positioning. For manipulation of weights in a page is what make-up is really all about. Anyhow informal balance is more popular and had been used extensively in designing pages.

Contrast

Contrast is the juxtaposition of dissimilar elements. It is the accentuation of an element in a page. Correctly employed, contrast contributes substantially to the attractiveness of a page. It indicates change or variety. In its absence all elements will look alike. It also helps emphasize stories and thereby guide the reader along the page. It is most important in headline typography. To differentiate different stories, it is necessary, variety of types may be used, otherwise one headline will merge with adjacent one, clashing with one another because both are in the same type face, same size and weight (weight here means bold or light face of a type)

In creating contrast, consideration should also be given to use of box items and graphics and illustrations, the interplay of heavy matter with empty spaces to highlight either news items or certain areas of a page, and to contrast them with others.

Hence contrast can be obtained by juxtaposing the three basic elements of make-up-type, graphics and white space or the dissimilar variations available within each element. Type placed next to a picture followed by type again is contrast. *Times Roman* used in one headline and *Universe* used in another headline is also contrast. Therefore, type-type contrast can best be obtained by alternating very heavy headline with very light headline. So is type-white space-type. More white space can be created between types. White space not only provides contrast, it also makes the types more legible and readable. Width, depth, design, size, weight are all aspects of type that can be used to obtain contrast.

But the degree of contrast obtained is important. A headline in *Times Roman Bold,* next to one in *Times Roman Medium* offers contrast in the strict sense of the word. Even layman can obtain very good type contrast in a page. This is to stick to the same type family. One great advantage of the English alphabet is that it lends itself to considerable variety within the same face structure. Indian languages also have been progressively achieving this. The variations are based on thickness and thinness as well as condensing and expanding to types. So we have *Times Roman, Times Roman Bold, Times Roman Extra Bold* and the Italics variation of each of these. Universe has a dozen variations.

Sometimes types families are deliberately changed in order to obtain contrast through a forced change of mood. This happens most often in pages set apart for special subjects such as sports, commerce and entertainment etc. A newspaper that uses *Times Roman* for its sports page, *Bodoni* for commerce page may switch suddenly to *Universe* headlines on its entertainment page. If done within limits, this can be a useful mood setter.

Unity

Page possesses a sense of unity when all the elements work together to form cohesive whole. Everything looks and sounds as if it belongs to the same page. Unity covers the way elements are laid out on a page as well as the character of the individual elements in the page, from the personality of the type used in headline to the background of a photograph or a cartoon used in a story.

Unity ties together the graphic elements of a two-dimensional layout. Elements should not appear crowded, but should have a "oneness" or a look of belonging together. Illustrations and type must be compatible and arranged in an order that complements each single element. Any switching of type families that interferes with unity cannot be good for the paper. This is why most papers stick to the safety of the same family. Departures should only be made when the designer is sure that the contrasting family picked by him matches the mainline family used by the paper.

*Eye Movement**

The habits of the reading eye have been extensively studied for the benefit of the make-up specialist. It has been established that the eye enters a newspaper page at the top left corner. The Americans call this the Primary Optical Area. After entry, the reading eye moves downward at a southeasterly incline until it reaches the bottom right of the page. The line from the top left to the bottom right is called the Line of Reading Gravity.

All this is merely a scientific way of describing practices which every reader of English and other left-to-right languages automatically follows while reading a newspaper. The make-up man analyses this eye behaviour to decide the way he should arrange his weights so that his page will be balanced and dynamic at the same time.

The point of entry at the top left explains why the day's main story, the lead, is usually at this corner. Only occasionally, for what is perceived as a 'change,' do subs place the lead at the top right corner. It is doubtful whether the eye really needs such change. Perhaps it will be better off if it is left to its accustomed entry point and line of gravity. American newspapers traditionally place the lead at top right—a deviation that must perhaps be attributed to America's distrust of all Leftist.

---

* *Courtesy:* George, T.J.S., Editing, New Delhi, IIMC.

Individual habits of course differ. There are any number of sport buffs who read their newspaper backwards. Elderly readers often start at the top of column 1, go to its bottom, then start at the top of column 2, work their way faithfully to the bottom and so on to the bottom of the last column, missing no word on the way. But, as in all scientific studies, we should not only go by the habits of the average reader, but accept them as the norm.

On that basis, it would be safe for a make-up sub-editor to visualize the reader's eye moving slowly from top left to bottom right and then taking one or two or three sweeps. It could make a loop towards the bottom left corner and then work its way against gravity to the top right; it could flip straight to the top right and then slide down a line of gravity to the bottom left; or it could swing in an erratic double loop from bottom right to bottom left and to top right.

A graphic approximation of these eye movements, as shown above, at once highlights the focal points of the page where appropriate weights will provide balance. Clearly the page has four equal quarters formed by a vertical line and a horizontal line intersecting at dead centre. Each quarter should be weighted appropriately.

But to do this mechanically would be to return to the days of symmetry. The modern trend is to alter the weights to suit the newspaper concept of balance. Thus the vertical line in the middle is only given notional recognition. Great importance is given to the horizontal line, the fold. Good layout men will never let the fold fall along a headline or the significant parts of a photograph lest they be disfigured by the ridge produced by the way the paper is folded after printing. 'Above fold' and 'below fold' are separate entities linked only by the unity of the total page. Balancing weights are distributed top to bottom, rather than quarter to quarter.

Sometimes considerations of balance take second place to the requirements of a strong focus. Especially on feature pages, the make-up editor may want to emphasise one overriding focal point, or simply provide an element of surprise. He can then use headlines, pictures or white space to achieve the desired effect. The drama of the focus may well camouflage the loss of overall balance in the page. This is the logic that operates on front pages when a narrow box goes on top of the page encompassing the primary optical area and the lead is placed below although it is weightier than all other elements on the page.

Layout

Layout is the device with which a newspaper achieves typographical dynamism and unity character. The secret of orderliness is layout. It is the art of arranging various visual elements to form newspaper page. Properly arranged, the elements will constitute an attractive layout. Badly done, they will present a jumbled page that puts off reader.

Layout is the spectacular side of a paper's personality that the reader sees. Because it makes the first big impact on readers for good or bad, layout is an aspect of newspaper work that engages the closest attention of editors. In other words, we can say that the layout is the master plan on which the make-up of a page is carried out.

In layout as in typography some in-built aptitude is necessary for a sub-editor to become an expert. Where none exists, extra effort needs to be put in so that one can develop a working understanding of what is competent in designing. Not everyone who looks at a tree can see its beauty. But if one knows that there is beauty in trees and then looks long enough and hard enough, one will eventually learn to see and enjoy the beauty.

Principles of Layout

(a) Never prepare a plan of the important pages without going through all the main stories and pictures.

(b) Each quarter of the page should have at least one good large headline.

(c) If there is a photograph at the bottom of the page it should be balanced by a bigger one at the top with a headline which is heavy.

(d) Advertisements can be balanced with photographs, box items or thick headlines.

(e) Give at least one dominating story with a large headline on each page.

(f) No photograph should touch an advertisement.

(g) Photograph in the exact centre should be avoided rather it should be given at the optical centre.

(h) A multi-column item should never be put immediately next to another double column or multi-column one. To avoid this, put a photograph or a single column top between the two. A box item also serve the purpose.

Purpose of Layout

The sole objective of layout is to help the reader to locate the news.The sub-editor should know what are the elements at his disposal to achieve the layout he wants. The elements that go into the make-up of a page and the headlines, blocks of body matter, pictures and other graphics, column rules or white space, and a fixed component in the day's advertising quantum on the given page.He must know how to use the elements he has to reach the make-up goal he sets himself. This is where expertise comes into play and the ability to choose wisely among contending schools of thought. Concepts about layout proliferate because of (i) changing standards of perception, (ii) the introduction of new technology, (iii) a paper's own background.

Steps in Layout

Thumbnail Sketches

Thumbnail sketches are simple idea sketches which help the sub-editor/ designer to obtain an attractive acceptable final print. Thumbnail sketches serve three primary purposes (i) They graphically preserve ideas, (ii) Visually portray ideas, (iii) choice among two three designs.Thumbnail sketches are prepared with the speed of brain.

Method of Preparation

(a) Prepare the pre-layout planning sheet and list the copy.
(b) Choose the final size of the printed product and plan to sketch the thumbnails 1/4 size.
(c) Use straight lines to represent type that is 12 points or smaller in size. Do not use lettering for the large or small type.
(d) Outline the space for illustrations or photographs. Within this space, sketch the illustrations or content of the photograph. Detail is not needed for thumbnail sketch illustrations or photographs.

It is important to sketch several ideas from which a final selection can be made. Preparation of many thumbnail sketches are extremely important. They serve as the foundation for the final usable printed material.

The Rough Layout

The second major step in layout is the preparation of a rough layout. This is an improvement or refinement of thumbnail sketch.

Purpose

The purposes of a rough layout are to

(i) force a selection of one of the several sketched ideas.
(ii) begin refining a specific idea.
(iii) provide a tangible item that can be studied and changed. Actually, a rough layout can be considered a predefined product.

Method of Preparation

Study the several thumbnail sketches that have been prepared.

Select the one that best presents the content of the final two-dimensional product.

Obtain a sheet of paper that will allow the layout to be drawn full size.

Outline the area that will be devoted to type and illustrations according to the thumbnail or combinations of them selected.

Sketch the illustrations within the outlined areas. They should be a higher quality and contain more detail than a thumbnail sketch illustration. The rough layout should reasonably resemble the finished product.

The Comprehensive Layout

The comprehensive layout is the most important step in the production of a printed work. It is the master plan or blueprint of the finished product, and therefore, its value cannot be overemphasized. After the designer made all decision, the comprehensive layout will contain all information needed to complete the printed product. It will guide specialists who will produce the final product.

Method of Preparation

Study the rough layout.

If the illustrations are in colours choose the colours and content for each. Use coloured pencils to represent the coloured illustrations.

Letter all type in the exact position desired. Make the type look like the actual kind.

Lines should be used to designate the correct position.

Draw the illustrations carefully in the correct position.

Block the space for the photographs, if they are used, and attach the glossy print if it is available.

Prepare an overlay sheet after all content has been placed on the layout.

Thoroughly review the layout. Be certain that you have included all copy and given full production information on the overlay sheet.

Hence the layout should be such that it permits last minute change without harm to the basic pattern. In newspapers, such flexibility is an important factor. Stories do not always shape out as expected. Their size may not be according to the space allotted; their importance may not be as thought earlier, or they may not fit into the association of the subject matter of other stories. A good sub editor bears these in mind and is able to make adjustments without disrupting the planned pattern. The soul of newspaper design is news and its communication to the reader. The approach therefore has to be communication oriented, not decoration oriented. Due to fast, technological developments, pages, these days are prepared on the computer itself with the help of Quark Xpress (a software programme for page making).

Types of Layout

Layout for a page is done with various styles. Since layout is the master plan on which make-up is carried out, you have to decide best layout among many, suitable for your work. A few types of layouts are being discussed here.

Top-and-bottom balance layout

In the style called top balance, attention is paid only to the top of the page whereas in the 'bottom balance' attention is paid only to the bottom of the page and the matter is allowed to flow conveniently on the rest of the page. In top- and-bottom balance the centre of the page seems to get ignored. The headlines, etc. are very carefully arranged all over the page except at the centre. As a change, this pattern can be interesting.

Off-balance layout

In an off-balance layout the page is divided into four areas. The only care taken is to have heavy material and light head lines in every area, but the heaviest item is always at the top. The placement of material within each area is not exactly similar in other areas of the page.

The broken page layout

The broken page layout needs great skill, although there is, planning, and the concept of balance is still at its base, headlines in a broken page are used or bigger items are placed ostensibly only to break the monotony and greyness, wherever it is needed to do so. Small items with heavy single column headlines are also useful for this.

Centre balance layout

This is opposite to the top-and-bottom balance layout. In this type of layout attention is drawn to the centre of the page and the centre becomes the 'heaviest' area. The front page of a newspaper can seldom be done this way, but it can be tried for an inside page with heavy advertisements.

Stepped layout

In 'stepped' layout stories are placed in such a manner as if they are stepping from larger ones to the smaller ones as in a staircase. This style is also known as 'the pyramid'. 'Heavy' headlines step down to 'lighter' ones as the bottom of the page is reached. It is not very easy to plan this type of page. When matter is large and a turn has to be avoided, it ends up by becoming an inverted pyramid.

Free-Style layout

Free-Style layout has no balance, no limitation of headline types and it seems to be just a matter of filling up the page. Even in this, care has to be taken that a sea of gray does not prevent in any part of the page.

Vertical layout

In 'vertical' layout matter generally runs in single columns down the entire page. There is not a complete absence of double columns or larger headlines, but most of the stories are run into single columns.

The photographs used are thin or narrow, received to one column size as far as possible. In double or larger size, they are not very deep. However, double column photographs are avoided if possible.

This is not a very popular layout as *Harold Evan* suggested in his book 'Newspaper design'. It is impossible to read long columns of texts on crowded buses and trains. He favoured horizontal layout.

Horizontal Layout

In horizontal layout, instead of running an eight inch single column story straight down one column, it is spread over four two inches pieces. Horizontal layout is opposite to vertical layout. In it there are mostly multi column headlines. The single columns are few, and the photographs, though not necessarily very broad, are certainly deep.

Hence, no newspaper follow the same pattern on every page. Often, individual pages have different patterns. Yet, the attempt is always to present a total personality, though sticking to fixed patterns for individual pages every day. At the same time care has to be taken to avoid exactly opposite layouts in the same issue. It would be a good practice to consult an artist who has specialization in layout to prepare ideas which can be practiced independently.

Make-Up

Make-up is the layout and designing of newspaper pages. In other words to arrange pictures and news matter in a page for maximum effectiveness is make up. Make up encompasses the choice of stories, size and styles of headlines, illustrations and their sizes and the relationship of these elements with each other.

Actually, layout is a trailer. It is rough plan of a page. Whereas make-up is the final plan. Make-up serves many purposes which are being discussed as follows.

Purposes of Make-up

- To ensure easy readability—a man in a hurry would prefer to read a page which is easily understood without having to read much.
- To identify the newspaper as different from its competitors.
- To attract the buyer so that he will be impelled to select one newspaper as more appealing over others.

- To emphasize through placement the relative importance of stories and photographs in the newspaper.
- To achieve variety and an artistic appearance for the newspaper, thereby relieving monotony.

While there are aesthetic principles in planning a paper, make-up keeps readership alive. It is only through definite designing that readers begin to recognize the newspaper. Thus, good design ensures easy readability, the attraction of the reader, sorting out of the news, creation of an identity for a publication and achieving variety.

Techniques of Make-up

After mastering the principles of design, one can learn make-up after practising techniques under the trial and error method.

*The basic purposes of make-up are to create variety and interest, while at the same time advising the reader regarding the relative importance of stories. Heads, of course, help advise of the story contents.

After selecting pertinent stories and photographs, editors dummy them on pages according to their relative importance: major stories and the most newsworthy photos go on page one or the first pages of sections, while the least important material is placed on inside pages. As indicated, a photograph should be dumped first as the main point on a page; news articles follow. The longer stories, which logically would have larger heads, go at the top of the page. Progressively shorter stories go lower on a page, with the exception of long ones which can "anchor" a layout by stretching across the bottom.

Irregular vs. Square Make-up

The two basic schools of thought on make-up can be described best as the "irregular," using headlines one, two, three, four, or more columns wide, and the "square," composed primarily of rectangular or square shapes in stories with mostly multi-column heads. The "irregular" is more traditional and produces more variety while the "square" offers more white space and therefore helps readability. More newspapers, both daily and weekly, use the "irregular" make-up than the "square."

While both types of make-up are acceptable, editors would frown on mixing them or even using them on alternate days in the same

* Courtesy : Spencer Crump, Fundamentals of Journalism, New York. Mc. Graw con. 1974

newspaper. Switching would interrupt reading habits and make it harder for the reader to find stories.

Pictures against Pictures

To create more interest, editors prefer not to use photos side-by-side on a page unless the pictures concern a related situation. The reasoning is that adjoining pictures suggest a relationship, and if it is not there, confusion will develop in the reader's mind as he seeks to find a link.

Use of Boxes

Editors create "boxes" with stories in several ways. One method is setting a two-or three-paragraph story narrower than the conventional column; the box is created by the white space of the indentation or by the printer's actually inserting a thin line (for instance, 2 points or 1/32 inch) on all four sides. "Boxes" two, three, or more columns wide can be used for longer stories by setting the stories 1/4 to 1/2 inch narrower than conventional columns. In offset printing, editors often use a 20 per cent tone to shade a story and thus give it emphasis over the articles that appear without the tone.

"Boxes" are used extensively to emphasize stories and create variety in make-up. They are regarded as "art" in dummying a newspaper, and consequently would not be used against each other or alongside photographs or cartoons.

Bumping Heads

Some journalists argue that "bumping heads," or headlines that appear directly opposite each other, should never be used. Placing heads against each other is also called "tombstoning."

Editors of virtually all major metropolitan newspapers and many weeklies and small dailies reject this injunction as unrealistic and too restrictive. They use a variety of techniques to eliminate the possibility of adjacent heads being read as one headline, which is the fear of those concerned with the problem.

Those claiming that heads should not "bump" would in effect mandate that a three-column head must appear under a three-column photograph. Modern newspaper editors reject this rule on the basis that a worse crime is putting an overly large head on a relatively minor article to avoid side-by-side heads. The better technique, in the case of the three-column picture, would be to use a two-column head with three lines; one head would be in Roman type, and the other in italic—either larger or smaller—to create contrast. An alternate method would be using a one-column "box" story with one-column heads of varying lines and type styles on either side.

Despite the fact that these heads may bump, the contrasts in type and headline styles make it obvious to readers that they are separate. At the same time, the head sizes are in accordance with the importance of the story.

Frequently there are inside pages where an editor has a choice of running one large headline across the top or using a group of smaller heads. Assuming that there was no "major" story worthy of a large head, the preferred method would be to use the smaller ones rather than a large headlines over an unworthy story. Variety can be achieved in these "bumping" heads through different head styles and type. A photograph or "box" story will also help to avoid the possibility that the heads would be read as one and thus be confusing.

Problems in Make-Up

Some aspects of newspaper make-up call for specialized heads or type. The purpose of these heads is to assist the reader and create interest.

Use of Subhead

Large story areas unbroken by conventional headlines will produce gray areas and give the reader a feeling or monotony while he is pursuing lengthy stories. Subheads, inserted by copyreaders, break these areas to create variety and increase readability.

One method of producing these "breaks" is by putting the first two or three words of every third to fourth paragraph in boldface (or blacker) type. Unlike italic, boldface type can be set without mechanical problems. The disadvantage for this method is that if paragraphs are discarded from a story after it is set in type, those with the boldface may be omitted. Another method is inserting in boldface type, two to four words between every three to four paragraphs. These words give some digest or thought regarding the material that is following. The type size is the same as in the text of the story. Two advantages for these subheads include their remaining if a paragraph is cut, or the fact that they can be discarded when it is necessary to shorten a story slightly so that it will fit in a designated spot. These points help make the "inserted" subheads more popular than those self-contained in a paragraph.

Both kinds of subheads can be all capitals or capitals and lowercase. The latter are more widely used because all capitals, regardless of how they are utilized, are more difficult to read.

Referral Lines

References to related stories or pictures are inserted at the beginning of a story or in the middle of it to guide a reader to another page. In the case of pictures, the photograph running on the front page may advise in its cutlines. "See Story on page 4," or the article may appear on page one with a referral line indicating that a photo is on a specific inside page.

"Jumping" a Story

When a story is too long for a front page, it may be continued to inside pages. Editors prefer never to jump less than 2 column inches of a story, with the reasoning that a short jump "cheat" the reader, who logically would expect to see more of an article. In the case of jump regarding a story on an election, lines such as the following would guide the reader:

(Continued on page 20, col. 2)

Example: For a story guided by page and column number, the jump head typically would repeat part of the article with a two or three-line head over one or more columns. The jump guided by the page number alone would have a large head corresponding to the line at the end of the story on the first page; in this example, it would be "ELECTION."

The origin of the story would be indicated at the top of the jumped material.

(continued from page 1)

Example: The soul of newspaper design is news and its communication to the reader. The approach therefore has to be communication oriented and not decoration oriented. A designer approaching the challenge without a full understanding of news and news value cannot work out a newspaper design, compatible with the primary aim of news communication. This is why many newspapers which have their basic designs made for them by advertising agency artists and executives of design institutes find themselves in difficulties later. The professional designer may propose, but the journalist must dispose. The best dispensation of all is when journalists develop expertise in the technicalities of design and look after their paper's layout. Design is another specialty in the cluster of specialties that add up to modern editing.

Computer Editing and Page Make-up

The introduction of computers have revolutionized the production of newspaper. These new techniques and concepts have swept away the traditional man-cum-machine methods. Now editing is done through computers only and the pages are made-up on computers using QUARK Xpress software.

In a fully automated modern newspaper sub-editors use VDTs (Video Display Terminal) on which they can call up both agency reports and stories by local reporters. Reporters also type their stories on computers and send them to their newspapers either through fax or through e-mail. The VDT has a keyboard resembling that of a standard typewriter. Text appears on the screen as the keys are pressed. The reporter or sub-editor corrects or alters the text as it is composed by moving the cursor backward and forward, upward and downward. They do not use pen or paper. The chief-sub or news editor in turn can call up any of these subbed copies on their own screens for checking. Copy so subbed and checked would be free of mistakes because no one but editor would have handled it. After story is completed it can be stored at the touch of a key.

The computer which stores all the typed material is called the Central Processing Unit (CPU). Editor, news editor and sub editors can recall copy from the CPU on their VDT, can roll the text backward and forward, review and alter it. It can be made to appear on the half of the screen while another version of the same story is recalled from CPU to appear on the other half for comparison or background material stored in the CPU, days or weeks before, may be recalled for modification and incorporation.

Under the electronic system of editing every sub-editor is assigned a VDT. Every story has a code number. The sub-editor directs the computer to produce the story he wants by giving its code number. As soon as the required story appears on the screen, the sub-editor will edit it on the screen and give it a headline. After copy is perfected, the same computer keyboard can be used to do 'pagination'. The sub-editor or art director, will assemble all types and headlines (photos and graphics will be added later) into a full page, employing formats already programmed into the computer. When the pagination is completed on the screen, all that needs to be done is to press the right buttons and output the page as a whole into machine which will deliver a negative ready for plate-making, or even a plate ready for printing.

The elimination of separate typesetting, proof-reading, bromides and paste-up not only speeds up the processes but also helps achieve higher quality and fewer mistakes.

The offset rotary press will print the copies as required. The system will also bundle and wrap the newspaper copies and deliver them addressed to the trucks allotted for delivery in each zone.

In the electronic newspapers, the process of handling a story from one person to another is more involved than in the traditional method, according to some observers. In the conventional newspaper newsroom, the news editor would demand to see a story and the copy would be handed over to him. But in the electronic newspaper the sub-editor has to send the story back to the computer and the news editor has to clear his VDT screen by returning the material on it to the computer and calling the story he wants to see. Giving back the story to the sub-editor requires substantially the same steps—another trip through the computer. This discourages supervision, close scrutiny and exchange of views, although it does not prohibit them.

A peculiar problem for the news editor or the editor in an electronic newspaper is that when a sub-editor edits a reporter's copy they would not know how it had been edited. What were the changes made and the additions and deletions in the copy for the material handled on the VDT is always clean. News editors will have no easy way to find out whether the clean copy is the reporter's work or the sub-editor's especially since the reporter would have fed his copy into the computer himself. The new system requires trained and mature staff especially on night shift. This system has made the desk job onerous and demanding. It requires precision and accuracy of the highest order. There is no scope for slippage. Mistakes of serious kind can prove disastrous for the paper.

Picture Editing

Few people today could visualize a newspaper without photographs or other illustrations on virtually every page. Yet the substantial use of pictures began only in the late 1890s and early 1900s when technical knowhow developed and newspaper czars Hearst and Pulitzer waged circulation battles. Photographs, increasingly important in recent years, help meet the visual competition of television and magazines. The average reader can logically understand a news situation better if it accompanies picture.

Two New York city newspapers, the Post and Daily News, are excellent examples of how appealingly displayed photographs will help impel people to buy from street stands. These publications almost daily display front pages dominated by large photographs that attract attention. Buyers are not disappointed, since inside pages are generously adorned with pictures supplementing stories. While few newspapers in America depend on street sales as much as those in New York City, editors throughout the nation recognize the value of photographs and use them to enhance their pages. In India also, almost every newspaper brings out pullouts increasing visual impact and series of photographs are carried out when some important event or tragedy occurs. For example, Olympic games, Godhra incident, Gujarat earthquake and riots and a year back Rajadhani train accidents between Kolkata and Delhi and Hyderbad and Bangalore. Television news gave additional impetus to the trend as journalists realized, more than ever, the importance of visuals.

Importance

Newspapers and magazines have become a part of most people's daily life. It does not mean that literacy is rising in India, for even the illiterate glance through any publication can get hold of it. To a large extent, it is their desire to 'see' things, even if they cannot read.

Photographs in publications not only appeal to this element in them, but give a visual dimension to an event, a happening. Journalism students are often told that a good photograph equals a thousand written words. This is true only to the limited extent that very few photographs qualify this.

Pictures are not just space-fillers, though on rare occasions, it becomes necessary to consider them just as such. They must be good in themselves. Even when a photograph is an illustration of an idea, it must have a quality which can enable an editor to choose it on its own merit.

Certainly, this cannot always be the case. Many a story needs, needs further 'explanation, which only a picture can give. Moreover, there is need to encourage 'asides' to stories. In such cases, they do not always become a part of the main narration.

Radio gives important spot news quicker than a newspaper can. Television shows them alive. The role that a newspaper can play with regard to these becomes limited. By bringing in 'asides', highlighting the human element through photographs, a newspaper can score over radio and television. Undoubtedly, the areas of influence of each of the three media of communication do not always overlap. But, where they do special care has to be taken.

Qualities of a photograph and its selection

Photographs are received mostly from staffers. Many large newspapers employ news photographers who are given the status of journalists. Photographs are also received from photo agencies, free-lancers, organizations and associations seeking publicity, and political parties. Magazines frequently give assignments to commercial photographers or to regular writers who make their own arrangements to obtain photographs.

Although photographs generally are considered on their own merit, they have to be used to break the monotony of the page. To illustrate an important happening to convey greater information than accompanying matter can, to highlight contrast to satirize or dramatize, to indicate facts of life not seen normally by readers and to present human nature. They may shock, surprise or agitate. In any case, they have to respond to matters of taste and decency. The assessment is made in the same manner as with news.

The news picture must create an action. It must tell a story. It should be possible for a clever photographer to get an 'active' picture even at a routine function like a dinner or birthday party. The best picture shows life happening. In the very best news picture the subject is not at all conscious of the camera. Life is not posed. Life moves. The people in the picture must be active.

The intelligent News Editor or Picture Editor must look for the dramatic element in a picture. He must look for movement. Action pictures lose their drama and excitement if they are not close-ups. If you can blow up the action, it is all right. If you cannot, then you must ask for a news photographer who can move in close.

While taking photographs, care must be taken that it must create an impact. If a picture does not affect you emotionally you should consider rejecting it. One must, keep oneself asking questions about the picture. Is it unusual? Does it arouse any curiosity? Does it arouse emotions or fear or sympathy? Does it make one smile? Does it tell about people? Does it sum up or symbolize any thing?

Every photograph must have one striking element. It can be just a face with an agonized look or a child symbolizing contentment and joy. It is important to bear in mind that staff photographers do not always have the imagination which the editorial staff has. Therefore, it is necessary to discuss with the photographer the types of pictures he should take and suggest the angle needed. These are necessarily based on a background knowledge of the subject covered.

In selecting photographs for use in a daily, the following some additional questions have to be kept in mind.

(i) Does it highlight any thing which the written story does not? (This is particularly needed in cases where a photograph is to accompany a news items.)
(ii) Does it tell story? Is it hot? In other words, is it of the type which is not normally available and which, if delayed can either become useless or be obtained by other newspapers?
(iii) In what size and on which page can it be used?
(iv) Is the quality of the print good enough to respond to enlarging or reducing it, and still appear clear and good?

In selecting photographs for use with features or in magazines, some more questions have to be asked?

(i) Will it go well with other photographs? Can it be a part of a group of photographs to be used in an article, or an individual one which can be made a member of the group?
(ii) Does it form a link in the story, feature or article?
(iii) Is it timeless? This is essential because magazines are produced over a stretch of time and, if the photograph loses its importance because of the delay, it is of no use. This means that it has to be topical in its own way.
(iv) Does it illustrate a point clearly?

In terms of picture stories, it must be remembered that the text is only supplementary in many cases. It is essential to choose the key pictures and decide the others that will go along with them. A haphazard selection will not help. The inclusion of human/subjects and maintenance of sequential order in photographs is particularly important. Having made the selection, you must see the arrangement in which they should appear and decide whether they really tell a story. It is probable that much juxtaposition in arrangement has to be done. Several patterns have to be considered. The written word is only a link between them, like a commentary for a documentary film.

Owing to limitations of space, it is sometimes necessary to prepare what is known as *photo-montage. Photo montage* is called when a number of pictures are put together and combined as one for a total effect. This requires skill. The artist cuts the required photographs in such a way that they can be put together to make a consolidated whole. This is used mostly in features. At times, this is needed because a single photograph is not suggestive enough thematically. It can happen that you have a large number of photographs, but owing to space limitations all of them cannot be used independently. So a few of them are arranged independently and the remaining are joined together in the form of a photo-montage.

Because of the utility of this method, there can be a tendency to overuse it. This can only cause confusion. Too many montage arrangements, or too many elements in them, can distract attention from one part to another, and the reader will still not be clear as to what is being said.

Editing photographs

In editing photographs, the aim should be to enhance the visual impact. Just as a skilful sub-editor may tighten or brighten a dull piece of writing, so imaginative editing can transform what at first sight was a disappointing print into an arresting picture.

The first task of the picture editor is to select the photographs to be used and to decide the relative prominence each to have—they must be judged not only on their technical excellence—bright, sharp, well composed but also on their editorial value, their news worthiness and whether they conform to accepted standards of honest reporting and good taste. The editor should recognize the legal implications of publishing a particular photograph; for example, will its appearance in the paper be held to be contempt of court or will it invite an action for libel.

Having made these decisions, he then proceeds to the editing. The photograph may have to be cropped, (cutting out unwanted background) scaled, enlarged or reduced. This is part of the editorial work.

Cropping and Scaling

A picture's value consists in its interest, composition and quality of reproduction. A small poor quality picture must be rejected because the flaws will be magnified in the enlargement. Because most news and feature pictures contain people, the picture editor strives to help the photographer depict them as dramatically as possible. He must decide how many persons to include in the picture, how much of a person to include and what background is essential. The picture editor makes the same kind of editorial judgement about a picture which the chief sub-editors in-charge of local and agency news make about a local story or an agency story. Does the picture tell the whole story or only a part of it? Does it distort, editorialize or mislead? Does it omit important details or include details that create an erroneous impression? In other words, is the picture loaded? A former editor of the *Washington Post* once said, *"The camera can be notorious, compulsive, unashamed, and mischievous liar. A picture may be striking and it may be narrative. But if it conveys a false or distorted impression it is better to be left unpublished."*

The picture editor must judge the photograph from editorial point of view as well as from technical point of view. The news editor must seek a picture which is technically perfect for newspaper reproduction. What is needed is a picture with sharp detail and large pattern. The detail must by crystal sharp and show a full gradation of tone. When a picture has news value but does not meet the technical requirements, the picture editor has to crop it so as to retain only the most interesting part and enlarge it in the reproduction. This allows the best use of a poor picture. There is one rule. 'If a picture is great it deserves to be played big. If it is an ordinary picture it needs to be played big.' It is fatal to print a picture small because it is of poor quality. It must always be used big.

A good news picture, like a good news story, should have prominent display big enough to bring out all the dramatic elements in it. It may be five columns wide and 12" to 16" deep. Most pictures that are received are horizontal and if it is felt that they would be good if used vertically then they must be cropped into that shape. Horizontal pictures can be made long and narrow spread over five or six columns as a strip. They are effective and look beautiful. Square pictures which cannot be cropped without damaging them are generally used as two column or three column pictures 6" and 7" deep. It is a good rule to make every picture a column bigger than one thinks it is worth. Big pictures help to break up headlines and types. Small pictures are just an irritant.

A photograph, as we have discussed earlier, is a composition. The composition should help the reader grasp the picture's message clearly and immediately. If the picture is too cluttered the reader's eye scans the picture looking for a place to rest. But if the picture contains a strong focal point the reader at least has a place to start. An important function of the picture editor therefore is to cut out unnecessary details to strengthen the overall view.

Scaling

Once a picture is cropped it needs to be 'scaled' to fit exactly into the page layout prepared by the desk. Scaling merely means measuring the picture for size. If it is decided to make a picture 3 columns across, it must be scaled to know precisely how deep it will be in the page. Correct scaling is important for the proper dummying of pages. It will also help visualize clearly how they will look on the page and whether the details in the picture will come out too big or too small.

It sometimes happens that a photograph can be conveniently cropped to the exact size required, both width and depth. Usually, however, there will be some reduction or enlargement, and the editor must then calculate the depth in relation to the required width and instruct the process department accordingly.

Although the general sequence of picture editing is to crop first and scale afterwards, the editor, after tentatively cropping for content, will be prepared to modify this in order that the picture fits the available space. It is usually a combined operation, with the hard realities of the page plan impinging on the aesthetic options offered by the photograph.

Scaling of photographs is done with the aid of a printer's proportion scale or, if that is not available, by using the less precise, diagonal line method. The principle of diagonal line method is straight forward. Draw a diagonal line from the upper left to the lower right corner on the back of the picture, measure the desired width along the top of the picture and make a vertical line. The point where it intersects the diagonal indicates the depth of the picture. Or the diagonal may be drawn from the upper right to the lower left corner of the back of the picture. The desired width of the picture is then indicated along the bottom of the picture. Pictures may be reduced in any proportion but generally newspapers adhere fairly closely to standard reductions such as one-fifth, one-third and one-half. There is one basic rule to remember, the narrower a cropped photograph is, the greater will be its depth when scaled over a given width.

Scaling instructions are normally written on the back of the photograph, with the width expressed in columns and then the depth in centimeters.

Caption Writing

Just as sub-editor sells a news story by means of a compelling headline so also the picture editor tries to attract the reader by the compelling caption he gives to a picture. It does not necessarily mean the head line above the photograph. It is the same as what is called the 'cut line' below the photograph, which gives details related to the photograph. The main objective of the caption is to make the reader respond to the picture in the manner intended by the photographer and the picture editor. A reader first looks at the picture at the focal points and then at the other parts. He then turns to read the caption to confirm what he has seen. The caption will provide the answers to the questions of who, what, where, when, why and how, unless some of these are apparent in the picture itself. The caption interprets and clarifies what the picture tells the reader. It helps to explain ambiguities and clarify what is not made clear in the picture and also mentions what it fails to show if that is necessary.

Writing captions or cut lines is an art. They must be brief and to the point, but not so short that they leave the reader wondering about the situation involved. Good cut lines supplement and even explain the pictures, but they do not repeat obvious information in the photograph.

While brevity is essential, cut lines, should not be telegraphic and omit words that are important for smooth reading.

People in the pictures should be identified by their full names and, if necessary for understanding, with their titles or other explanation of who they are.

When a story accompanies the photo the cut line writer must take care not to repeat lengthy facts from the article. The cut lines are not intended to be condensation, but are expected to supplement.

Subjects should be identified as to their places in pictures, because most readers will not know them well enough to recognize them.

Present tense must be used. Only on rare occasions is the past tense required, specially when it is a historical photograph highlighting something what happened many years ago. In any case, change of tense within the caption is not proper. At times a photograph on the front page only refers to a report or article that appears inside. In such instances, it is essential to mention this by saying : Story on page - - - - -

While working out a caption, it is best to obtain details from the photographer and the reporter concerned. The man behind the camera was on the spot. He knows exactly what happened and in what circumstances he took the photograph. Bearing those details in mind and studying the story that goes with it, jot down the details that you would incorporate in the caption. You must consider where and how the photograph will be used. It is good to write precise instructions for the printer to let him know that the matter is a caption and that it has to be set in the style required for the photograph.

Just as eyes are said to be the windows to the soul of a person, photographs can become a part of the true quality of a newspaper or magazine. Used properly, after careful selection and editing, they can also brighten and enliven the visual impact of a publication.

Do's and don'ts with regard to Picture Captions

Do not tell the obvious. If the girl in the picture is pretty or attractive that fact will be obvious from the picture. The picture will tell whether or not a man is smiling. It may be necessary, however, to indicate why he is smiling.

- Do not editorialise. The caption writer cannot know whether someone is happy, glum or troubled.
- Use specifics rather than generalities. It is better to say a 5 Kg. book than a huge book. A man, 70, is a better description than 'an old man.'
- Because the reader knows you are referring to the picture, omit phrases like 'pictured' 'is shown' and 'the picture above shows.'
- Say 'from left' rather than 'from left to right'. The first means as much as the second and is shorter. The words 'left' and 'right' should not be overworked.
- One of the worst things that one can say about a person in a picture is that he 'looks on'. If that is all he is doing he is superfluous.
- Do not deceive the reader. Give the date when the picture was taken. Also let the reader know where the picture was taken but not how.
- Caption in the present tense enhances the immediacy of the picture.
- Make sure the caption is accurate. Mistakes happen because someone, the photographer or the reporter accompanying him, failed to give the picture desk enough or accurate information from which to write a caption.
- Double check the picture with the caption in regard to identification. If the persons appearing in the picture are wrongly identified it may create problems for the news editor and editor.
- Writing a caption requires as much care and skill as writing a story or a headline. The reader should not be puzzled by the caption.
- Captions should be bright if warranted by the picture. Humour and sarcasm have no place in captions.
- The caption should describe the event as shown in the picture and not the event itself. Readers will be puzzled if the caption describes action they do not see.

- Because a lapse occurs between the time a picture of an event is taken and the time a reader sees it in the newspaper, care should be taken to update the information in the caption.
- The person responsible for checking page proofs must make sure that the correct caption goes with the picture. It is not unusual to see picture captions transposed with disastrous results.

Exercises

1. Visit a local agent where several newspapers are displayed in stands; note the varying appeal of make-up.
2. Invite the news editor of any regional newspaper and discuss with him the make-up techniques as practiced by his staff.
3. Assemble samples of any three national dailies and note:

   (1) Contrast in their head types and styles;
   (2) to what extent they use 'bumping' heads and how they contrast type when doing so;
   (3) how they use 'referral' lines;
   (4) the methods used for 'jump' head;
   (5) the similarities or differences in column widths;
   (6) the kinds of sub-heads used;
   (7) Whether they use 'irregular' or 'square' make-up.

4. Identify newspaper page as follows:

   (i) Top balance.
   (ii) Top and - Bottom balance
   (iii) Off- balance.
   (vi) Centre balance.
   (v) Vertical.

5. Remake the layout of the pages which are unattractive, using the same items, to make them appealing.
6. Convert a symmetrical balance into a asymmetrical balance.
7. Analyze local newspapers to determine their styles of writing and setting cut-lines.

SECTION II

BASIC SKILLS

4

STRUCTURE OF NEWS STORY

STRUCTURE

The news story is written in the inverted pyramid style with the most significant facts at the top. The other facts follow in order of importance except in special circumstances. This enables a story to remain self-contained, no matter how much of it is deleted from the end. For this reason the first part or the opening paragraph of a news report must bring out the dramatic importance of the event.

The inverted pyramid style has developed in journalism over the years. In stories written in the above style the climax is at the beginning in the lead. The reporter gives the most important information at the top, then less important details. The least required information is given at the end of the story. Presenting the story in this fashion carries two advantages. One, the reader need not to read up to the end. He first scans the headline then lead. If lead is interesting he reads the middle of the story. And if it still holds his attention he will read the least important details given at the end—called the tail of the story.

This format has been criticized as being old fashioned and traditional. However, the inverted pyramid has survived and will probably do so in future as well.

It is essential to incorporate all details in your report related to the event or happening, which ever element or type of news you are writing about. They are as under:

WHAT (the nature of the happening)
WHERE (identifying the place)
WHEN (the day and, if possible, the time)
WHO (the persons involved or affected)
WHY (the causes, the background)
HOW (the sequential record of exact happening)

In this context Rudyard Kipling's rhyme outlines the entire nature of news writing.

- *"I can keep six honest serving men*
- *They taught me all I knew*
- *Their names are: What and why and when*
- *And How and Where and Who"*

It is natural—to think that when we come back to the office with a good story, it is going to be the best story in the next issue and that everyone will want to read it. But good stories often go unread. Many readers just skim through the paper, picking at what takes their fancy. The page is to them like a shop window in which the newspaper displays its wares. The headline and the opening paragraphs of a story represent the packages of the goods. If they are attractive, the story will be "bought."

So to the reporter, the opening paragraph is of vital importance. Many experienced journalists spend more time in fashioning the lead than they do for the remainder of the story.

Some newspaper organisations try to lay down rules for intro and lead writing. A common rule is: "The intro must tell the story." Strict adherence to a rule of this sort, however, can make nonsense of a story and cramp a writer's individual flair. A much better principle is that a lead or intro must capture the reader's attention. With a "hard" news story this means going straight to the heart of the matter, stripping it of all unnecessary detail and presenting it in a clear and concise way in a paragraph of not more than forty words.

Here is a story in which the writer has failed to cut away the details: "Tension prevailed in Shimla today, the sixth day of the students' strike over fee raise, and most of the shops of the Summer-hill remained closed as violent incident resulted in injury to 10 students and a policeman."

What was the real story here? Surely not that tension prevailed in Shimla? The intro should have been: Ten students and one policeman were injured in violent clashes in Shimla today—the sixth day the students' strike."

That goes to the core of the story, to the fact that people were injured. It is only in this light that the tension and the closed shops make any sense.

Directness is the most natural form of expression in every day conversation. A man coming from the scene of an accident would most probably say to his friend: "A man has just been killed in a crash down the road." But reporter, coming from the scene of the same crash, far frequently writes an intro like this: "A collision between two motor vehicles in Cart Road, Shimla, yesterday resulted in fatal injuries being sustained by one of the drivers."

Writing the Lead

The lead should try to answer the six basic questions : What? Where? Who? When? Why? How? The order which it answers them will depend on the relative importance of each. In the above example, the question "What?" (killed) is clearly the most important. "How?" (in a car crash) obviously follows. "Who?" and "Where?" are probably of equal importance. This would yield an intro like this: "A man was killed when the car he was driving collided with another in Cart Road, Shimla yesterday He was Mr..."

If the dead man had been a prominent public figure, the question "Who?" would need to be answered first. "When seldom takes priority except in rare instances."

So the lead should convey the kernel of the story, convey it briefly and concisely and also authoritatively. Vagueness seriously damages the intro, as in this example: "It is understood from usually knowledgeable sources and reliable quarters that the strength of the Congress Legislature Party in the Gujarat State Assembly will increase and reach the figure of 100."

The opening words immediately shed an element of doubt on the whole story. The reporter himself is clearly not as certain as he would like to be. There are other obvious weaknesses. The increase in party strength could mean anything or nothing, depending on the previous strength. Did it increase by one, or by ten, or by twenty? In this case the story did not enlighten us at any point in the narrative: The intro ought to contain facts, not speculation.

Definition

It is the beginning of a story which may be a sentence, a part or several paragraphs depending on the elements forming the story, In other words, it is the intro or the first paragraph of a story.

Importance of lead

The structure of a story succeeds or fails primarily on the basis of the lead, which plays the main role. Most leads tell what has happened in such a way as to make the reader curious about what else has happened. A lead aims at projecting a definite happening, guides the sub-editor in giving headings, directs the attention to what has to follow and sets an emotional tone for the news item.

Reporters spend much time on the opening paragraph. They often write and rewrite it, because the first 30 to 50 words can tell whether a reporter understands what he is writing or not. Headlines appear ahead of leads and sometimes condition the reader. Therefore, the leads become all the more important for retaining readership interest. The present tendency is to make headlines cryptic and small. They cannot arouse enough interest. The burden of doing so falls on leads.

Need

Years ago, reporters attempted traditionally to crowd as many facts as possible into a lead. The effect was burdensome and difficult to read, because all the facts were not necessarily that the lead should be confined to the facts vital for telling the reader the story's contents. If interested, the reader can continue the article; if not, his eyes will move to another item. Leads, not only give a good idea of the story's contents but also give briefs.

The readers expect all the basic facts in a story's first one or two paragraphs. If the story begins with preliminaries or unimportant facts their interest never develops; they turn to an article with a lead offering provocative facts. Leads which lucidly digest a story give the reader an opportunity to decide which articles to pursue from start to finish. If the salient facts were in the closing paragraphs of stories, readers would never find them because it would be impractical to consume every article in its entirety.

Lead variations

Despite its usefulness, suitability or desirability for all news situations, there are numerous types of stories, to which varied leads can give sparkle and flavour, adding to the mood of the article. Sub-editors, like their readers, enjoy variety. Some news events by their very contents, deserve different treatment. Working journalists would seldom consciously attempt to categorise leads, despite their ability to handle many varieties.

The 'Inverted Pyramid'

It is also called the 'summary lead' because it presents the pertinent facts in the earliest paragraphs. The inverted pyramid is the basic format for news stories. The reader learns the conclusion or major points in the first paragraph or two; introductory points are at the bottom of the story. It is very popular lead and is used in approximately 90 percent of all news stories. The summary lead is widely used on radio and TV newscasts because it enables the broadcaster to give the facts concisely in the brief time allocated. It normally answers the five Ws and one 'H'.

The origin of the summary lead can be debated. One logical theory goes back to the early days of telegraphy, when reporters gave the basic facts in the first paragraphs of their stories for fear that the transmission would be broken prior to completion of the message.

Another attribute of this format is that the copyreader can easily cut the story from the bottom and yet retain its readability. With the important facts at the top of the story, and those of decreasing interest closer to the end. Such deletions cause no harm. Moreover, this format is the delight of the make up editors and printers, who must trim stories to fit over, above, and around other articles. Since the least important facts are at the bottom of the story and the competent journalist uses short paragraphs, to make the story readable.

'Emphasis' Lead

This lead highlights generally the 'who'. This implies personality, other details follow. In this form of writing, the approach has to be casual and light-hearted. The feature style is conversational. It does not have to highlight any of the important elements. The attempt is to make the beginning the most interesting part. With greater emphasis being laid on human interest stories, this style is becoming popular.

The 'Upright Pyramid' or 'Sequence Lead'

Some stories can be told effectively in the order in which the events occurred. This is the opposite style of most newspaper articles. A short story or a novel follows the format of this type of lead. The reader begins with preliminary or introductory facts and finds out the facts at the end.

'Quotational' Lead

As the name implies, a quotational lead starts with a dramatic statement made by someone who matters. It picks up possibly, a policy announcement, or declaration on bahalf of the government, official plans or decisions. A direct quotation lead that contains abstract ideas, or is unclear, will turn the reader away whether used in the lead or body of a story. This type of lead runs somewhat as follows:

India has lodged a strong protest with the U.S. about the latest supply of arms to Pakistan. This was declared by the Foreign Minister, Mr...- This is one of the easiest ways of starting an item.

The 'Direct Address' lead

Although quotation marks are not used, the second person ('you') approach reaches one to involve the reader and capture his attention while occasional direct-address leads help add sparkle, overdoing them can create monotony and cause them to lose the impend of involvement.

The 'Dialogue' lead

This type of lead begins with a dialogue. Dialogue lead can add flavour to many stories with a human interest.

> Example : "It was so cold in Shimla, that the coffee froze almost as soon as we poured it."

The 'Crowded' lead

When many points are boiled into a single paragraph. The advantage of crowding a great deal of information into a lead is the use of less space. Its disadvantage is the loss of impact for important material that would be more readable in shorter sentences.

The '1-2-3-4'

Often a story situation contains a number of news-making elements which the reporter would like to emphasize. By listing them in '1-2-3-4' order, the writer concentrates them all.

The 'Shirt Tail' lead

An alternate to the crowded and '1-2-3-4' lead which contains several news items is to include them in two or more brief paragraphs. This type of lead can be used as a compromise to the above two leads; it permits the combining of a number of news elements without using a great deal of space.

'Bang' lead

This is also called cartridge lead. It is brief and contains one single news incident, to be expanded later in the story. Its impact makes it a lead to reserve for important stories. If this lead is used for minor news, it can magnify an article, cause the reader to lose interest, as well as faith in the newspaper's integrity when he reads the full article.

'Negative' lead

This type of lead is required only in order to clarify certain situations. If there have been earlier reports about a possible government decision, and then the government declares that 'no possibility exists,' it is essential to have a clarification. In general, this is not very effective, unless the proposed government step has gained a degree of unpopularity. The exception is when, for example, firmness is demanded towards a neighbouring country. Then, it becomes somewhat like 'India has not accepted the terms proposed by Pakistan. This was disclosed by ......'.

The 'Preface' lead

A brief quotation or a few appropriate lines from a poem or familiar saying, preceding a story can form a background that helps increase enjoyment of the article.

The 'blind' lead

The blind lead permits the writer to hurry in to the story without crowding too much into the first paragraph. The purpose of a lead is to both inform and interest the reader. This is a difficult job in an age when readers have so many distractions in their lives and when the newspaper has so much competition for readers' time. Readers spend very little time with newspapers these days and tend to read only stories that look especially interesting. They skim and skip. If a summary lead is packed too full of details, if it looks too formidable, the reader will hurry on the something that looks more appealing.

The blind lead, by limiting the information in the first paragraph and picking it up in the second, attempts to give the reader the summary in two stages: a partial summary in the first paragraph and details in the second.

The 'delayed-identification' lead

Somewhere between the blind lead and the summary lead lies the delayed-identification lead. Here the name is given in the first paragraph of the lead, but full identification is held back and given in the second paragraph—or sometimes later. Delayed-identification leads leave out some information and by so doing make the first paragraph of the lead more concise and more readable.

The 'Substantive Clause' lead

A substantive clause, usually starting with 'that' or 'when', helps achieve variety and usually contains interpretive elements.

The 'Familiar sanging' lead

A familiar quotation or sanging can be woven into a story to help create a light touch. Care must be taken that the effect comes naturally and is not strained.

The 'Parody' lead

Brightness can be added to appropriate stories with leads parodying well-known motion pictures, songs, or books, or sayings by noted people.

The 'Punch' lead

One method for attracting attention is concentrating with a brief, to the point lead sentence and developing details later in the story.

The 'Cumulative interest' lead

This type of lead starts with a brief news fact and lead the reader's interest to the end of the story.

The 'Suspended interest' lead

Unlike the previous construction, the 'suspended interest' lead contains no news element. The reader must obtain the news by reading to the end of the story.

'Historical or literary' lead

It draws some character or event in history of literature in relation to an event or person in the news.

The 'Question' lead

This lead starts with a question addressed to the reader and is highly popular with budding journalists. Question lead can be good or bad according to the news situations involvement and how the questions are phrased. This type of lead can lead editor when used occasionally, many editors frown on them on the basis that people read newspapers to get answers not to be asked questions.

They argue with great merit, that unless the question used in the lead is provocative, it may bring a subconscious 'no' report from readers whose eyes would skip to another story.

Opponents of 'question' lead contend that the reporter tempted to use such a beginning should ask himself the question silently and write the reply as the lead to be submitted to the editor.

Journalists should avoid leads using 'dead' verbs that say little and have no action, or which drag because they contain needless past perfect verbs. For example:

'The burglars had been climbing through a hole in the roof when the police had arrived and caught them.'

This lead lacks impact because the past tense is emphasized needlessly.

By using 'action' verbs and de-emphasizing the past tense, the sentence could be rephrased to attract more interest.

Example : *'The police caught the burglars climbing through a hole in the roof.'*

Forms of the verb 'to be' (was, is, are, has been) also carry little action and therefore tend to slow interest in a lead.

The use of direct, action, expressive verbs invariably will make a lead more readable and understandable.

Writing the Remainder of the story

While a story's lead attracts a reader and provides a summary, the remainder of the article must hold the interest by furnishing details clearly and concisely. The reader will lose interest in the article, if the details fail to justify the lead. After an appropriate lead, the body of the story should be accurate and understandable. Some of the other essential points in developing news and feature stories as a journalist are:

The use of the third person

All news and feature stories are written in the third person. The main reason for doing this is to maintain the air of fairness and objectivity which would not be present in a first person story. "I", "you", "my", "we", "us", "me", "our" are not used and "our" are used in editorial and refer to the newspapers staff or owners. "I", "mine", "my" and "me" words are appropriate for regular columns or letters to the editor. They are not used in news or feature stories.

Write for the reader

The reporter must remember that he will not be present with the reader to explain any vagueness, confusion, or references. The reader's understandings and impressions will come only from that story, unless there is an unusual situation where he may have an independent knowledge of material in the article. Reporters write, of course not for that isolated knowledgeable reader but for the bulk of subscribers.

Use of technical information

Most readers, though they are knowledgeable, have little knowledge of technical subjects. The reporter must serve as "middleman between the technician and reader to put information into meaningful words. Stories should be fair and understandable as well as accurate.

In writing a scientific story the reporter will use layman's terms so that the reader will not be forced to consult a dictionary. News stories, the reporter should remember, inform and entertain average people. They are not intended as technical trade articles.

Readability

The reporter thus avoids words, phrases, questions, or sentences that he does not understand, if the writer lacks comprehension of his own story, it is doubtful that the reader will understand the meaning. The reporter gathers many facts and sorts out the meaningful ones, translating this information into words and sentences that the average reader will understand and enjoy.

Short-paragraphs

Reporters find that the first requirement of their jobs include "breaking", long paragraphs. The news writer must develop a "habit" of almost automatically terminating one paragraph when it becomes lengthy and starting another. Four type-written lines is a good average for a news paragraph, and six lines, with a rare exception is maximum.

Avoid "Wordy" or lengthy sentences

Lengthy sentences also are undesirable for journalistic writing because they create difficulty in reading. Skillful reporters can delete unwanted words from a sentence and instead of altering the meaning, strengthen it. Removing unwanted words and phrases from stories not only makes individual articles more readable, it also helps provide more room for other stories. "Tight" story construction is an art that writers can develop by being conscious of "wordiness" when they write and read. An excellent way to form an awareness of the possibilities for dropping words and phrases is by checking one's own copy and that of others.

Shorter sentences

Editors do not expect reporters to count words or follow formulas for writing but they rightfully demand that the writers construct sentences which will be readable. The Associated Press explained it this way:

"Our first duty is to tell what has happened, in a language the average reader can grasp at first reading. Every lead and every subsequent paragraph should be clear and incisive. We must not delay him with wordiness, confuse him with imperfect sentence structure or discourage him with dull, technical phraseology. We must give him the drama and colour that comes from judicious selection of detail, and a relaxed, conversational technique. We must not over feed him by forcing who-what-why-when-where into a single sentence. It is better to use words

that are generally used in everyday conversation. But, if you have to use a word that is unfamiliar to an ordinary reader, explain it. Good writers develop the habit of writing readable sentences by examining their copy for logical sentence breaks. They soon are able to write a readable sentence almost automatically. The reader can better absorb the information when words are simplified and are into short sentences using the words and phraseology that people would choose in ordinary conversation will make the sentence understandable."

Choice of words

Using his tools of words, phrases, and sentences to build stories, a reporter constructs stories to give readers maximum information and understanding. "Padding" or adding words merely to lengthen an article wastes valuable space. Journalists develop the habit of selecting the most expressive words and cutting extraneous phrases. Readers want facts, not speculation.

Do not make readers "guess"

Reporters should avoid using words that are unfamiliar to the average reader, if the writer has more to say, he should give it to the reader but should not expect his audience to imagine what was left out of the story.

Avoid unnecessary words

Journalists pride themselves on "tight" writing, or being able to delete unwanted words. One can develop this skill by carefully reviewing his own copy and by having others check it. A reporter also can note the long sentences of others to see how extraneous words and phrases can be deleted. Deleting words and phrases that say little or nothing will make room for more facts in that story and more stories for the reader.

Use correct spelling

Misspelled words block understanding of stories and slow reading time. They also cause the reader to question accuracy of facts since they indicate carelessness. Do not use "manufactured" abbreviations which are not given in dictionaries or style books because they create confusion. When there is a question over spelling, seasoned journalists instinctively consult a dictionary. After looking up a problematic word once or twice and using it, the spelling thereafter comes almost automatically.

Avoid repeating words

An elementary rule for writing is not to use the same word twice in a sentence, but substitute a synonym on the second usage. Journalists go a step farther to avoid repeating words or parts of the same words in a paragraph. This makes for less monotony and smoother reading.

Avoid "Overworked" words and phrases

Slang and figures of speech can add punch to a story if these are not overdone. Some of the words they detract, rather than add to stories. "Very" is also a very overworked word which no longer has great meaning. If a story deals with "very high attendance", the reporter would do better to substitute an estimate of the number present. Often "very" means very little: "a very good example," "very fresh juice" or "very interested." The use of "very" frequently does little than clutter sentences, which usually are already crowded. Ordinarily by removing "very" there is very little change in the meaning of the sentence.

"Interesting" is another word that says little. People may be "interested" in a story or they may receive "interest" from a bank, but beyond those uses the word is virtually meaningless. A play that is "interesting" can be described as "funny", "hilarious", "frightening", "dramatic", or "well-structured". Each descriptive word tells the reader that it is "interesting" and why it is. Readers are intelligent enough to judge from the facts whether or not the programme is "interesting".

Use of names

Stories without names lack interest. People are important and so are their names even though they may not be famous journalists. Therefore, names are generously given in their articles. Names are used in their entirety when initially used in a story, Mr. A.B. Vajpayee. In subsequent uses in the same story, people are identified only by their last name. If the man or woman has a doctor's degree, "Dr." would be used. In their cases, "Miss", "Mr." or "Ms." as appropriate would precede the name. Men are identified only by their last names, with no "Mr." being used.

Attribution

Every news story has a source and must be attributed to the person who provided the information. Otherwise, the reader may assume that the newspaper is vouching for the accuracy of the information instead of only publishing it. If the story is lengthy, the attribution should be reinforced by quoting the source after every three to four paragraphs. This attribution is particularly important when dealing with controversial material.

Statements that are controversial, dubious, or questionable should be attributed to their sources, thus permitting the reader to weigh their validity and not credit the information to the newspaper or writer. Care should be taken to credit each such statement so that the reader will know the source.

The reader does not know who provided the story unless the reporter tells by attributing the source, using either direct or indirect quotations.

Ending the Story

When a reporter has used all his facts, he simply ends the story. Assuming that the story is written in the inverted pyramid format, the article could end even before all of the facts are used. The presumption is if any deletion is to be made to fit the story in the space given it should be at the bottom of the story.

Writing Headlines

Good headlines are written in vigorous, conversational, idiomatic language. Good headlines should be capable of being read aloud which the mind does subconsciously.

—Arthur Christiansen

"A newspaper may be judged pretty accurately by its headlines", writes Allan Holcomb, copy desk chief of the *New York Herald Tribune*.

Giving headlines is not as simple as it may seem. Even the most competent sub-editor finds it difficult. The influence that a newspaper exerts can be made or marred by headlines. Most of the people merely glance at the newspaper headlines. They arrive at judgements based on this. Their opinion is moulded by headlines. Writing good headlines is a very challenging task. Reporters supply the raw material to the newspaper. It is the sub-editor who gives the proper shape to the story and writes its headline.

Headline Defined

Any line or collection of lines of display type that precedes a story and summarize it or introduces it can be called a headline.

Characteristics

Although headline writing practices vary from newspaper to newspaper within a small range of differences, newspaper headlines have certain distinguishing characteristics:

- The headlines should be simple and informal.
- They should have maximum impact on the readers.
- They must fit the space available to it.
- They are skeltonized primarily to save space.
- They use the present tense to show the sense of immediacy.
- They must be adjusted to a pre-determined typographical style.

Headlines are the display windows of the newspaper

The modern reader sees the headlines and expects to be able to take in their message almost at a glance. They are also a major source of information for a newspaper reader in a hurry. They certainly have to perform certain *functions* as follows:

Indexing: The headlines guide the reader into the stories in which he is interested and steer him away from stories of marginal or no interest for him.

Capsule Information: The headlines must give an idea of what the story contains, must give an accurate information for the headline scanner.

Attraction: The headline must provide readers variety in the newspaper's design and make pages attractive.

Identity: It must create an identity or character for the publication through the use of distinctive types. The consistent use of familiar headline structures give the newspaper a relatively familiar and welcome personality.

To Convey Significance: The headlines convey to the reader the relative significance of the news. This is done by expressing editor's own expert opinion of a story value in terms of type display and the relative size of the headline used.

To Convey Seriousness: They convey to the reader the relative seriousness of the news. This is accomplished by the choice of headline styles. The use of italics and various typographical devices such as boxes, star dashes etc. indicates that a story is used for its entertainment value, primarily, rather than its significance.

To Sell Newspapers: The headlines make a person select the paper from a news stand in preference to a competing publication.

Excellence in Headlines Writing

Writing headline is a skill. Nobody ever achieves perfection. But more than that, it is a skill basic to communications. The headline uses minimum of language symbols to convey a maximum of meaning. Headline writing does not employ a "language of its own". Headline must employ language symbols people can understand. Some of the skills that point to success in head line writing are:

Accurate perception of the story

He must first of all be able to see the story clearly and stripped down to its essentials. He must be able to recognize what parts of the story are more newsworthy, dramatic, significant and new. To make this judgement he needs to know the background to the news item he is editing: if it is a developing story he must be fully aware of the previous developments. As he reads the copy the deskman sums up the news in his mind and scribbles on notepaper at his side the sentence, words, phrases or ideas which are at the heart of the story. These notes will serve as the basis for constructing the headline.

Strong Sense of Appropriateness

The headline wording must not only be accurate; it must have a sense of appropriateness for the story. Funny headlines do not fit happily on sombre events: it is wrong to indulge in puns when the subject is death, injury, physical affliction or religion.

Broad and Deep Vocabulary

The layman's vocabulary is not sufficient to the head line writer's task. Constructing sentences within the structures of the headline requires not just a vocabulary of many words, but precise knowledge of the meanings of many words and a keen sense of their connotations. The sub-editor must pay more attention than ever to both denotations and connotations of words, and examine the words he uses for their exact meaning and for special meanings in the light of their immediate context.

A Sharp Sense of Sentence Structure

Headlines are written in sentences. Sentences take many structures. The sub-editor spends on flexibility, not only in the choice of words but in the choice of structures also.

A Keen Eye for Ambiguity

The copy editor must review his work endlessly to detect sources of ambiguity. He must be able to put himself in the place of many potential readers. What is meaningful and clear to him may not be to others.

Rules for Writing Headlines

There are lots of 'rules' for headline writers. In some cases these are rules indeed, since office style requires conformity; in other cases they are just guides. No effort will be made to separate rules from guides in the enumeration which follows:

Put the key facts at the top of the headline

The top of the story should be reserved for the most important details. The headline over a straight news story is usually based on the lead, but there are times when the sub-editor is justified in taking a leeway. When he does he must take pains to see that he does not go beyond the story.

Build the headline around a strong verb

Active, meaningful verbs in headlines reflect the freshness of news. Good sub-editors choose the vigorous, active, positive, colourful words. All headline words—even the little ones—are selected with care but verb is the key on the entire head. If the verb is weak, the headline is weak. The normal headline has no palm for adjectives. Its colour and spice must come from a rich verb. All forms of the verb 'to be' (is, are) and particularly the past tenses (were, had been) are avoided because many are passive and tell little.

Use present and future tense

Most headlines are in the present or future tense. 'CM dies' is better than 'CM has died'. The headlines use the present tense to describe events that have already happened. There are good reasons for this. First the present tense is active. It puts the reader into the middle of the action. It gives him a feeling of participation. Secondly, the event may be past, but it is recent past, and the reader is learning it for the first time. He perfectly well understands the connection and will imply from a present tense headline that the event occurred within the publishing time of the newspaper.

Use active voice

Generally speaking, headlines demand the active voice, rather than the passive. In other words, write headlines with somebody saying something or being something, rather than having it told to them or done to them. Passive voice breeds extra words, excess weight which exhausts the headline.

Do not over abbreviate

Despite limited space in headline, arbitrary or rare abbreviations are not acceptable. To produce an understandable headline, the copy editor must use better known abbreviations and rephrase it.

Use subject

The subject should be there. If the name is known, use the name and not other title. If there is doubt about whether a man is well known enough, the good sub-editor will use a title, since his doubt will become a certainty for the average reader. The weakest form of subject in a headline is "he" or "she". It is not an identification. It should be avoided.

Give single thought

Simplicity in headlines does not merely mean simple words. It equally means the simple expression of a single thought. Effectively to convey one single idea in the limited space, of a headline, requires skill; to convey two ideas in the same space with the same intelligibility requires a rare genius. Just as a sentence becomes difficult to follow when it is overloaded with separate ideas so does a headline. The attempt to combine two thoughts may not always be so confusing but often it lessens the impact of the news.

Use of quotation marks

When slang or portion of direct questions appears in a head, the copy editor uses quotation marks. In story the marks would be used in double fashion like this "Hey". In headlines most newspapers use only single quotation marks. One purpose of using the single quote marks is to save space in the head. A second reason it to avoid excessive symbols which could 'clutter' a head.

Quotation marks are also used occasionally to indicate that a word is being used in some special way; for example :

Tohra 'adjourns' Jind meeting

Use of periods

Periods are used in many abbreviations to help make them more understandable. It is not used in headlines to indicate the end of a sentence. Sentence breaks are indicated with the semicolon, instead.

Use of comma

Comma is often substituted for 'and' to save space. It also separates dependent and independent clauses. Example : Deve Gowda defends Government, says it's on track.

Apostrophe

It is used in the usual ways: to show possessive case and to denote contractions, for instance. The latter is a convenient headline device where space must be saved. Many desks allow use of the apostrophe in headlines to denote contractions that would not be allowed elsewhere. For example: It's a witch-hunt : Kojo Annan.

Hyphen

The hyphen can be especially useful in headlines in linking together two words: As Nathpa-Jhakri staff stir 'politically motivated'.

The Question mark

The question mark comes in for some special uses in headlines. Example: Colombo blast, a message for Government?

The Colon

It is specially useful in the headline. It can help save space by shifting part of the sentence around into an introductory term. For instance: Cane diversion to *gur* units: Govt. acts to plug losses.

Some desks allow the colon to be used in attribution, as,

Tehri project near completion: Tiwari.

Shun the lazy habit of padding

Padding the headline means finding ways of filling out space with something besides additional facts. Don't substitute the space, consuming words for the economical one when the line is short. Don't make an unnecessary lengthy identification when a shorter one will do.

Be as specific as possible

Give facts instead of abstract material as much as possible. For example, use the exact number instead of 'many' in the headline. When using numbers, figures are better than spellings because they are easier to read in headlines.

Use only well known names

If the person about whom a story is written is reasonably well known, use the names in the headline. Avoid using names of the individuals who are unknown to the average newspaper reader.

Avoid repetition

Do not repeat the same or similar words in headlines. Repetition in headlines as in stories, detracts from readability and indicates sloppy writing and thinking.

Avoid 'splits'

Avoid splitting prepositional phrases or infinitives between lines. Doing so makes heads difficult to read and understand.

Counting the Head

Constructing headlines that fit the space and tell the story requires patience and flexibility. Headline writers have developed a system for predicting whether a line will 'go' (can be fitted into the required space). They 'count' each line, using any system that will predict with reasonable accuracy. Types vary: some are extended and some are condensed. An extended type across a single column will yield a few units; while a condensed type across two columns will yield many more. The 'unit count' system begins by giving a unit value to every letter and figure in the alphabet. It is based on a count of one for most letters, with adjustments for thinner and fatter letters, and for capitals when they are mixed with lower case letters.

While a typewriter makes an equal space regardless of the letter, printing does not. For instance "i" takes just half the space required for "e" and a capital "M" will cover approximately twice the space of a lowercase "a". Those who write headlines, use a count schedule to compensate for letter variances. These "counts" are standard regardless of the size or style of type used.

Sub-editor uses the following table in writing headlines.

All lower case letters	-	1 unit
except f, l, i, t which takes	-	½ unit
and m & w takes	-	1½ unit
All capital letters	-	1½ unit
except I	-	½ unit
M & W	-	2 units
All numerals	-	1 unit
except 1	-	½ unit
symbols ($, &, %)	-	1 unit
Punctuation (., ;, :)	-	½ unit
Single quote	-	½ unit
Hyphen	-	½ unit
Dash	-	1 unit
Space between words	-	1 unit

Obviously before beginning to write the headline we should know the number of units we have to play with. Normally one column (11 ems) accommodate 11 units of 18 pt. Century Bold all capitals and 14 units in one column of 18 pt. Century Bold upper and lower letters.

Method of counting heads

There are at least three ways to count heads; or to determine whether the words will fit in the allocated number of units. The number of units may be 10,15, 18, 24 or whatever is indicated by a particular sample on the head schedules. The count is given by the line. For example, if a particular head counted 10 units, the sub-editor would have room for 10 units per line and methods used to put six units on one line and four on another.

The first method used by many veteran copy editors in counting heads is to go over each letter with a pencil and add the number of units mentally. Practice builds proficiency in using this technique.

A second method is to place a mark over a full count letter and a mark under a half count. The sub-editor counts the marks to determine whether the head will fit without the need of mental arithmetic.

The third method is the key word method, which uses words matching the number of units in a specific head. For instance an 11 unit head may use the words "Many Returns," containing 11 units, as its key; these key words would be on the head schedule. The sub-editor types the keyboards, then types the proposed head beneath it. Adjustments necessarily must be made for half, one-and-a-half, on double unit letters. Each head used by the newspaper would have key words of varying length according to its units. The advantage of this method is that the key words eliminate the need for looking at calibrations, and there is no need to count manually or in one's head.

To emphasize the first or mental count method is the most popular with journalists. After writing heads for several months, many sub-editors are able to judge whether a line will fit in the space provided, almost by looking at it. In computers, thousands of type families are available. Headlines are adjusted simply by touching the keys.

Headline patterns

Newspapers of a half century or more ago featured heads composed of many layers or decks, each developing different phases of the story. Today's newspapers use simpler heads with a minimum of decks.

Headlines pattern vary according to newspapers and many even change with editors. Readers subconsciously become familiar with the styles, which help identify the newspaper. Radical changes in headline patterns should not be made frequently. Once a newspaper adopts a particular style for writing headlines, it clings fairly tenaciously to the standards because of reader identification. When a decision is reached it changes styles, the entire paper adopts the heads so that the readers will not be disturbed.

The various styles of headlines are discussed as under:

Deck

A deck is a distinct headline on its own, as such it may consist of one or more lines. A headline of six lines is a single deck if the lines are in the same type and read one on to the other. If the six lines of type are divided into two units, each of three lines, each making some kind of sense-contained, then we have a double-deck headline. A multi-deck headline is any with more than one deck.

Strapline

It is the subordinate line above the headline, usually one line in smaller type (say 14 pt. or 18 pt.). It is also called kicker or eyebrow line. It adds a new thought but does not repeat the words or information in the lines below. Strapline has the following characteristics:

- (i) This line is in type approximately one-third to one-half the size of the main head;
- (ii) It is underlined
- (iii) It is in the opposite kind of type from the main head;
- (iv) While straplines are frequently used with feature stories or those with humour, editors also put them over straight news articles.

Reverse Kicker

It is reverse strapline. The general effect of this head is similar to the above except that the overline is larger than the two lines of type below it. The kicker overline for instance, might be in 30 point italic capitals, while the two lower lines, would be in 18 point roman capitals and lowercase. This head is essentially for feature-type stories.

Flush left

The flush left heading is a heading of one or more lines in which all the lines are set flush to the left. The flush left heading has become more popular, being recommended by Allen Hutt as easier to write and by ED Arnold as 'optically better.' The typesetter can work more easily with such head. This style of head can tell more, since the sub-editor is not confined with rigid mechanical requirements. Example:

Badal to speak
at dedication
of main library

Here the symmetry of all lines is on the left side.

Flush right

Each line is pushed against the right hand margin to create a stepped effect on the left. It has very limited application. It is all right as an occasional variant but not as a regular style. The flush right is slower to set.

It is opposite to left flush. The symmetry is on the right side of the lines.

Flush head

This head is difficult to write and causes problems for the printer who sets it because of its mechanical requirements; it theoretically must fill the column so it is flush left and right. The sub-editor, therefore, must work longer with words to accomplish the goal. Because of this difficulty, flush heads are seldom used in modern newspapers.

Single line

This is normally used for small news items appearing in single column as a filler.

Inverted Pyramid

This is headline style of centred lines in which each successive line is shorter than the one above; also story structure which arranges facts in descending order of importance. The mechanical requirements make this head difficult to write, and it requires more time in typesetting. Relatively few modern newspapers use it. Example :

Badal to speak
at library
sites

Crossline

Early American newspapers relied heavily on this head, and it continues to be widely used for short stories. This head is a single line of type, originally centered but now popularly used flush left. Example:

Badal to speak

Banner head: A large headline of one or more lines extending across a page or almost the full width of a page. Also called a 'Streamer.'

Blanket head: This type of head is the most common in USA. This headline covers all columns occupied by a story.

Pyramid head: line form resembling a pyramid with lines succeeding short, longer and longest.

Cross head: These are the sub-headings placed in text, between paragraphs.

Turn head: This is a headline on inside page identifying resumption of story continued from another page. In USA this term is jump head.

Label head: A dull, likeless headline, usually lacking a verb.

Drop head: A type of headline in which each line is stepped back to the right.

Caption head: The headline appearing over a piece of art.

Exercises

1. Cut out six leads from newspapers. Identify what questions are answered (who ...). Identify what is not answered. Identify the kind of lead (summary ...).
2. Count the number of 'Emphasis' leads appearing in any regional newspaper during a one-week period.
3. Using your any national daily, clip and label examples of 'direct quotation', 'dialogue', 'summary', 'punch', 'contrast and 'crowded' leads.

4. Select any three national dailies and note:
   (i) The style of headlines used in those dailies.
   (ii) Compare the types used.
   (iii) Readability of the headlines.

5. Compare the headline of any one story which appeared among all three dailies on the bases of the following :
   (a) From editorial point
   (b) From style point
   (c) From point size
   (d) From importance point;

6. Identify the who, what, where, when, why and how, if they are present in the following para:
   A personal assistant of the Union Minister of State for Finance, G. Ramachandran, was arrested by the Central Bureau of Investigation in Delhi while allegedly accepting a bribe from a senior Indian Revenue Service Officer.
7. Note the 'headlines' or abbreviations and word selections, used in the heads of any three regional newspapers.
8. To introduce yourself to head writing, compose heads for your own stories; ask third parties to decide whether the head given them an idea of what the stories contain.
9. Cut out large reports without their headlines. Give your own headlines and compare them with the ones actually given. Which are better and why?
10. Convert every headline without a verb to one with a verb to make it 'active'.

5

EDITING NEWS

Your editor hands you a news story with the following advice. "The lead is buried and the copy is full of holes. Clean up the copy and cut it to 500 words." Where will you begin? How will you decide what to keep and what to cut out? What needs to be changed and why?

When a reporter finishes writing, the publication process is far from complete. The production phase, when writing is scrutinized, amended, corrected and sometimes restructured can profoundly affect the piece of writing that is eventually published. The person responsible for overseeing this process is known as a sub-editor.

All types of a copy reach to a sub-editor, from copy that is clean ready-to-print to that which is clumsy, heavy and badly worded. He does not have spare time on a newspaper desk and must immediately know what to do with it, when to leave it as it is, or when to rewrite it.

The dictum never to be forgotten is: all copy has to be made clear, precise and accurate.

It is necessary to understand the general type of problems that can arise in copy and to recognise specific errors to be dealt with. It needs to be stressed again that a mind with discipline in the use of language, understanding, perception of ideas and clarity of judgement is required for any copy. It is more so when dealing with complicated copy. Great skill is required in this.

Ideas are abstract. Sometimes they cannot be presented clearly and appear diffused or scattered. They have to be grasped and put together in a comprehensible form. This can necessitate paragraph re-arrangement, language other than what is used in the copy and the elimination of expressions that tend to confuse.

The writer seldom feels happy unless he has used adjectives, or 'strong' expression; but they only distract from the flow of language. This results in bad copy. Accurate phrases and fewer, but more effective, adjectives have to be used. The exact meaning of every word must be understood by the sub-editor before he can be satisfied with his work.

Burns (2002) says, "A well–written news story has the facts, written in the right order and with the right emphasis and tells those facts simply'.

The Editing Process

The editing process is used to correct over-writing, clumsy sentence construction and faulty grammar. It translates jargon into plain English, and explains technical or complex ideas. This process includes deleting unnecessary words and checking the vocabulary of a story to ensure it suits the audience. Sub editors also ensure that punctuation, grammar and spelling are accurate. Most news organizations have 'style guides' that offer preferred usages and spellings. For example, newspaper style dictates that numbers from one to nine are spelled out while two-digit numbers such as 10 are expressed numerically. Readers want to comprehend immediately. Simple sentence structures and transparent paragraph structure lead the reader to continue reading.

Rules for Editing Process

There are some simple ground rules to guide the editing process. The first step is to understand exactly what the writer intended. A sub editor does not impose his or her own interpretation of the facts, but aims to make the writer's intention clear. A good way to begin is to read what the story is about. Once you have a clear idea, you can evaluate how successful the writer has been in getting the story across.

You as a sub editor apply your news sense to the facts and evaluate the choices made by the reporter. Sometimes copy needs to be restructured or re-ordered to emphasize the most newsworthy aspects. Newsworthiness is a relative value and your decision is partly based on your understanding of the audience, their interests and values.

Third, you know a news story must contain who, what, where, when and why. If this information is in the story but not at the beginning, you need to rework it. Decide in what order those elements should be presented. Does 'who' come before 'what'? Is 'where' more important than 'who'? Sometimes 'when' is the most important fact but rarely does a story begin with 'why' although 'why' should never be left to the end of the story. Often 'why' is followed by the sixth element of news, 'how'.

Fourth, sometimes a report contains answers to the five Ws but the reporter has missed the main point. Ask yourself again 'What is the most interesting part of the story?' The ideas in the story should flow logically and easily. Are the ideas in rational order? Do they lead on naturally from one to another? If you were telling this story, where would you begin? If the place where you would start the story is not at the beginning of the story in front of you, then the 'lead', or most newsworthy information, is said to be 'buried' in the story. It must be 'on top' or in the first sentence.

Fifth, if the order of information needs improvement, you may be able to fix it without rewriting the whole story. Try re-ordering the paragraphs. Once the paragraphs are in the right order, look for gaps in the way the story is told. You will probably need to reconstruct some sentences or change their direction so that the new order makes sense. You will need to write a new introduction. Some information may need to be moved from one paragraph to another, tenses may need correction, nouns and pronouns may need to be re-arranged. If you attend to the structure first, you avoid wasting time correcting typographical errors in paragraphs that you cut out or change for structural reasons.

The Butcher's Art

A Sub editor also edits copy to a required length. This is done by first removing any information that is not essential to the meaning of the original story. If the story is still too long, the sub editor looks to the construction of individual sentences to find ways to reduce the number of words required to tell the story.

> *"Gibson describes, if you edit – your own copy or someone else's you must learn to chop fearlessly to cut out duplication, to eliminate the inconsequential, and you must do the work on your material as well as that from the farthest outposts covered by a wire organization."*

The relationship between writers and sub-editors is often contentious. Sub editors complain they are made into scapegoats for lazy journalism. Writers complain that the sub editor has deleted the best parts of their work. Reporters face the wrath of the public after editing errors change the meaning of a story. Your aim is to take things out in such a seamless way that even the writer will be hard pressed to recognize the deletions.

"Gibson suggests, You can keep a lot of your sentences down to a reasonable length with some careful trimming, and a little thought. Practice helps. You need to get the habit of eliminating excess baggage in your prose. If you learn to delete it when you see it soon, you will learn to avoid it as you write."

Dealing with Redundancies

This is not the job of the journalists alone. Every writer bears this in mind. According to Goethe, the first sign of the master was compression.

If the sub-editor comes across writing which is loose, and full of words that are incorporated without justification, he has to remove them. At times, it is a long phrase, which can be reduced to one word. Thus 'at the hour of sunset' can be 'at sunset' and absolute monopoly is only 'monopoly'. Reporters sometimes say: 'the stabbing was fatal and the man 'died'. Well, it was fatal it is obvious that the man died. When the sub-editor sees 'new invention', he must remember that an invention is always new. 'A box with a round shape' is a 'round box'. There is doubt sometimes about the use of 'in the meantime' 'in the meanwhile' or 'meanwhile'. The last one is most suitable and in the meanwhile is wrong. The following redundancies are common.

'the actual fact'
'8 P.M. in the evening'
'The immediate past'
'In close proximity to'
'It is likely to be most probable'
'Enclosed in box in which it was kept'
'Repetition of the same thing'
'Detailed research',
'Antiguated idea'
'sing together in chorus' etc.

An 'unseen' difficulty arises when stories are written in a profound obvious learned manner. It is not easy to make changes at the first reading, even if they contain errors and redundancies.

Cutting the Straight News story

Cutting, trimming, boiling, slashing are among the terms used in the newsroom for reducing stories in length and the terminology is not entirely uniform. In some newsrooms, cutting is the generic term, with trimming, boiling and slashing indicating increasing degrees of cutting. You trim by cutting out excessive wordage and minor details; you boil by doing the same thing more intensively; you slash a story to the bone by retaining only its hard essentials. Garst and Bernstein explain at the New York Times:

> *Trimming is a general tightening up of the story, chiefly by eliminating superfluous words and replacing loose phrases with single words that express the thought adequately.*

... boiling down is more drastic and is the process of close paring of all sentences and the sacrifice of minor facts.

... Cutting means the elimination of all but the most important facts, those without which there would be no story or an incomplete one. Often there is nothing left but the bare bones of the story with a shred or two of clothing.

Bitting Off

Most straight news stories are still arranged in inverted pyramid form, but increasingly stories not in that form cross the desk. Part of the logic of the straight news, inverted pyramid structure is to permit the story to be cut at any point. In fact some newspapers once left it to printers to chop away paragraphs to make stories fit on the page. No self-respecting newsroom will permit this today, except under most unusual conditions. But whoever does it, bitting off is the easiest way to cut a story.

Boiling

Although chopping away at the end of the story is a legitimate professional solution, it is only one way. The fact that it is also the easiest way that has prompted some bad copy reading. If a copy desk knows no other way to reduce a story's length, or if the routine is so pinched that it allows no time for careful editing, he deletes the last paragraph sacrificing its pertinent details. The straight news story is pyramid form frequently needs a more complicated type of handling. For reasons either of content or structure, it cannot be chopped of. Boiling is done not only to adjust a story to fit the available space, it is also done in the interest of clarity.

The editor is always alert for chances to remove wordage that not only doesn't contribute to the story but actually gets in the way of telling it. The fact that the story is shortened is merely a by product. The Chief reason for all this labour is to make the story better—simpler, more direct, easier to read, easier to understand.

Most judgement on whether a word or phrase stays or goes are based on considerations not only of space but of the quality of the story. Nevertheless, wholesale cutting simply to fit space is frequently necessary. Even when cutting at the end the editor should give special attention to the last paragraph of what remains. It should put a finishing touch on the story if possible.

Newspapers are much more concerned with good beginnings than they are with good endings, and that is as it should be; many more readers are affected by beginnings, since relatively few who start a story read through to the end, especially in the case of long stories. However, a touch of craftsmanship at the end can improve the total impact of a story for the reader who does want all the details.

The editor must be sure that whenever something is deleted from a story, its loss will not affect another part of what remains. Hasty deletions can wreck a good story. The damage is especially devastating when editor cuts details that broaden out lead materials. Leads built around more than one aspect of the story are particularly tricky.

Westley in his book 'News Editing' offers following solutions

The editor must wield a scalpel, not a butcher knife. In cutting, it is the total impact of the story on the reader that must be taken into account, in addition to the need to save words and sacrifice only non-essential details. No simple set of rules could ever be adequate for all the space saving requirements of a busy copy desk. The situations are extremely varied – and there are many more variations than space permits here. But although this list is not exhaustive, here are some points to remember:

1. Do your cutting in such a way as to preserve the essential facts, leaving just enough details to answer the reader's most pressing questions.
2. Don't assume that a story can be chopped off anywhere just because it seems to be arranged in inverted pyramid form.
3. Try to preserve the broad outline of the story when the structure is not the routine inverted pyramid form.

4. Try to preserve the flavour of the story when it is built around a feature treatment.
5. Read the new version carefully. The process of cutting may have raised new problems. Read past the cuts to determine whether changes are necessary in what remains–in antecedents of pronouns, for instance. The new structure may require the insertion of new connective words and phrases. Supply them where they are needed.
6. Remove excess wordage at any time, whether or not you have been given general instructions to reduce the story in length.
7. Try to preserve or supply an ending that fittingly closes the story.

Re-writing

Re-writing is a factor in dealing with complicated copy. It has to be borne in mind that many times the information given may appear to be useless, but is not only really so. The writer has all the knowledge about what he has written. He is writing with the background of that knowledge. The sub-editor sees the copy only at its face value and some statements might appear to be giving useless information. Before re-writing it may be necessary to contact the writer and see the points clarified.

In re-writing change of tenses is sometimes involved. This is not easy; again, because the author is in the know of the actual time of happenings. In his carelessness, he may have mixed up the tenses. The sub-editor has to understand the actuality of the happening, and then change the tenses suitably.

A good re-write job calls for incorporation of important related facts. They may be inserted in the story in individual paragraphs, but should not hamper the flow of the narrative. In case this is likely to happen, it is worth considering the possibility of carrying the additional information in the form of a box to go alongwith the main item.

Sum Up

Sub-editing is a production tool used by journalists to ensure that reporting fits the style, length and news priorities of the publishing organization. Editing is also the process by which writers polish and refine the messages they create. Developing editing skill and processes for evaluating the strengths of various parts of your writing is important from the beginning.

The better the editor you are, the more effectively you can see your writing as the sum of its parts, the better writer you will be.

As a reporter, you should apply the same process to your work as sub editors do, before you submit the story. Never assume that others will pick up your mistakes or that you can abdicate responsibility for errors.

Most of the time, the writer does not have the opportunity to negotiate changes with the sub editor. However, sometimes the editing process is a collaboration between a writer and the person who commissions the work. One final piece of advice – always proofread your writing twice.

Exercises

1. Compare the presentation styles of several newspapers. How does your edited version differ from the published one?
2. Take a piece of news agency copy and cut it by 40 percent.
3. Write a few paragraphs in usual manner. Re-write them to make them (a) light hearted, (b) fast paced and (c) serious and persuasive.
4. Pick out a few reports from your daily newspapers. Now, rewrite them in a biased form, both for and against.
5. Pick up complicated pieces of writing done by those you know. Strip the language down bare to the bone.
6. Convert complicated writing into simple language, with small sentences and paragraphs.

6

ELEMENTS OF GOOD WRITING

Too much of what we put on newsprint these days is dull, awkward and pedestrian. As a result many editors believe they need to improve the writing on their papers. Because dull writing is more common than writing that has vitality. Editors are looking for those unusual people who can combine reporting and writing skills. Good writing begins with good reporting. The journalist whose prose jerks around the page like a mouse trapped in a room with a cat has no future in the business.

On newspapers around the country today, small but growing numbers of journalists are producing literature daily as they deal with everything from accidents to artists imagination and the dedication to learn how to combine them, you too may produce literature. We should all try to improve our writing. If we succeed, newspapers will not only be informative, but also enjoyable; not only educational, but also entertaining; and not only bought but also read.

In this chapter you will learn the basic characteristics of good writing and how the skills of good reporting make good writing possible.

Good Writing has the following characteristics:

It is precise

It is clear

It has a pace appropriate to the content.

It uses transitional devices that lead the reader from one thought to the next.

Precision

Words should be used precisely. They should mean exactly what you intend them to mean. You should never use 'uninterested' when you mean 'disinterested.' Nor should you use 'allude' for 'refer', 'presume' for 'assume', 'farther' for 'further.' If you report that fire has destroyed a house, you mean it must be rebuilt, not repaired.

Precision, however, means more than knowing the etymology of a word, it means knowing precisely what you want to say.

Incorrect: The Bill will make it illegal. . . .
Correct: The Bill would make it illegal. . .

The use of 'will' is imprecise because the legislation has not been passed. By using 'would' you are saying "if the legislature passes the Bill," it would - - -

Precision means using the correct sentence structure to communicate explicitly what you mean. The following sentence is technically correct but imprecise.

The state government passed the Ordinance, and the 150 supporters cheered.

It is imprecise because the compound sentence gives equal importance to the two thoughts expressed. Because the writer meant to show cause and effect, he should have used a complex sentence:

Because (or when) the state government passed the Ordinance, the 150 supporters cheered.

When you write implicitly, you force the reader to make inferences. Say what you are thinking.

Clarity

Before typing a single word, reporters should remind themselves of three simple guidelines:

- Rely on simple sentences.
- Use correct grammar and punctuation.
- Avoid cliches
- Think clearly.

The result will be clear writing; such as: in fact, nevertheless, however, for instance.

There is pretty fine difference between the colon and semi-colon. The semi-colon marks a longer pause than that indicated by a comma while the colon indicates an even longer pause than the semi-colon. The semi-colon is more useful in double sentences where there is no conjunction. For instance:

Rumours spread that the army had mutinied; the crowd believed it.

The principal function of the colon in newspapers is that it should always be used before opening quotes.

The Prime Minister said: "This is a very good result." The colon is also useful if you are listing things in a story, Ramesh sold every thing: his house, his car, his scooter and even his clothes.

Full stop denotes the end of a sentence. A sentence is a complete

....

Simple sentences

One remedy for unclear writing is the simple sentence. Simple sentences create an impact on the readers. So the message should be stated clearly in a simple sentence.

Grammar and Punctuation

Errors in grammar are far too common in newspaper writing, and because of them, meaning is obscured. No one who aspires to be a writer will succeed without knowing the rules of grammar. Dangling participles, split infinitives, noun verb disagreements, pronoun-antecedent disagreements and misplaced modifiers are like enemy troops. They attack your sentences and destroy the meaning. The best defence to construct tight, strong sentences.

Here are some typical errors and ways to correct them.

Incorrect : Each of the boys brought their sleeping bags.
Correct : Each of the boys brought his sleeping bag.
Incorrect : The Mayor told the taxpayer to submit a claim to the clerk, bringing it to her before noon.
Correct : The Mayor told the taxpayer to submit a claim to the clerk before noon.
Incorrect : The Major agreed to soon submit his resignation.
Correct : The Major agreed to submit his resignation soon.

Improper punctuation also creates ambiguities at best and inaccuracies at worst. The most important punctuation marks are: the comma, the semi colon, the colon and the full stop.

Commas are more used than any other punctuation marks and many of them are superfluous. A comma replaces the word 'and' to separate a series of words.

A reporter should ensure that his stories are clear, concise, easy to read and accurate. A comma is essential in words or phrases. Yet again, you will write a good sentence much more easily if you make a conscious effort to make it short. There are plenty of excellent one-word sentences. Some of these are:

Yes.
No
Rubbish!

All these words are complete thoughts, completely expressed.

Cliches

It is almost pointless to warn reporters to avoid cliches. The problem is, just what a 'cliche is' there are a few to be going on with:

blow by blow
bitter end
Crying need
each and every
fair sex
interesting to note
last but not least
long years
marked contrast
ones and above
true colours
matter of life and death
acid test.

There are hundreds more. Reporters should try to alert themselves to spot cliches in their copy and take them out before handing the story in.

As bad as cliches are jargon. Jargon is the specialist language which particular groups of people use in their own trades or professions. It is most noticeable in handouts. Fortunately, jargon is easier to eradicate than it is to avoid cliches. The reporter should train himself to spot jargon and then translate it into terms that can be understood by a common man.

When a reporter is interviewing someone who uses jargon the reporter does not understand (for example, a scientist explaining some complicated technicality) he should not take refuge in playing safe by scrupulously ensuring that at least he has the correct spelling of the particular term or word which he does not understand. When he does not understand a particular term used by a man, the reporter must say: "Could you please put that in words which the average reader of my paper will understand." The reporter who says that he is not displaying his ignorance; he is displaying his skill.

Good spelling is primarily a matter of remembering. No reporter is going to get very far in his career if he is bad at spellings; for if he cannot spell he almost certainly does not know the meaning of many of the words he cannot spell. He thus has a smaller supply of words upon which to draw than he will often need in his work.

Listed below are a selection of words, frequently miss-spelled and almost as frequently mis-used. Test yourself on them.

Accommodation	Humorous
Acquiescence	Hysterical
Annihilate	Innocuous
Benefited	Jeopardize
Cemetery	Manoeuver
Debatable	Meanness
Descendant	Miscellaneous
Destructible	Noticeable
Discreet	Occurred
Eligibility	Recommend
Emissary	Supersede
Exhilaration	Unnecessary
Fallacious	Vociferous
Harassed	Separate

Clear Thinking

A story must have a beginning, middle and end. Put in a maze, rats make many mistakes before they find their way out. So do writers who start a sentence, a paragraph or a story without knowing where it will end. The problem is most obvious when the reporter is unsure of the lead. The result usually is a story that jumps from one idea to another without transitions and without supporting evidence for each idea introduced. When you are sure of your lead, the rest of the story often will fall into place.

Too many reporters would try to work with so many elements in the lead and then would not know where to go in the second and third paragraphs. Rank the elements in the order of importance. Then take them one at a time.

Pacing

The untrained observer looking at a new car may see the glossy finish, flashy chrome and stylish lines. An engineer may see the hundreds of complicated working parts under the hood.

Like the untrained observer, the reader enjoys a story because of the message. Another writer will recognize the author's skillful use of techniques that make the story readable.

One of those rarely noticed but important techniques is pacing sentences, as much as the words themselves, give a story mood. Short sentences convey action, tension, movement. A series of long sentences conveys a more relaxed mood, long sentences slow down the reader.

Between these two extremes are sentences of varying lengths, and good writers use them all. Not all sentences should be long or short. Nor should they all be of medium length. An abrupt change in sentence length draws attention to the sentence. Giving precisely selected words the proper pace is a skill of the creative writer. Some writers read their copy aloud to themselves. Their ear tells them if the story has proper pace and variety. The beginning writer should count the number of words in each sentence.

Transitions

Besides being well-paced, good writing also uses transitions to lead the reader imperceptibly from one thought to the next. Transitions assure the reader that the writer has a sense of direction. A transition is a bridge. It can be a word, a phrase, a sentence or a paragraph.

These linkages help you achieve coherence, the logical connection of ideas. The linkages transfer you from one sentence to the next, from one paragraph to the next. The different types of linkages are called transitions. Writers unfamiliar with transitions merely stack paragraphs, like wood, atop one another. Transitions keep the story if not the woodpile, from falling apart. Repeating a word or phrase is one way to keep the story from falling apart.

Repetition of a phrase or of sentence construction, called

parallelism, is another way to guide readers through a story. Writers frequently use parallelism to achieve coherence.

Chronology and references to time are other ways to tie a story together. Words and phrases such as 'now', 'since then', and 'two days later' are invaluable in helping readers understand where they have been and where they are going. Chronology is important in everything from reports of automobile accidents (which car entered the intersection first?) to recaps of events that occurred over months or even years.

Exercises

1. Analyze the front pages of any four dailies to see;

   (a) Editors' understanding of each paper's audience by looking at the selection of stories.
   (b) If you find stories on the same topic on two or more front pages, determine if they are written differently for different audiences.
   (c) Are there any attempts to localize national stories? Suggest any possibilities you can think of:

   On the basis of what you have learned in this chapter, do you agree or disagree with the editors' news judgements? Why?
2. Go to your library and look at both- a recent issue of 'The Times of India' or the "Hindu" and an issue of the same date five years ago. Describe the differences you find in subjects and sources of stories.
3. Interview the editors of two dailies about how they decide the value of news stories, how they assess the reliability of sources and how they try to ensure accuracy.
4. Puntuate the following sentence:
   In the Lok Sabha the Speaker Somnath Chatterjee recalled the sacrifices made by the nine persons killed in the attack on the temple of Indian democracy due to the supreme sacrifice and the exemplary courage shown by the security personnel of the central reserve police force the Delhi police the Indo-Tibetan Border police and the Parliament watch and ward staff the terrorist attack was foiled.

7

ART OF INTERVIEWING

"The key to a good news interview," says the *Seattle Times*' Mike Francher, "is to make it possible for the source to say what he really thinks rather than having to think about what he says."

Journalists agree that good reporting is about 80 percent interviewing. It is the key to many stories you will write. Your ability to get people talk to you is the difference between mediocre reporting and good reporting.

Although you already have experience interviewing some one, you probably haven't thought much about how or why you have been doing it. And you probably haven't had much experience trying to get information from someone who wants to withhold it.

Sometimes journalists are denied information they stomp out of the room; they shouldn't, they must find other resources. A skillful questioner often can obtain information, the source does not want to divulge or does not even realize he or she is giving. Interviewing is an imperfect process. As in the city water-works system, there is plenty of leakage. When the city pumps a million gallons of water, not all of it reaches the customers. Some evaporates, some leaks through decaying pipes. In the same way information also leaks out, too, as it is passed from source to interviewer to editor to reader. The source may not want you to know everything. Sometimes differences in cultural and ethnic backgrounds change the meaning. You must work hard to refine your skills.

Interviewing does of course, require a certain courage when you are meeting people you don't know and talking about subjects of which you have little knowledge, you run the risk of having your ignorance exposed. But not asking question is worse, you run the risk of remaining forever ignorant of matters that could have well fascinated you. You also miss the opportunity to meet interesting people. A special kind of reward awaits the person who asks questions. You learn not only facts and opinions you will use in your story, but you also add to your reservoir of knowledge.

According to a Chinese proverb, " He who asks is a fool for five minutes; the one who does not, is a fool forever."

Definition

Interview is defined as a conversation in which a journalist puts questions to someone to elicit information. It is an exposure of the personality, whom you are interviewing. The word interview has been derived from the French word 'entervue', which means between sight. It is a meeting between two persons with a specific purpose. It may be defined as any purposeful communication between two individuals. The word 'Interview' may also be treated as an acronym. Each letter denotes an important element of the art of interview.

I — Investigative
N — Natural
T — Topical
E — Enthralling
R — Realistic
V — Vibrant
I — Interactive
E — Expressive
W — Warmth

"An interview is a conversation, usually between two persons, to elicit information on behalf of an unseen audience. It is often a conversational exchange of information that can produce a level of intelligence that neither party could achieve alone."

Ken Metzler in his book—*Newsgathering*

The second part does not mean reporters should do a lot of talking, quite the opposite is true most of the time. It does suggest, however, that the reporter has a serious responsibility to do homework in preparation for the interview so that the level of conversation is beyond kindergarten. It further suggests that reporters, with an eye toward the needs and interests of an unseen audience, will ask the kinds of questions that will get answers suitable for the readers. And finally it suggests that sometimes reporters literally are the experts after having explored a topic exhaustively. In such instances, people are more forthcoming if you are open and candid.

Interviewing Skills

Information is the merchandise of a journalist. While some of the information is gathered from records and some from observation, most of it is gathered in person to person conversations. For that reason, every journalist needs to develop interviewing skills. He should develop a personality that is acceptable to enable him to meet others with confidence and friendliness. It is the beginning of a relationship. The relationship survives on the foundation of mutual respect and non-aggressiveness. Interview is conducted to study background details or to use the information somewhere. Interview with the people clear up things and help readers to understand the prevailing situation. The reporter must be able to devise questions that will draw revealing answers. In order to be able to do so, he must be familiar with the total situation within which he is operating. The reporter must be clear about what he wants to know, and the problem has to be carefully formulated in his mind. He must work hard to refine his skills. He should simultaneously ask questions, digest responses, record answers, cajole the source, gauge reactions and look for detail.

A few Precautions

An interview is not necessarily a formal event, but covers any situation where the reporter talks with someone face to face to obtain information. Most people involved in news meet reporters for the first time and as a result may be nervous and apprehensive. They may hesitate to talk fearing that what they say, may be wrong and reflect against them in a story.

People who have met reporters earlier may not be so apprehensive. They know that journalists do not bite, and that most are good ones who only write, must put the subject at ease. Even using the term 'interview' can frighten some story subjects because it connotes a formal event. Thus reporters should create a relaxed and informal atmosphere. One may be able to do this is to suggest a 'talk' which really is an 'interview'. Another is to postpone any suggestion of taking notes until after the reporter establishes rapport with the subject. The most productive and newsy interviews develop when the subject is at ease with the reporter. People are naturally tense because most are not accustomed to the prospect of having their words taken down for a news story that thousands will read.

Interview on Telephone

Personal interviews, which give the reporter a better chance to achieve rapport and watch facial expression are impossible because of such obstacles as difficulty in reaching the subject, or distances. Sometimes there is little to be gained in a face to-face meeting.

By using telephone, reporters can achieve a great deal, both in time saved and information gained. A practical way to conduct phone interviews is by avoiding preliminaries or lengthy explanations. The reporter simply identifies himself, digests the problem, explains the deadline, or other problem, and asks the questions. In some situations, reporters may make an appointment for a personal interview after obtaining the information needed for a deadline.

Consideration of the kind of story

How you prepare for the interview depends on what kind of a story you intend to cover. It may be a news story, personality profile or an investigative piece. In each case you check the newspaper library and search the data bank, talk to other reporters and if there is enough time, read magazine articles and books.

To prepare for a news story, you pay more attention to clips about the subject of the story than to those about the personality of the individual to be interviewed. To prepare for a profile, you look for personality quirks and the subject's interests, family friends, travels and habits. To prepare for an investigative piece, you want to know both your subject matter and the person you are interviewing. In all these stories, don't overlook other reporters and editors who know something about the person or subject.

If a potential interview involves discussions of a particular event at a site, you should try to visit the site first to get a good mental picture of it. This will help you to formulate questions and make you aware when an interviewee's answers conflict with something you have observed first hand. You should consider, if necessary, preparing an interview schedule or a questionnaire to help you. Interviewing requires patience, confidence and an ability to listen, participate, observe and absorb. Reporters must be able to ask a question and then listen to the entire response, all the time concentrating on the key points.

Three-fourth of an interview is only listening

—Tim Sebastian

Tim Sebastian, the B.B.C. anchor of *Hard Talk, Badshah of all Talk Shows,* in an interview with Nikhat Kazmi, in *The Times of India,* 16 April 2000, says that three-fourth of an interview is only listening.

Some interesting excerpts from the interview

> *Surprisingly, people want to share their stories. All you have to do is push at the door and it will open. You know, it's funny how people keep talking about the art of interviewing but they don't realize three-fourths of an interview is only listening. Only one-fourth is about talking. And sometimes, you've got to let the long silences remain because silences can be very telling too. You don't have to fill the entire programme with talk. Essentially, you've got to create moments of great intimacy with people you've never met.*

The rich, the famous, the powerful: do you ever feel intimidated at the prospect of grilling them. Any butterflies in your stomach?

> *I am always nervous before an interview. But that's not because I'm talking to certain people. No, I have always been nervous about broadcasting. Do you know I was a shy little schoolboy who was terrified of reading out loud in class?*

As the Hard Talker, do you envisage your role as an interrogator, a friend, a counsel or an inquisitor?

> *I see myself as a catalyst who is trying to get people to talk about themselves in the most effective way. Now I have to find the key to unlock the person sitting in front of me. Rarely can you unlock the front door, which is always closely guarded. So you've got to go in through the back or side door and somehow, find a key for it. You see, interviewing is not an exact science. It is largely intuitive. You have to engage with the other person and it's impossible to engage with everybody. People aren't robots. People aren't computers.*

Art of the Interview

People think that interviewing is easy, that it's simply a matter of going somewhere and asking someone a few questions. Anyone with a little nerve can do that. The truth, however, is that to interview is an art, and a difficult one. Let us think first of all what the interview is News interviews and feature interviews have different objectives, but in general you want three things from them.

The aim of an interview is to provide, in the interviewee's own words, facts, reasons or opinions on a particular topic so that the listener can form a conclusion as to the validity of what she/he is saying. The opinions of the interviewer are not to be counted here and he should not get drawn into answering the question himself/herself. Within the present definition, it is the interviewee who must come through in the programme and not the interviewers.

Preparing for the Interview

Never go without preparation. A reporter who begins an interview without proper preparation is like a pilot flying a bomber without a navigator. Analyse the subject you are going to discuss with him. A source who thinks the reporter is knowledgeable about the subject of the interview is more likely to speak frankly and fully than one who must explain everything as the conversation progresses. If he knows that you are completely ignorant, he may either get away with bluffs, or feel insulted that he is being interviewed by someone who is not even interested in the subject.

In formulating your problem, keep some basic questions ready. It is not necessary to write all of them, only a few important ones, will do. Many other questions are bound to arise when the interview develops into a conversation. Do not tie yourself only to the questions you have on hand. Jot the questions on paper and leave space for the answers to be put below them.

The environment, too, is important. Most interviews are conducted in the interviewee's office. Especially, if the story is a profile or a feature, it usually is better to get the source away from his or her work. In some interviews, it would be an advantage to get the source on neutral territory. If the reporter has some questions for the public official, suggest meeting in a coffee shop at a quiet time. A person has more power in his or her official surroundings. It is important, too, to let the source know how much time you need and whether you expect to return for further information.

After doing the appropriate homework, write down a list of questions which are to be asked. The list will guide the reporter through the interview and prevent him from missing important topics altogether. The best way to have a spontaneous conversation is to have questions prepared. Having questions prepared relieves the reporter of the need to be mentally searching for the next question as the source is answering the last one. If the reporter tries to think of the next question, he will not be paying close attention to what is being said, and he might miss the most important part of the interview. The source should also know the exact reason why you are meeting him. This can be helpful in complicated problems because it enables him to get the necessary information to make the interview more purposeful.

Preparing questions will benefit the reporter in two ways. It shows the seriousness of the reporter and the work he did. Thinking of the questions help prepare him for the interview. On the basis of the information the reporter has already gathered he knows what he wants to ask, now he must be careful about how he should ask the questions.

Phrasing the Question

Listen to an accomplished lawyer, ask questions. How the question is structured often determines whether the lawyer will win the case. Journalists face the same challenge. Reporters sometimes do not know how to ask questions. Quantitative researchers have shown how just a slight wording change affects the result of a survey. Before you interview a person you must be clear whether going for open-ended question or for closed-ended questions.

Open-Ended Questions

Open-ended questions allow the respondent some flexibility. In response to such type of questions, the source often reveals more than he or she realizes or intends to. Open-ended questions are less direct and less threatening. They are more exploratory and more flexible.

Closed-Ended Questions

Eventually the reporter needs to close in on a subject to pin down details, to get the respondent to be specific. Closed-ended questions are designed to elicit specific responses. Asking a vague question invites a vague answer. By asking a specific question, you are more likely to get a specific answer. Knowing exactly when to ask a closed-ended question or when to be less specific is not something you can plan ahead of time. The type of information you are seeking and the chemistry between the interviewer and the interviewee are the determining factors. You must make on the spot decisions.

Rules for Asking Questions

Questions must be asked clearly. Ambiguity would be disastrous. The subject must be encouraged to talk. The meeting has to be more like a conversation than a question and answer session. Never ask the subject his name, job or title. You have sought an interview with the source and are supposed to know all these. Link the topic of interview to what he is interested in. Clarify what "off the record" really means. Often when the person says something is "off the record," he secretly expects to see it in print the next day. If you ask him directly whether he would have any objection to those being published, he may not really mind it. If you do not obtain this clarification, you may miss an important detail. Jotting down points may cause nervousness to the subject, he may speak in a long and complicated manner. Here cleverness has to be used. Make your questions brief and put them one at a time. There will be digression (deviation from main subject) you have to keep the subject in mind, if necessary bring him back to the main topic. Always get the full meaning of the statement made as well as produce hard fact as well as opinions. The reporter should never imagine that he knows all.

Establishing a Rapport

The relationship between the reporter and the source—is crucial to the success of the interview. The relationship is sometimes relaxed, sometimes strained, often it is somewhere in between. The type of relationship you try to establish with your source is determined by the kind of story you are doing.

For most news stories and personality profiles, the reporter has more to gain if the subject is at ease. Often that can be accomplished by starting off with what you talk about. If you think the subject might be skeptical about your knowledge of the field, open with a question that shows you have done your homework. Reporters who can show sources what they have in common also have more success in getting information.

Rapport also depends upon where you conduct the interview. Many persons, especially those unaccustomed to being interviewed, do not feel comfortable in their work place. Persons who are seldom interviewed are often nervous, edgy or even scared. When you are doing an investigation, you may want the key characters to feel easy.

You may pretend you know more than you actually do. You want them to know that the material you have is substantive and serious. Seymour Hersh, a Pultizer Prize-winning investigative reporter, uses this tactic. Time magazine once quoted a government official commenting on Hersh. *"He wheedles, cajoles, pleads, threatens, asks a leading question, uses little tidbits as if he knew the whole story. When he finishes you feel like a wet rag."* In some cases, however, it is better even in an investigation to take a low-key approach. Let the source relax. Talk around the subject but gradually bring the discussion to the key issues. The surprise element may work to your favour.

Starting for the Interview

The reporter must judge when the interviewee is at ease and ready to answer questions. If he or she appears tense, the wise reporter chats leisurely about other things before leading into the areas of concern. This procedure often is necessary even with people involved in non-controversial situations. On the other hand, some interviewees are eager to talk, but their conversation wanders to areas that have nothing to do with the matter at hand. The journalist must politely, but firmly, provide questions to direct the person into the areas to be covered.

Reporters have few problems with "professionals," or those who, because of their place in life, frequently meet journalists. These individuals usually are cooperative, even in unfavourable situations, because they are accustomed to talking with reporters.

Taking Notes

Since few people have "photographic" memories that retain substantial amounts of information, some method is required for accurately preserving the important points an individual makes during a contact with a journalist. Unless an accurate record is made, the news story obviously will be wrong-to the unhappiness of all concerned from the interviewee to the reader.

Whatever method is used, the reporter should strive to maintain a relaxed setting by having a preliminary talk with the story subject before making any move to take notes. While everyone wants his words taken down accurately so the story will be correct, the average person has never had such attention. He may "freeze," refusing to say anything of importance. Seasoned journalists overcome this fear by talking without attempting to make notes: when the story subject appears at ease, the reporter suggests that taking notes will help accuracy. By this time the interviewee should be relaxed and trustful and the conversation can be continued with notes being taken.

Use of Shorthand

The ideal way to take notes is in shorthand, and the journalist who masters this skill will find it much easier to handle stories. Few reporters, unfortunately, have achieved this: they are consequently forced to devise their own shorthand symbols and combine them with conventional writing or printing. In making hasty non-shorthand notes, journalists often find that the quality of their handwriting suffers. They must transcribe the jottings, promptly to ensure the accurate story that all concerned expect.

Shorthand skill is invaluable to a reporter and moreover, will distinguish him from others who have not done so and may be competing for a job.

Reporters usually take abundant notes but base their stories only on those they decide are pertinent. During an interview, reporters have no way of knowing the major story element and must have adequate notes for "insurance" when they sit down to write the story.

Use of Tape Recorders

Many newspapers and radio stations equip staff members with tape recorders, an increasingly valuable tool for the reporter. Recorders not only eliminate the burden of taking detailed notes, but they also help assure the story subject that his speech or replies to questions will be reported accurately.

While tape recorders help accuracy, a disadvantage is that the reporter must go over lengthy tapes to find important segments of a talk. Some writers take notes while using a recorder and after completing the story listen to the tape to check for accuracy.

Just as the sight of a notebook and pen requires preliminaries to reassure the interviewee, the plan to use a recorder also should be explained to avoid distrust from those not accustomed to dealing with the press. The reporter who begins an interview by thrusting a microphone in front of the subject is almost certain to terminate the talk before it begins. One way to win the interviewee's confidence is to begin a discussion and develop rapport. When the interview is going well, the reporter suggests the use of a tape recorder to avoid any possibility of misquoting.

The recorder then can be placed into operation, with the interviewee's full knowledge and consent.

Those accustomed to dealing with the press prefer using a tape recorder in the interest of accuracy. These "professionals" know from experience that they shouldn't tell secrets to a reporter, and realize what they say will be used, if it is newsy, whether or not a recorder is used.

Those in the spotlight at public meetings and press conferences usually are accustomed to tape recorders, just as they are to TV cameras. Many public agencies not only expect recorders but even make their own tapes of meeting for the use of reporters and to compose their official minutes.

Reporters or their editors usually retain tapes at least until the story is published. If there is a likelihood that a controversy could develop, tapes are retained indefinitely.

Hidden Tape Recorders

For conventional interviews, it is far wiser, to bring the recorder into the open or not use it at all than to lose the subject's respect if he finds that it was hidden. The reporter dealing with honourable people has more to lose than to gain with hidden recorders.

In the case of controversial interviewee or investigations, the concealed tape recorder may be necessary. These exceptions should be weighed carefully in view of state laws and in consideration of personal and journalistic ethics.

Taping an ordinary telephone interview after the reporter has identified himself can be justified on the basis that there are no implications of "surveillance," and the recording helps, just as do written notes which the subject does not see being taken, to produce an accurate story. The lack of a face-to-face meeting that allows explanations is a disadvantage to any phone interview. To discuss the use of a recorder, in view of these disadvantages, probably would cause most subjects to refuse to talk.

Concealing a tape recorder during a personal interview is another matter. Reporters who defend the practice, in many cases with great merit, contend that the technique helps to arrive at the truth with individuals involved in questionable activities who would deny statements made to a writer carrying only a notebook. This, they argue, serves community interests by shedding light on situations which otherwise would never be brought to public attention.

Those who oppose the use of concealed recorders argue that the instruments constitute an invasion of privacy and deprive the interviewee of his rights, even though the subject may realize that he is talking with reporters.

Ensuring Accuracy

Accuracy is a major problem in all interviews. Both the question and the answer may be ambiguous. You may not understand what is said. You may record it incorrectly. You may not know the context of the remarks, your biases may interfere with the message. Some possibilities for making errors or introducing bias are unavoidable, but others are not. To ensure the most accurate and complete reporting possible, you should use all the techniques, available to obtain a good interview including observing, understanding what you hear and asking follow- up questions.

Don't be embarrassed to admit you haven't grasped something. It is better to admit to one person you don't understand than to advertise your ignorance in the newspaper in front of thousands. Once you have written the story, check with your sources, check the facts, check the concepts, catch your errors before publication. You will impress your editors, you will serve your readers better, your newspaper will have more credit, ability, and your source will be happy to talk to you the next time. Many dull interviews become interesting after they end. There are two things you should always do when you finish your questions: Check key facts, figures and quotes and then put away your pen but keep your ears open. You are not breaching any ethical rule if you continue to ask questions after you have put away your pen or turned off the tape recorder. That is when your source loosen up. Many reporters find they get their best material after the formal interview has ended and they are having a cup of coffee with the source.

Before you leave, if there is anything you forgot to ask, put the burden on the source; you are also doing your subject a favour by giving the person a chance to contribute to the direction of the interview. You may have missed some important signal, during the conversation, and now the source can be more explicit about what he or she wanted to say. Sometimes this technique opens entirely new subjects.

Quickly review your notes, check facts, especially dates, numbers, quotes, spellings and titles. Besides helping you get it right, it shows the source you are careful. If necessary, arrange a time when you can call to check other parts of the story or clear up questions you may have as you are writing.

As a matter of courtesy, tell the source when the story might appear you might even suggest you can send him an extra copy of the article.

Remember that although the interview may be over, your relationship with the source is not. When you have the story written, call the source and confirm the information. Better to discover your inaccuracies before you print.

Students of journalism should make it a point to read interviews in newspapers and magazines written by well-known journalists. Some of these interviews are reported in the questions and answer format. Some are titled as 'Face to Face'. They should also watch interviews being conducted on television. Some of the well-known programmes are:

The popular Hindi news channel ***Aaj Tak*** conducts a weekly programme ***Seedhi Baat***. In this programme a well-known journalist Prabhu Chawla interviews eminent persons from politics, business cinema and other celebrities. Like wise the BBC interviews—***Hard Talk*** by Tim Sebastian are watched worldwide with great interest.

These interviews will help you understand clearly the techniques of interviewing.

Examples of Interesting Interviews

Here are some examples of interesting interviews published in newspapers and magazines. These have been selected out of a large number of interviews for being interesting, informative and of human interest value.

I. Tim Sebastian, anchor of Hard Talk spoke to Shailja Bajpai, Special Correspondent of the Indian Express that when he tried some Talk with Indian Politicians on the eve of the polls, none of the biggies gave him time. *The Indian Express, April 3, 2004*

Some people find it hard talking to him. People who, otherwise speak all the time on air. People like L.K. Advani, Sonia Gandhi, Anil Ambani and Tony Blair. Or UN Secretary General, Kofi Annan. A pity, really, because Tim Sebastian would love to talk to them.

"For seven years, Blair has been saying it is not convenient to appear on the show," says the host of BBC World's Hardtalk, "And, if other U.N. officials do the show, why not the big man himself? There's a huge list of people who won't talk to us. They find it too hard."

Sebastian, in India to record a series of interviews just before the General Elections, asked for meetings with Deputy Prime Minister Advani and Congress President Sonia Gandhi, "and I think Rahul Gandhi too," but was turned down in each case. Advani had initially agreed to meet Sebastian in Porbander at the start of the second leg of his Uday Yatra. The interview was fixed for an early morning 7 a.m. "We called his bluff and agreed. At the last moment, he pulled out," reveals Sebastian 'no reason given. This is something of a pattern with Mr. Advani: he does not like to come to our table. He has avoided us in England and in India. Personally, I am really sorry."

In the face of these refusals, Sebastian had to cast his net much wider: he ensnared a few of the usual media suspects- BJP's Arun Jaitely, Delhi Chief Minister Sheila Dixit- as well as VHP's Vishnu Hari Dalmia and Syed Shahabuddin. You will also see NASSCHOM chief, Kiran Karnik in forthcoming episodes of the daily talk show. "Outsourcing is a big issue- you're pinching our jobs," Sebastian pauses, grins, "That' a joke". Naturally.

What did he think of his guests? "Politicians are the same everywhere. You don't have an extra mole in the neck. We hear the same arguments, the same excuses." Press him to be up close and more personal and he says Dalmia was "Quiet, calm consistent in his line. What he said may not be a surprise to audiences here but it is potentially explosive for outside audiences." What to know more? Watch the show.

Sebastian admits that this, his fourth trip to India in almost as many years, is unusual. What brings one of BBC's most famous personalities so frequently to this country? "It is a mark of the importance BBC gives India," he explains, "and when 675 million people go to the polls, the world should take notice." Regular viewers of Hardtalk may have noticed two recent phenomena: the show is more political. It has an agenda: Iraq and WMD- "we don't intend to forget them", terrorism and human rights violations. It does not include soft personalities. You won't see Sebastian interview a cricketer. "I know it is hugely important in India but personally, I would not like to do it." Here, Sebastain shares a secret: "As a child I played cricket I hated it."

Sebastian has reduced the number of Hard Talk appearances. He wants time out for "other things". If you've read about him before, you'll know the TV host is also an author. "Written eight books," he says, "thrillers. I began when I was in Russia during the Cold War. My son calls it 'airport trash'. Probably is."

Don't be fooled by the banter and soft touch. Sebastian is a commited TV journalist. Ask him if the Hutton Report's criticism of BBC's role in the David Kelly affair has led to editorial changes or interference: "No change whatsoever for me. If there is, that's the day I walk out."

II. Let us look to the future, says Musharraf, *The Hindu, 1 April, 2002*

Another memorable interview, given by the President of Pakistan Pervez Musharraf, to the executive editor of ***The Hindu***, Malini Parthasarathy in March 2002. The exclusive hour-long interview, being the first such interview given to an Indian publication since July 1999, naturally made headlines. The excerpts from the interview were reported in the form of a lead story, splashed across six columns, with a picture of the Pakistan President, General Musharraf at the interview made available by special arrangement in ***The Hindu*** on 1 April.

Details of the interview were covered extensively on the two inside pages. The interview was followed by an editorial in the newspaper on 2 April, the reaction of the Indian Government was again page one news on 3 April.

Thus the interview was a first rate media event of its kind

Let us now analyse some of the important aspects of the interviews for which, Malini Parthasarathy had to fly all the way out to Dubai to reach Islamabad, thanks to the ban on direct flights between India and Pakistan. The colour and atmospherics are all there in the beginning of the interview:

> *At Army House, the wait is not long and General Musharraf emerges, in informal attire. For someone who has been in the eye of the storm since September 11 and has found himself pitchforked to the centre of international attention, some unwelcome, he appears curiously stress-free and in fact eager to put his message across through this interview to a wider audience in India. So conscious was he of the fact that this interview represented an opening to public opinion to India that he was quick to seize upon examples that illustrated his arguments.*

After this interesting beginning, all issues between the two countries were discussed.

> *General Musharraf made clear many times in the course of the interview his deep sense of disappointment with what he characterized as a negative official Indian attitude towards him since September 11 which he saw as being fuelled by a calculation that the post-September 11, international context would give India*

an opportunity to have Pakistan 'sorted out' and which was belied subsequently.

Malini Parthasarathy sums up the crux of the interview as under: President Musharraf wanted this particular interview to contain the message to the Indian people that he was 'open to peace in the region' and that he wanted 'to resolve all disputes', he was 'ready to discuss every issue', provided Kashmir was accepted as the main issue of contention between the two countries. The Pakistan president also said 'we sincerely want friendship... in the immediate context, we need to de-escalate in the interests of both countries, in the interests of the armies of both countries." Pakistan wanted to 'live in harmony' with India which ought to behave like the 'elder brother' and show magnanimity to the smaller country.

A look at the format of the interview on pages 12-13, along with pictures goes on to show how much research and preparations would have gone into before the interview got going and also in putting it together after the interview was over.

Question-Answer Format of Interview

The newspapers are increasingly taking to the question-answer format for conducting interviews.

III. ***An upbeat Punjab Chief Minister Amarinder Singh talked to Special Correspondent Rohit Parihar on his campaign against corruption directed at his predecessor Parkash Singh Badal. Excerpts from India Today, July 21, 2003.***

Q. How is your Target Akali campaign going on?

A: I am targeting corruption, not the Akalis. Everyone who comes under the purview of corruption will be investigated. Only nine corruption cases out of 241 registered are against the Akali ministers, and just one is against Parkash Singh Badal.

Q. It seems like a witchhunt as you have not been too quick in booking Badal despite your tall claims against his corruption.

A: There is no witchhunt. I could have framed a case long ago, but I want to go strictly by facts that stand the test of law.

Q. Do you actually have any worthwhile evidence against corruption by the Badal family?

A: Yes, we know about benami properties but are gathering evidence to establish a clear link with the Badals. It is taking time to expose the offshore companies and money laundering, but we are close. Badal cannot explain even his Indian properties; fake companies were set up in which shareholders did not have investments exceeding Rs. 50,000 to circumvent tax laws. As for the foreign investments, I know where and how suitcases of cash were delivered, who was involved and how money travelled from Hong Kong, US and Mumbai before arriving in Chandigarh. Even a bank was set up at the Cook Islands, New Zealand, to help Badal's transaction.

Q. Have you sent teams abroad? Are their governments helping?

A: Yes, my teams have been abroad and foreign governments, particularly the US, are cooperating in bringing out tainted money.

Q. Badal does not like the way you are treating a political rival. Why don't you set up a judicial commission?

A: Why is Badal running away from the Vigilance Department? I have asked the chief justice of the Punjab and Haryana High Court to provide a designated court to try the corruption cases on a day-to-day basis. Badal wants a judicial commission to delay the matter as even in the past, despite his indictment by a judicial commission, he was not tried.

Q. So will Badal go to jail?

A: I will not arrest him, only interrogate him, his family members and whoever is involved in corruption. Then let the court decide the cases.

Q. Badal may gain the sympathy of the masses. He may use religion to turn the masses against you?

A: He cannot do that. He has launched many morchas but have you ever heard of something like a "corruption morcha" to save oneself?

NDA Govt. Sabotaged reservation Bill for women: Brinda Karat. *The Tribune,* February 8, 2004.

For almost two decades as the General Secretary of the All India Democratic Women's Association (AIDWA), Brinda Karat has lent her voice of reason to empower unorganised textile workers, handloom workers, street vendors, disabled women and those from the minority community. Member of the Central Committee of the Communist Party of India (Marxist), Brinda is proud to be associated with the AIDWA. Brinda was drawn to politics in the late sixties while working in England. "At the time of the Vietnam War, I was influenced by the anti-war movement. I started thinking seriously about politics and getting attracted to the ideology of Marxism," she says, recalling her change from an apolitical being to a political person, in an exclusive interview to The Tribune.

Excerpts:

Q. Why is the government dillydallying on the passage of the Women's Reservation Bill?

A: Well, there can only be one interpretation. The National Democratic Alliance government in spite of the best opportunity, a pledge given in writing by the main Opposition party that they will support the Bill, refused to put it to vote. Therefore, it is primarily responsible for the sabotage of the Bill. Worse, it came up with an alternative of double member constituencies.

Q. Will women organisations be able to persuade political parties to give more tickets to women in the ensuing elections?

A: Frankly I'm not very hopeful because if they refused to pass the Bill, they are not interested in increasing the representation of women. There may be a token increase in representation but it would certainly be inadequate to strengthen the democratic processes.

Q. How will women organisations convince political parties of the winnability of women candidates?

A: I can only speak on behalf of the AIDWA. Our understanding is that at present, we have to make a difference in the political agenda of parties along with women's reservation. Elections are a time when we have to assess the performance of political parties on various fronts–political, social, legal and economic. On all these fronts, the NDA government has failed to help women. The Bill on Domestic Violence has been put in cold storage. The original draft was most atrocious on domestic violence. The right to residence (matrimonial home) of a woman who is being assaulted was not even mentioned in the Bill. When women's organisations raised an objection, the government set up a parliamentary select committee. Though it submitted its recommendations a year ago, it has not been implemented. Why is the government not recognising that today in India more women are killed in cross bedroom terrorism than all those killed in terrorist attacks or wars that India has fought?

Q. Is the CPI (M) open to the idea of giving women a legitimate chance to contest in the polls?

A: We fought only 70 seats in the last Lok Sabha elections. There is a limited number of seats that we contest. So the scope for tickets for women is limited.

Q. The National Commision for Women has initiated a debate on the review of the legislation on dowry. Is this a meaningful exercise?

A: The killing of women is the end result of the practice of dowry. A survey by AIDWA on dowry in 16 states last September indicated that dowry has even spread to communities where it was not practiced (it is mostly practiced in the upper caste urban communities). The study concluded that it is now being practiced among the minority community besides tribals and dalits.

Q. What is your stand on death penalty for rapists?

A: The conviction rate is well below 15 per cent. There is reluctance by the authorities concerned to give maximum punishment under the existing law. If death penalty is included in the statute book, it would be a guarantee to further leniency because no one pronounce a death sentence. Secondly, it would increase the vulnerability of the rape victim to murder.

Q. Why has the NDA government failed to provide meaningful economic opportunities to women?

A: Wage workers are facing problems of unemployment and lack of work opportunities. We have just completed a survey of two villages, one each in Hisar and Rohtak in the supposedly prosperous state of Haryana to look at the women in 500 households. In both villages, we found that agricultural workers are not getting more than 35 days of work in the entire year. What do they do for the rest of the year? They are eating much less than they did ten years ago. Nutritional deficiencies are on the rise. The rural per capita calorie intake has come down by 300 calories. This would be much lower for women.

Q: About honour killings, the AIDWA passed a resolution upholding the human and democratic right of every adult to choose his or her partner. How did this come about?

A: The convention is part of the whole struggle against honour killings and self-proclaimed lawgivers. The most horrendous case was reported from Hoshiarpur in November where a gang of Rajputs killed a Jat Sikh youth who had married a woman from their community. The struggle for women's emancipation is very closely linked to the abolition of the caste system. Personal assertions as choice of marriage partners, friendships, relationships, interaction are very closely and strongly shaped by the iron framework of caste. Where a woman rebels and crosses the caste rekha, the community perceives it as a crime and thinks that she has to be taught a lesson to maintain the so-called purity of the caste. In the caste system, women's chastity is equated with women's honour and the centre of the entire caste system is control over women. We have found the most savage and barbaric violence wherever upper caste women got married to men from lower caste. This is happening particularly in North India and states like Punjab and Haryana. An extremely dangerous development has been the proliferation of caste panchayats in Haryana and all areas of Western Uttar Pradesh where there is a challenge to democratic and judicial processes. The extra-constitutional authorities take the law into their hands and meet out murderous sentences.

Union Finance Minister, Jaswant Singh spoke to Editor Prabhu Chawla on the feel good factor. The interview was telecast on *Aaj Tak* under a weekly programme *Seedhi Baat.* India Today: February 23, 2004 reproduced the following some of the excerpts.

Q. What is the feel-good factor?

A: Feel good is not a ploy to win, votes. The current mood is one of self-confidence and self-reliance.

Q. Is this same as Bharat Uday or India Shining?

A: That is a totally different programme. It is meant to make people aware of India and the parliament-approved "India development initiative".

Q. So it advertises your government's work.

A: No, it merely gives information.

Q: Is "feel good" not attached to this?

A: No. We are not the ones doing the talking. But yes, the Opposition is definitely not feeling good.

Q. Where will you get the revenue to fulfil the promises riding the feel-good factor?

A: Customs duty. When the volume of imports increase the revenue will go north.

Q: Is your budget not for political security?

A: No economic policy is without political input.

Q: Is it inspired by economic or political policies?

A: It is based on reality and today's needs. The country is on the track of progress.

Congress President Sonia Gandhi spoke to Shekhar Gupta, Editor-in-Chief of The Indian Express, on how she came to the centre stage of Indian politics, her relationship with Indira Gandhi and Varun Gandhi joining the BJP. Some of the Excerpts from Part I of the interview telecast on *NDTV 24x7's Walk the Talk* and reproduced in the Sunday Express: February 29, 2004 are as under:

Since you know my guest today so well let me first tell you about this remarkable setting. This is Swaraj Bhavan, part of the larger Anand Bhavan complex in Allahabad, the home of the Nehru-Gandhi family, and my guest today, somebody who carries that formidable dynasty on her slender shoulders if I can put it like that:

Welcome to Swaraj Bhavan

- ***Thank you for finding the time in the very busy election season***
  Yes, very busy. In fact I have been touring Uttar Pradesh, Orissa and other states...only yesterday I was in Benaras, Badhoi, Mirzapur. And it's going to carry on like this till the end.
- ***Life changes a great deal. Let me go back to where it began, when did you first come to Anand Bhavan?***
  I came to Anand Bhavan in 1970 and that was when Indiraji dedicated Anand Bhavan and Swaraj Bhavan to the nation, in

terms that it became a museum, open to the public. That was 1970, I had been married for two years, I was mother of a young baby, Rahul.

- ***Tell me, what did you learn from your mother-in-law? She was a tough woman.***

  She was a very strong woman, but she had a very gentle side to her...... a side that, very few people know. She had an eye for detail. If someone was unhappy or unwell, she would immediately notice and she would immediately do something about it. Perhaps by jotting down two lines. For instance, I remember when I got married, my mother came to the wedding and she stayed for a month. And when she was going, obviously it was a sad moment for me. And my mother-in-law sent a little note to me: 'Hi Sonia, this is just to tell you that we all love you'. And that totally melted me. It gave me a lot of strength, that I am loved and cared for.
- ***Do you have any recollections from that time of her responses to things that were happening in India which showed her character to you... something that made her angry, something that made her very determined?***

  She was at her best when faced with challenges. If she was pushed to the wall, there was pressure on her, she would come out and really fight back.
- ***Give me some examples...***

  When there was a split in her party...
- ***In 1969***

  Yes, she came out and fought. I remember the elections for the president at that time.
- ***Sanjeeva Reddy and Nijalingappa... Reddy was the presidential candidate.***

  Yes, that was a time when she came out strongly and aggressively.
- ***Was that the first time when you saw her as the iron woman as she came to be known as later?***

  Yes.
- ***And the Bangladesh war, do you recollect any of that?***

  Yes, Bangladesh war was a very exciting moment for all of us, we lived every moment of that crisis in our family. And I remember when Mujibur Rahman came to Delhi from London, there was a big reception at the airport, even though I was about to deliver my other child the next day, I made it a point to be there at the airport. There was such excitement.

- ***What was the conversation on your dining table like during the days of the war?***
  Well, mostly we were getting reports of the atrocities by the Pakistani army on the people of Bangladesh. Then the crisis of—I think we had 10 million refugees—coming in from Bangladesh. Nowadays when you read about 3 million refugees; a couple of hundred thousand refugees, the whole world...
- ***But during those 13 days of the war is there something that Mrs. Gandhi said at the dining table that you remember?***
  Obviously, she won't come out with the details, but she would certainly talk that today this happened, they have killed so many people, so many refugees have come in. Throughout that period she was composed, calm.
- ***The other turning point in her political career, the Emergency. What side of her did you see then, and how did you and Rajiv respond to the Emergency?***
  Well, my mother-in-law herself, after she lost the elections, she did herself say that she had a rethink on that. And the very fact that she declared elections proves that she had a rethink on the Emergency.
- ***Do you think that she really thought that it was a mistake?***
  I think she did think it was a mistake. Don't forget that, at least the Indira Gandhi I knew, was a democrat at heart, to the core. I think circumstances compelled her to take that action. But she was never quite at ease with it.
- ***But did it come across at conversations at home, that she was not at ease with it? That she wanted it to be over?***
  Yes, there were instances, through what she said, her comments, from which one could understand that. I can't recall any particular instance but I can recall that at times she was uneasy about it.
- ***After that, the Opposition, the public opinion responded to Emergency. Remember that slogan? Emergency ke teen, dalal, Indira, Sanjay, Bansi Lal, that public rejection... was that a low moment in the family as well?***
  Well, there is no way we can say that the Emergency was right. She herself said it wasn't right. But there was a great deal of propaganda against Mrs. Gandhi, deliberately done. And I think there were even some reports post-Emergency that went into details of the family planning programme, which turned out to

say that the problems were magnified. Yes there were problems, but not in the scale that the Opposition had built up.

- ***But Emergency was a lesson that no government will repeat such a thing. It is not possible to bring in so much authoritarianism in India, the Indian system will not accept it.***
I guess yes, but those were different times.
- ***Do you remember this coming up between Mrs Gandhi and Rajiv or between Sanjay and Rajiv at that point?***
I do remember, but I wouldn't like to disclose it.
- ***25 years have gone past, may be you should.***
May be another 25 years, may be I'll write it some day.
- ***But can you say that this is something that one can make a reasonable guess as to what the conversation was?***
Well I said I wouldn't like to discuss it now, may be another time.
- ***But there is a certain irony to the fact that one member of your family who was so involved in the Emergency, namely Sanjay, his family is now on the other side.***
Well, I can only say what I said the other day, he (Varun Gandhi) is a young man, he is embarking on a political career, I wish him well.
- ***Does it cause unhappiness—I won't say bitterness—in your mind? These are visceral issues in our politics: to be with the BJP or not with the BJP. And if one section of the immediate Gandhi family goes that side, does it hurt you? Not politically, I mean personally or ideologically?***
In some ways, it is painful. You are here in this house where the freedom movement took place, where strategies for the course of the movement were envisaged, this house symbolises the freedom movement... it symbolises not only the fight against the British, , but also a fight against communal forces. My mother-in-law was born here and other members of the Nehru family, stalwarts of the freedom movement came here, they lived and died upholding certain principles... and secularism, this principle, the fight against communal forces of all kind, was very much core of...
- ***And direct descendants of that family go and join the BJP now, does it amount to betraying that legacy?***
I would not like to comment on this, I wish my nephew all the best.

That you should even if he were a political opponent. But I am just talking in philosophical terms? Would it hurt less if he were in another party than the BJP?

I would rather not go beyond this.

Exercises

1. List ten open-ended questions you would ask the chief Minister.
2. List ten closed-ended questions you would ask.
3. Select a local or state issue and develop background material on it. Who would you interview? List some open-ended and closed-ended questions you would ask.
4. How would you prepare yourself when you would go to interview captain of the cricket team who has just returned after losing world cup?

8

FINDING STORY IDEAS

Sources and Reference Books

"There is no such thing as an original story idea", a prizewinning, editor told a group of journalists, assembled for a workshop. "We all steal ideas from each other."

There is a certain amount of truth in that statement. Although every good story must start somewhere, good ideas are valued in journalism. The reporter or editor who regularly comes up with good new story ideas, or fresh angles for old ones, quickly becomes a valued member of the newsroom staff.

Now how do reporters and editors come up with those ideas or find those fresh angles? The answer should be obvious: They are curious people who are aware of the world around them. They read their own publications, and they read what others write. They watch television and listen to radio and they also do a lot of talking with colleagues, fellow friends, neighbours and even casual acquaintances. They take time to chat with the service station attendant, an electrician, the grocer and the plumber. All can be good sources of story ideas. The good reporters and editors, it is said, have a "nose for news."

Those trained to sniff out stories know that good ideas are in abundance. Every person has a story to tell; good reporters find the person with a story worth retelling.

Finding the story

Readers bring some story ideas to the newspaper office. Most story ideas, though, are the result of an active imagination, a lively curiosity and a little help from friends. Journalists soon learn to recognize how stories written for other publications can be written for their own. They get in the habit of carrying a little notebook to jot down ideas when something somebody says strikes to them. But even for good journalists, the wellspring of ideas sometimes dries up.

Although every reporter will have his own contacts, the news editor supervises and keeps a list of all the paper's regular sources of news. A lot of news comes from well-defined sources and it is the news editor who must ensure that these sources are cultivated by his reporters. The reporter must know where to go for what information; which authorities have to be contacted, if they are not available, what the alternative is. Every country has a number of public personalities and leaders. Discretion and discrimination has to be practiced in choosing any of them to obtain information.

Reporters are given definite 'beats' in which they operate. Some specialize in news from police sources, others attend courts and the rest confine their activities to the civic body, assembly, secretariat, trade unions, sports or commercial or general functions. The division of duties depends on the size of the newspaper and the place of its publication. Smaller publications do not have large enough staff. In many cities the areas of coverage are not so diverse.

In larger newspapers, sports and commercial sections are independent of the rest. They have their own reporters and sub-editors. There is further specialization in cricket, table tennis, hockey, football and other games.

Working on 'beats' does not mean that the reporters will not operate in other areas. The beats are decided upon to obtain proper coverage of all possible sources; but there are many unforeseen happenings, for instance, accidents, demonstrations, tragedies etc. The reporting of these is allotted by the chief reporter as per the needs of his newspaper. Collection of information for news or for features depends not only on the beats, but also on the newspaper's attitude. For example, a rightist newspaper will naturally want to give greater coverage to items that are not in favour of communism. Though newspapers are said to be objective and should be willing to publish all types of items, subconsciously their choice is determined by their policy.

Background details in covering the event are sometimes more important. Here you need to do some research. For instance, you have to cover the train accident near Allahabad. On the spot visit to the scene of the happening is not always enough. You must know how to reach there, the importance of the rail link, which have been blocked and relevant details about Allahabad. This can be done before you go to the spot to see things for yourself.

Brian S. Brooks in his book '*News reporting and Writing*' has given a list of sources of story ideas, good for any time and any place, for the day that happens to you. Some of these are as under:

Other People: As a journalist you meet many persons. What are they talking about when they are talking business? What have they heard lately? Journalists must know what interests people? There is no better source of story ideas than the people you meet while you are off duty.

Other Publications: Stories are recycled across the country. Read other newspapers, magazines, books, pamphlets and the magazines and newsletters of businesses and organization.

Not all stories will work in every community. You have to know your own readership. The problem of water supply in Shimla could not be adapted to make a story somewhere else where there is no such problem.

When you are reading other publications for ideas, remember that you should not duplicate a story. You are looking for ideas. Think of a new angle.

News Releases: Some news releases from public relations people are used, but many of them are not. Yet they can be a valuable source of story ideas. News that one company has posted increased profits may be worth for one or two paragraphs; news that several companies in your community are prospering may be a front page story.

A Social Services Directory: Many cities and states have a composite listing of all agencies providing social services. Look beyond the pages. There are stories of people serving or not serving people. Each of those agencies and their clients is a story.

Government Reports: Government departments issue brochures and other materials, which can be a good source of story. The census reports for instance, list not only the number of people in a community but also their income and education. They tell much more, too. Besides these, the district gazetteer can be helpful. It deals with places of interest, the district's history, unusual factors connected with the district, the people, their customs and faiths, administration and so on. A study of these can help formulate a plan of presenting the news item. At times, the Chief Reporter or the News Editor helps by making suggestions.

Stories in your own Newspaper: Many stories are reported in your own newspaper. Ask yourself if the human-interest angle has been reported adequately. When your newspaper is concentrating on the election winners, may be you can get an interesting story by talking to the losers and their supporters. After the story of the car accident has been written, perhaps there is a feature on the victims whose lives have been changed.

And when the unemployment statistics are reported in your paper, remember that behind each of those numbers is a person without a job.

Wire Copy: The newspaper keeps itself open to all possible sources of information. Of course, objectivity is always borne in mind and experienced reporters and sub editors are the best judges for this. The press also gets information from news agencies. In India those are United News of India (UNI) and Press Trust of India (PTI). Besides these English news agencies, vernacular newspapers are also fed through their Hindi news agencies: Univarta and Bhasha.

You: In the final analysis you are the one who must be alert enough to look and listen to what is going on around you. What are people thinking about? What are their fears, their anxieties? When that happened, what else was going on? Reporters who are attuned to people rather than institutions will find the world around them a rich source of human-interest stories. Don't tune out.

Besides the above sources, there are other sources which the news editor controls.

Government Ministries: Many stories come from the government in power or in opposition. These are generally covered by senior persons in the newspapers. Many of the best stories in newspaper offices come from people with very modest positions.

Official Agencies: There are a number of 'Official agencies' which provide news to newspapers. These are: the fire brigades headquarters, the police control room and information section, public relations and other departments in the civic body, the Vocational Guidance Bureau, the employment exchange, the labour commissioner's office, hospitals and ambulance services, the tourist department, government offices and secretaries to the various departments in the government. In the municipality, the most rewarding are public relations, health, education, markets and water supply departments.

Police: In the police there are various police stations, the headquarters, the information section and police courts in the city. From the coroner's court, details can be obtained about cases referred to it. When a dead body is found and taken to the coroner, he examines the details pertaining to it, obtains police evidence, and decides whether the death was due to an accident, a suicide or a possible murder. On the recommendation of the coroner further action is taken. Besides the police courts, there are the others: the city civil court and the high court.

Press Conferences: Press conferences, cocktail parties and other functions are generally sources of routine items or those for which publicity is sought. They are given by political parties, trade unions, social welfare organizations, industrial manufactures and diplomatic representatives of foreign countries.

Social Welfare Organizations: Among other sources are social welfare organizations: charity trusts, trade agencies or associations, benevolent and cultural bodies and research institutions. Research work being done, cultural programs planned, welfare projects, details of manufacturing industries etc. can result in readable news items.

Political Parties: Political parties are seldom shy of wanting publicity. Their leaders and office bearers can become sources of information. The same applies to trade unions and labour organizations. It can be fruitful to interview personalities.

Hotel Receptionists: These can be very useful people in an age where some odd and interesting people are moving about the world.

The numerous sources mentioned above, on the spot visits and meetings with officials and personalities indicate that a journalist is not helpless. There is a wide ocean of possible information. Awareness of what to get where is all that is necessary.

Reference Books and Checking Facts

A wealth of information is available for the reporter who wants to develop the sound habit of checking every verifiable fact that goes into a story. Some of that information can be found in the reference manuals maintained in most newspaper libraries. A good reporter will learn quickly what materials are available. It is not possible to buy all that are needed; therefore, they have to be consulted in libraries.

ALA glossary defines 'Reference Book' as a book 'designed by its arrangement to be consulted for definite items of information rather than to be read consecutively'. According to Winchell, 'Reference books' are meant to be consulted or referred to for some definite piece of information.' Gates says, 'A book which is consulted for aid or information on a topic, an event, a person, a data, a place or a word is reference work.'

To Dr. S.R. Ranganathan, 'it is a book designed to be looked up for specific information... It does not lend itself to continuous reading.... It is characterized internally by an ensemble of disjointed enteries of short, though varying lengths. The sequence of the enteries is not determined strictly by intimate thought sequence. It is determined by the scheme of arrangement chosen.'

Characteristics of Reference Book

1. Its exposition of thought—content is not continuous.
2. It is usually not used for reading consecutively.
3. It is a miscellany of information organized for quick and convenient use.
4. Its entries are disjointed. They are usually short, though of varying length.
5. It gives only a bird's eye-view of the topic. And rarely it considers the subject in any depth.
6. It concentrates on facts. For it is compiled for finding facts and answers to questions. Hence it does not raise its own questions.
7. Its arrangement, usually, does not follow some consistent plan. Such as in dictionaries and encyclopedias, it is alphabetical, in bibliographies, it is either alphabetical or subject-wise or classified or chronological, in atlases it is regional.
8. It is consistently used in answering reference questions.
9. Usually it has a detailed alphabetic index to facilitate in finding out answers to questions without much loss of time.

The list of reference books that you must remember to have beside you

Dictionary: A dictionary is a book containing the words of a language or terms of a subject. It is arranged in some definite order, usually alphabetic. It gives meaning of words with explanation and sometimes their origin, use, pronunciation, etc. It is used for answering language questions such as meaning and definition of words, their origins, spellings, etymology, pronunciations, usage, synonyms, antonyms, homonyms and other things such as proper names, foreign terms, phrases abbreviations etc. For example:

1. Webster's New International Dictionary.
2. The Concise Oxford Dictionary.
3. Chamber's Twentieth Century Dictionary.
4. Roget's Thesaurus of English Words and Phrases.
5. Fowler's Modern English Usage.

Encyclopedia: It contains informational articles on subjects in every field of knowledge or it may be limited to a specific field or subject. Usually it is arranged in alphabetical order. Sometimes it is arranged topic-wise. It is used for knowing about a subject. It is helpful for background information of a topic. For example.

1. Encyclopedia Britannica.
2. Encyclopaedia Americana.
3. Pear's Cyclopaedia—A book of reference and background information for every day use.
4. Encyclopedia of Social Sciences.
5. Van Nostrand's Scientific Encyclopedia.
6. Guinness Book of World Records (Guinness superlatives). World records listed in countless categories.
7. McGraw—Hill Encyclopedia of Science and Technology.

Yearbook: It is an annual publication and reviews events or developments during a year. It gives current information in descriptive and/or statistical form. It is helpful in answering trend questions such as past year's developments, recent happenings and current events. Some of the important yearbooks are:

For Example:

1. *The Statesman's yearbook.* London: Macmillan.
2. *India: A Reference Annual,* New Delhi: Publications Division, Ministry of Information, Govt. of India.

Almanac: It is an annual publication and contains a calendar. It is frequently accompanied by astronomical data and other information. Here are a number of well-known publications in this category:

1. Information Please; Almanac. N.Y. Farrar, Strauss.
2. Whitaker Almanac. London, Whitaker.
3. US Almanac.
4. The World Almanac and Book of Facts (Newspaper enterprise Association) published annually.

Biographical Dictionary: It is a dictionary of concise biographies of noteworthy persons. It is useful for getting information about important people, socialites, specialists and others. Here is a list of few biographical dictionaries.

1. International Who's Who. London : Europe Publications.

2. SEN (SP). Ed. Dictionary of National Biography. Calcutta : Institute of Historical Studies, 1972-74. 4 V.
3. Indian Who's Who (INFA)

Gazetteer: It is a geographical dictionary or a dictionary of places of cities, towns, rivers, lakes, mountains etc. It gives indication of their location along with brief description of them. Some of the gazetters are listed below:

For Example:

1. Columbia Lippincott Gazetteer of the World. N.Y : Columbia University Press.
2. The Gazetteer of India. New Delhi : Publications Division, Ministry of Information and Broadcasting.

Guide Book: It is a handbook for travellers. It gives information about a place, a city, a town, a state a region or a country.

For Example:

1. Fodor's Guide to India. New Delhi : Publications Division.
2. Murray's Guide or a Handbook for Travellers in India, Pakistan, Burma and Ceylon. London, Murray.

Atlas: It consists of maps, charts, tables, plates etc. It helps in answering geographical queries.

Some of the important Atlases are as under:

1. Goode, J.Paul. Goode's School Atlas. Chicago, McNally.
2. Harmond's Complete World Atlas. N.Y.Hammond.
3. Oxford School Atlas of the Indian Peninsula. Bombay, OUP.

Map: It represents surface of the earth planets/moon. It helps in understanding location of a place on a flat surface.

For Example:

1. Political Map of India. Calcutta, Survey of India, Govt. of India.
2. Relief Map of the World. London, Geographical Institute.

Globe: It is the only relatively accurate representation of the earth. It also helps to know location of a place.

Liberty. Denoyer.

Directory: It gives addresses, affiliations etc. for individuals, officers, and organizations. Its arrangement is either alphabetic or classified. It is helpful in answering questions about the full name, address, telephone nos. etc. of an organization, a political group, a firm or an individual, description of a particular manufacturer, product or service; year of formation, history and current data about an institution, firm or political group. It is also used for selecting a list of individuals or organizations for an approaching or mailing in a particular area. It also helps in answering questions such as : The name of the chairman of the organization, his address and telephone number etc.

For Example:

1. The Times of India Directory and Yearbook including Who's Who. Bombay : Times of India Press.
2. World of Learning. London : Europapub.

Handbook and Manual: These books contain miscellaneous facts and figures on one or many subjects assembled for ready use in response to popular interest or to a specific need for concise handy information. They serve as a ready reference source for a given field of knowledge. They also give background material and are helpful in answering such questions such as how to do a job? They are addressed to experts and not to laymen. For Example:

1. Kana J.N. Famous, First facts. N.Y.H. Wilson.
2. Harvey, Paul. Oxford Companion of English Literature. Oxford Clarendon Press.

Bibliography: It is a list of written, printed or otherwise produced records of civilization. These records may be books, serials, pictures, maps, films, recordings, manuscripts and other media of communication. It is used primarily to identify, verify, locate and select documents.

Some of the important bibliographies are as under:

1. Indian National Bibliography. Calcutta, Central Reference Library.
2. British National Bibliography London : British Library.
3. Cumulative Book Index a World list of Books.

These useful publications, and many others like them, enable reporters to verify data and to avoid the unnecessary embarrassment caused by recognizable errors.

Computers and Data Base Searches

Computer data bases provide reporters and editors with a wealth of information at the touch of a button. Electronic data bases have unlocked doors that many never thought would be opened. Because of the deadlines under which reporters operate, there seldom is time to trek to the local library to research a story. So, while a great deal of information may be there, the opportunity to tap that resource may not be available. Electronic databases, however, are as close as the nearest modem-equipped computer and telephone lines.

In the United States and Canada, thousands of data bases offer unaccountable tidbits of information. The reporter who learns to use them will be able to produce many stories that would have been impossible to do in past years. For example, while it would take a reporter using conventional means thousands of hours to search through all the nation's medical journals for information on a particular disease, a well-trained librarian could find the same information in a database in a matter of minutes or seconds. Of course, not everything is available in databases, but each day more and more material is.

Although large metropolitan newspapers have been leaders in the field, smaller newspapers are beginning to realize the importance of tapping into the wealth of information available in databases. The reporter who fails to learn what databases can do soon will be outclassed.

Data base search saves much time. Such a search also greatly reduces the chance that an important article will be overlooked. Data base searches make simple the kind of searches that were seldom made in the past because they were too time consuming or too unproductive. Database searches also help small newspapers that in the past have been unable to afford to give a reporter the time to conduct such searches in traditional ways.

Clearly, database-searching techniques will be increasingly important to learn as newspapers and radio and television stations begin to go about the task of researching their stories more scientifically.

Exercises

1. Write a biographical sketch in 250 words of each of your Governor and Chief Minister of your state.

2. You have to interview the local leader of the ruling party. Write the subject area of your questions. What details would you study about him in advance?
3. You have to interview the richest industrialist in your city. What questions would you ask him? Which leading personality would you like to interview and why?
4. Choose any story in your local newspaper, and tell how that story could have been improved with a date base research.
5. If you were interested in determining where PRINI is located, what is its importance? Where would you look? What other sources of information would you search?

SECTION III

BASIC REPORTING

9

REPORTING SPEECHES, PRESS CONFERENCES AND MEETINGS

Though speeches, press conferences and meetings are similar, but they have some distinguishing characteristics which you must keep in mind while reporting.

SPEECHES

A speech is a public talk. Someone stands and speaks to an audience in person or on radio or television. Regardless of the medium the nature of a speech is the same. It is a one-way communication, the speaker speaks, and the audience listens.

Reporting speeches is easy. Reporting them well is a still too often underrated. The commonest trap for reporters is to be taken in by the importance of the occasion or the supposed importance of the speaker. But important speakers do not always say important things and quite often rely heavily on their own standing in the public eye to try to get by with indifferent speeches.

Not every speech you are assigned to cover will demand a great deal of research. Many speakers and speeches will be dry and routine. The person giving it will be someone you know or someone you have covered before. At other times you may be given an assignment on short notice and may be forced to find background information after you have heard the speech. But never take the speaker or the topic for granted. The failure to get enough background on the speaker and the speech may prevent the reporter from making a comprehensive report on the speech.

Speeches are generally the most uninteresting way of imparting information. The real content of the speech that is, the revelation of any thing new which the audience does not already know is just a tiny proportion of the speech. Many speeches . . . of course do not have anything new to say at all. And yet newspapers all over the world continue to give undue space to speeches, whether from politicians, officials or anybody else.

Frank Barton in his book. The Newsroom said, "what journalists should remember is that a speech is designed to be heard and not read. So a reporter reporting a speech should attune himself to the fact that there is likely to be very little news in at anyway and even if there is any news it may be wrapped up in so much verbiage that it would be almost meaningless if served up in the newspaper the same way."

Steps in Covering Speeches

- The first step in covering speeches is to get the right person. Check the name, surname, father's name and address etc. One reporter wrote about the wrong person because he did not know that a father and son shared the same name at the same address.
- Before doing research on the speaker, contact the group sponsoring the speech and ask for the topic. You might find you need some reading to prepare yourself to understand the subject better. If you are lucky, you may get a copy of the speech ahead of time. Also check your newspaper library to see what your paper has done on the speaker. If you have access to a data bank, use it.
- Whether you are reporting a speech or re-writing it from a handout, the first thing you should remember is that the speech should not be tackled in the order in which it is presented, that is, do not necessarily start your story with the first part of the speech and then take the other parts in the order in which they were presented by the speaker. The most interesting element should form the intro and thereafter the other parts of the speech should be presented in order of interest and or importance. Politicians, particularly even when they have something to say, rarely make speeches presenting the facts in order of importance.
- If there is no hand-out and a note has to be taken, it should be taken with discrimination. The important thing is to take sufficient notes to follow the thread of the speaker's argument. Then, when he comes to a significant part of it, should a verbatim note be taken and later presented, in quotes, as direct speech.
- Few newspapers can carry reports of complete speeches. As a reporter, you must decide what is significant. And to do this you must know something of the subject. Make some marks in the margin of your notebook when the speaker covers important ground. It

can be very helpful when you come to write your story and even more helpful if you have to dictate it directly into a telephone.

- Beware of impressive oratory. Resounding phrases that bring a cheering audience to its feet can look uncommonly dull in cold print. Try to invest your report with some flesh and blood by describing the speaker and if necessary, some of his mannerisms. Was he obviously angry? Did he thump the table? Was he nervous? How did his audience react to him?
- Accurate recording of this kind of detail and use of direct speech can help to transport the reader to the meeting. You can help by objective interpretation. Say why this speaker's views on this particular subject are relevant. If he says something which marks a departure from his earlier views, tell the reader that too.
- If the subject is important enough try to catch the speaker after the meeting and ask him to elaborate on that or any other point. That is the way to beat your rival.
- Try not to be so preoccupied with your note taking that you lose the thread of the speaker's argument. The reporter with selective notes and thorough understanding is more useful than the man with a book full of words he doesn't understand.
- If an important politician visits a village and makes an insignificant speech, it may well be more revealing not to report the speech at all but to concentrate in the actual visit, on his reception by the villagers, on the people he talked to, on the reasons for the visit and on its likely results.
- In other words, while going to report a speech do not close your eyes to other possibilities. The story of the reporter who returned from a meeting and said there was nothing to report because the speaker was shot is probably untrue. But there are plenty of near parallels. In cases like these such journalists do no credit to their profession.
- Keep an eye on the audience and on what is happening around the edges. You need to measure the mood of the audience by noting the tone of the questions. Are they sharply worded? Is there much laughter or applause? Does the speaker remain calm and in control at all times? Is there a casual bantering or joking with the audience? Is the audience stacked with supporters or detractors?
- Note the size of the audience. Reporting a 'full house' means little unless you indicate the house capacity. One way to estimate attendance is to count how many people are sitting in a row or in a

typical section. Then you simply multiply those members by the number of rows or sections in the hall.

Here is an example of Sonia Gandhi's inaugural speech reported by *Vepa Rao* of The Statesman on *Vichar Manthan Shivir* in Shimla dt. July 8, 2003.

Sonia trains gun on NDA

Inaugurating her party's three-day *Vichar Manthan shivir,* Mrs. Gandhi said corruption had crossed all limits under the BJP-led government "whose track record on probity, accountability and transparency had been deplorable". Recalling the long list of scandals and scams on UTI, petrol pumps, co-operative banks, disinvestment, DDA, telecom, defence sector and others, the Cong chief lamented that "even the Taj Mahal has not been spared".

Referring to the speculations about advancing the Lok Sabha elections, Mrs. Gandhi said her party was fully prepared, "stands ready at any time, this year or next".

She highlighted "just seven of the most glaring failures" of the Centre beginning with the failure to tackle terrorism. Recalling the Kandahar hijack episode in which the then foreign minister had escorted three hard core terrorists to freedom, she said: "These very terrorists continue to kill innocent men, women and children in our country".

The people of India, Mrs. Gandhi said, are waiting for the White Paper on ISI activities in India promised four years ago by the home minister—the only home minister to be chargesheeted. The government failed to spend Rs. 24,000 crore from the defence budget for modernisation in the last three years, considerably weakening the country's security. Referring to the Rs. 4,200-crore collected from people as the "Kargil surcharge" last year meant for "preventing future Kargils from taking place", Mrs. Gandhi said the money was spent for other purposes "in a gross betrayal of the people of the country". She mentioned the "grave intelligence failures identified by the government's own review committee on the Kargil war".

Condemning the BJP and its organisations like the VHP, RSS and Bajrang Dal for "grievously damaging the secular fabric of our society and severely disturbing social peace and harmony", the Congress chief said whatever they "preached and propagated had nothing whatsoever to do with Hinduism and liberal Hindu way of life. Deliberate distortions of

Hinduism is part of their evil and cynical designs". The entire country knows how these outfits are "injecting the poison of communalism into our entire education system at all levels ... Only the Congress can protect India's religion from these merchants of hate."

Attacking the Centre's foreign policy "for lack of consistency, conviction and clarity", Mrs. Gandhi said the government's approach to Pakistan had "vacillated from one extreme to other". This despite the Congress' consistent support for the Prime Minister's peace moves "including his most recent initiative from Srinagar". The Prime Minister and the Deputy Prime Minister "say one thing at home but when they go abroad they talk about compromises and give-and-take on J&K." Mrs. Gandhi said: "What are these compromises, and what are we expected to give?" Mrs. Gandhi announced her intention to set up a "Bapu Sadhbhavana and Shiksha Trust" comprising eminent men and women committed to the "vision of a modern secular progressive India". The trust will give shape and direction to enlightenment and excellence in the education system—based on values empowered by "our founding fathers". This will be part of the battle against "seeds of bigotry, intolerance." Mr. Jaipal Reddy.

Another example of a speech delivered by The President of India *Abdul Kalam* at the IPI-India Award for Excellence in Journalism 2004 and produced as such.

Can Media to be the Partner in National Development?*

I am delighted to participate in the Award Ceremony for Recognizing Excellence in Jorunalism 2004 organized by the International Press Institute (IPI), India Chapter. My congratulations to the award winner—the NDTV and greetings to noted Editors, publishers, academicians, columnists, writers, media specialists and distinguished guests. I would like to share with you my thoughts on the topic "Can media be the partner in National Development". Media has to know the dreams and aspirations of our people, particularly the youth of the nation.

The Profile of Developed India before the year 2020

Developed India is a Nation where the rural and urban divide has reduced to a thin line. A Nation where there is an equitable distribution of energy and quality water. A Nation where agriculture, industry and service sector

---

* president of india.nic.in

work together in symphony, absorbing technology thereby resulting in sustained wealth generation leading to higher employment potential. A Nation where education is not denied to any meritorious candidates because of societal or economic condition. A Nation which is the best destination for the most talented scholars and scientists all over the world. A Nation where the best of health care is available to all the billion population and the communicable diseases like AIDS/TB, water and vector borne diseases, Cardiac diseases and Cancer are extinct. A Nation where the governance uses the best of the technologies to be responsive, transparent, easily accessible and simple in rules, thereby corruption free. A Nation where poverty has been totally alleviated, where illiteracy and crime against women are eradicated and where the society is unalienated. A Nation that is prosperous, healthy, secure, peaceful and happy. A Nation that is one of the best places to live in, on the earth and brings smiles on a billion plus faces.

Present Economic Scenario

In the Indian history, very rarely we have come across a situation, all at a time, an ascending economic trajectory, continuously rising foreign exchange reserve, global recognition of technological competence, energy of 540 million youth, umbilical connectivities of 20 million people of Indian origin in various parts of the planet, and the interest shown by many developed countries to invest in our engineers and scientists including setting up of new R&D centres. The priorities of the Government emphasize on economic development by ensuring growth rate of 7 per cent to 8 per cent annually, enhancing the welfare of the farmers and workers and unleashing the creativity of the entrepreneurs, business persons, scientists, engineers and other productive forces of the society. Also a dynamic technology powered dynamic media is in place.

This is the time the nation has to focus all its technological and financial growth towards the Vision, Vision of transforming India into a developed nation before 2020. Media can definitely become a great partner for promoting this Vision, as it played its role during the independence movement 1857-1947. Hence, I thought of highlighting two vision components—one is India 2020 Mission and the other is PURA (Providing Urban Amenities in Rural Area) programme.

Our National Mission—Challenges

Our nation is going through a major challenge of uplifting of 260 million people who are below the poverty line and also to give better life for many millions who are on the border line of poverty or just above the poverty line. They need decent habitat, they need work with reasonable income, they need food, they need health care, and they need education and finally resulting into a good life. Our GDP is growing at more than 6 per cent per annum on an average. Whereas, the economists suggest that to uplift the people from below the poverty line, our economy has to grow at the rate of 10 per cent per annum consistently, for over a decade.

Integrated action

To meet the need of one billion people, we have the mission of transforming India into a developed nation. We have identified five areas where India has a core competence for integrated action: (1) Agriculture and food processing, (2) Reliable and Quality Electric power, Surface transport and Infrastructure for all parts of the country, (3) Education and Healthcare, (4) Information and Communication Technology, (5) Strategic sectors. These five areas are closely inter-related and if well done would lead to food, economic and national security.

PRESS CONFERENCES

It is an interview session, also called a 'news conference' in which someone responds to questions from reporters. It has become an accepted means of issuing information to the press. In a press conference, invitation to the general public are not sent but to the members of various news media. The invitees to the government press conference are normally all accredited journalists including foreign correspondents, accredited cameramen and representatives from radio and TV etc. In the case of private organizations all correspondents who normally cover the organization are invited to the press conference. Official invitees to the press conference should be reduced to the minimum. The person holding the press conference often begins with an opening statement and then usually accepts questions from reporters. A news conference is meant to be a two-way communication.

A press conference should never be called merely to handout a development or information which could be covered equally well by a press release. The main justification for holding a press conference is that the subject is an important one likely to elicit plenty of questions from the journalists present.

Covering the Press Conference

First of all, get the position in news conference because it may help you get the attention of the person holding the conference. Next, you need to know the up-to-date background of the person holding the press conference, and you must learn why the news conference is being held. Often the person holding the press conference has an announcement or an opening statement. Unless that statement is released to the press, you will not know its contents ahead of time. But you can do some intelligent guessing. Check out any rumour. Call the person's associates, friends, secretary. The more prepared you are, the better chances you have of coming away with a coherent, readable story.

A problem you will encounter at news conferences is that every reporter has a line of questions to pursue. Your editor may want certain information, and other editors may want something else. You will not have time to think out your questions once you are there. The job of recording the responses of other reporters, questions will keep you busy.

It may be impossible, as well, to arrange an interview before or after the news conference. If the person holding the news conference wanted to grant individual reporters interviews, he or she probably would not have called the news conference. But you can give it a try. You never know and you may end up with some exclusive information.

Writing the news conference story

Remember when the news conference is finished, you will have a story to write. Piecing together notes on dozens of unrelated topics can be difficult, if not impossible.

Writing the news conference story may be a bit more of a challenge. Because you will come to the conference with different questions in mind than your fellow reporters, you may come away with a different story. At least your lead may be different from those of other reporters.

A news conference often covers a gamut of topics. Often it begins with a statement from the person who has called the conference.

After you come away from a news conference that covered many topics, you have the job of organizing the material in some logical, coherent order. Usually you will treat the most newsworthy subject first and deal with the other subjects in the order of their importance. Rarely would you report them in the chronological order in which they occurred.

Pay particular attention to making proper transitions from paragraph to paragraph so that your story is coherent. If one of the subjects is of special interest, you may want to write a sidebar, a shorter piece to go with your main story. With a longer or more complicated story, you may want to make a summary list of all the main topics covered and place them in a box or sidebar.

Remember, your job is to give readers the news, as simply and clearly as possible. Sometimes what happens at a news conference is more newsworthy than anything the person holding the conference says. What happens there might well be the lead of your main story, or you may want to place it in a sidebar.

Here is an example of a press conference of P. Chidambaram, Union Finance Minister, covered by Arup Chanda, in The Tribune, dt. December 19, 2004.

Economy has improved, but inflation worrisome: FM

Union Finance Minister P. Chidambaram said here today the Indian Indian economy had greatly improved this year though plagued by the rate of inflation.

Addressing a press conference, Mr. Chidambaram said the growth of 7.4 per cent during the first quarter during this fiscal was better than that of the corresponding period last year while the growth in the core industry in the first seven months from April to October was 5.9 per cent.

He said the rupee had also strengthened against the dollar and foreign exchange reserves stood at an unprecedented $ 130 billion.

The Sensex had crossed 6,400 points for the first time and the government was well on its way to meeting the loan disbursement target of Rs. 1,05,000 crore this year, he added.

The Finance Minister claimed, "Even a Bharatiya Janata Party MP openly acknowledged in the House that the Indian economy has further strengthened this year."

However, he admitted the continuing inflation was a cause for concern and said, "Inflation had gone up from 5.56 per cent on December 6 last year to 7.02 per cent on the same day this year."

He felt it was due to the sudden spurt in international crude oil prices adding that the government was making all efforts to bring down inflation.

But he pointed out that while crude oil prices had gone up by 40 per cent in a year, the rate of inflation had gone up by only 1.5 per cent.

Replying to a question on why the subsequent decrease in international crude prices was not reflected in the pricing of fuel in India, he denied that the crude prices had gone down.

He said, "The crude price fell to $ 42 a barrel a few days ago, but within two days, it had once again shot up. And the relevant factor for Indian imports was that the Indian basket had gone up from an average of $ 27 a barrel in 2000 to an average of $ 37 this year."

MEETINGS

Unlike speeches and news conferences, meetings are not held with an audience in mind, even though an audience may be present and allowed to participate. A meeting is primarily for communication among the members of a group or an organization; whether a local parent- teacher association or the congress party meeting of the Himachal Pradesh. If reporters are permitted to witness a meeting, they are there to report to the public what is of interest and importance. The task of the news media is especially important if the meeting is of a governmental body that deals with the public money collected through taxes.

Preparing for the Meeting Story

You never know what to expect at a meeting, either. But again, you must do your best to prepare for it. Who are the people holding the meeting? What kind of an organization is it? Who are the key figures? Contact some of the key figures. See if you can find out what the meeting is about. Perhaps the president or the secretary has a written agenda for the meeting. If you know the main subject to be discussed at a meeting you will be able to study and investigate the issues before arriving, knowing what to expect and being familiar with the issues will make covering the meeting much easier.

A reporter with a regular beat, or assigned area of responsibility, usually covers the meetings of more important organizations and of groups like the school board meeting or the syndicate meeting of the university. A beat reporter has a continuing familiarity with the organization and with the issues involved. Often the meetings of important organizations are preceded by an advance report dealing with the subjects and issues to be dealt with in the upcoming meeting.

In short, to cover meetings you must arm yourself with information concerning the people involved and the issues to be discussed. Do your homework.

At a meeting you should be in a position to see and hear the main participants. Ordinarily a board will sit facing the audience. Before the meeting starts you should know which members are sitting where, you may want to assign each participant a number so that you do not have to write the person's name each time he or she speaks, you also can draw a sketch where they are sitting. In this way you will be able to quote someone by number, even if you do not know the name until later. Know who the officers are. The president or the secretary may have some handout before the meeting. You may receive copies of resolutions for consideration at the meeting. After a meeting, sometimes the secretaries can help you fill in missing words or information.

As a general rule, when the speech, news conference or meeting is over, don't rush off. Hang around awhile. Some of the best stories happen afterwards. You may have some questions to ask. You may want some clarifications, or you may arrange to interview a key spokesman, listen for reactions from those in attendance.

Common principles for covering Speeches, News Conferences and Meetings

- Get the content correct. Tape recorders can be helpful, but always take good notes. Quote people exactly and in context.
- Note the background, personal characteristics and mannerisms of the main participants.
- Cover the event. Look around the edges at the audience (size, reactions) and sometimes at what is happening outside the building.
- Get there early, position yourself and hang around afterwards.

The story is often told of the reporter who prepared well for a speech assignment, contacted the speaker, got a copy of the speech, wrote the story and spent the evening in a bar. He didn't know until after the speech story had reached the office, that the speech had been cancelled.

There is another story about a reporter who was assigned to cover a meeting and came back to tell the editor there was no story. "Why not?" the editor asked. "Because the meeting was cancelled." "Why was that?"

"Well", replied the young reporter, "When the meeting started, some of the board members got into argument. Finally three of them walked out, The president then cancelled the meeting because there was not quorum."

The reporter had been sent to cover a meeting. But the cancelled meeting and the circumstances surrounding its cancellation probably were of more interest to readers than the meeting itself would have been.

Preparing to cover events is only the beginning. Knowing what to do when you get there is the next step. Remember this: covering the content of a speech, news conference, or meeting often is only half of the job and sometimes the less important half. You must cover the entire: event the time, place, circumstances, number of people involved and possible consequences of what was said or of the actions taken.

NEWS RELEASES

Reporters do not go out and dig up all the stories they write. Many stories come to them. They are mailed, telephoned, telexed or hand delivered by people who want to get some thing in the paper. They come from different offices, for instance, public relations departments, public information offices, corporations, press agents, press secretaries and publicity offices.

Good publicity is so important that private individuals, corporations and government agencies spend a great deal of money to obtain it.

Definition

A news release is an official, authorized statement about the policies and activities of an organization whose purpose is to disseminate information in ready to publish form. Editors of print and broadcast media to whom news releases are sent judge them on the basis of news interest for their audience and timeliness, and in some instances on their suitability to the medium's form. As the company or the government has to stand by the information, the news release must be factual, correct and project the policy clearly and without ambiguity. No payment is made to the publication or station if the material appears in print or on the air. If an organization or individual purchases space in a publication to present its material this is a paid advertisement and the purchaser controls the content.

Releases should be prepared so that the media could relay their news content to audiences easily, with confidence in their accuracy. Editors want the main facts stated succinctly in the opening paragraph of a release, for quick understanding. A news release is a purveyor of information, not an exercise in writing style, except in those cases of longer releases that are clearly intended to be feature stories.

Skilled public relations or public information practitioners know how to write news, and they apply all the principles of good news writing in their news releases. A good news release meets the criteria of a good news story.

As a reporter you must recognize that a news release is both a help and hindrance to a newspaper. It helps because without a news release newspapers would need many more reporters. It is a hindrance because it sometimes contains incomplete or even incorrect information. Most of the time, in one way or another, it is self serving and, unlike objective journalism, starts with a point of view.

A news release faces intense competition when it arrives on an editor's desk, against scores or even hundreds of other releases. As they scan the releases, editors make almost instant decisions, assigning each release to one of three categories:

1. *Obvious news.* Copy that is certain to be used.
2. *Maybe.* Stories possibly worth developing if a reporter has the time. Otherwise, thrown away after a second reading, because the key information is poorly developed.
3. *Discard.* Releases of insufficient interest to the audience and those of marginal value that would require too much effort to develop. These go into the wastebasket.

News releases that are prepared according to the criteria described in the following sections have the best chance of being accepted for publication, assuming that their content is newsworthy.

Criteria

Physical Appearance

There is a standard format for a news release:

- Use plain white 8½-by-11-inch paper.
- Identify the sender in the upper-left-hand corner of the page, listing name, address, and telephone number. Many releases also include a fax number and an e-mail address. Especially if the sender is a large organization, also give the name of an individual within the organization as a point of contact. It is important that the listed phone be answered by an informed person, usually a public relations specialist, not by a recording.
- Below the identification state *For Immediate Release* if the material is intended for immediate publication, as most news

releases are. If a time restriction is necessary, as with an advance copy of a speech to be delivered at a specified hour, indicate the desired publication time; for example. *For Release at 6 p.m. Feb. 12*. This is called an *embargo*. Media recipients of embargoed material have no legal obligation to obey its restrictions, but they normally do so out of courtesy and mutual convenience unless they believe that the embargo is an obvious effort to manipulate the news. Embargoes should be used only when genuinely necessary.

- Leave 2 inches of space for editing convenience before starting the text.
- Start them with a clearly stated summary lead containing timely, relevant, important information.
- Leave at least a 1.5-inch margin. Double-space the copy to give editors room in which to edit the material.
- Never split a paragraph from one page to the next. Put *(more)* at the bottom of each unfinished page.
- Place an identifying slug line and page number at the top of each page after the first.

Some public relations practitioners place a summary headline above the text, to tell a editor quickly what the release contains.

Content

There are a few essential rules for content:

- Begin the news release with a tightly written summary lead and state the fundamentals—who, what, when, where, and why—early in the copy. The first sentence should state the most important point in the story. *Do not bury the lead.* The opening paragraph should not exceed five lines, at the most.
- Be concise. Edit the copy to remove excess words. A competent editor would cut them out, anyway. Few news releases need to be more than two pages long: most can be written in a single page. A reporter may obtain additional details by telephoning the number listed at the beginning.
- Caution: Avoid cliches and fancy phrases. When editors receive a news release using such terms as "unique," "revolutionary." and "state-of-the-art," they are likely to throw it away.
- Never use excessively technical language in a release for a

general audience. The objective is communication, not confusion.
- Be absolutely certain that every fact and title in the release is correct and that every name is spelled properly. Check the copy closely for grammatical errors. Errors can be embarrassing and costly.

For protection against errors and misunderstandings, a public relations counsellor is wise to have the client initial on a file copy of each news release before its distribution. In company public relations departments, similar initialing by a superior is desirable and in some cases mandatory. Corporate review can become excessive, however. *Writing in Editor & Publisher*, Ron Cantera, a former public relations executive who became a journalism professor, reported: *"In one corporate job I held, my news releases were reviewed by at least six different insiders—my boss, his boss, a product manager, the marketing vice president, an agency copyreader and, believe it or not, a word-processing supervisor... that led to communication by committee."*

Those who issue news releases should welcome follow-up inquires from reporters and be able to provide additional information. Often reporters complain that the public relations personnel aren't available or don't promptly return phone calls.

To counter this complaint, many public relations people make it a point to list contact numbers on news releases. These contact numbers are direct lines of a real person instead of voicemail or an answering machine. In addition, many practitioners also provide a number where they can be reached after regular business hours.

Types of Press Releases covering Government news:

1. Press Communiques
2. Press notes
3. Handouts
4. Unofficial stories or unofficial handouts.

Press Communiques are issued when some important government decisions or announcements are made such as cabinet appointments, conclusion of the foreign dignitaries visit, etc. The press communique is formal in character. It carries the name of ministry or department and the place and date at the bottom left hand corner of the release. Generally the press is expected to reproduce the press communique without substantial change. No heading or sub-heading is given on press communiques.

Press notes are less formal in character. They are issued on important matters. They also carry the name of the ministry/department and the place at the bottom left hand corners. Headings or sub-headings are given in press notes.

Handouts are issued on a variety of subjects and on day-to-day activities of the ministry/department. VIP speeches, questions and answers in Parliament, etc. The handout is a less formal type of release and not issued under the government's formal authority. It bears the name of the PIB or other releasing agency on the top without any mention of the ministry/department to which the release pertains. The place and date are indicated on top at the right hand side. One of the most important common categories of handouts relate to the speeches of ministers or other high officials. The handout is released only when the speech is connected with governmental activity. No official handout is issued if the minister has spoken in his personal capacity as a member of a political organization. The speech when released to the press in the form of handout is summarised and properly edited. Formal, introductory and concluding remarks are omitted and redundant and repetitive material taken out. A proper title and sub-title are given. The important aspects which are to be stressed are included in the beginning paragraph or in the lead. The full text of the speech is not released unless the subject is of great importance.

Unofficial handouts are issued on the subject where the government would not like to assume official responsibility in the matter but feels that there may be positive advantages in making information public unofficially. These handouts are supplements to oral briefings. The unofficial handouts do not have the imprint of the PIB or of other releasing agencies. The date and place are indicated at bottom left hand corner.

Timing of release is very important. All releases should, as far as possible, reach the desk by 6 or 7 p.m. The PRO should finalise it at least one hour in advance of the official delivery time.

Non-News Releases

These are such releases which do not cover news but give information in an indirect way and help in building the image of the government. More widely known releases of this type are back grounders, biographical sketches, contradictions, articles and features, newsletters, releases on reports, broadcast talks, etc. The releasing agency's name is given at the top. The place and date are indicated on the top right hand side. Title and sub-title are also given.

Exercises

1. How would you cover the Prime Minister Manmohan Singh's speech on Pravasi Bhartiya Divas to be celebrated on January 9, 2005? What steps you would take and the information you would gather?
2. You learn Aaishwarya Rai becomes the first Indian actor to be member of the Cannes Film Festival Jury. She holds a press conference before going there. Prepare to cover the conference. Write the steps you would take and the information you have gathered on Aaishwarya Rai.
3. Find out when the University is having its next Executive Council meeting. Prepare to cover it. Write the steps you would take and the information you have gathered for the meeting.
4. Your professor will give you a local release. Using local sources and resources, report and rewrite the story.
5. Collect any two press releases from your local public relations department. Rewrite each of them.

10

REPORTING ACCIDENTS, DISASTERS AND OBITUARIES

Why to Cover

Stories about accidents, fires and disasters are very common. These have been principal ingredients of newspapers for many years. There is good reason for that: when people hear sirens, they want to know what happened and perhaps more important, whether their friends or acquaintances were involved.

Newspapers also cover these events in their capacity as watch dog for the public over government agencies. If the police were slow in responding to an accident, is it because there are not enough officers or because they are poorly supervised?

Did someone die needlessly because police, fire or ambulance personnel were slow, poorly trained or inefficient? To ask these questions on behalf of their readers, reporters must observe the way public officials perform their duties.

In newspaper bureaus throughout the country, editors and reporters stay tuned to the police and fire brigade services provided for that purpose. When they hear something out of the ordinary, reporters and photographers are dispatched to the scene.

How to Cover

Editors have varying ideas about which stories about accidents, fires and disasters are worth reporting and which are worth developing into major articles. A story about an accident in which no one was killed will take a little space in the newspaper than a story in which numbers of people were killed. For instance, derailment of Howrah—New Delhi, Rajdhani Express near Gayaji in which number of people was killed. For instance, derailment of Howrah—New Delhi, Rajdhani Express near Gayaji in which number of people were killed. Now on December 15, 2004, another train accident near Mukerian town of Hoshiarpur district in Punjab in which many people are killed and many injured. Such stories run into many paragraphs and occupy the front page mostly. Streamer headlines are given to such stories. Numbers of photographs of the different scenes are also carried out.

As a beginner you almost certainly will be assigned to cover an accident or fire. You even may become part of a team of reporters and photographers assigned to cover a disaster. Consequently, you need to know what to expect and how to get the information you need.

In many ways covering accidents, fires and disasters is the simplest form of reporting. The subject matter lends itself to the classic inverted pyramid writing style. But you also can produce far more interesting accounts of the pain and suffering of people who have encountered crisis.

As a reporter assigned to cover an accident, fire or disaster, you must report the effects of the event on the victims. Only then you can write a story that tells the event in terms of the human experience. For example, in train accident in Mukerian a labourer, Bijuria from Madhya Pradesh brought his family to earn better livelihood but she never knew she would meet such a tragic end. She had lost her daughter, daughter-in-law and two grand children.

Whether your are assigned to cover an accident, fire or disaster, many of the facts are gathered at the scene. By being there, you will have a better picture of what happened. Too many reporters, however, cover accidents and fires as purely passive observers. You must observe. But you also must actively solicit information from those who are there. Many of them, including those directly involved, you may never be able to find again.

COVERING AN ACCIDENT

When you reach the site of an accident, you first must concentrate on gathering the facts. Collect the following information as quicly as possible:

The names, ages, addresses and conditions of the victims.

Accounts of witnesses of what happened.

When the accident occurred?

Where it occurred?

Why it happened?

How it happened?

Who was at fault, as determined by officials in charge of the investigation?

After getting the above information, a visit to the scene is essential, if the accident has just taken place. The following suggestions will help you in collecting information.

Question the person in charge of the investigation

This person will attempt to gather much of the same information you want. A police officer, for example, needs to know who was involved, what happened, when it happened and who was at fault. If you are able to establish a good rapport with the investigator you may be able to secure much of the information you need from this one source. Check the spellings, names, addresses and similar facts which may be verified later.

Interview witnesses

Police and other investigators may lead you directly to the best-witnesses. The most accurate account of what happened usually comes from witnesses, and the investigators will try to find them. You should, too, and a good way to do that is to watch the investigators. Listen in as they interview a witness, or corner the witness after they are finished. If there is time, of course, try to find your own witnesses. You cannot always rely upon investigators to do your work for you, and you should not.

Interview friends or relatives of the victims

These sources can be quite helpful in piecing together information about the victims. Through them you often get tips even better stories.

If possible, interview the victims

Survivors of an accident may be badly shaken, but if they are able to talk, they can provide first hand details that an official report can never give. Make every attempt to interview those involved.

Others at the scene

If someone has been killed, medical examiner may be able to give you some indication of what caused the death. At least you can learn from them where the bodies or the injured will be taken. That may help, because later the hospital official may be able to provide information you need for your story.

Of course, your deadline will have a major impact on the amount of information you are able to gather. If you are to meet the deadline, you probably will be forced to stick to the basics of who, what, when, where, why and how. For that reason, it is important to gather that information first. Then, if you have time, you can concentrate on details and colour information to make the story more readable. A true example of a train accident is given as under :

Howrah-New Delhi Rajdhani Express Derails 150 Feared Killed

Soroor Ahmed and Anand Mohan Sahay in Patna

"Nearly 150 people were feared killed in one of the worst railway accidents in Bihar when 15 bogies of the 2301 Up Howrah – New Delhi Rajdhani Express derailed on Monday night on a bridge near Rafiganj station between Gaya and Dehri-on-Sone in the Mughalsarai division of Eastern Railway.

The train, which left Howrah at 1700 IST, derailed at about 2240 IST on the Grand Chord section soon after it had passed through Rafiganj station in the Naxalite-infested Aurangabad district.

At least 35 bodies have been fished out so far, Magadh Divisional Commissioner HC Sirohi said.

The mishap occurred on a 300-foot-long bridge over the Dhave river about 80 km west of Gaya junction. The train had left Gaya as scheduled at 2210 IST after a three minute halt. The driver of the train informed the railway control room at Mughalsarai about the accident at 2254 on his high-frequency telephone.

Reports said that two coaches fell into the river while three more were hanging precariously from the bridge.

Additional Director General of Police (Patna zone) Ashish Ranjan Sinha said the exact number of causalities could not immediately be ascertained, but confirmed that it would be large.

"The bridge was considered weak for a long time," a senior railway official told rediff.com on condition of anonymity. But police did not rule out the possibility of sabotage by some extremist outfits active in the region either.

Railway Minister Nitish Kumar, who was returning to Delhi from Bihar, was informed of the accident at Mughalsarai Junction in the night and reportedly headed back to the accident site.

Accident relief trains have left from Mughalsarai and Gaya stations. Some local people had reached the spot and started rescue work, but had to contend with rain, the darkness and strong currents in the river.

Railway sources said 125 passengers had been rescued by early morning by local people and the first rescue teams to reach the spot. Since the accident site is not accessible by road, medical teams are having trouble reaching it.

Meanwhile, Northern Railway has arranged for a special train to ferry relatives from New Delhi to Dehri-on-Sone. The train was scheduled to leave New Delhi at 0900 IST on Tuesday.

*This is the second such accident to take place on a bridge in less than four months. On May 12, the Patna-Delhi Shramjeewi Express had derailed near Jaunpur, killing 12 passengers."**

COVERING FIRE

Accidents and fires present similar problems for the reporter, but at a fire of any size you can expect more confusion than at the scene of an accident. One major difference, then, is that the officer in charge will be busier. At the scene of an accident, the damage has been done and the authorities usually talk with you. The investigation will not even begin until the fire is extinguished. In many cases the cause of the fire will not be known hours, days or weeks. The train burning near Ludhiana in Punjab in 2003 was one of such example.

Five killed in fire incident

KANPUR, MAY 22. Five members of a family were burnt alive and eight houses gutted in a devastating fire that broke out in Bilhaur police circle, police said here today.

"The fire started from the kitchen of Ram Nath, a resident of Nathu Jhal village late last night and spread to seven other houses due to dust storm, Senior Superintendent of police M.K. Bashal told PTI.

Those killed include Ram Nath's wife Ramwati, his three sons and a daughter. Ram Nath was also suspected to be under the debris of the house, he said adding about one dozen houses of the village were damaged partially.

Villagers tried to control the fire which also killed twenty goats by throwing water from buckets but failed to control the flames.

—rediff.com: Howrah-New Delhi Rajdhani Express derails; 150 feared killed

Though fire tenders from Fazalganj fire station were pressed into service they couldn't reach the village on time due to uprooted trees blocking the way, sources said.

Senior district and police officials have rushed to the spot and distributed exgratia and relief to the victims.

An example of the follow up story of fire runs as under:

Frontier Mail fire: Witness supports sabotage theory

RAILWAYS is coming around to the theory that the fire that killed 38 people on Frontier Mail on May 15 was the result of a sabotage. Now they have at least an eyewitness to back it too.

Joginder Pal Mehta, a passenger from Amritsar who lost his wife in the fire, told the Railway authorities that just as thick black smoke started emanating from the S4 coach, he saw three young men run out of the coach. The witness will be called to Delhi when the Commission holds its extended inquiry on May 24 and 25.

Even, the Commissioner of Railway Safety (CRS), Bhupender Singh, who's completed his four-day inquiry at the station, did not rule out such a possibility.

Meanwhile, the probe team has picked up fresh specimen from the debris, including a nylon saree and a glass bottle, after it was found that the smoke had started emanating from this heap.

Mehta, who was contacted by the Railway Police, said: "I deal with waste, and burning all kind of stuff is part of my daily work but the smoke which filled our bogie that day was of a nature I'd never encountered before. Those who were sleeping never shrieked, no one ran for escape, the smoke simply consumed them."

He said: "I was on my berth No. 62 and was trying to go back to sleep after having woken up at Ludhiana Railway Station. Suddenly, I saw smoke and three men sneak out to the next coach with their heads down. I woke up my wife, who was sleeping on seat no 55 and asked her to follow me. The train had halted by then, but she could not make it, and when I went back inside to get her, the smoke nearly killed me. I managed to come out just in time," he said.

Today, Mehta was called by GRP at the railway station. He was also called up by a railway official from Ferozepur to report at Delhi before the commission of inquiry going into the episode of May 15, but Mehta has expressed his unavailability since he has to perform the last rites of his wife, Asha Mehta.

Asked whether he would be able to recognise the three men, Mehta was not sure since it was still dark outside. "But they were definitely there, and I did not see them thereafter", he said. Incidentally, there is also a difference between his version and the police's on where the fire started.

Railways, meanwhile, have burnt down two more coaches of Frontier Mail, trying to figure out the cause of the fire. And by the entire exercise they are driving at the conclusion that it was sabotage which could have caused the fire. And also attempting to give a clean chit to their coaches, which they claim are "adequately fire resistant."

Sources said that Bhupinder Singh tried his best to simulate the exact conditions of the fire but did not succeed in completely burning down the coaches to their shells. The simulation was done near the Ludhiana railway station.

"Kersosene was sprinkled on the coach and high-speed pedestal fans were used to create the right wind velocity. The train had been travelling at about 90 kmph when it caught fire. The fire had encompassed three coaches within 10 minutes. So Singh tried to create the exact conditions but the coach was only partially burnt," disclosed railway sources.

Not satisfied with the result, and also wanting to see the reaction if inflammable material was kept inside the coach, Singh set fire the second coach after putting kerosene soaked rags and cotton in it. "This time the fire was definitely stronger but still not as fierce as the accident. The coach was not burnt down to its shell," sources added.

Though the CRS is supposed to give his report within 10 days of the accident, railway authorities have already started hinting at the possibility of sabotage. "Singh had also spoken to the kin of some of the victims. One constable, who lost his two children in the fire, told him that he had seen a bag lying inside S-4 coach and smoke was coming out of its," a senior official said.

Another problem you can face is that you may not have access to the immediate area of the fire. Barriers are often erected to keep the public—and representatives of the news media from coming close to a burning structure. The obvious reason is safety, but such barriers may hamper your reporting. You may not be able to come close enough to fire fighters to learn about the problems they are having or to obtain the quotes you need to improve your story.

These problems will make covering a fire more difficult than covering an accident. Despite the difficulties, you cover the scene in much the same way, interviewing officials and witnesses at the scene. You should also try to interview the owner. Because the official investigation will not have begun, you must conduct your own. When covering any fire, you must learn.

- The location of the fire.
- The names, ages and addresses of those killed, injured or missing.
- The name of the building's owner.
- The value of the building and its contents.
- Whether the building and contents were insured for fire damage.
- The time the fire started, who reported it and how many firefighters and pieces of equipment were called to the scene.
- What caused it, if known.

As in any story, the basis are who, what, when, where, why and how. But the nature of the fire will raise other questions that must be answered. Of primary importance is whether life is endangered. If not, the amount of property damage becomes the major emphasis of the story. Was arson involved? Was the building insured for its full value? Did the building comply with the fire codes? Were any rare or extremely valuable objects inside? Were there explosives inside that complicated fighting the fire and posed an even greater threat than the fire itself?

Your job is to find answers to these questions for the newspaper's readers. You will be able to obtain some of that information later or from the official fire reporters if they are ready before your story deadline. But most of it will come from interviews conducted at the scene with the best available sources.

Another important source in covering fire stories is the fire marshal, whose job is to determine the cause of the fire and, if arson is involved, to bring charges against the arsonist. You should make every effort to talk with the fire marshal at the scene, if he or she is available. But more likely the marshal will be the primary source of a second day story.

As in covering spot news story, in which news is breaking quickly, deadlines will determine how much you can do at the scene. If your deadline is hours away, you can concentrate on the event and those connected with it. But if you have only minutes until your deadline, you will have to stick to your basics like what, when, where, who, why and how. For that reason, it is important to collect the information first.

COVERING DISASTERS

Disasters present special problems because investigators themselves may have difficulty determining where to begin. When, for example, cyclones slice through cities, efforts may be concentrated on finding those trapped in the rubble of buildings. No one may know for certain. Who is trapped or where they are, or, in fact, whether anyone is trapped at all as happens at the coastal areas usually. Orissa is also one of such instances where several people were killed in a disastrous cyclone. Similarly in cloud bursting disaster in Himachal Pradesh many precious lives were lost during August 2003.

In such cases confusion makes your job more difficult. Officials often are caught up in the turmoil of the moment and overestimate the number of people killed or the amount of damage. In some instances you may find yourself in the unusual position of being a heat of the investigations. You may be in a better position to determine the death toll or estimate the damage. At least you will be able to make an informed judgement about the accuracy of what you are told. Many newspapers are filled with incidents of reporters quoting inflated estimates of deaths and damage. Failure to make informed judgements about the accuracy of those estimates leaves your newspaper open to charges of irresponsibility.

In addition to confusion you may well encounter hazards to your personal safety as a reporter at the scene of a disaster. After a cyclone, for example, electric wires may lie on the ground for hours until repair crews are able to reach them. At the scene of an earthquake you may be frighteningly close to a wall about to collapse or, in the aftermath of that earthquake, decaying bodies may present serious health hazards as reporters found when covering the Gujarat earthquake of 2001. As you go about your work, you must avoid all such hazards.

At the scene of a disaster, you can expect the unexpected. Presence of mind is very important in such situations. Fortunately, when disasters strike, you may not have to shoulder the entire reporting load. In such cases editors usually mobilize their other reporting staffs to gather as much information as they can as quickly as possible. You probably will be assigned a specific responsibility, such as interviewing witnesses or survivors you may then be asked to write a sidebar, a secondary story that runs with the major story and usually captures the personal side of an event. Other reporters may focus on the damage involved and compile lists of the dead and injured.

Examples of disaster stories:

Cloud Burst in HP Floods 3000 : Lives with Grief

Ashwani Sharma

Chirgaon, Aug. 15. Screams of women and a trial of death are all that is left behind in Chirgaon. When the cloud burst came on Monday night in this bustling, up-coming trade centre in Shimla district after three days of rain, it swept away the entire township and left its population of 2,500-3,000 homeless.

The death toll varying from 115 (officials) to 200 (locals) is expected to rise further as people are missing. Where houses used to be stand five-six ft mounds of mud and stones. Big boulders and uprooted trees complete the picture. The Andhra river, the culprit for the floods, has broken its banks and now runs through Chirgaon.

Three minutes, says a survivor, Sohal Lal, is all it took for his world to come tumbling down. "I tried to save my wife when gushing water entered our house around 8.30 p.m. But she was swept away before I could do anything".

Puran Chand lost his wife Sandhya and daughter Sharda, whose marriage was arranged for this month. Village Pradhan Kesar Singh, his wife and child also could not save themselves.

A woman survivor recalls Singh had rushed to the root of his house to warn the villagers to shift to safer places. But he found his own house crumbling and cried for help. However, before anyone could do anything, his wife, a child and two guests had been washed away.

Nearly 50 families have been completely wiped out, and dozens others have lost half their members. Nine people of the families of Mansa Ram and Ganga Ram, seven of the family of Nand Lal, seven of the family of Vir Singh, five of the family of Vidya Nand, six Nepali labourers and six Kashmiri labourers are till now among the dead.

—The Indian Express

Downloaded from internet

EMBASSY OF INDIA

Gujarat Earthquake

Information on Earthquake in India

A devastating earthquake hit India in the early morning of January 26, 2001, killing more than 20,000 (based on news reports) and injuring

200,000 people as it toppled buildings and houses. The quake, measuring 7.9 on the Richter scale with epicenter around 20 km north-east of Bhuj in Gujarat, occurred at 08:46 IST (Indian Standard Time) according to the Indian Seismological Department.

The quake struck as many cities were celebrating India's 51st Republic Day. The terrible caused high-rise buildings to shake from New Delhi to Mumbai, Chennai and Kolkata. Reports of aftershocks came in from around the country.

Prime Minister Vajpayee visiting some of the earthquake ravaged areas, described the devastation as "a massive tragedy". Prime Minister said that the need of the hour was that everyone should join hands to save the people. Indian armed forces have been playing key role in all aspects of relief work in Gujarat. Preliminary estimates indicate that about 40 million people have been affected.

Many non-governmental organizations are involved in relief and rehabilitation efforts. International organizations have also rushed relief materials and medical personnel to Gujarat.

—File://A:\ Information on earthquake in India – January 2001 htm

Another disaster story loaded from internet runs as follows:

BOMBAY BOMB BLASTS LEAVE 46 DEAD

By Ramola Talwar Badam (Associated Press)

Bombay, India – A part of car bombs ripped through lunchtime crowds in India's financial capital, Bombay, on Monday, killing 46 people and wreaking havoc at a crowded jewellery market and a popular historic landmark. More than 150 people were wounded.

Police Commissioner Ranjit Sharma blamed India's longtime rival, Pakistan, saying suspicion in the blast fell on Islamic militant groups "let loose by the enemy country".

The groups are the focus of the investigation, but victims from the explosions were almost certain to include both Muslims and Hindus.

The bombs were hidden in the trunks of two taxis and exploded within five minutes of each other, police said. Several people were being interrogated, including one taxi driver. No one immediately claimed responsibility for the bombings.

The timing raised concerns that the blasts were linked to a dispute over a religious site in the northern city of Ayodhya claimed by both Hindus and Muslims that has been the source of much bloodshed in the past. The bombings came hours after the release of a long-awaited

archaeological report on the site that itself showed divisions over the site's history.

Sharma, the police commissioner, specifically mentioned the Students Islamic Movement of India, or SIMI, a militant Muslim students' group outlawed in 2001, and Lashkar-e-Tayyaba, one of more than a dozen Islamic rebel groups fighting Indian security forces in Kashmir since 1989, seeking independence for the Himalayan province or its merger with Muslim-dominated Pakistan.

The reference to Pakistan could increase tension between the nuclear-armed neighbours at a time when the two countries are taking steps to improve relations. Pakistan has condemned the attacks.

On Tuesday, police declared a special alert in New Delhi and several other cities as police checked vehicles, stepped up street patrols and urged citizens to be on guard for possible bombs.

Follow up stories

A great deal of the news the reporters write is of little significance in isolation. A happening is often of importance only in relation to its effect on people. A rounded picture of news tells not only what happened but why happened and just important, what happens next?

Reaction to the news may be immediate or may take a day or two to crystallize. So today's story should be followed up tomorrow. This is essential as most editors expect their reporters to initiate follow up to major stories of accidents, fires and disasters. Sometimes the follow ups are as good as or better than the original stories.

If a story has aroused reader's interest the paper has a duty to keep them abreast of current developments rather than abandon it completely in favour of the next day's news.

The commonest type of follow-up is that of checking, the day after an accident, fire, disaster or of any other type of mis-happening, to see how the injured are faring, to discover whether traffic has returned to normal at the scene of crash, to find whether any blame is being apportioned or any inquiry to be held. This kind of follow-up is obvious. The reporter should make it a practice, when reading his own—and rival-papers, to ask himself questions about every story to decide whether some point might be worth pursuing further. Such type of articles will not only please editors but will interest readers also.

Many stories lose their full impact if not properly followed up. Follow ups demonstrate that a newspaper is wide awake, and builds its reputation for providing a valuable service, and produce a far more readable newspaper than full of lengthy reports of speeches and official pronouncements. More important, they yield a 'feedback' of public reaction to new developments—a function which is supposed to be one of the primary aims of the press in a developing country.

REPORTING OBITUARIES

In a newspaper office, death is a daily occurrence. Many newspapers do not publish a news obituary even of well-known persons. At those papers the advertising department handles obituaries as paid notices. Many metropolitan papers have adopted this policy because to publish obits on everyone who died in the area would require a substantial amount of space. At papers where obits are handled as advertising, the skill and creativity a reporter brings to the reporting and writing of the story are missing.

Still there are many reporters who wish their papers would handle obits as advertising matter. These are the reporters who look at obits as a tedious exercise in formula writing often that attitude is fostered by editors who assign the obits only to new reporters.

Not always, of course. The death of a celebrity, a major public official, a notorious criminal- all these may call for long stories recapping an extra ordinary life. The wire services and many newspapers maintain biographical files on prominent citizens who are in their mature years so that obituaries can be prepared quickly. Indeed, obits of the most important people are already written, should one of them suddenly die, the editors need only add the circumstances of death to the beginning of the story.

Most obits, however, are routine, based on information provided by the mortuary in charge of the funeral arrangements. The information comes to the newspaper in the form of a questionnaire filled and by the family or as an obit already prepared by the mortuary. Often the mortuary will call by a phone if a deadline is close. The mortuary's information usually includes circumstances of death, highlights of the person's life, names of survivors, and details of funeral services. A reporter may supplement this information by check-ing clips in the newspaper library or by interviewing the family.

Obituary Style

The routine obit follows a fairly standard story organization. You should apply the same standards to crafting a lead and building the body of an obituary as you do to other stories, you begin the lead by answering the same questions you would ask in any news story. Who (S.K. Gupta, 54, Vice-Chancellor), What (died), Where (at Indira Gandhi Hospital, Shimla), When (Tuesday morning) Why (heart attack) and how (suffered while going to office). With this information, you are ready to start the story.

The fact that Gupta died of a heart attack, while going to the office may well be the lead, but the reporter does not know until the rest of the information essential to every obituary is gathered. You also must know:

1. Time and Place of funeral services
2. Time and burial place
3. Visitation time (if any)
4. Survivors
5. Date and Place of birth
6. Achievements
7. Occupation
8. Memberships

Any of these items can yield the nugget that will appear in the lead. However, if none of these categories yields notable information, the obituary probably will start like this:

Shimla, Sep. 14, S.K. Gupta, 54, Vice-Chancellor of H.P. University, Shimla died here today morning at Indira Gandhi Hospital, Shimla., due to heart attack.

However, good reporters often find distinguishing characteristics of a person's life. It may be volunteer service, an unusual or important job, service in public office or even just having a name of historical significance. Whatever distinguishes a person can be the lead of the obituary. Writing approaches can be as varied for obituaries as for any other news story.

- After deciding on an interesting lead, you should proceed by including the information basic to every obituary: funeral arrangements. For example; funeral will be held at Summer-hill crematorium grounds, Tuesday at 11 A.M.
- Next comes a recap of the person's life, brief or extended depending on the prominence of the individual. This includes details of employment, place of birth, civic honours, awards, public service, professional and social affiliations.
- Survivors come next. Most newspapers confine the list of survivors to grand-parents, parents, brothers, sisters, spouse, children. Sometimes the number of grandchildren is included.

Because this information normally is obtained directly from the family it generally is accurate. But you still should check the spelling of all names, addresses and the deceased's age against the birth-date. You should also never print an obituary by phone from someone purporting to be a funeral home representative. Too many newspapers have been the victims of hoaxes. Always call the funeral home to confirm the call. Following is a story covered by the *Tribune.*

Tribune scribe dead

T.V. Lakshminarayan, Special Correspondent of *The Tribune,* died here today after battling with lung cancer for over two years. He was 39 and is survived by his wife Ranjana and two sons.

Lakshminarayan, who was popularly called in journalistic circles by his initials "TVL", was cremated at Nigambodh Ghat tonight. He joined *The Tribune* in 1994 as a Principal Correspondent and was promoted as Special Correspondent in 2001.

TVL had worked for a Malaysian newspaper at the beginning of his more than 17-year-long journalistic career, but he flowered when he joined by United News of India in 1986. UNI staffers had nicknamed him "All-rounder" because he covered such diverse fields as sports, courts, crime and politics.

The President of the Editors' Guild, Mr Hari Jaisingh, and Editor-in-chief of *The Tribune* described TVL's death as "a huge loss to journalism."

Examples of Obituary are as follows:

'Life should be great, not long'

God, it is said, also needs good people and calls them to His abode much earlier than other people.

Otherwise, what else can explain the sufferings of T.V. Lakshminarayan and the trauma of his family, particularly his wife Ranjana, who virtually moved mountains in the past two years in a vain bid to cure him of lung cancer?

Hindu philosophy, which talks of the life-death-rebirth cycle, says that your previous births influence your present birth and the present birth would cast a reflection on your future births.

The life (and death) of Lakshminarayan, better known by his initials "TVL", is a glaring example of this and a fit case for metaphysical researchers. This is because a noble soul like TVL, who never harmed even a fly, went through hell for the past more than two years since he tested positive for an advanced lung cancer.

The life of TVL raises an important metaphysical question: Why a man who has not harmed anybody and has led a virtuous, sinless life should suffer?

I first met T.V. Lakshminarayan at his B-98 Gulmohar Park residence in 1983. He was in school then. What struck me most, apart from his towering physique, was the confidence with which he talked to me on various subjects at our first meeting. His elder brother, T.V. Sriram, had introduced TVL to me saying, "Meet my younger big brother."

Three years later, TVL joined United News of India (UNI) and very soon became the most sought-after "reporter" though he was on the Central Desk. He impressed everybody with his all-rounder skills. Those in charge of different beats like courts, sports and economics used to fight among themselves to ensure that TVL covered their assignment only. In the nineties, when I was in charge of legal reporting in UNI, I confess to have fought with the sports chief and economics chief to have exclusive "rights" over TVL. Such was the halo around TVL.

He was willing worker who never said no to any work at any time of the day or night. Year after years, he would be given early morning assignments which other reporters loathed. And yet, he would willingly go for the late night assignments too.

TVL was extremely popular among girls, but he never chased any girl. As far as I know, Ranjana was the only girl in his life.

But the most striking thing about TVL was that during the 20 years of my association with him, I did not come across a single person who ever talked ill of him.

So many times I thought that a day would come when he would lose his battle against cancer. Once I asked him whether he had seen the popular Hindi film "Anand" in which the hero Rajesh Khanna is a terminal cancer patient and is loved by all and sundry.

He replied in the negative and disclosed that whenever the film was being telecast, Ranjana would immediately change the channel. Once I asked him whether he had read a recent book, "The Joy of Cancer", he said Ranjana does not keep a single cancer-related book in the house.

Today that day has come. TVL has lost his battle against cancer. But as the "Anand" protagonist said in the film: "Zindagi lambi nahin badi honi chahiye" (The life should be great, not long). TVL did not have a long life. But he definitely had a great life. TVLs donot die.

—Rajeev Sharma.
The Tribune
April 27, 2003.

He served man to serve God

In consonance with his altruistic way of life, his last wish was to bequeath his body to the PGI, Chandigarh, for study and research so that even his mortal remains would be of some use to humanity. But God wished it otherwise for Aloysius L.Fonseca, a Jesuit priest.

He was destined to spend the evening of his life in war-ravaged Afghanistan to bring succour and relief to the helpless and the hopeless. And there the Lord called him for his eternal reward on February 8.

There was nobody to deliver a panegyric. Nor was there a funeral procession as his mortal remains were laid to rest in the cemetery adjacent to the Italian Embassy. Perhaps, that must have been his untold wish.

Punjab has a solid reason to be grateful to Fr. Aloysius. The Balwadi programme he started in Ropar district in 1990 drove away the darkness of ignorance and lit the light of knowledge in the minds of thousands of children. He devised a system, which helped to bring such children into the mainstream. It envisages preparing preschool children to go to regular schools, thereafter following them up with remedial classes to prevent them from dropping out so as to improve the educational standards in the rural areas; At present it is quite successfully working in 55 villages.

When Fr. Aloysius relinquished his charge in June 1997 his noble legacy of service was handed over to his worthy successor, Fr. Joseph Kalathil, the former Provincial of Jamshedpur and the first Chancellor of JalandharDiocese, who is continuing the work with a plethora of other developmental activities for rural upliftment under the Guru Kirpa Society.

On February 15 thousands of people of different religions from far and near gathered at the Loyola School premises in Kotla Nihang village, which was his 'karmabhoomi'. Leaders of Sikhs, Hindus, Muslims, Jains and Christians prayed and paid their last respects to a man who never thought of his own comforts, but always the welfare of others, who preached a message of love and service not so much by words, but by actions leaving thereby a noble legacy for the posterity to make it a better world.

—K.J. Thomas

Pitfalls to avoid

Avoid platitudinous eulogies in your own writing, and use them sparingly in quotations, for example, "Loved ones", "passed away", "our dearly beloved brother and father", "the departed", etc. These euphemisms may be fine for eulogies, but such terms are out of place in a news story. Try to make your article a recap of the highlights of a person's life, not a grim report of death.

"A good obit is like a good personality feature," explains one editor -teacher, Professor Lillian (Lee) Wilkins of the University of Colorado. "The only difference is that the subject doesn't show up for the final interview."

Watch your language, too, when you report the cause and circumstances of a death. Unless the doctor is at fault a person usually dies not "as a result of an operation" but "following" or "after" one. Also a person dies "unexpectedly" but not "suddenly". All deaths are sudden. Note, too, that a person dies "apparently of a heart attack" but not of "an apparent heart attack". And a person dies of injuries "suffered," not "received".

Consult your wire service style book when you have a question. The style book prescribes usage in another instance, too. A man is survived by his wife, not his widow, and a woman is survived by her husband, not her widower. In fact, you will need to consult the style book often when you are writing an obit.

Newspaper Policy

Newspaper Policy often dictates what will—and will not—be included in an obituary. Those newspapers that do have written policies may prescribe how to handle everything from addresses to suicides.

Because of threats to the safety of property and the individuals involved, in some cities even information essential to the obituary no longer appears in the paper. Some newspapers specifically tell reporters not to include the address.

Criminals have used information taken from the obituary columns to prey on widows. Knowing the time of the funeral and the address of the deceased makes it easy to plan a break-in at the empty residence during the services. Therefore, this information also may be withheld.

Two other kinds of information newspapers may have restrictive policies on are the *cause of death* and *potentially embarrassing information.*

Cause of Death

It the person who dies is not a public figure and the family does not wish to divulge the cause of death, some newspapers will agree. That is questionable news judgment. The reader wants to know what caused the death. A reporter should call the mortuary, the family, the attending physician and the appropriate medical officer. Only if none of these sources will talk should the newspaper leave out the cause of death.

A death certificate must be filed for each death, but obtaining it often takes days, and some states do not make the cause of death public records. Even if the state lists the cause of death and the reporter has timely access to the death certificate, the information is often vague.

If the death is caused by cancer or a heart attack or is the result of an accident, most families do not object to including the cause in the obituary. But if the cause is cirrhosis of the liver brought on by heavy drinking, many families do object, and most papers do not insist on printing the cause.

If the deceased was a public figure or a young person, most newspapers insist on the cause of death.

If the death is the result of suicide or foul play, reporters can obtain the information from the police or the medical examiner. Some newspapers include suicide as a cause of death in the obituary; others print it in a separate news story, and still others ignore it altogether.

Embarrassing Information

Another newspaper policy affecting obituaries concerns embarrassing information. If you discover that the person you are writing about was 77 and had served a short jail term for breaking and entering when he was 21, your editor probably would not include it in the obituary. It is a relatively minor offense committed years earlier. However, if you discover that your subject had served a term for child molestation and was well-known since then for having spent hundreds of hours as a volunteer with youth groups, the question would be much less clear-cut. Some editors would include it; most would not. In fact, many would not run the featured version of the obituary at all because of that piece of information.

The crucial factor in determining the extent to which you should report details of an individual's private life is whether the deceased was a public or private person. A *public figure* is one who has been in the public eye an officeholder, a participant in civic or social activities, a person who spoke out at public meetings or through the mass media, a performer, an author, a speaker—these all may be public figures.

Policy Options

1. Run an obituary that ignores any embarrassing information and,

if necessary, leave out the cause of death. If circumstances surrounding the death warrant a news story, run it separate from the obituary.
2. Insist on including embarrassing details and the cause of death in the obituary.
3. Insist on including embarrassing details and the cause of death in the obituary only for public figures.
4. Put a limit on how far back in the person's life to use derogatory information such as a conviction.
5. Print everything newsworthy that is learned about a public figure but not about private figures.
6. Print everything though newsworthy about public and private figures.
7. Decide each case as it comes up.

It is the reporter's obligation to be aware of the newspaper's policy. In the absence of a clear policy statement, the reporter should consult the city editor.

Exercises

1. Find an accident story in any newspaper of your choice. List all the obvious sources the reporter used in obtaining information for the story. List additional sources you would have checked.
2. Talk with a fire official in your city about the department's media policy at fire scenes. Based on what you learn, write instructions for your fellow reporters on what to expect at fires in your town.
3. Compare the coverage given a disaster story in two national daily newspapers. In your analysis, explain which one had the more effective coverage and why?
4. Write a lead for an obituary from the following information. Ashok Kamath, born August3, 1921, New Delhi. Kamath died following a cardiac arrest June 5, 2003. Funeral services will be June 7. He was Resident Editor, The Times of India. Kamath had also been a former Associate Editor (News), Hindustan Times.
5. An obituary notice comes from a local association. it contains the basic information, but under achievement it lists only former member of Lion's club, your editor tells you to find out more about the deceased. Whom would you call and Why?

6. If Kamal Aggarwal, private citizen, committed suicide while alone in his home, would you include that in his obituary? Why or Why not?
7. Write a two page advance obituary of one of the following:-

   (a) Nirmal Mukary
   (b) Swami Satchidanand
   (c) Haren Pandya
   (d) Balwant Gargi
   (e) B.C. Sanyal
   (f) Krishan Kant

At the end, list your sources.

11

SERVICE JOURNALISM

The questions that preoccupy people day by day are not necessarily the ones that make big headlines. They are personal questions like these: What shall I wear today? What shall we have for dinner tonight? Where can I get ideas for decorating my apartment? Where can I spend my winter vacations? How can I meet somebody new, make new friends, enjoy new relationships? How can I make more money, or save the money I have, or invest it wisely? How can we make sure our children are getting the best education?

Often the answers come in an expanding branch of reporting known as "Service Journalism". The term means simply the reporting of information that helps people cope with their daily lives.

In truth, all journalism is supposed to do that, more or less. But service journalism does it more directly and personally. Regular journalism may report that the economy is down and that the jobs are hard to find, service journalism tells you what to do if you got laid off or how to find your first job out of college in a tough economy. Regular journalism may report that food prices are up by 10 percent this year; service journalism tells you how to make your food rupees stretch. Regular journalism may report a new study in alcoholism, service journalism makes it more personal; what to do about the alcoholic in your family.

Service journalism is not new. It is indeed the bread and butter of magazines. Newspapers have carried food, home and garden sections for years but newspapers have pursued service journalism with new vigour recently.

A survey released by the American Newspaper Publishers Association in 1977 asked readers what they would like to see added to the regular coverage of newspapers. "More consumer information" stood at the top of the list. It was particularly important to the younger (21-35) of the two age groups studied.

And the younger group showed more interest in how-to-do—it stories, feature stories, and movie reviews than the older (35) group. The young showed less interest than the older group in the traditional fare of newspapers, local news, national news, and editorials. A 1984 study by the American Society of Newspaper Editors reiterated the desire for more stories on health and business. In India, several newspapers bring out special supplements on service articles like Career Guide, travel, food, consumer rights, health, business, sports and education etc.

Toward a New Definition : Utility Journalism

Service journalism, though it has expanded, tends to be thought of as 'utility' journalism—how-to-do—its on leisure, fashion, food, home and garden, child care, family health, and the like. But something has been added to the definition of late.

That something might be called the 'spirit of service'. It means a change in attitude among reporters and editors. In essence the attitude has changed from mild arrogance ("Here's today's news; take it or leave it!") to a more modest, audience oriented approach ("Here's the news we think will interest you- we hope you like it"). Arrogance won't work in this era of intense media competition.

The spirit of service, moreover, means greater attention to how the news will affect readers personally. The reporter who thinks will often have different criteria for what is news. The selection of stories may be different, or the story angles will focus more on personal impact.

Types of Service Articles

Service articles generally fall into four categories; the straight how-to, the case history, the feature with how- to emphasis and the list.

The how-to: This is the most common service feature, the staple of the food, home and garden pages. You address the reader directly, and the headlines are equally direct and to the point. " How to guard against termites" or plant now for spring daffodils or "Ten ways to keep healthy."

The case history: Here you write about someone who has already done something that others might try. The basic theme is "they did it, and so can you". Suppose, for instance, that you interview a young couple who have just returned from a two week motorcycling trip in Himachal Pradesh. Your story is about them, written in third person, but the content is definitely how- to. That is, your questions and your story focus on the traditional how-to elements. How do you plan such a trip? How much does it cost? Where do you stay at nights? What are problems to watch out for? What advice have you for any who might follow your path?

The feature with how-to emphasis: Two types are involved here. One is the straight news story that happens to deal with how-to information. The tax assessor develops a new form for use in paying one's property taxes and calls a press conference to tell the public, step-by-step, how to use it. The second type is the story in which the writer consciously includes service information.

Lists: They have become ever more popular in the media, they are both fun and utilitarian. They are often controversial, which enhances reader's interest. What are the ten best week-end vacation spots? What are the five most dangerous intersections in your study? What are the ten quiet places to study? and so on.

Covering the Service Beat

Some reporters make service their full-time beat. they keep in touch with experts in their fields of interest. A 'shelter' writer covering homes and gardens, would keep in touch with college nutritionists, architects, home economists, agricultural extension agents, and similar sources. A reporter specializing in people problems would keep develop sources from among counsellors, doctors, psychologist and the like.

Ideas also come from ordinary circumstances. A journalist once remarked that ideas come from the most tenuous of sources: "There is an idea in what keeps you wake at night." If worrying about money keeps you awake, perhaps writing about it how to save it, how to make it go farther, how to get more—will keep you sleep better. Ideas come from the people who deal with the public. What are the most frequently asked questions of the tax assessor's office for example? If lots of people are asking a certain kind of question perhaps it's time to write an article that would share the answers with everyone.

Writing the Service Article

Many service articles are written the same way as regular news or features. One exception is the list, but probably no advice is necessary on preparing a list. The other major exception is the how-to article.

A how-to starts with a good idea, even a novel one, backed up by good research. Research is vital, you must have sufficient detail to tell the readers how to make that motorcycle trip in Himachal—anticipating all their insecurities; things like taking enough money, speaking the language, finding safe places to spend the night, protecting health. Many of the details are strictly utilitarian. For a building project you include such elements as what materials are needed, their cost, where to get them, how to assemble them step by step. The writing itself must be simple, clear, direct.

The structure of the how-to is similar to that of the feature. You usually start with a statement of the problem or an anecdote that illustrates the problem. You then propose a solution (which becomes the theme of your article). You then take to the reader through the solution in chronological order, an easy step at a time. When you have delivered your last bit of information, you summarize quickly and stop.

Finally, the development of a good how- to piece suggests the inclusion of such practical details as the phone numbers of sources of information, or books pamphlets; and other materials that would help the reader.

Some of the articles on service journalism, published in various newspapers during the recent months are given below as examples :

Explore the Himalayas

Do you want to discover the Himalayas with something to do for everyone in the family? Here's something then ... from May to July 2003.

The Tons-Sutlej watershed damarcates Garhwal from Himachal Pradesh and the "Himalaya River Runners (HRR)" base camp in a pine forest on the banks of the Tons river at 4,000 ft above sea level. Located in the secluded Tons valley, it makes for an ideal summer getaway.

There is white river rafting on the "river without peer", trout fishing, a swim in forest pools, bird watching, rock climbing and rappelling, as also mountain biking, day hikes and over night treks.

Some of the well known treks that originate from the Tons base camp are the challenging Buran Pass, the moderate Ruinsara and other alpine meadow treks such as the Kedar Kantha trip.

How to get there:

Road: *About 450 km from Delhi and in your own vehicle or a hired coach/taxi.*

Rail: *Dehradun Shatbadi Express: Departure from New Delhi railway station. Arrival at Saharanpur, and then transfer to camp by an "HRR" vehicle.*

Air: *Daily flight to Dehradun*

Tons packages:

Tons getaway (three days)

Tons Great escape (four days)

Tons Alpine Experience (Eight days)

Other packages:

Longer trips for rafting, trekking, Mhaseer fishing, birding and corporate team building.

Booking:

Contact "HRR" Office in New Delhi for cost details and reservations. Travel and transport cost extra.

Full advance payment before the trip.

Payment in cash/cheque/bank draft/traveller's cheques.

All packages can be modified.

About the camp:

Temperature: *Day: 24° to 29°C. Night: 12° to 18°C.*

Deluxe tents on a twin share basis and set apart for privacy.

Meals: *Buffet meals that are a mixture of Indian and continental.*

Showers: *Simple and rustic but efficient. Hot water is provided twice a day on request.*

Toilets: *Dry pit western style.*

Established in 1988, the "HRR" is one of the first rafting outfits in India. Yousuf Zaheer, the founder and managing director of "HRR" is a trained river professional. The company uses imported equipment like helmets, life jackets, wet-suits, paddles, kayaks and catarafts under the supervision of full-time Indian and international guides.

For more details contact:

Himalaya River Runners (India) Pvt. Ltd.
N-6, (First Floor), Green Park Main, New Delhi – 110016
Ph: 011 – 6854643, 6852602, 6968169, Fax: 011 – 6865604
E-mail: riverrun@vsnl.com
Website; www.hrrindia.com

—The Hindu
June 1, 2003

Eat Smart

Isn't it interesting how we grow up thinking something is true and never question until someone comes along and tells us our thinking was wrong? If you like to learn new things, even if they fly in the face of what Mom taught you, read on:

- *Cottage cheese is not a good source of calcium. Hard cheeses usually have two to four times as much calcium as cottage cheese and milk and yoghurt are still the best (300-400 mg per cup). Cottage cheese is still a good source of protein and is much lower in fat than other cheese. This makes it a good food to include in your diet, but not as a major source of calcium.*

- *Vine-ripened tomatoes are not necessarily more nutritious tomatoes. They may taste better than the kind that are shipped green, then gassed with a plant hormone called ethylene to complete the maturing process. But the amounts of vitamin C and beta-carotene are nearly the same.*
- *Eating lots of sugar does not cause diabetes. But being overweight does tend to increase your risk for diabetes and if you are overweight primarily because of your sugar intake, then the two may be related.*
- *Drinking carbonated liquids when you are nauseated will not make you feel better. In fact, all fluids, especially the bubbly ones, are hard to keep down when your stomach is upset. The better remedy is a cracker or other dry food.*
- *Fresh-squeezed juices are good for you but they are not better than whole fruits and vegetables. They cannot cure arthritis, migraine or other chronic maladies. Salesmen who sell expensive juicers would have you believe that juices are medicines. They are not. Ounce for ounce, the juice of an orange, has as much vitamin C as an orange but you lose some other nutrients that remain in the solids.*
- *In the case of carrot juice, one carrot has less beta-carotene than a cup of carrot juice because it takes more than one to make a cup of juice. But you lose the fibre unless the carrot is pureed.*
- *Vitamins do not provide quick energy. Vitamins do not have any calories and thus provide no energy at all. The only way to get energy is by eating carbohydrates, fat and protein. Many vitamins are coenzymes, which means that they work with other nutrients to release energy. But the body can only use a certain quantity of vitamins and if you take more than your body can absorb, the excess will be excreted or stores in fat.*

—Sheldon Margen
Dale A. Ogar
Lats
The Hindu
April, 4, 2004

Tips to Avoid Constipation

There is widespread misconception that one daily bowel movement with good quantity of evacuation is essential for normal health. It is a general belief that if bowel is not cleared daily with good quantity of evacuation, toxins from the intestine are absorbed into blood and this causes all types of diseases. So, it is commonly said that chronic constipation is the root cause of all types of diseases.

Due to the fear of such misconceptions and disbelief if one does not get one's bowel cleared with good quantity of evacuation, one generally complains of headache, giddiness, head heaviness, body-ache, weakness, sleep disturbances, palpitation, reduction in efficiency, etc. On the advice of a quack, he take a strong purgative and passes good quantity of stool and is relieved of complaints caused due to the tension from chronic constipation.

As a result of purgative, the whole intestine becomes empty. It normally takes two-three days to fill the empty intestine resulting in no bowel movement for two-three days or so. Due to the fear of chronic constipation the person complains of tension again and again and is compelled to take some stronger purgative (even enema). So, he becomes a purgative-addict.

In fact, the frequency of bowel movement and the quantity of evacuation of stools depend upon the diet taken. Those who take a very refined diet pass stool once in two-three days. Those on a very high fibre diet (high roughage/residue) past stool two-three times a day. Both are medically normal. No toxins are absorbed from the intestine in such cases at all. So, the frequency of bowel movement and the quantity of evacuation of stools depend on a refined and high fibre diet. It is only very hard or watery stools which need medical advice.

In general private clinics every fourth patient complains of chronic constipation with symptoms of tension due to some disbelief. So, it is essential to understand the following points regarding normal bowel movement.

Stools are made of residue of diet and water. So, a refined diet and lack of water is a major cause of chronic constipation, it is advised that one should take a high fibre diet (10-12 gm of fibres daily). Seasonal vegetables, salad, fruits, bran, unsieved flour (not maida) and plenty of water should be taken to keep stools soft.

Lazy rectum is also a very important cause of chronic constipation. If one does not attend to the call of nature in time and properly, after some time even rectum is full. It stops sending a call, resulting in constipation. Regular, timely eating and an elimination (going to toilet) habit are very important. Enough time and privacy for complete evacuation are necessary. Incomplete evacuation in a hurry causes lazy rectum.

To squeeze out stools, good tone of abdominal and pelvic muscles is important. In bed-ridden patients, very old people, persons with their tummies protruding out, doing no physical activity or walking, constipation is very common. it can be prevented by undertaking proper physical activity. It improves the muscular tone.

When anything reaches the stomach, the colon is stimulated, resulting in a call for evacuation. Manu people take a glass of water, a cup of tea or smoke a cigarette before going to toilet. This is helpful in avoiding a purgative.

In the case of certain diseases when constipation is common, treatment of the disease is essential. Among these diseases are chronic amoebiasis, irritable bowel syndrome, intestinal obstruction, anal fissures, fistula, chronic depression and diabetes mellitius. Even a sudden change in the surroundings, lack of rest or sleep can cause constipation.

—Dr. Vijay Sharma
The Tribune
April 4, 2004

Exercises

Write a how-to feature for the campus newspaper on a topic of interest to college students. Some possibilities:

1. How to take an exam.
2. Five quiet places to study.
3. How to get along with your roommate.
4. Books you ought to have read before graduation.
5. How to listen and take notes during lectures.

12

CIVIC JOURNALISM

Meaning

Civic journalism is an effort to reach out to the public more aggressively in the reporting process, to listen to how citizens frame their problems and what citizens see as solutions to those problems.... and then to use that information to enrich news stories. Civic journalism is practiced by newspapers and radio and television stations around the world. What can encourage these people to take part in their own system of governance, a democracy that depends on the participation, as well as the consent, of the governed?

Civic or public journalism, holds that delivering the news to the doorstep may not be enough, that journalism organizations need to develop innovative ways of drawing a reluctant citizenry into their public affairs.

As defined by Jay Rosen, a leading theorist: *"Public journalism is not a settled doctrine or a strict code of conduct but an unfolding philosophy about the place of the journalist in public life. This philosophy has emerged most clearly in recent initiatives in the newspaper world that show journalists trying to connect with their communities in a different way, often by encouraging civic participation or regrinding the coverage of politics in the imperatives of public discussion and debate."*

Edward M. Fouhy, former executive director of Pew Center, said, *"Civic journalism is an effort to reconnect with the real concerns that viewers and readers have about the things in their lives they care most about—not in a way that panders to them, but in a way that treats them as citizens with the responsibilities of self-government, rather than as consumers to whom goods and services are sold. It takes the traditional five w's of journalism--who, what, when, where, why--and expands them--to ask why is this story important to me and to the community in which I live?"*

In effect, civic journalism's efforts to motivate people to get involved in civic life are in addition to such traditional press responsibilities as ongoing coverage of issues and watch dogging public officials. The philosophy, as applied, would have a news organization purposefully use its resources and activities to educate and interest people in the public sphere.

Civic journalism is rooted in journalists' concerns about disconnections, not only between citizens and their government but also between people and their news media. So it must be said that civic journalism is self-interested in that it seeks to make the participating media more valuable to consumers by connecting them to their community.

Techniques of Civic Journalism

- Soliciting and harvesting suggestions and ideas from citizens in the initial process.
- Providing access to our air for citizens to interact with policymakers, raise questions, make suggestions, etc.
- Holding community gatherings and forums at which some of the activities in the above items take place.
- Serving as a venue where citizens can discuss public policy initiatives and comment on their implications—involving them in a public civic conversation that in recent years has tended to exclude them.

Suggestions for Civic Journalists

(1) Journalists should offer solutions to the community problems they write about in their stories;

(2) Journalists should see their jobs as that of initiators of public debate;

(3) Journalists should get directly involved in helping solve the problems of the communities that they report in;

(4) Journalists should see themselves more as participants in the democratic process, rather than as watchdogs of democratic government;

(5) Journalists should write more on what affects ordinary citizens rather than on the major news events of the day...similarly,

civic journalism relies more on intense local coverage than on news from national and international bureaus; and

(6) Journalists should not view people as potential customers of news, but as potential actors in the democratic process who can solve community problems.

However, there remain some questions to be answered:

- Can civic journalism be reinvented to suit the contemporary political and social scenario?
- Can this journalism technique truly involve people in their public affairs, or is it just novelty?
- Does civic journalism affect the credibility of the news media positively or negatively?
- Is civic journalism powerful enough to overcome the growing trivialization and manipulative-ness of campaigning and politics?
- Can this empowerment of the people make public officials more responsive?

Beside these, there are some vital questions to be answered with respect to the extent a journalist should play a pro-active role in the citizens' lives and his/her new role as partner with the public: Should reporters be investigators of system failure or initiators of solutions? Should journalists be detached observers or activist participants? Should newspapers be independent watchdogs or conveners of public forums? There has also been a brewing debate on the appropriateness of this "community-reporter partnership" in terms of its impact on reporter objectivity. The questions encompassing this ethical debate are not easily answered for they strike at the heart of traditionally held journalistic values: objectivity and the watchdog concept.

But at this juncture the answer to these questions would be far easier if one acknowledges that journalism has an obligation to public life. These obligation, according to the Pew Center for Civic Journalism, goes beyond just telling the news or unloading lots of facts. The way we do our journalism affects the way public life goes. Journalism can help empower a community or it can help disable it. It is here that civic journalism has helped reinvent journalism to suit the contemporary political and social scenario and involve people in their public affairs, thereby empowering the electorate and making public officials more accountable.

Civic Journalism and Socio-Political Relevance

In the present day social and political flux, according to Carter, civic journalism becomes all the more important as:

— It says that the people who live in a neighborhood know as much, and probably more, about what is wrong with it and what might be done to fix it than city officials and certified experts.
— It says that good reporting only begins with databases and phone calls; it is made more accurate and relevant by person-to-person contact with those whose lives you impinge upon and alter with your coverage.
— It says that asking people to tell you what they think matters to their community, and adding those opinions to the mix that guides your coverage is at least as useful as polling them about their political preferences.
— It maintains that such surveys are more relevant to a newspaper's basic mission than those that measure our consumers' tastes in horoscopes, comic strips and canned editorial features—or their preferences among local, state, national and international news.
— it calls attention to the neglected role of journalism in deliberative democratic procedures. Public journalism presents something of a puzzle, since its advocates see journalists as central catalysts of deliberative democracy.

However, one must be careful while analyzing the affects public journalism would accrue. Civic journalism does not—and must not—promise a quick fix or a sudden explosion in civic participation, circulation, love between our brothers and our sisters—or ethical journalism.

Jan Schaffer, Executive Director, PEW Center for Civic Journalism has suggested 10 ways in which civic journalism can be used rebuilding and fortifying the frameworks of society:

(1) Let ordinary people see themselves in your stories doing ordinary and extraordinary things: rescuing survivors, searching for the missing, overcoming obstacles, grieving their losses. Let them see the capacity they have to transcend tragedy.
(2) Give people space to tell their own stories. They need to share their joy or grief, their despair or triumph.

(3) Stay interactive. Create zones of connectivity where people can trade information, chat, vent or ponder. This might include chat rooms, talk-back sections of the paper, e-mail invitations to write for the newspaper, etc.
(4) Chronicle history at large; explain, as well as condemn, the terrorists.
(5) Toss out old taboos and let your readers and viewers see that journalists are human, too. You are not seeking to profiteer off calamity, rather you share in the suffering.
(6) Likewise, let public officials be human—unvarnished in their uncertainty, tentative in their approaches.
(7) Ban rubbernecking coverage; citizens want to do more than ogle. Celebrate the capacity of individuals to heal, to rebuild, to make a difference in your community.
(8) Rise above petty competition. Set more overarching priorities.
(9) Position your news organization be a good citizen in your community.
(10) Create a forum for people to share their ideas, values and aspirations.

Conclusions

Civic journalism reflects a new investigative style of journalism—an investigative style that requires the watchdog concept, but one that goes beyond this press function to solve the uncovered or discovered (community) problem. It has helped in keeping public discourse alive while talking to and listening to people. In such an instance where the community problem might revolve around some form of police or government corruption, civic journalism holds potential for adding another layer of accountability and a mechanism for retaining media's watchdog function. In a philosophical context, some journalists frame these ethical issues in terms of organizational culture, identifying that media must change conventions about what is news and how it is covered.

As the need has arisen to suit it to the changing times, journalism has had to be redefined and categorized into sub-disciplines or specialties. That's why today, no journalist, lest he be thought outdated, will be caught doing plain journalism; it has to be interpretative, explanatory, conceptualised, investigative, in-depth, perspective, or other journalism on some such order.

Indeed, as life modernizes and becomes increasingly complex, people demand more from the journalist. Basically, they now want him to not merely recount yesterday's events, but help them understand what those events mean to them, how they affect them, not only as individual citizens but also as a community. Public journalism is not a settled doctrine or a strict code of conduct but an unfolding philosophy about the place of the journalist in public life. Journalists will have to redefine their own standards of proper conduct, (and) draw new and imaginative lines that mark off their special functions.

As it happens, there has emerged lately a kind of journalism that tries to strike that precise balance. It employs all the tools of good journalism, but it's not afraid to get more involved with the community—in listening, in being a catalyst for activity, in helping community build its own capacity. And it's not afraid to say: If the old journalism is not working, let's re-invent it.

Exercises

1. Bring out the significance of civic journalism as a public service function.
2. How the techniques and practices of civic journalism can be reinvented to suit the contemporary political and social scenario?
3. Is civic journalism being practised in the newspaper you read or news channel you watch? Explain with examples of such stories.

SECTION IV

SPECIALIZED REPORTING

13

INVESTIGATIVE REPORTING

Investigative reporting is the most glamorous form of journalism. It may well be the most important form. It publicises information about wrong doing that affects the public interest. But the work of investigating is hard, often dull, sometimes risky. Days may be spent tracking down leads that prove fruitless. Pressures and even threats are common.

Ever since the two enterprising reporters of the *Washington Post*, Carl *Bernstein and Bob Woodward* committed themselves to unravelling the *Watergate* scandal which ultimately led to the resignation of US President Nixon, investigative journalism got a boost. The idea that investigative journalism became important only as a result of Watergate era of 1970s is a misconception. Journalists have always been society's watch dogs and they have always been investigating wrong doings. Quite often they have to spend months to ferret out the truth. ***Ashwini Sarin*** vetern journalist of *The Indian Express* got himself arrested on a flimsy ground to investigate wretched conditions in the Tihar Central Jail. Likewise ***Sucheta Dalal,*** formerly with *The Times of India* revealed manipulation of the market by a Stock broker in connivance with stock exchange and Indian and foreign banks. This phenomenal rise in the value of shares she noticed while going through the stock market quotations. Arun Shourie, *of the Indian Express, has made the newspaper the cutting edge of opposition to the government tackled issues like corruption, prison reforms, bonded labour, the plight of undertrials through sustained investigation and the hard team work. When he wrote of the Muslim Women Bill he had read the Quran, the Hadi, the parables of the Prophet so that he could not be faulted for superficiality.*

Seymour Hersh, vetern investigative journalist, from New York, was able to achieve his fame and reputation as a man who could dig out any information from government sources. He ascribes his success to his sole objective of " I just want the people to know the truth". Some of his notable stories on the front pages of several American publications are the massacre of My Lai, the secret bombing of Cambodia by American fighter aircraft, the wire tapping of the staff of Dr. Henry Kissinger, the theft of papers from Kissinger's office by the Pentagon, the CIA's involvement in the coup against President Allende of Chile and his assassination and the CIA's involvement in domestic spying.

In India he earned notoriety, when the then Prime Minister Morarji Desai, sued him for libel when Hersh named him as the "mole" in Jawaharlal Nehru's cabinet spying for the US. But Morarji Desai failed to win his case against Hersh.

Electronic media is also not lagging behind in exposing malpractices. The Indian Express reported in its November 21, 2004 issue that NDTV got second IPI India award for outstanding work in Journalism in 2003. This award has been given in exposing the baby swapping racket in Hyderabad, and also in the corruption trail of the Telgi stamp scam.

Investigative journalism matters because of its many contributions to democratic governance. Its role can be understood in keeping with the Fourth Estate model of the press. According to this model, the press should make government accountable by publishing information about matters of public interest even if such information reveals abuses or crimes perpetrated by those in authority.

From this perspective, investigative reporting is one of the most important contributions that the press makes to democracy. It is linked to the logic of checks and balances in democratic systems. It provides a valuable mechanism for monitoring the performance of democratic institutions as they are most broadly defined to include governmental bodies, civic organizations and publicly held corporations. The centrality of the media in contemporary democracies makes political elites sensitive to news, particularly to bad news that often causes a public commotion.

The publication of news about political and economic wrongdoing can trigger congressional and judicial investigations. In cases when government institutions fail to conduct further inquiries, or investigations are plagued with problems and suspicion, journalism can contribute to accountability by monitoring the functioning of these institutions. It can examine how well these institutions actually fulfil their constitutional mandate to govern responsibly in the face of press reports that reveal dysfunction, dishonesty, or wrongdoing in government and society.

The Process of Investigative Reporting

Few editors assign beginning reporters to investigative work. It is the most demanding kind of reporting. Many of the techniques can be used as well as to produce good stories from what would otherwise be routine assignments.

Formulating Hypothesis

Most investigations start with a hunch or a tip that something or someone deserves a close look. No good reporter sets out on an investigation unless there is some basis for suspicion. That basis may be a court proceeding that leaves something untold or a tip that some public official is on the take. It may be a sudden upsurge in share process or it may be long festering problems in the school. Without some idea of what you're looking for investigation is too likely to turn into wild goose chasing.

Based on the tip or suspicion together with whatever background material you have, you form a hypothesis. Reporter hardly ever use that processes of investigative reporting and scientific investigation. In both, the hypothesis is the statement of what you think is true. Your hypothesis may be, "The mayor is a crook," or, "The school system is being run incompetently." It is a good idea to state clearly your hypothesis when you start an investigation. By doing so, you focus on the heart of the problem and cut down on the possibility of any misunderstanding with your editor or other reporters who may be working with you.

Once the hypothesis is stated, the reporter – like the scientist–sets out to prove or disprove it. You should be open to the possibility of disproof. Reporters – like scientists – are not advocates. They are seekers of truth. No good reporter ignores or downplays evidence just because it contradicts his or her assumptions. In journalism as in science, the truth about a situation is often sharply different from what is expected. An open mind is an essential quality of a good investigative reporter. Remember, too, that you may have a good story even if your hypothesis is disproved.

Stages of Investigations

The actual investigative work usually proceeds in two stages. The first is ***sniff.*** You sniff around in search of trail worth following. If you find one, the second stage is the ***serious investigation***.

The preliminary checking should take no more than a day or two. Its purpose is not to prove the hypothesis but to find out the chances of proving it. You make that effort by talking with the most promising source or sources, skimming the most available records, consulting knowledgeable people in your news room. The two questions you are trying to answer at this stage are, "Is there a story here?" and, "Am I going to be able to get it?" If the answer to either question is no, there is little point in pursuing the investigation.

When the answer to both questions is yes, the real work begins. It begins with organization. Your hypothesis tells you where you want to go. Now you must figure out how to get there. Careful organization will keep you on the right track and will prevent you from overlooking anything important as you go. Ask yourself the following questions:

1. Who are my most promising sources? Who am I going to have trouble with? Who should I go to first? Second? Last?
2. What records do I need? Where are they? Which are public? How can I get to the ones that are not readily accessible?
3. What is the most I can hope to prove? What is the least that will still yield a story? How long should the investigation take?

Now draw up a plan of action. Experienced reporters often do this mentally. But when you are a beginner, it's a good idea to write out a plan and then to go over it with your editor. The editor may spot some holes in your planning or have something to add. And an editor is more likely to give you enough time if he or she has a clear idea of what has to be done.

Carry out your plan, allowing flexibility for the unexpected twists most investigations take. During your first round of interviews, keep asking who else you should talk to. While you are checking records, look for references to other files or other persons.

Be Methodical Many investigative reporter spend an hour or so at the end of every day adding up the score, going through their notes and searching their memories to analyse what they have learned and what they need next. Some develop elaborate, cross – indexed files of names, organizations, incidents. Others are less formal. Virtually all, however, use a code to disguise names of confidential sources so that those sources will remain secret even if the files are subpoenaed. The method you use isn't important, as long as you understand it. What is vitally important is that you have a method and use it. If you fail to keep careful track of where you're going, you may go in the wrong direction.

Accuracy Accuracy is very important. It is the most essential element in good journalism of any kind. In investigative reporting especially, inaccuracy leads to embarrassment, to ruined reputations and, sometimes, to lawsuits. The reputations ruined often are those of the careless reporter and newspaper. Most investigative stories have the effect of accusing somebody of wrongdoing or incompetence. Even if the target is a public official whose chances of suing successfully for libel are slim, fairness and decency require that you be sure of your facts before you put them in print. There is no excuse for an error.

Personal Integrity and Motivation

The doyen of investigative reporting in America, Clark Mollenhoff, considers personal integrity and motivation for the investigative reporters as essential for the craft. Any actions by the reporter or the newspaper that are illegal, politically partisan, or even unfair by generally accepted standards can undercut or destroy a valid journalistic inquiry. The investigative reporters must believe that it pays to be honest and ethical and know that any illegality or dishonesty is dangerous for the reporter, the newspaper, and the cause in which they are interested. He makes it clear that sources and the public will be disillusioned if the reporter or newspaper misuses the power and intentionally distorts the picture or engages in superficial sensationalism. It is essential for the reporter to ask himself if he has been fair with his dealings with the confidential sources, public sources and with persons who have been subject of an enquiry. Investigative reporting must avoid superficial sensationalism. It needs balanced judgement and in-depth understanding. Investigative reporting may be reflective even speculative but always based on hard – core evidence.

Writing the story

Most investigative stories require consultation with the newspaper's lawyer before publication. As a reporter you will have little or nothing to say about the choice of your paper's lawyer. That lawyer, though, will be an important part of your investigative career. The lawyer advises on what you can print safely and what you cannot. Most editors heed their lawyers' advice. If you are lucky, your paper's lawyer will understand and sympathize with good, aggressive journalism. If he or she does not , you may find yourself forced to argue for your story.

Writing and Rewriting

The last step before your investigation goes public is the writing and rewriting. After days or weeks of intense reporting effort, the writing strikes some investigative reporters as a chore – necessary but unimportant.

That attitude is disastrous. The best reporting in the world is wasted unless it is read. Your hard–won expose or painstaking analysis will disappear without a trace unless the writing attracts readers and maintains their interest. Most reporters and newspapers that are serious about investigative reporting recognize this. They stress good writing almost as much as solid reporting.

How do you write the results of a complicated investigation? The general answer is , as simply as you can. One approach is to use a hard lead, displaying your key findings in the first few paragraphs. Another approach, often used; is to adopt one of the alternative story structures.

Writing an investigative story so that it will be read takes the same attention to organization as any good writing. Here are a few tips that apply even more to investigative stories than to other writing:

1. *Get people into the story.* Any investigation worth doing involves people in some way. Make them come alive with descriptive detail.
2. *Keep it simple.* Look for ways to clarify and explain complicated situations. When you have a mass of information, consider spreading it over more than one story- in a series or in a main story with a sidebar. Think about how charts, graphs or lists can be used to present key facts clearly. Don't try to print everything you know. Enough to support your conclusions is sufficient; more than that is too much.
3. *Tell the reader what your research means.* A great temptation in investigative reporting is to "lay out the facts and let the reader draw the conclusions." That is unfair to you and your reader. Lay out the facts, of course, but tell the reader what they add up to.
   If the facts are there, drawing the obvious conclusions is not editorialising. It is good and helpful.
4. *Organize.* Careful organization is as important in writing the investigative story as in reporting it. The job will be easier if you have been organized all along. When you are ready to write, examine your notes again. Make an outline. Pick out your best quotes and anecdotes. Some reporters, if they are writing more than one story, separate their material into individual folders, one for each story. However you do it, know what you are going to say before you start to write.

Think of writing as the climax of a process that begins with a hypothesis, tests that hypothesis through careful investigation, checks and double- checks every fact, and satisfies the concerns of editors and the lawyer. Every step in that process is vital to success.

The Sources

Investigative reporters-like any other reporters- get their information from people or documents. The perfect source would be a person who had the pertinent documents and was eager to tell you what they meant. Don't count on finding the perfect source. Instead, count on having to piece together the information you need from a variety of people and records- some of the people not at all eager to talk to you and some of the records difficult to understand. Let's consider human sources first.

Human Sources

Suppose you get a tip that the mayor received campaign contributions under the table from the engineering firm that just got a big city contract. Who might talk?

Enemies. A person's enemies usually are the best sources when you are trying to find out anything bad about him or her. More often than not, the enemies of a prominent person will have made it their business to find out as much as possible about that person's misdeeds and shortcomings. Frequently, they will share what they know with a friendly reporter.

Friends. Surprisingly, friends are sometimes nearly as revealing as enemies, in trying to explain and defend a friend's actions, they may tell you more than you knew before. Occasionally you may find that someone your target regards as a friend is not much of a friend after all.

Losers. Like enemies, losers often carry a grudge. Seek out the loser in the last election, the losing contender for the contract, the loser in a power struggle. Bad losers make good sources.

Victims. If you are investigating a failing school system, talk with its students and their parents. If your story is about nursing home abuses, talk with some patients and their relatives. The honest and hard-working employees caught in a corrupt or incompetent system are victims, too. They can give you specific examples and anecdotes. Their case histories can help you write the story.

Experts. Early in many investigations, there will be a great deal you may not understand. You may need someone to explain how the campaign finance laws could be circumvented, someone to interpret a contract, or someone to decipher a set of bid specifications. Lawyers, accountants, engineers or professors can help you figure out technical jargon or complicated transactions. If they refuse to comment on your specific case, fit the facts you you have into a hypothetical situation.

Police. Investigative reporters and law enforcement agents often work the same territory If you are wise, you will make friends with carefully selected agents. They can—and frequently will—be of great help. Their files may not be gold mines, but they have investigative tools and contacts you lack. When they get to know and trust you, they will share. Most police like seeing their and their organization's names in the paper. They know, too, that you can do some things they cannot. It takes less proof for you to be able to print that the mayor is a crook than it may take to convince a jury. Most police investigators want to corner wrongdoers any way they can. You can use that attitude to your advantage.

Managing Human Sources

As an investigative reporter, you cultivate sources in the same ways a reporter on a beat does. You just do it more quickly. One excellent tactic is to play on their self-interest. If you keep in mind that, no matter how corrupt your target may be, he or she is still a human being, it may be easier to deal sympathetically with that person's friends. That attitude may help ensure that you treat the target fairly, as well.

Experts just want to explain the problem as you present it. And you just want to understand. People in trouble want sympathy and some assurance that they still merit respect. No reporter should have trouble conveying either attitude.

Another way to win and keep sources is to protect them. Occasionally, a reporter has to pay a high price in order to keep a promise of confidentiality. More often, the threats to confidentiality are less dramatic. Other sources, or the target of the investigation, may casually ask, "where'd you hear that?" Other reporters, over coffee or a beer, may ask the same question. Hold your tongue. The only person to whom a confidential source should ever be revealed is your editor.

Human sources pose problems as well as solving them. They may lie tc you. To get at an enemy or protect a friend, to make themselves look better or someone else look worse – and sometimes just for fun – people lie to reporters. No reporter is safe and source is above suspicion. They may use, too, just as you are using them. The only reason most people involved on any side of a suspicious situation will talk about it is to enhance their own position. That is neither illegal nor immoral. Sources may change their stories as well. People forget. Re-collections and situations change.

Pressures can be applied. Fear or love or ambition or greed can intrude. A source may deny tomorrow – or in court. What he or she told you today.

Finally sources will seldom want to be identified. Even the enemies of a powerful person often are reluctant to see their names attached to their criticisms in print. So are friends. Experts, while willing to provide background information often cite their codes of ethics when you ask them to go on the record. Police usually will co-operate fully only if you promise them anonymity. Since they are not supposed to prosecute people in the newspapers. Stories without identifiable sources have less credibility with readers, with editors, even with colleagues.

Written Sources

Fortunately not all sources are human. Records and documents neither lie nor change their stories. Many useful documents are public and non-public records. Both may be available thorough your human sources upon request.

Even when you can obtain them, records present problems. They are usually dull. Record give you name and numbers, not anecdotes or sparkling quotes. They are bare bones, not flesh and blood. They can be misleading and confusing. Misinterpreting a document is no less serious error than misquoting a person. And it is easier to do.

Most investigative reporters use both human and documentary sources. People can explain what records cannot. Documents prove what good quotes cannot. You need people to lead you to documents and people to interpret what the documents mean. And you need records to substantiate what people tell you. The best investigate stories have both.

Exercises

1. Imagine that you are working as a reporter for a newspaper at Shimla. And you have been asked to write an investigation story about child labour. How would you go about your job and what kind of information you would seek?
2. Investigating journalism of the present times is another form of muck-raking. Comment. How effective is this type of reporting in the context of Indian public affairs?
3. Investigative reporting has its own perils. Discuss.

14

DEVELOPMENT REPORTING

The training kit, prepared by the Thomson Foundation/UNICEF for Human Development Reporting, discusses development reporting in terms of PEOPLE. The emphasis in such examples is on people because it is after all the **people** who are building the nation.

> *"Development journalism seeks to report a country's progress and setbacks in both urban and rural areas in a factual and readable way. It should create an information bridge between the authorities and the public, between urban and rural communities. Long term, it aims to contribute to improvements in people's lifestyles."*

If development means anything, it must mean development of a better framework of existence for people – the men, women and the children. An effective news organization should record their progress. It must give them information which will enable them to improve their productive capacity. It must show them how to improve their bargaining power with society.

The former CNN's South Asia Bureau Chief, Anita Pratap, defines development journalism as, "reporting of issues such as population, healthcare, illiteracy, poverty and environment..." (*Outlook,* 18 January 1999).

Most of the countries of the third world are today witnessing a tremendous upsurge in the development activity which should not be ignored by newsmen. Critics of development reporting say that it is *hand out* journalism—the replication of the flattering half-truths put out by official information agencies. It is equated with the reporting only of *positive* news, to the exclusion of the negative or unflattering news.

However, development reporting does not mean governmental publicity in the old fashioned sense of publishing the achievements of a development or its plans for further. Development in the sense means the whole range of economic and social change and, therefore, development reporting involves the social conscience of the reporter.

Development is much more than just the passage from poor to rich from a traditional economy to a sophisticated urban one. It carries with it, not only the idea of economic betterment but also of great human dignity, security, justice and equality. There is a difference between economic growth and development. Growth is a quantitative process involving mainly the extension of an already established structure of production, whereas development suggests a qualitative change for a better human life.

Development is measured in the improvement of the lives of the people and the strengthening of the family's or the individual's capacity to deal with the rest of the society and of the nation's capacity to deal with the world. This can include issues like the removal of poverty, the lessening of disparity between regions and classes, the building up of the technological infrastructure, modernization of society through shedding feudalism, tribalism and superstition as well as the gradual achievement of economic self-reliance.

One of the most inspiring books on the subject—*India 2020: A Vision For the New Millennium*- is devoted to an action plan where by India can reach a developed country status by 2020. It spells out what developed status means under:

"What does the developed nation status mean in terms of the common man? It means the major transformation of our economy to make it one of the largest economy of the world; where the countrymen live well above the poverty line, their health and education is of high standard; national security reasonably assured and the core competence in certain major areas enhanced significantly so that the production of quality goods, including exports, is rising and there by bringing all-round prosperity for the countrymen. What is common link needed to realize these sub-goals? It is technological strengths of the nation, which is the key to reach this developed status."

Definitions

"A manual for News Agency Reporters" published by the Indian Institute of Mass Communication defines the purpose of development reporting as follows:

1. The purpose of development reporting is to create a sense of involvement, to spread the realization that the future comes out of present efforts, that development can be nobody's gift, least

of all of the aid given by affluent countries, but is the result of one's own labour. Destiny does not descent from above; it grows out of one's hands.

2. Development reporting must concern itself with the people. It must show them how to improve their bargaining power with society. It must make them realist that their future is in their hands. It must describe the process of backbone building.
3. Development reporting must describe the people actually at work in new projects and processes. It must describe the processes of change and modernization, the new discoveries and the products. It must describe terms and concepts of development.
4. An important aspect of development reporting is success stories of people who have adopted new technologies, tried new methods, and benefited themselves and helped society.
5. Development reporting, by its nature, is devoid of the kind of sensational interest than an eruption or a calamity or a political confrontation produces. Secondly, it does not carry the stamp of immediacy that 'events' do.
6. Development reporting, to be effective, requires considerable investigative and research skill on the part of the journalist, apart from firm grasp of trends in economic thought, planning and development.

Why Development Journalism

Development Journalism has to cover the whole complex and interlocking web of economic activity, catalytic forces unleashed by technology and industrialization, the tides and under-currents of social change, the momentum of urbanization, and its impact on politics, society and religion. Development journalism has to include these larger and more relevant areas of reality and not the traditional concept of *bad news is good news.*

Development Journalism calls for an honest collection, intelligent processing and interesting presentation and interpretation of information. Interpretation here means making the report relevant to the readers, situating it in the daily experience of the readers, the creation of traditionally recognized meaning by giving voice to thoughts of the people and also the creation of new meanings that affect all our lives. A development reporter has to take ideas to the people and the people to ideas.

Development Journalism should not be one sided or propagandist. It should not be superficial. It should have depth. Devoting a couple of paragraphs to the inaugural speech of a minister is not development reporting.

Since development is multi-dimensional phenomenon, development journalism calls for new approaches and responsibilities on the part of reporter. It is a relatively new and a varied field and, therefore, provides unlimited scope of innovations. It will thus entail more background reading, more legwork, and often greater understanding than conventional reporting of political goings-on in the capital of country or in the metropolitan centers of the world. Development reporter has to work hard to get his facts and needs skill to present them interestingly and in logical order. He has to be especially careful while dealing with the social aspects of development. e.g. when loans from international agencies are finalized for development projects, background, plans to utilize such loans and the estimated benefit should be included in the story.

Development Journalism has been a part of the western journalistic scene for a long time. It gathered prominence in recent years in India because it was generally believed that Indian newspapers were too pre-occupied with political events to give much thought to what was happening in the economic field and that Indian political reporting took a substantial percentage of space in the daily columns. Newspapers were accused of not caring enough for development reporting especially at a time when India was making rapid progress in industry and commerce. It was only after India went through a succession of Five-Year Plans that thought was, at last, given for assessing the result of planning. To what extent did planning benefit the common man? Did he get adequate compensation for the fruits of his labour? The Planning Commission itself had a house magazine *Yojna.* This magazine was primarily devoted to development reporting. And while other magazines and dailies did report on economic development, sporadically as it turned out, it was only in recent times that development reporting has reached respectable proportions. It is not unusual these days to read development reports in the Indian press.

Development journalism is primarily socio-economic reporting giving the Why, When, Where, What and How of deep structural changes in our society.

Development Journalism need not be confined strictly to socio-economic issues. Any reporting pertaining to development in fields as diverse as medicine, science, industry, and technology would come under that heading. The stress rightly is placed on the term "development". Has company X discovered a new process of instant photography? Has company Y discovered a fresh use for lasers? What is the latest in heart transplants? Answers to all these necessarily are part of development journalism. To think of it in narrow terms as pertaining or relevant only to developing countries is not only erroneous, but is self-defeating.

Rules for Writing a Development Story

Certain rules may be laid down for writing a development story. These rules are as follows:

1. Development reporting must describe the people actually at work in the projects and processes. It must describe the processes of change and modernization, innovations and improvements.
2. If you are writing a development story, see that the story is meaningful to the community that your paper is serving. A development story that is readable but has no relevance to your readers fails its very purpose.
3. Research the background of the story from the pre-development stage to its current status and find out whether schedules have been met, expenditure properly audited and if schedules have not been met, the reasons should be explained.
4. Try to seek the version of all those involved in the development project including government servants, plant managers, workers, representatives and the people for whose benefit the project had been undertaken in the first place.
5. Development journalism is not a public relations exercise. Therefore, be careful in using the public relations handouts making out tall claims. He must not use phrases directly from official handouts.
6. If two contrary opinions are expressed by two different sets of people, state them impartially. Do not take sides.
7. A development journalist must maintain regular contacts with a wide range of persons and institutions, non governmental organizations, voluntary and civil society organizations.
8. Whenever possible, quote profusely. Let the reader know that you have actually been talking to individuals and not generalizing on what you may have heard.
9. A development journalist should acquire basic understanding of terms used in agriculture, environment, science, economics and other related subjects.
10. Avoid the temptation to rewrite handouts; treat these as basic raw material on which to build the superstructure of your own well-researched story.

A reporter should not be guided by his personal prejudices and his likes and dislikes should not intrude into his reporting.

Development reporting deals with a wide variety of situations. It covers individual projects, the entire planning process and its implementation, difficulties faced by people and efforts made to remove them; economic and social change in rural and urban areas, impact of development efforts in backward and tribal areas and various aspects of development and its socio-economic impact.

In a developing country like India, the importance of development reporting should not be understated. Some of the well-known newspapers like *The Hindustan Times* pioneered developing reporting through their features like "Our Village Chhatera" which is considered as a unique contri-bution in this area. Likewise, the eminent journalist P. Sainath has been writing extensively from India's poorest districts.

Grassroots—Reporting the Human Condition

The Press Institute of India journal – regularly publishes stories on development subjects. The first issue of the journal appeared in May 1999, its primary mission being "to promote and disseminate media reportage of human development and empowerment at the grassroots of society". Reporters are commissioned to cover vital engines of empowerment, like Panchayati Raj and literacy that normally receive little media attention. Their reports are published in Grassroots and distributed to regional newspapers through the Grassroots Feature Network. A prize of Rs. 5,000, contributed by the National Foundation of India, is awarded to the best item published.

EXAMPLES OF STORIES FROM GRASSROOTS—REPORTING THE HUMAN CONDITION

Children forced to clean toilets

Mari Marcel Thekaekara

Trailed behind them over four states – Uttar Pradesh, Madhya Pradesh, Bihar and Rajasthan. Our most pathetic children- the bhangis, doms, mehtars of India. Everywhere they were the same. The children of ugly India who have had their childhood snatched from them. We see them everywhere, yet we have ceased to be shocked. They are so common place that we do not notice them. They are invisible children.

I have been in the balmiki trail since 1997. Even for the outsider, the writer merely recording their plight, it is a nauseating, depressing round. I thought I had seen everything. Then I came to Sikar, Rajasthan. Manual scavenging anywhere tends to shock you, the sheer ugliness of it, the degradation of an entire people. But this was worse. In Sikar, little girls, eight, nine, ten years old – were working with their mothers.

I met Pooja. She thought she was 12. She had the saddest eyes of any little girl I have ever seen. And as she talked haltingly, slowly, shyly, I finally realized what it was all about. Not just the four endless years of cleaning human shit every morning from the age of eight. It was a combination of many things. Pooja had never ever had a childhood.

Pooja's dress had faded and had obviously seen better days. Her hair was neatly combed but it had the blonde, straw textured streaks, a tell tale sign of malnutrition and vitamin deficiency. She was going to the school started by the Manabadhikar Sampark Kendra to help balmikis. She was pleased to have stopped working the latrines. She wrote her name painstakingly, with pride and concentration.

I asked her what she would like to be when she grow up. Even as the question left my lips, I could have bitten my tongue off. She looked at me blankly. She was 12. Girls like Pooja are married off immediately after puberty. She could barely write her name at 12. Unless there was a radical intervention in her life, what could she hope for? A stupid, thoughtless, pointless question.

In and around, Sikar there were 70 little girls like Pooja working the latrines. The scenario was the same in U.P. and Bihar. There are still one million people working as manual scavengers all over India. Prime Minister Vajpayee, like other before him, declared from the ramparts of the Red Fort that manual scavenging would be abolished by 2002. The deadline is one year old. Nothing has changed for India's one million balmikis.

An Action Aid led campaign has successfully highlighted the problem in U.P., M.P., Bihar and Rajasthan. But even where activists have successfully sealed dry latrines, the fate of the people is pathetic. For the children, it seems hopeless. Merely admitting them in government schools achieves nothing. The children are victims, picked on, beaten up, laughed and jeered at. I met Reena as about the age of Pooja. She looked less defeated than her friend. That may have been the effect of her bright orange top and black trousers. She had been to the government school for one month. "Why did you leave?" I asked her. "The teacher used to beat me". "Why did he do that?" I asked. "I was not very good with lessons," she answered.

Twelve years old with one months of schooling in all her life. And the first teacher she encountered beat her because he thought she was stupid and lazy. That what education means for average balmiki child. In addition, they have to sit and eat separately. They are not allowed to take water from the pot because it would be polluting. The teaching is minimal.

Near Lucknow, I met another group of bright, laughing kids. They had all been admitted to a school by a well-meaning social worker who had used a blend of threats and cajoling to convince the headmaster that the kids had to be admitted. He reminded the principal about the existence of the Prevention of Atrocities Act by which practicing untouchablility is punishable by law. The kids were excited, delighted as any kid would be at the prospect of not cleaning latrines.

A months later all of them had dropped out. The teacher beat them. Called them stupid. And rarely taught them anything. None of them could read or write after six months at school. They were now out every morning collecting plastic from garbage dumps. Earning Rs. 20-30 a day. They went to the movies sometimes. School was a distant dream with not very pleasant memories.

I thought of our President's inspiring speeches to children in cities. To toppers, super intelligent, elite kids in "good schools". Girls like Pooja do not know what gold medals or high first classes mean. She wrote her name painstakingly with pride. For her that was huge achievement. Kids like Pooja can not dream big. A good life means enough to eat, hoping that they won't be ill and that they can sleep without being beaten or brutalized by a drunken father. The President's targets will be met in Hyderabad and Bangalore and IITs.

If bhangi kids have just one center of excellence where could they not go? What is desperately needed is a kind of bridge school designed for older children who have never been to school before. More than the teaching, they need kind, loving, nurturing teachers.

All these children beat the scars of being told "keep your distance, go back to the slum". They barely believe that any other kind of life exists. There are thousands of kids like Pooja and Rina. Putting them into ordinary schools is not enough. Only a dedicated, committed group of people can heal the wounds and scars that centuries of scorn, degradation and derision have left in their psyche. Anyone with compassion and sympathy can empathize with them. But it means a long-term commitment to an uphill task, a long, lonely and difficult road. Are there any takers?

Courtesy: The Hindu

Radio changes the face of this village forever

Rama Lakshmi

Boodikote, Karnataka

After three years of drought, the villagers lost patience when the public water pipes were dried up last June. For eight days there was no water. There were murmurs of protest everywhere. Women came out from their homes with empty pots demanding that old pipes be fixed and new wells dug. Men stood at street corners and debated angrily. The village chief made promises, but nothing happened. Then a young man ran over to the village radio station and picked up a recorder. "Women complained and shouted into the mike and vented their anger at the village chief's indifference. There was chaos everywhere. But I recorded everything"., says Nagaraj Govindappa, 22, a jobless villager. He played the tape that evening at the small community radio station called Namma Dhwani or Our voices. The embarrassed village chief ordered the pipes repaired. Within days, water was gushing again.

India's first independent, community radio is in this millet and tomato growing village in Karnataka. It is a cable radio service because the Government forbids communities from using airwaves. A media advocacy group, with the help of UN funds, laid cables, sold subsidized radios with cable jacks to villagers and trained young people to run the station.

"The power of community radio as a tool of social change is enormous in a country that is poor, illiterate and has a daunting diversity and language and culture", says Asis Sen, Director of Voices, the advocacy group. Emboldened by a Supreme Court ruling in 1995 declaring airwaves to be public property, citizens' groups and public activities have been pushing for- a legislation that will free airwaves free from Government control. Two years ago, the Government auctioned its FM stations to private businesses. And late last year some elite colleges were allowed to set and run campus radios. But the airwaves are still kept restricted.

Radiophony, a lobby for community radio., claims villagers can set up a low power, do-it-yourself radio station with a 0.5 watt transmitter, a microphone, antenna and a cassette player for approximately Rs. 1,250.

The group says the station can reach more than 500 meters and cover a small village. Last year the group supplied a low wattage transmitter to a World Bank supported Women's group in Oravakal, a village in Andhra Pradesh. Mana radio or our radio ran for five months before officials from the Communities Ministry seized the equipment and shut down the broadcast last February.

"We have to tread very cautiously when it comes to community radio", says Pavan Chopra, Secretary, Communication and Broadcasting Ministry.

"As of today we do not think that village people are equipped to run the radio stations. People are unprepared and it could become a platform to air provocative, political content that does not serve any purpose except to divide people. It is fraught with danger.", Chopra says, communities could buy time from All India Radio service and run their programmes under state supervision.

Since 1999, two groups of villagers, one in Gujarat and the other in Jharkhand, have been using time slots on AIR to run programmes in their local dialects. But activists say the central principle of community radio is to own and run a radio station freely. "Community radio in India is not about just playing alternative rock music", says Seema Nair who helps the villagers run the station at Boodikote. "It is a new source of strength for poor people because it addresses their most basic development need,"

Since it began broadcasting in March, Our Voices community radio has crackled with the sounds of schoolchildren singing songs and giggling to jokes; of young girls talking fearlessly about the evils of dowry and admonishing boys for teasing them at school; of women giving out recipes and teaching others how to open a bank account; and of farmers debating the vagaries of weather and of fluctuating crop prices.

"The radio station is ours because it speaks about us—in our language and in our accent. When I turn it on, I hear the voices I know," says Triveni Narayanswamy, 28, as she twirls the dials of her tiny transistor. Narayanswamy used to sell milk until her only cow died three months ago. "But when I went to claim insurance money for my cow, the agent tried to cheat me. He said he owed me no money," she says, "I went up and down at least a dozen times in vain. Then I spoke my problem at Namma Dhwani radio. The next day, the agent gave me the insurance amount." She says it was about Rs. 12,000.

"Our radio is more powerful than the inefficient village council," she says proudly. "They hold secret meetings and do not spend money on our welfare. I want the proceedings of such meetings to be recorded. We all have right to know what happens to the money that comes in."

Courtesy: The Indian Express

In Kerela women drive buses

Savitha

Thrissur, Kerela

A row of buses stand ready for departure with the conductor of each calling out the destination, creating quite a din that is characteristic of all bus stands. But above the noise is heard clear and strong woman's voice. Armed with a conductor's bag she stands by her bus; the woman in the drivers seat revs up the engine waiting for the whistle from the door checker. At a glance, it is only the attire that makes them different from their male counterparts, and so it is at closer inspection too.

These are only three of the thirteen women who from the Women's Transport Co-operative Society, Thrissur, Kerela- the first ever women transport company in India. Formed in 1998, it was conceptualized by the Thrissur District Panchayat during 1997-98. By March 1999, it had taken up 13 apprentices- three as drivers and 10 as conductors. The team were out on the roads with two buses in November of the same year. The only difference the three years has made is the increasing amount of confidence in women.

The two limited stop buses run along the Kodungallur – Thiruvilvamala (towns within Thrissur district) route. Starting at six o'clock in the morning, they run three rips each along this route. The president of the Society, Fathima Abdulkhader talks with pride about "our girls", it was during her term as District Panchayat president that the activities of the society were launched. "We did not have a model to follow, we ourselves were setting up one," she says adding that over the years, the Society has learnt a lessons too.

The Women's Transport Co-operative Society is a result of the role of the People's Planning programme in the area of women's development. As per the programme, 10 percent of the plan outlay of every local body is kept aside for development projects for women. Under this facility, the District Panchayat gave a grant of Rs. 25 lakh to the Society with which it was able to buy the two buses that ply the roads now.

Ms Fathima says that there is also a training school for women masons in the district, where, at present women from other states also come and stay for training. This center was also launched during 1997-98,. To date, about 10,000 women have been trained in masonry here, says Ms Fathima. She goes on to explain that though women mix cement and help carry it up the different storeys of a building, when it comes to putting the bricks together, it is forbidden territory. "We have broken that norm, our women masons are just as competent as the men," she adds with a triumphant smile.

Involvement in public transport had been totally alien to women. Completely monopolized by men till recently, the aim of the society to introduce to women this new and so fear unexplored realm. To make a women realize her worth, what she is capable of doing- that is what we wanted," says Ms Fathima.

To Misriya, one of the drivers a bus did not come as a challenge. "It was not to prove anything, nor was it a test of power. It was something new and I felt that I would be able to do it well," she says with a smile. She recalls that it was her father who helped her to learn driving. For conductor Shreekumari, the only regret that she is unable to spend much time with her children. "I leave home early in the morning and get back very late. My family hardly gets to see me," she says.

How have the men in this field handled the entry of women into their territory? "They have been quite co-operative," says Shreekumari. "It is only in the roads that there is some shouting. But then it is not because we are women- everyone shouts at everyone when there is traffic jam." Misriya shares this opinion as she says that it is one in a hundred people that they ever run into a problem. "Incidents like that are not restricted to this field," she adds.

The Society is currently training two more women as drivers as it is difficult to manage only with three. With only one person as stand-by to relieve the drivers if both buses, they have had to hire a man to drive at times The Secretary of the Society, AC Satidevi says that the buses are running on a no loss no profit basis. "We are not looking for profit through this anyway," she adds. The pay of the employees depend on the number of days they work on and a driver can earn up to Rs. 5,000 a month, explains Ms Satidevi. The Society has also started a driving school of its own, providing classes on two wheelers, auto rickshaws and cars. In time, they hope to have classes for driving heavy vehicles too at the school.

—Grassroots Feature Network

Exercises

1. How does a development journalist find story ideas?
2. Explain different dimensions and scope of Development Journalism in India.
3. What are different rules for writing a Developmental story?

15

BUSINESS REPORTING

Business journalism is not a narrow and dry recitation of stock quotes and company earnings, it includes broader stories about the national economy and how the economic trends and policies affect the citizen.

Business journalism is also known as economic reporting, financial reporting or commercial reporting.

With the growth of commercial activity in India, the importance of business journalism has increased manifold. Several newspapers, magazines, news channels and online news sites cater to economic news. In the case of newspapers, these days it is a general trend that at least one page carries news stories related to business and commerce. It is an important section and cannot be ignored. *The Tribune,* an English daily, has a special page devoted to business news— named *Business Tribune.* Certain newspapers, magazines and news sites specialize in business and economic reporting. e.g. *The Economic Times, The Financial Express, Business Standard, Fortune, Forbes* and *Business line.* The news channels are not lagging behind. Certain channels like *Star News, Aaj Tak, BBC World, CNN, NDTV India and Zee News* provide business news. Channels like *CNBC* are business news channels. News agencies also give importance to economic reporting for they have many business news subscribers and they have commerce page in newspapers. **Reuters,** a leading news agency, earns much of its profit from commercial service.

Evolution of Business Journalism

Business reporting in America dated to the latter years of industrialization, when the *Wall Street Journal* was founded in 1889. The brief business and consumer boom of the 1920s led to a new breed of business publications such as *Forbes* and *Fortune* that were geared to the expanding business and investor class. However, these publications had extremely limited readership, and business reporting in major newspapers such as *The New York Times* generally was confined to stories about the stock market and major companies. Concepts such as a national economy and national income, or the idea that broader economic trends might affect society in different ways, were either unknown, ignored, or seen as vaguely Marxist and subversive. Economics was still a young discipline, not quite free of political economy or philosophy. The basic economic measurements and data such as the GNP were developed only during the late 1930s and early 1940s.

Although business journalism continued to expand in the years after 1960, the double-digit circulation growth of the postwar era was largely at an end. The *Wall Street Journal*, whose circulation had grown 14-fold during the 15 postwar years would little more than double in the next 40 years. During the intervening years, the journalists played a major role in shaping a generation of Americans' ideas about their economy and society.

In the meanwhile even prominent daily newspapers began to devote increasing resources to business and economic coverage during the 1980s, personal-finance magazines such as *Money* and local business newspapers proliferated and new media emerged in the 1990s such as Bloomberg Business News and CNNfn. But the days when millions of middle-class Americans were reading about—and becoming interested in—their economy for the first time were over.

Since 1970s business reporting has seen the most dramatic growth. Earlier, the financial dailies existed only in Bombay and there were a handful of economic journals, none of which could claim a large circulation. Since then business reporting has moved out of the back-waters of journalism into the mainstream. There are financial dailies from major cities- Mumbai, Delhi, Kolkata, Chennai, Bangalore, Chandigarh and Ahmedabad. The Economic Times today has one of the largest circulation amongst all English language business newspapers in the country. The Financial Express, and Business India are other financial publications which enjoy a place of prestige in this segment. The general purpose newspapers themselves have doubled their economic and commercial coverage. In a fundamental sense, business journalism is a new frontier in India.

Attributes of a Business Journalist

Being an economic reporter means being a good writer, a good communicator, not just someone who is knowledgeable about the subject matter.

A good communicator means we have to be expert journalists, not experts in finance or economics. And we have to keep doing what all journalists do—expertly judging things with the same instincts—Is it new? Is it big? Is it different? Is it interesting? Is it entertaining, even? And why does it matter?

And we should approach the information we are given with the same caution and concern: Where did it come from? Does the source of the information have an interest in seeing the story presented in a particular way? Who else can I talk to so that I can confirm that the information is accurate, fair and balanced? Have I spoken to everyone involved in the story, or at least enough people to get a fair cross-section of opinion? Have I asked experts (since I am not the expert) what they think about it? Have I got some good quotes? What is my lead going to be?

One way of thinking about this is to say to yourself: This is my story. You might have been given some information to start with, but you build the rest of it yourself. You begin by asking yourself—or your news editor or colleagues – all the questions you can think of that might make the story better, more interesting and easier to understand for your readers. And if there is something you don't understand, don't just put it in your story and hope for the best. Take command of the story and build it from a variety of sources, not just the one that issued the press release or held the press conference.

Ten Steps for Improved Business Reporting

Get a clear picture of what the story is about

The most common single problem with poor stories is that the reporter hasn't been clear in his/her own mind what it was about. One way to get it clear is to tell someone else what the story is. In an ideal world, that means your news editor. S/he should be asking you questions, all of which are designed to judge whether you have a story and if so what it is. Sounds simple, but it's not. If you are not lucky enough to have an excellent news editor then do the job yourself. Imagine you are telling a friend or a family member who is not particularly interested in or involved in business or finance. But don't be tempted to pump the story up into something it isn't.

Widen the story

Make the story your own – what we call "adding value". You start asking questions that arise from the information you have been given. The first place to start is to take it beyond the specific person or government department or country involved.

So you start asking questions like:

- Is this the first time something like this has happened in this part of the economy?
- Is it part of a trend?
- Or is it against the trend?
- Or does it signal a change in the course of events?
- Now that this has happened, what might the consequences be for the economy or country or region?

And if that sounds difficult, remember that you don't have to know everything—if you have good contacts, you will know someone who does. Ask "stupid" questions when you are building your story rather than look stupid in print. And don't print anything you don't understand.

Decide on what details you will need for the lead

Give the story real substance without cluttering the lead. You need just enough for readers to know who or what you're talking about, but not so much that they find it too much to take in. Well-informed, expert readers do not find it irritating when all the names and numbers are not at the top of the story. They "scan-read" down through the bits that are simple or which they know well until they find the details they want.

Tell the reader why the story matters

This is the most added-value bit of the actual writing of the story. It is the "So-what?" element of the story that tries to tell the reader in a nutshell what it means. It's the justification for the story being published. It's the help, the guidance and the interpretation you offer to the busy reader who has all these questions churning around in his/her head but not enough time to put them in any order, let alone find out the answers. That's your job, and it's an important one. If you do your job properly, you will find out from the experts what it means. For example, *This is the first time the deficit has gone beyond 3 per cent of GDP and analysts say it reflects a loss of control by the government over the public finances. The figure will also be greeted with dismay by the IMF, which is trying to negotiate a loan deal with the government.*

Provide background

Many readers of a news story are what we call "new readers"—ones who have just begun to venture into reading financial news, or have just come back from travelling abroad or some of his or her private affair. Help them. The skill is to boil down the information you have gathered from the archives and from your reporting into sentences and paragraphs that "remind" readers of what has happened. It is important that you think of it as reminding, because many readers will already know what happened yesterday or last week. So you don't want these paragraphs to sound repetitive. That means you should drop the background into the story as you go, often as clauses within sentences that are giving the latest information, sometimes as well-timed sentences, sometimes as whole paragraphs.

Provide context

Just as important are the "surroundings". Economic decisions are not taken in a vacuum. Often they are intended to address a particular problem or to give in to political pressure or follow from some event. Tell the reader about those things, otherwise they will not understand all the implications of what has happened. e.g. The unemployment figure, higher than expected, comes as the ruling coalition is preparing its election strategy. The opposition has already attacked the government for its poor economic record, and there have been signs from the opinion polls that the government is scoring low on economic policy among voters.

Keep it balanced

No one knows all the answers to all the economic questions – not a fraction of them. So ring around, ask different experts, follow your own doubts and concerns. And when you have a variety of opinions and interpretations of significance of something, represent the main ones in your story. The best way to inform is not to be seen trying to "make a point". Intelligent readers can spot a story with a particular bias from a thousand paces, and dismiss the whole thing.

Use numbers well

Numbers constitute an essential part of the context. All good financial journalism needs a certain amount of solid, properly measured statistical information to emphasize it. Make the numbers serve the story not the other way around. Think: what is the story about? And then, at first, answer without using any numbers. Even if it is a story about the latest economic indicator, you will be forced to say the story is about why the economy has grown or why inflation has risen. In other words, think of the numbers as instruments for telling the story, not as the substance of the story. Here are some guidelines:

- If you think the numbers are essential to the understanding of the story, don't have more than two in the lead.
- Distribute the numbers through the story. Don't bunch them. Make it easy by separating them from one another with pace-changing quotes (see below).
- Keep numbers together that belong together.
- Remember that numbers are just one "turn-off" factor for readers. Others are long sentences, unfamiliar names and technical language. Keep these things apart from each other as much as possible. Where you have any of these, try to keep the numbers down to a minimum.
- Consider taking out some of the numbers and getting them made-up as a table or graphic so that the information is there and the story can flow.
- Check, double-check and triple-check them all.

Give the story life by using quotes

Stories without quotes are dead. Find one to put high up, possibly as the second paragraph, straight after your lead, or by the third or fourth paragraph at the latest. If you have done your research and reporting properly, you should have plenty of quotable things in your notebook—in fact the problem should be what to leave out, not what to put in. Quotes lend a sense of authenticity. They change the pace and give colour to a story. They also capture things in everyday speech, which is often hard to convey in economics and finance.

Define and explain

Too many financial journalists still believe that their readers know what all the technical terms mean. They don't. Many readers buy and skim the financial press for news that directly affects what they do. The rest they leave, unread, even if they have the time to read more. That's because while they might be highly paid experts in industry, finance or government, they are only experts in one thing. A good accountant or banker doesn't necessarily know anything about what's going on—or what the jargon is—in trade policy. A good agricultural economist doesn't necessarily know anything about how pension funds invest their money. And a good manager in the retail sector doesn't necessarily know how foreign exchange markets function. So we have to define and explain as we go.

Helping the reader with the technical bits doesn't have to be a complex process. There are several ways it can be done:

- Rather than stop the story and insert a definition, use a phrase that defines the technical term as part of a sentence in the normal flow of reporting. For example: *The trade deficit rose 65 per cent to a record $271 billion as the country's strong economy pulled in foreign goods much faster than exports expanded.* In other words, make the definition part of the information.
- Use the technical term in a normal sentence and then in the next sentence, use the defining phrase as an alternative while giving further information. For example: *Inflation was 6 per cent last year. This is the first time the government's measure of the change in prices for goods and services has exceeded 5 per cent a year in the last decade.*
- Insert a crisp, clean and clear definition at just that point in the story when you think readers are in danger of turning the page because their ignorance makes them feel either uncomfortable or irritated. Just stop the story and define the term. For example: *A non-performing loan is one on which neither the principal nor the interest has been paid for a specified period – such as two consecutive quarters.*
- Sometimes what the reader needs is not just a technical word, but understanding a process. An example is when shares fall because of a threat of an interest rate rise. Even this reasonably widely known process could do with some explaining, for example: *Investors do not like interest rate rises because they make borrowing by companies and spending on credit more expensive, damping demand—and ultimately profits.*

Essential terms a reporter should be familiar with

Familiarity with economic terms is essential. A dictionary of economic terms would be a handy tool to resolve some of these difficulties.

Ad Valorem Duty: Duty charged on the basis of value of the goods or subject matter.

Annual report: Report sent by a company to its members every year.

Annual return: A return which must be made annually to the registrar of companies and must contain statutory particulars.

Bank rate: The official rate of interest charged by Reserve Bank of India as lender of last resort.

Banker's cheque: A cheque drawn by one bank on another either for clearing purpose or for transferring customer's money.

Bear: A stock exchange term for an individual who sells shares in the belief that prices will fall, then he will replace them. The act of selling can affect the confidence of public and cause the prices to fall.

Blue-chip investment: A term used for those types of investments which are considered to be safe. They are usually shares of well-known and financially sound companies.

Bull: A stock exchange term applied to an individual who buys on a short term hope that the shares will rise quickly in price, enabling him to make profit. He can force the price to rise by buying sufficient quantity. Thus, by creating an artificial demand, he leads others to believe that shares are worth buying.

Caveat emptor: Means 'let the buyer beware'. The law presumes that a man uses common sense while buying goods, if he suffers loss then it is his own fault. He will not find the remedy in law.

Cover note: A provisional document issued by an insurance company to cover the time between the acceptance of a risk and the issuing of a policy.

Devaluation: The alteration of the value of the currency of one country in relation to the currency of another. By devaluation the rate of exchange alters and the currency becomes cheaper from the point of view of other countries. The purpose is to encourage exports and discourage imports.

Endorsement: A term used in reference to bills of exchange. When the bill is negotiated, the person who negotiated the bill will write the matter in the bill in favour of the other person on the reverse of the bill. This transfers the property in the bill to endorsee.

Financial year: A general term normally meaning the year of account or accounting period. Financial year of the government starts on 1st April and ends on 31st March of the next year.

Floating charge: When a loan to a business is secured on floating or current assets rather then on a particular item, there is said to be a floating charge.

Liquid ratio: The ratio of quick current assets to current liabilities. Quick current assets are cash and the items readily convertible into cash but stock is excluded.

Liquidation: This is effectively the insolvency of a company.

Managing director: The director of a company with specific responsibility for management.

Merger: The amalgamation of two or more business organizations with a view to be more efficient or creating monopoly.

Mortgage: Any transaction by which land is given as security for repayment of loan.

Nationalized industry: These are the industries owned by the public that is in direct control of the government.

Net worth: An accounting term for the total of share capital and reserves or the difference between total assets and the outsider's liabilities.

Patent: A patent gives patentee the sole right to make use or sell his invention during the period patent remains in force.

Security: It would affect a citizen.

Stag: A stock exchange team for who buys heavily on a new issue of shares in the expectation that the price will rise very quickly and earn him a large profit.

Standing instructions: An instruction to bank to pay a certain sum of money at certain intervals to the said person or institution.

Window dressing: The word used in company finance for lawful manipulation of accounts to make the balance sheet favourable and to attract investment or to increase the share value.

Sources for Business Journalism

Sources of news are innumerable, if one has nose for news he can get it while walking on the road or talking to people. The innumerable sources can be classified into various categories depending on the criteria applied. Sources can be hard or weak.

A source is hard when the facts of the report come from the horse's mouth where they are ascribed to the concerned person or person by name. On the government policies, for example, the prime minister or other ministers, top officials of the concerned ministry are the hard sources.

When a general opinion within a particular group with a wide base is to be given, the practice is to quote "circle" for example, political circle, trade circles. Such sources can relate to reaction, comments but not any hard news. These are considered to be weak sources, e.g. The phrases like "it is learnt", "it is believed", "it is stated", "it is gathered" or "it is reliably learnt".

A business journalist must pursue his sources on a regular basis. The government ministeries and offices are a major source of business news. Political parties generally offer their views on matters on economic policies, budgetary announcements and issues like inflation, rising prices and difficulties encountered by general public. Their reactions are always covered by the media.

In this age of liberalization and privatization, where economic scenario is undergoing fundamental changes, business and commercial organizations like FICCI (Federation of Indian Chambers of Commerce and Industry), ICI (Indian Confederation of Industries) and ASSOCHAM (Associated Chambers of Commerce and Industry of India) play a leading role in helping shape the economic policies of the country.

Apex national institutions like the Reserve Bank of India, Stock Exchange Board of India, Annual reports and Quarterly Reports of the business houses, all constitute important sources of information.

Likewise important international bodies influencing economic policies at the global level—World, International Monetary Fund, International Labour Organisation and several other such bodies bring out reports and publish findings on important economic aspects. A business journalist must keep himself abreast with the important developments at the global level. Trade unions also influence the government policies and do lobbying on behalf of their constituents. Their perspectives should be covered as and when they have something significant to say.

Since business journalist has a wide range of subjects to cover, he must keep himself in touch with his sources regularly. It is essential for a business reporter to adopt a writing style which his readers will find it easy to understand even on topics related to annual budget, deficit financing and other such terms.

In this context it will not be out of place to make a mention of the writing style of Nobel laureate Amartya Sen. His book, *India—Development and Participation,* discusses issues like economic reforms and policies in a language and style which makes the subject clear and easy even for a non-specialist reader.

Exercises

1. Discuss the meaning, scope and importance of business journalism in detail.
2. Write a note on evolution of business journalism and where it is headed with particular reference to developments in India.
3. What are the various steps involved in writing for the business page?
4. Enlist the various important sources which a business journalist must cultivate in the course of his duties.
5. Make a list of terms and jargons used in business reporting and trace their meaning.
6. Collect at least five news stories which are related to economics and would affect a common man.
7. Write a feature for business page on the eve of festive season about market trends and consumer behaviour.
8. Visit the stock exchange and prepare a report on its functioning.
9. Read a business paper and analyze the news story of your choice. How is it different from a daily newspaper like The Tribune, The Hindustan Times?

16

SPORTS REPORTING

Sports are one of the best media of entertainment, recreation and keeping oneself positively engaged. It has gained an exceptional distinction and visibility across the world, and is considered as an element of inter-cultural dialogue. Sport provide superb opportunities to learn to communicate, cooperate, work in teams, respect others, acquire discipline and accept defeat—all aspects that are becoming daily more important in a world of globalization in which cultural identities are under threat and in which learning to live together in peace and harmony is a prerequisite.

Another specialty about sports is that apart from playing, it is equally interesting to watch games. Normal activities come to a standstill during Cricket Test matches, The Wimblendon Tennis Tournament or The World Cup Soccer contest. Not only this, sports have become a significant economic activity too. People love sports and their sporting heroes. They take pride in honest achievements in sports and for producing champions. The fans, the coaches, the administrators and the athletes all despise cheating, in all of its forms and understand the worth of pure performance and sportsmanship. They understand that values and ethics are essential ingredients in the cocktail of sporting success.

Importance of Sports Journalism

Sports journalism is a popular field. One of the important as well as interesting beats in journalism is sport reporting. Sports Journalism can be defined as gathering, selecting, interpreting and disseminating sports news. As far as readership preference is concerned, the sports page comes next to the title page. Earl Warren, an American Politician and Judge, remarked, *"I always turn to the sports page first, which records people's accomplishments. The front page has nothing, but man's failures".*

Sports news along with political and economic news makes a newspaper what it is. Most of the young people probably prefer to read the sports pages with greater interest than any other page. Inevitably, the make up of sports page and its content are quite often brighter than the rest of the paper. It is as if the sports writer is given a sort of "poetic license", a concession usually not shown to other correspondents.

Often the sports section in a newspaper is termed as a miniature of the news department. Now it is hailed as a specialized branch of journalism. There is a phenomenal growth of interest in sports at all levels—be it local, national, or international. It has become almost binding for newspapers to plan in advance, the coverage of sports events.

In the present era of fast communication, people immediately come to know about the final scores of the most of the sports events from Radio or Television and now on Internet, much before the publication of the newspaper. So the task of newsperson acquires a new dimension. He is expected to go beyond the mere story.

The importance of sports news is itself evident as most of the major sports stories always make it to the front page of the newspapers despite the fact that there are separate pages exclusively devoted to sports. To catch the pulse of ardent sports fans, the news-hawk is quick enough to add special supplement pages for the time when national and international sports events like Olympics, ASIAD, Cricket World Cup and Common Wealth Games etc. are hosted. Like other branches of journalism, Sports journalism too has grown with time, is evident from the fact that the contemporary sports journalist is not just confined to reporting events only..

As most of the newspapers especially devote a few pages for sports news, one must be wondering that how sports events will be found enough to fill these pages. The answer is no as sports pages contain sports news, articles, features, pictures, special columns by expert writers. Not only the sports events rather anything concerned with sports or sportspersons makes a place on the sports page. These could be like the following:

Kalam felicitates Anju Bobby

Star athlete Anju Bobby George called on President APJ Abdul Kalam at the Rashtrapathi Bhavan on Thursday.

Kalam congratulated the long jumper for winning the bronze medal in the Paris World Athletics championships. Later, she met Sports Minister Vikram Verma and thanked him for all the help given to her for training abroad.

Anju's husband Bobby George, who accompanied her, assured the Minister that they would try to return with an Olympic medal.

Montoya alleges sabotage

Berlin: *Colombian Formula One driver Juan Pablo Montoya has accused Heinz-Harald Frentzen of helping his fellow German and five-time world champion Michael Schumacher win last week's Italian Grand Prix at Monza a victory that could have a major impact on the outcome of this year's title race.*

He slowed me down at the decisive moment of overtaking, Montoya told Thursday's Bild newspaper. Williams driver Montoya finished second in the race behind Schumacher but now trails his Ferrari rival by three points with just two races left in this year's world championship.

He was referring to what happened on the 40th lap of the Grand Prix when Frentzen, driving a Sauber which is powered by a Ferrari engine, slowed down to allow Schumacher to pass.

Montoya believes he was then slowed down at three curves. If he did it on purpose, it is cheating, said Gerhard Berger, the director of Williams engine suppliers BMW.

BMW director Mario Theissen was equally scathing. The driving of Frentzen was legitimate but not very skillful, he said. At the time of the overtaking, he intervened in the result of the race.

However the sports news could be divided into two major groups. First, there are those which precede the event perhaps by months or days. Second, there are those which report it, explain it, interpret it. Both are concerned directly with the sports event, not with related angles.

The importance of the sports could also be gauged from the fact that even there are separate TV channels like Star Sports and ESPN for airing live matches of different tournaments in progress. But readership surveys indicate that sports fans who have seen a game on TV are not satisfied only to watch it, as they also like to read about games they have seen. Sports have so much craze that one could see markets flooded with magazines. Even one could find magazines especially devoted to one game, as in case of cricket.

Sports journalism also contributes to other branches within journalism. Sport journalism has a huge audience and reaches viewers and listeners that are unreachable by other kinds of journalism. This gives sports journalists an opportunity, and a responsibility, to include other topics in their job apart from traditional sports reports. In this job they have a lot to learn from other journalists.

Today there are many sports TV Channels. These include: Sky sports TV, BBC Sports TV, Channel 4, ITV Football, Angila Sports, etc.

Sports Page

A newspaper remains incomplete without a sports page and a sport page remains incomplete until all the sports events are covered. A special feature of sports page is that it has to cater to the tastes of all types of readers, for interest in games varies from person to person. Some are lovers of cricket, others hail hockey while some are avid lovers of tennis, chess and football. Sports events, meets and festivals dot the calendar of the entire year, so the sports page is a great challenge to the correspondents to present the events in an interesting and critical style. The sports editor is an all-rounder. He is in-charge of a team and the sports page is the result of earnestness of all those who work with him. Sports pages in USA have produced some to the best writings in American journalism.

Sports page is the result of the endeavour of all those who work in the sports department and for this very reason, everyone involved in making sports page, whether it is reporter, sports editor or page designer. Sports pages don't mean mere sports news as visuals have an important role to play. Selecting and correcting the pictures in a right manner is extremely important as one picture is equal to thousand words. Moreover, it is field of sports, which gives the opportunity to lensmen to click one of the best pictures. It is generally seen that maximum pictures on sports pages or even sports picture on page one are those clicked by the agency photographers like that of Reuters, Associated Press, AFP, All Sports, PTI etc. The reason for it is, if a photographer devotes sufficient time in covering an event, he is sure to get a page one picture and here comes the role of agency photographer who have to cover extremely important assignments and can thus give time in covering an event. Thus, in today's cut throat competition, no newspaper wants to lag behind, just for not having good pictures, therefore, they take the services of news agencies for the purpose. Besides full fledged news stories or sports features, the sports pages now invariably also carry sports briefs, many a time without any dateline even or with the place or agency of origin mentioned at the end. Some such news are reproduced as follows:

India's shuttlers lacking focus, motivation: Coach

Bangalore, September 19: India's top badminton players-barring Pullela Gopichand are complacent and lack focus and motivation, says chief national coach U. Vimal Kumar, who is now pushing the game's top brass to crack the whip.

"I feel at the moment that our players are playing international tournaments without purpose. They are just going and coming back. Their performance is not monitored properly," Vimal Said in Bangalore.

Pak drop Zia's son

Pakistan's selectors today dropped the son of Pakistan Cricket Board Chairman Tauqir Zia from the team for the fifth and final one-day international against Bangladesh. Junaid Zia (19) was a controversial choice when selectors chose him over other notable performers.—AFP

PAP, Bathinda boys in final

PAP Jalandhar and Bathinda in the men's section and Ludhiana and Faridkot in the women's section won their semifinal encounters to set up the title clash on the penultimate day of the first Parminder Yadgari State-Level Invitation Basketball Championship being held at Malout.

India TFA White lose

Uzbekistan stormed into the final drubbing India TFA White by a brace in the four-nation JRD Tata Cup International Invitational Football Tournament (U-19) at the JRD Tata Sports Complex here today.

Archery meet

"Diet money for sportspersons will be increased and a new pension scheme for sportspersons will be introduced soon," said Minister of State for Sports Jagmohan Singh Kang. He said this while inaugurating the 26th Junior National Archery Championship here today.

Aussie Choice

Sydney: *Australia's big decision ahead of next month's two Test cricket series against Zimbabwe is the choice between batsmen Damien Martyn and Martin Love, chief selector Trevor Hohns said on Friday. Martyn was established in the Australian batting line-up before he missed the Test series wins over the West Indies and Bangladesh with a broken hand. Martyn broke his hand while batting in Australia's victorious World Cup campaign in southern Africa in March. He returned to the Australian one-day team and scored an unbeaten 92 against Bangladesh last month and has been in great form for Yorkshire—**AFP***

What about other news on the sports page? Many of them are about the people in sports. Actually they may be personal—about a vacation trip; society stories—about a wedding, a story of illness—an operation on arm; a story of business; a player's negotiations for a better contract. It is important to mention here that news on the sports page also concern business firms, educational institutions, government agencies, and numerous organizations, which have an interest in sports. The newsmen may interview officials attend meetings, examine records, and glance at news releases, just as he might in covering business or government. Thus, in one sense the sports page contains sports news and sports related news.

Sports Reporting

The sports writer is different from the general reporter in one general aspect; he is at the same time a reporter and a critic. He is giving his opinion about the game at the same time as he is describing the facts of it. He judges the quality and skills of the players , who in this sense are actors in a public spectacle. But opinion must be authoritative to be effective. An important thing for the newspaper is to employ sports writer who perfectly knows the sport he covers. Those who read a sports story might know what happened before they glance at the lead or box score. They may have been present or they may have heard the outcome in a newscast. Thus the sports writer is expected to tell why and how one team won and the other lost, explaining just what happened despite previous predictions. These types of minute details actually make a newspaper favourite among the readers.

Sports fans are gluttons for statistics. That is why sports pages—specially on Sunday present so many figures. Newsmen writing sports naturally must be sure that all figures are accurate. Avoid using jargon without explaining it for the benefit of readers who may not be familiar with the game. Most readers of the sports pages will probably be familiar with the rules and the jargon of the major sports, such as Football and Cricket—but never assume that they are.

The careless writer who fails to check the number of foul shots, base hits, or yards gained may be exposed by a competing reporter who is sure of his facts. Reporting a cricket match involves a lot of statistics. Here are three typical stories on cricket match coverage:

Mumbai on top

Chennai, September 19

Rest of India paid the penalty for lack of application as they conceded a 95-run first innings lead to Mumbai in the Irani Cup cricket match at the MA Chidambaram Stadium here today.

After wrapping up Mumbai's last wicket and restricting the Ranji Trophy champions led by star batsman Sachin Tendulkar to a modest 297, Rest saw their top order batsmen commit a harakiri and be bowled out for 202 in the first innings.

At stumps on second day, Mumbai were 11 for no loss—a lead of 106 runs—with Vinayak Mane (6) and Wasim Jaffer (1) at the crease.

The might of Tendulkar notwithstanding, Rest are the favourites to win the trophy based on their superior batting and bowling line-up.

But the Rest batsmen lost their wickets due to poor application on a wicket that offered turn and bounce, and was double paced.

With Mumbai Cricket Association president Sharad Pawar and cricket board's TRDO chairman Dilip Vengsarkar witnessing the match, Mumbai bowlers were up to the task.

Off spinner Ramesh Pawar looked more impressive than the duo of Anil Kumble and Harbhajan Singh, who went wicketless in Mumbai's first innings.

The blame for Rest's debacle lay on their batsmen. Their captain Saurav Ganguly proved that he is still to shed the outside the off stump trap as he played Powar away from his body, giving a simple catch to Nishit Shetty at second slip.

Scoreboard

Mumbai (1st innings): *V. Mane c Kumble b Bangar 26, W. Jaffer b Balaji 43, N. Shetty c Sehwag b Zaheer 5, S. Tendulkar c Dravid b Zaheer 94, V. Kambli lbw b Zaheer 2, A. Agarkar c Patel b Zaheer 0, S. Bahutule c Laxman b Kumble 58, R. Morris c Harbhajan b Balaji 31, R. Pawar b Kumble 0, V. Sawant lbw b Zaheer 4, A. Salve not out 2.*

Extras: *(b-16, lb-3, nb-13) 32 Total: (all out in 97.2 overs) 297. Fall of Wickets: 1/32, 2/59, 3/91, 4/98, 5/98, 6/247, 7/260, 8/260, 9/265. Bowling: Zaheer 24-6-77-5; Balaji 20.2-6-47-2; Bangar 10-2-35-1; Ganguly 9-5-11-0; Kumble 22-6-64-2; Harbhajan 12-2-44-0.*

Rest of India (1st innings): *S. Bangar c Mane b Morris 29, V. Sehwag b Salvi 16, R. Dravid c Tendulkar b Pawar 41, V.V.S. Laxman c Pawar b Agarkar 5, S. Ganguly c Shetty b Pawar 0, Yuvraj Singh c Jaffer b Pawar 27, P. Patel c Samant b Salvi 26, A. Kumble LBW b Agarkar 1, Harbhajan Singh LBW b Pawar 4, Zaheer Khan c Shetty b Bahutule 34, L. Balaji not out 12.*

Extras: *(b-2, nb-2, w-3) 7. Total: (all out in 73.2 overs) 202. Fall* *of wickets: 1/16, 2/87, 3/89, 4/90, 5/123, 6/125, 7/134, 8/141, 9/159. Bowling: Ajit Agarkar 18-7-29-2; Avishkar Salvi 13-3-52-2; Sairaj Bahatule 9.2-1-35-1; Robin Morris 10-2-23-1; Ramesh Pawar 23-6-61-4.*

Mumbai (2nd innings): *V. Mane batting 6, W. Jaffer batting 1. Extras: (b-4) 4. Total: (for no loss in 4 overs) 11. Bowling: Zaheer Khan 2-0-5-0; L Balaji 1-1-0-0; Harbhajan Singh 1-0-2-0.—PTI*

Ajeetesh tightens grip on Golf title

Ajeetesh Sandhu played a one over card of 73 to tighten his grip on the title after the third day's play in the Chandigarh Junior/Subjunior Golf Championship here today.

Ajeetesh had a three-day tally of 223 with Gaganjeet Bhullar four strokes behind with a tally of 227. Jaskeerat Dullat who played a card of 79 was at third spot with a tally of 232.

In category 'B' also Ajeetesh Sandhu led the field. Fatehbir S. Dhaliwal with today's score of 76 was placed 2nd. Raghav Wahi went ahead of Viraj Gadhoke and was placed third with today's score of 79, one stroke ahead of Viraj Gadhoke.

In 'C' category Kanishk Madaan was overtaken by local lad Rahul Bakshi. Rahul Bakshi with a round of 80 went ahead of Kanishk Madaan, who today played 86. Madhav Soi with a round of 85, still held on to his third spot.

In 'D' Category Viraat Badhwar played a round of 82 to hold on to his first position. He was followed by Raghav Bhandhari with today's round of 89. Ankur Chadha with a round of 94 was at the third spot.

The top five spots

Category-A: Ajeetesh Sandhu (CGC) 76+74+73=223, Gaganjeet Bhullar (RCF, Kapurthala) 76+77++74=227, Jaskeerat Dullat (BEGC, Patiala) 75+78+79=232, Himmat Rai (DGC) 77+81+75=233, Aditya Singh (DGC) 81+74+78=233.

Category-B: Ajeetesh Sandhu (CGC) 76+74+73=223, Fatehbir S. Dhaliwal (CGC) 76+78+76= 230, Raghav Wahi (BSF, Jammu) 81+80+79=240, Viraj Gadhoke (DGC) 81+80+80=241, Sidharth Seth (DGC) 81+81+82=244.

Category-C: Rahul Bakshi (CGC) 81+83+80=244, Kanishk Madaan (DGC) 81+81+86= 248, Madhav Soi (DGC) 84+84+85=253, Amanvir Guron (CGC) 86+92+92=270, Mohd Asif (AGC, Meerut) 92+94+92=278.

Category-D: Viraat Badhwar (DGC) 86+82=168, Raghav Bhandari (CGC) 92+89=181, Ankur Chadha (AGC,Delhi) 97+94=191, Hemendra Chouwhary (RGC, Jaipur) 99+98=197, Tarundeep S. Chadha (CGC) 108+101=209.

HPCA register 19-run victory

Himachal Pradesh Cricket Association beat Piccadily Cricket Club, Chandigarh, a last minute entry into the tournament, by 19 runs in a closely fought match in the 10th All-India JP Atray Cricket Tournament at the PCA Stadium, Mohali, today.

Piccadily XI skipper Arun Tuli won the toss and elected to field. His move paid rich dividends when they curtailed Himachal Pradesh Cricket Association to a modest total of 165 in 50 overs. The Himachal innings was propped up by their skipper Vikram Rathore (23), Richi Kapoor(27), Vishal Bhatia (24) and Vinod Minhas (21). For Piccadily Club Sanjay Gill (2 for 42) and T Anand (2 for 29) were the main wicket-takers.

Chasing a none to difficult target, Piccadily Cricket Club folded for 147 runs in 46 overs. Their skipper Arun Tuli was the highest scorer with a well made 37. Tuli was tragically run out when he was taking his team close to the victory target. For his valiant effort of 37 runs and one wicket for 17 runs he was declared Man of the Match. For Himachal Kapoor Singh (3 for 32) and Nischil Gaud(2 for 28) were the main wicket-takers.

Brief scores: Himachal 165 all out in 46 overs (Richi Kapoor 27, Vikram Rathore 23, Vishal Bhatia 24, Vinod Minhas 21, Sanjay Gill 2/42, T. Anand 2/29). Piccadily XI 147 all out in 46 overs (Arun Tuli 37, Rahul Arora 20, Shashi Ranjan 19, Kapoor Singh 3/32, Nischil 2/28).

In the second match of the day played at the cricket stadium in Sector 3, Panchkula, between Associate Banks, Mumbai, and Bihar Cricket Association, the bankmen coasted to a huge 85-run win which fetched them an additional bonus point.

Associate Banks after winning the toss and electing to bat were all out for 198 in 49.2 overs. C.P. Sahu 34 off 40 balls and Anil Sinha 31 off 39 balls were associated in a second-wicket partnership of 56 runs. Their innings were propped up by some lusty hitting by M. Matithia, who scored an unbeaten 29, inclusive of two fours and a towering six. Sanjay Gupta (3 for 38), Sumit Panda (2 for 32) and Anshuman Raj (2 for 21) were the main wicket-takers for Bihar.

Replying to the Associated Banks' total Bihar were bundled out for 113 runs in 41.3 overs. There rout was plotted by left-arm spinner Anand Kati who returned an impressive figure of 4 for 20 in eight overs and was ably supported by right-arm medium pacer Davinder Bundela who got two for 15 runs. The only resistance came from C.M. Jha, who scored a polished 34.

Brief scores: Associated Banks 198 all out in 34 (Anil Sinha 31, M. Matithia 29 not out, Sanjay Gupta 3/38, Sumit Panda 2/32, Anshuman Rai 2/21). Bihar 113 all out in 41.3 overs (C.M. Jha 34, Nikhlesh 17, Anand Kati 4/20, Davinder Bundela 2/15).

Saturday's fixtures: Rajasthan vs Indian Oil Corporation at PCA Stadium, Mohali, 9 a.m.; PCC vs Associated Banks at Sector 16 stadium, Chandigarh, 9 a.m. and PCA Colts vs Piccadily XI at Dhruv Pandove Stadium, Patiala, 9 a.m.

The importance of covering sports doesn't end by just devoting separate pages to sports news. Almost all the newspapers take the services of experts in the way of regular sports columns. For instance, Sunil Gawaskar, Ravi Shastri, K. Srikant, Dilip Vengsarkar, Pardeep Magazine, etc. are renowned columnists for various newspapers.

Many sports columnists review books on athletics, predict winning teams, and promote local sports events. Public interest in sports justifies the space given not only to straight news but also to articles. There are as many articles for sports, as there are article in general. Those sports stories, which are critical, analytical or are revealing are put in the form of an article, in order to make the sports pages equally important as any other age. Three typical news stories/write-ups illustrating different angles in sports reporting are as follows:

India, Pak keen to resume sports ties

Wagah, September 19. Olympic associations of India and Pakistan have decided to resume sports ties, including hockey, between the two nations, which had been snapped many years back, according to the secretary-general of the Indian Olympic Association Mr Randhir Singh.

Mr Randhir Singh, along with two other members, Mr Mohamad Aslam Khan, and Mr B.S. Ojha, returned from Pakistan here today after holding a comprehensive dialogue with their Pakistani counterparts at Islamabad. Briefing newsmen, Mr Randhir Singh said though Pakistan had decided to back India's claim for hosting 2016 Olympics jointly, rules of the International Olympic Committee do not permit such an arrangement.

The secretary-general said Asian countries must come together to convince the international body to allow India to host the 2016 Olympics. He said Pakistan had confirmed their participation in the Afro-Asian Games to be held in Hyderabad on October 24. Reciprocating their goodwill gesture India had confirmed participation in the South Asian Federation (SAF) Games. He said it was after a gap of three years that the SAF games would be held in Pakistan from March 29 to April 7 next year.

He said Pakistan had shown keen interest in organising regional level meets and suggested that teams from Indian state of Punjab and Pakistan's Punjab province should take a lead by sending teams for encouraging sports in this area. He said Pakistan had desired to resume hockey ties with India.

CCI membership for Ehsan Mani S Iyer

The Cricket Club of India has conferred life membership on International Cricket Council President Ehsan Mani of Pakistan and ICC CEO Malcolm Speed.

Mani is in Mumbai in connection with the ICC's cricket committee meeting.

Mani was conferred the honour by Mumbai Cricket Association (MCA) President and Nationalist Congress Party chief Sharad Pawar. Malcolm Speed was conferred the life membership by former Indian captian Nari Contractor. Former Indian Test players, Madhav Apte and Madhav Mantri, were also conferred life membership.

The dignitaries who attended the function, apart from the delegates from the 10 Test playing countries and three non-Test playing nations, included former Indian skippers Sunil Gavaskar, Dilip Vengsarkar, Cricket Board (BCCI) President, Jagmohan Dalmiya, and secretary, S.K. Nair.

The two-day meet of the ICC's cricket committee—management (CC-M) has important items on the agenda like the ICC Champions Trophy in England in September 2004; ICC U/19 World Cup in Bangladesh in February and March 2004, suspect bowling actions process; performance analysis of match officials and player associations. According to UNI in a significant move, the ICC today turned down suggestion to prune the number of participating teams in the World Cup and instead raised the limit to 16 teams for the next edition of the cup to be held in West Indies in 2007.

Brian Lara says Tendulkar is phenomenal

Brian Lara holds many sparkling gems on his crown. He's famous for his moods and tantrums, too. But the Brian Lara who breezed past Delhi today projected a different image—that of a sober, softer man who lent a willing ear to all the probing questions put at him and replied with candour and modesty.

The West Indies captain, who came to Delhi on a brief promotional tour for MRF, made an honest appraisal of another cricket "legend", Sachin Tendulkar, and conceded that the Indian star was a cut above him. "Sachin is phenomenal", Lara said, though he did not try to hide his own importance among the pantheon of cricketing greats, adding that "we are the top two (batsmen, obviously!)".

Sachin apart, Lara was also impressed with the new breed of Indian cricketers like Virendra Sehwag and Yugvraj Singh, who he described as "attacking, exciting cricketers, who have a different approach to the game, than the players of old."

Lara has high opinion about the Indian team as a whole "as the Indian team is much matured, now that they have crossed the bridge at the ICC Trophy". He said the Indians were really good playing on home ground, but "met with a kind of psychological disadvantage", while playing away from home.

Lara conceded that though Indian cricket was rich in many respects, it was a different experience "playing in front of 80,000 fans in Melbourne, with everyone rooting for Australia. There you don't see the money, you don't see the fans, only the harsh reality of the match and in such conditions the Indians have been found wanting"

Lara, who sees a resurgence of West Indies cricket after languishing in the doghouse for a quite some time, particularly after the series against Australia and Sri Lanka, was optimistic about his team's prospects in the upcoming series against South Africa, whom he described as the "second best Test-playing country" in the world. Lara said his knock of 153 against Australia at Barbados in 1999 was his "best" and Wasim Akram of Pakistan was the "best" fast bowler he had ever played against. Lara said his own batting was a "lot better now", and the West Indies team were on the upswing.

Lara had high praise for India's very own Javagal Srinath "who has served the country for very long and admirably", and added that players like Zaheer Khan and Ashish Nehra were also talented bowlers. Lara, however, admitted that India were yet to produce fast bowlers of the calibre of Brett Lee (Australia) and Shane Bond (New Zealand), despite all its efforts to shape up genuine fast bowlers. "But Srinath has been very loyal, and India have a pretty good side", he remarked.

Lara said that it was unfair to make comparisons, say for example, between Walsh and Ambrose "as every one has his own image, his own individual character". Lara also took the stand that "sledging" was part of cricket "as it has been there for a long time". But he noted that he did not carry forward the on-field happening off it to nurse any ill feeling. Lara, who along with Sachin Tendulkar, have been netted by MRF, plans to visit India "as often as I can", on business trips.

In major events there come a number of sports personalities. Many of them can be interviewed. Interviews of sports stars are not only confined to sports magazines. They add colour to a sports page of newspapers also. Lewis Jordan, news editor of **The New York Times,** says, "He wants the story to reflect the tension, the cob; the excitement, the joy, the sorrow of the context. He wants the plays analyzed and the players performances criticized. Luckily, the sports reporter has the latitude to do this. Like the drama or the music critic, he is an expert who can speak his mind."

It is a must for a sports correspondent that he should be present during the time of the event in progress. Besides this, a sportswriter must possess fundamental knowledge of rules and technical details of the games he is covering.

Qualities of a good Sports Journalist

Sport is a very wide field and a vast area comes under news. Red Smith of the New York *Herald Tribune* advocates, "Be a newspaperman first and a sports writer second." The sports writer not only covers games, but almost all the typical types of news stories. For a new sports hero, the sports writer becomes his biographer. He interviews the hero, chronicles his marriage, announces the arrival of an heir, and reports on his illness or accidents. Similarly, sports writer reports on business as and when a top sportsperson holds out for a better contract. When the hero awaits the surgeon's scalpel, sports pages contain reports on science. The sports writer also may write an obituary if the sports hero is not a forgotten man when he dies. He even may record crime news when the hero mingles with questionable company. Thus, the sports writer does much more than merely covering one game or the other.

The sports writer is a specialist who is expected not only to know the wide-ranging outlines of rules and regulations of games, but also to appreciate the subtle nuances of play and the special strong points of the player. A good sport journalist is expected to critically examine the entire scenario of the playfield, new techniques involved, the best performance of a team and the cause of its superiority. He also investigates the major causes of failure of a renowned player and the quality of sportsmanship and the standard of judgement. The role of referees and coaches of the game, political interference, natures of selection of the team and other factors that contribute to the success or failure of a particular team or nation are also observed. The sports writer should know the rules of the game just as well as the coach, players, and referee. He should be able to follow the plays and, when necessary, keep his own statistics. Moreover, he should have some knowledge of the history, traditions, records, and statistics of the sport, including those of local significance. By incorporating all these details, a sports writer could make a sports copy much interesting.

Sports journalism is not just limited to reporting sports events. A sports writer has to cover organizations, their meetings, elections, appointments, controversies, decisions etc. All this is part of sports news as readers, sports lovers and players are curious to know about latest happenings. Features on sports pages are liked by the readers very much and they are therefore not new on the sports pages. Even the Saturday and Sunday supplements contain sports features. It is extremely important that the sportswriter must owe a peculiar and good style so that readers show their courtesy towards reading the sports stories filed by him. In other words, he must develop a good style of writing, which attracts readers. In order to develop this talent, a good sportswriter should try to read as much as possible of sports-related stuff including sports magazines and journals. Apart from this, all sorts of techniques which are used for reporting other fields, could be employed in sports reporting. But a sports correspondent should not take it for granted that everybody knows about sports as he does. With the exception of a few cups and trophies, they must mention clearly the name of the game along with the trophy and the cup.

According to Wainwright (1986), the best sports reporting captures the atmosphere as well as the facts of the game. But remember that the reader wants to know the facts first. Big sporting events today are rituals and like all rituals, they have rules and conventions. It is must for the sports reporter to learn these conventions. Apart from this, the sports correspondent must find out which players are in form and who could not perform well in past games. The sports reporter must therefore do as much as research as he can before the game starts.

According to Mencher (1990), for the budding sportswriters the important lesson is that good sports writing is good writing. This means getting to the point quickly stressing human interest, avoiding sports jargon and clichés, and giving the readers some insight into the game or the personality being described. In other words, sportswriters just follow the principles of good writing. Imagination is vital to the sports story. Further, sports are the story of men and women straining mind and body to reach beyond limits, of unusual people and strange events and the story must reflect all these.

Parthasarthi (1996) said that the sports correspondent of a newspaper has to be an experienced one, versatile in reporting all kinds of games and sports, having a flair for description in language-smooth, flowing and readable. Only the sports critics and correspondents enjoy complete freedom in reporting and comment. There is no readership more critical than sports fans that demand the writer to be absolutely accurate and sound in judgment. Sports reporter produces a copy for readers who think they know as much as the reporter. To keep up with their expectations, the sports reporter must understand not only the rulebooks but also the record book containing statistics of what players and teams had done in the past. Otherwise the reporter will not know if a particular achievement is unusual.

A sports reporter is a specialist writer. Therefore a sportswriter is expected not only to know the broad outlines of the rules and regulations of any game, but also to appreciate the subtle nuances of play and the special strong points of the players. It goes without saying that a correspondent who is not up to date in his knowledge of a game and its players is not much of a correspondent. Sports journalists also have something to learn from their colleagues when it comes to research and sources, critical reporting, ethics and investigative reporting. In certain countries, the biggest obstacle for sports journalism is the lack of resources and the lack of journalistic experience and training.

Challenges to Sports Journalism

Theodore Roosevelt, the twenty-sixth President of the USA, stated that aggressive fighting for the right is the greatest sport in the world. Tactics, fitness, stroke ability, adaptability, experience, and sportsmanship are all necessary for winning. Today, sometimes, the sports journalism is blamed for failure of Indian teams. It is alleged that sportspersons pay more attention to media coverage and less to their training. Their pre-occupation with media leaves less time for practice. This has been discussed at higher levels and situation has reached such a stage that many a times coaches strictly instruct the players not to interact with media. One such story released by UNI and published by The Tribune (September 20, 2003) is placed below:

Keep media at bay, hockey team told

Kuala Lumpur, September 19

Title contenders India, led by ace forward Dhanraj Pillay, arrived here with an express directive from their hockey federation to keep media at bay and "concentrate on the game".

The 6th edition of the Cup begins here from Sunday and India will try to capture it which has so far eluded them.

The title winners here will qualify for the 2006 World Cup.

The Indian players were barred from speaking to media while they were undergoing a trial camp in New Delhi and that ban still continues.

"It is high time we produce results and then the players will have ample chance to talk to media" said coach Rajinder Singh.

The Indian media had held Rajinder Singh responsible for the "media shut out" during the camp and the coach is not apologetic about it.

"All the players have been specifically told not to talk to the Press," Rajinder said adding" The tournament (Asia Cup) is very important for us and we want all the players to be focused".

"It is not as players will not be allowed to talk to the Press but let us first settle down, get out act together and then we will see" the coach said.

"We have been runners up in first four editions and finished third in the last edition which was also held here, I want that this time India should win, victory here will save us from a hassle of going through the World Cup qualifiers" he said.

"My aim is to see that players remain focused on the tournament. I don't think not allowing the players to talk to the press is a big issue. The players understand the importance of the tournament and realize that what is being done is in the interest of the team"

Rajinder said that he was confident that team would make it to the semi-finals.

Training in Sports Journalism

Before deciding to join sports journalism, one need to be asked such questions: Are you passionate about sport? Would you like to work in the fast developing world of sport journalism? The budding sports journalists should learn the basic skills and processes of a journalist and relate them to the coverage of sport. They must also study sport so that they become knowledgeable about its structure, evolution and organization. They should be exposed to all media and to topics such as lifestyle and fitness, legal issues for the coach and research methods. Finally there should be strong emphasis on options enabling students to personalize their programme to suit their vocational aspirations. Again, a strong vocational element should be emphasized in the training of sports journalists. The course should have a strong multi-disciplinary structure. Students must receive a rounded education designed to enhance their journalistic abilities and sporting profile. The ability to pursue vocational qualifications gives graduates both academic and sports-related strengths. There are also other related courses like sport sociology, sport planning, sport administration, sport management and sport economics. There are courses which develop student's academic understanding of aspects of sport including: psychology, physiology, sociology, coaching and nutrition. These also teach professional journalism skills including writing for radio, TV and the web. Finally, one must understand the ways in which sport and the media interact.

Trainings in sports journalism are also carried out regularly by different newspaper groups as well as journalism institutes. There are two main objectives for such trainings: to strengthen and professionalise sports journalists in their role as commentators, interviewers and broadcasters, and to support the trend to broaden sports journalism from sports results and live commentary to also include social issues such as HIV/AIDS and gender and to help sports journalists in addressing issues that are important in their respective societies by using sports. Among the issues raised include ethics in sports journalism; sports as a part of the society—the role of the sports reporter; live commentary and research and sources.

Exercise

1. Define sports journalism and its importance in the modern world.
2. What are the qualities of a good sports journalist?

3. Discuss various challenges to sports journalism and the role of a good sports journalist.
4. How is training vital in reporting sports?
5. Write a brief note on the sports page of your favourite newspaper.
6. Report at least three different sports activities held in your institution.
7. Compare at least two reports of a sports event published in different newspapers.
8. List the names of five sports feature writers.

17

ONLINE REPORTING

Online journalism is a generic term often used loosely to describe digital information access, retrieval or dissemination. It is also known as cyber journalism, e-journalism, web or internet journalism.

If you sit at home and access the internet via your modem and telephone line, you are going *online.* Similarly, if a newspaper has a web site to compliment its published editions, this is seen as an *online* version of the paper.

It can also be hailed as new media-mediated journalism. Online Journalism has steered journalism to new heights of easy and all time accessibility of news. With the fast pace of life, more and more people are turning to the web for their daily news. And the number of net news users is increasing everyday. The news on the net is for free and latest news can be accessed any time from anywhere. News can even be accessed according to one's own interest. These days one can subscribe to online news sites for daily or weekly news according to one's own interests and needs, e.g. stock quotes, medical news, etc. can be subscribed.

Web and Internet

The internet is not just the World Wide Web. There has been confusion in the past between the web and the internet. They are not the same thing. The internet is a the infrastructure that allows computers to talk to each other throughout the world. The web is the interface that allows people to exchange data, text, pictures, graphics, audio and the video in the internet.

Online journalism has evolved over the last decade, and development in technology has revolutionized the world of information. Today, masses thrive for latest news. And people want all time availability of all news, so that they can read it whenever they get time.

The technology of online journalism makes a marked departure from the mass targeting technology to an individualized technology that has potential of reaching out to a greater audience without being insensitive to the idiosyncrasies of the individual news consumers. This technology negotiates a change from 'massification' to 'individuation' of news. Cyber journalism involves two separate aspects: 'journalism online' and 'online journalism'. The former implies to web as a secondary publishing site and simply transforms conventional journalism while latter is applied to virtual 'e-zines' and 'e-newspapers'. Today both aspects are combined by large media organizations like CNN.

Online journalism invites readers to deliver information directly to anyone through a computer and imagine a world in which everyone can be his or her own journalist. Journalism in short, is being reinvented

Online Journalism and Journalists

Here a journalist is seen as a media professional, earning at least half of his or her monthly income as a journalist, working in the context of a newsroom or editorial board within a media organization and performing at least one of four selected journalistic 'core' activities: newsgathering/ research, selecting, writing/processing, editing. The definition is more or less taken from a journalism survey project in Germany. The online journalist is, therefore, a professional performing journalistic task within and for an online media outlet.

Exclusive online news venture are still very rare. Generally, at the most eight people can easily make an online venture work, and they can grow at the pace of 40 per cent per year. Mostly, newspaper organizations host their own websites e.g. those of *The Times of India, Indian Express, Hindustan Times, The Hindu,* etc. Some websites provide complete version of print publications along with archives that run back a year. *Indian Express online* is one of them. *The Times of India* made available all the information contained in the *Education Times* along with the data bases of Indian educational institutions.

Evolution and Future Projections

The emergence of online journalism has not been an abrupt event. It has been evolving through three stages. Initially, newspaper establishments looked at the Internet only as a means to have an electronic presence, and in many cases it was a 'me too' kind of situation. Such organizations did not invest much and that got reflected in their sites. In stage two, the journalists create original content and augment it with such additives as **hyperlinks** (with which reader can instantly access another website); **interactive features** such as search engines, which seek out material on specific topics; and a **degree of customization**—the ability to choose what categories of news and information you receive.

Traditional vs. Online News and Journalism

The three keywords in the debate about quality online content and the difference between traditional media and the net is as under:

- Interactivity
- Personalization or individualization
- Convergence

When looking at online news, the interactive element seems to be of essential importance. The key to understanding this, is to see interactivity as a purely audience related feature. It has not so much to do with the speed of news and journalistic activity although it does facilitate fast work—but it has to do with the fact that online news has the potential to make the reader/user part of the news experience. Better interactivity increases the feedback to the site and helps it improve upon its mistakes and content, as journalists get more and more ideas through e-mails.

The second key element is also an audience related feature i.e. 'personalization' or 'individualization' of content according to one's own interests. This implies blurring of lines between public and private spheres especially in the media. With this, individual preferences of clients can be deciphered.

Convergence is not so much an audience feature but more of a journalistic feature. Convergence in the context of online journalism vs. traditional journalism is the meeting of these traditional media forms (moving) image, text, sound—in one story told online. Imagine a story with pictures offering links to a video shoot of the event described, excerpts of the interviews that were held and links to other stories and back-ground material of related topics. With this every single story can have a different angle, a different way of telling the story. Whereas a bombing could start with a video shoot, a court ruling could begin with the voice of the judge and the response of the lawyers, to give an example. The technology for full con-vergence is not fully available, but will be in a matter of years.

Even the ways of newsgathering are changing due to a variety of interactive tools present in online journalism. With these tools there is interactive communication between the journalist and readers, as the time for response is drastically reduced. You can ask questions, enter a discussion forum, cast opinion poll, chat, read bulletin board, form interest groups, do video conferencing, send e-greetings, form e-club, and to much more. Some of the tools used for the above purpose are:

E-mail: It is a one to one, a synchronous means of inter-personal communication. You can exchange text, graphic and even voice. You need not be present on the net to receive e-mail: You can type a message and send it very quickly, ranging from the instantaneous to the relatively fast depending on connec-tion times. It is global and yet personal. You can send the same message instantaneously to as many people as you want.

Chat: In this people can do real time communication i.e. have discussion. Journalists are asked to be present at a particular time when they can be asked questions by the readers. It is a synchronous mode of interaction. Both parties need to be present on the net to chat.

Opinion polls: You can cast your opinion on a particular subject.

Online forums: Readers can post their opinions on bulletin boards and enable other readers to know their opinion. This enables reader-to-reader communication.

Audio facility: Means audio supplementing text on the web page.

Video facility: Links to moving images (not animated) increase interest in the story.

Hyperlinks: To stories give detailed information.

Search tool: Allows searching previous editions e.g. a particular news, article etc. It is a type of search engine.

Messages posted: to a newsgroup, bulletin board are within hours made public and are available to the majority, around the world.

Usenet: Is a collection of hundreds of different discussions that travel around the world via electronic mail to millions of people in dozens of countries.

Whole Earth 'Lectronic Link (Well)': is a computer conferencing system that enables people around the world to carry on public conversations and exchange private e-mail.

Writing for the Web

Writing for web is not the same as writing for print because people read differently on the web. The most obvious difference is that the web offers readers the opportunity to access information non-sequentially. Everyone who observed, tested, or studied online reading agrees that people behave differently when online. When viewing a new page, they don't read—they scan. They look at headings and subheadings first; they scan for hyperlinks, numerals, and keywords. The challenge for the web writer is to overcome reader's impatience by keeping things as brief as possible. People rarely read web pages word by word; instead, they scan the page, picking out individual words and sentences. In online writings, following instruments help entice the reader to read more.

- Highlighted keywords
- Meaningful subheadings
- Bulleted lists
- Hyperlinks
- One idea per paragraph
- Use of pictures, video links
- Half the word count (or less) than conventional style

Another difference is the ability to link directly to source material and outside resources. It is also possible to navigate archives for previous stories and other details. For example if you are publishing an article about some new legislation, you can link directly to the online text of the law as well as the web pages you've published yourself.

- In short, judicious use of convergence can help.

Web sites are about saying something that's important for the visitor. If you have nothing to say, what's the point of having a site? On the web, the reader wants to know "What's in it for me" not "What's in it for you". Text plays a key role not only in terms of a site's content, but also in reader orientation. In this regard, the role of text is somewhat different in the online world than it has been in print world. In online net content you cannot have a story in **linear fashion** as in print. Here you write in chunks or net jargon where every paragraph has a separate theme and links to details—in the form of "read more", see background, check archives, etc. (non-linear style of writing).

The information given in separate paragraphs is brief, concise and teasing the reader. Remember that people can enter a web site at any time. So there should be text that answers these questions:

Whose site is this?
What kind of information does this page contain?
How much information is there on this page?
Whom is the information intended for?

Points to be Kept in Mind

Certain points are to be kept in mind for making the text on web user-friendly and interesting.

Write conversationally: Casual, conversational style of writing seems friendly and is easy to read. It leaves a mark on the reader.

Write in "Inverted Pyramid" Style: With most important information or conclusion in the beginning and less important things in succession. The practical reason for this is that your readers get the most important information first. And also, people scan on the net, and this is an easy way of providing the conclusion of the story first to your readers.

Shorter the better: Write to the point on net. If you have to give details you can use links like 'read more' links.

Use shorter sentences and paragraphs: It's generally more convenient to use shorter sentences and paragraphs on the web—that's easier on the eyes, and works particularly well for sites that display text in thinner columns. This also makes it easier to "Chunk" content, so readers are presented with digestible and navigable sections of content rather than an unbroken river of content.

Cut short anything that's not essential: Redundancy is unforgivable in journalism, be it print, electronic or online.

Simple, common words are better than long, unusual ones: You don't want people to have to pick up a dictionary just to understand your. "Eschew obfuscation" means the same thing as "avoid confusion". Guess which one is more effective—the one most people understand. Big words won't impress people; they'll just confuse them.

The material can be plain text: or it can be contained in images (logos, buttons, image maps etc.).

Role of micro-content: Another important thing for good writing and editing on the web is the role of micro-content. This includes headlines, subheads, links text, navigation bar text etc. Basically, on the web micro-content should be as self-explanatory as possible.

Beginning with questions and exclamations: Although this is a taboo in conventional journalism, but is sure a good bait to lure readers to read or see more. This can be done by giving hyperlinks to pictures, text, cartoon strips, etc.

Use of 'emoticons': There are discussions about the use of non-verbal icons, symbolizing emotions, in journalistic writings. For example a smile :-) a wink ;-) surprise 8-) and many more.

Not using the last name only on second reference: When one writes online—which generally means having a piece cut up in different segments or having to scroll down the screen to read on—one should be aware that a name can be seen first in different parts of the online story, so it should be printed, told or shown in full every single time.

Use maps/graphs to show where the place is: You can make complicated figures easier to understand by making a paragraph or a chart.

Make your page easy on the eye: Use short paragraphs and do not clutter up the screen.

- Use of interactive tools to expand content such as discussion groups, web-chats and so on.
- Always answer readers' e-mail.
- Allow the reader to trace back the reporting and newsgathering process.
- Offer hyperlinks to sources, background material, related content and archives.
- Always offer extensive 'About Us' section.
- Sending out e-mail teasers and reminders as personalized e-mail services.
- Online news sites should serve as community resources.
- Layer the content i.e. cut the story into multiple chunks the user can scan through any story or topic easier and read whatever he wants. For example, he can see the video shoot and go to the editorial and leave the chronology of events behind.

Advantages of Online Journalism

Updated Information

Most of the newspaper sites update the news constantly every hour. For instance, over 1.1 million users had access to the MSNBC.com news website on August 17, 1998, the top story being Clinton-Lewinsky affair, when the President testified and addressed the nation on his relationship with Lewinsky.

Hyperlinks

These are highlighted words or phrases, which when clicked, provide more information related to the given word or phrase. Then a window filled with new text pops up on the screen. But the extra material does not appear unless the reader asks for it. With hyperlinks one can have detailed information about different aspects of news e.g. one can see audio-video clippings, read an editorial on it, see a cartoon, enter a discussion, etc.

Archival Facility

Whole of the morgue is virtually present on the web and you can search for any article, news link, and editorial published in the past and read it. You can, for instance, see all news, articles editorials, cartoons related to *Tehelka* scandal.

Interactive Editions

In an interactive online newspaper, you can see what you want, how much you want, the font size that you are comfortable with, you can see the details of ads which you wish and just zero-in to a particular item without going through all the pages, participate in an opinion poll or send feedback to the editor etc.

Easy skimming and scanning

An e-newspaper facilitates hunting, browsing, and/or grazing. An 'Autopilot mode' would flash headlines at a speed set by the reader (who might also set filters, such as 'no sports' and 'news since last Tuesday night'). If something seemed interesting the reader could press a button to stop the flow and read the entire story.

Job opportunities

More and more web-editors, web-designers, content providers, web-visualizers are needed. For this, one needs the knowledge of HTML, Java, photoshop, frontpage and flash.

Mostly news sites offer free news and their income comes from ads, some value added services like archives are charged. But high subscription magazines like *The Economist, Science* and *Lancet* are open only to subscribers of their print editions. Similar is the case with *Time* magazine and *Readers' Digest.*

Some news sites offer an advertisement banner for as little as Rs. 150 for 1000 impressions

Challenges before Online Journalism

Copyright and intellectual property rights

The biggest concern today is the copyright infringement and protection of intellectual property. Since the Internet is in the public domain, there are serious issues regarding copyright on content. Then, there are legal issues like how to deal with defamation on the net. Defamation cases across national boundaries may be a complex issue to resolve since there is no ownership or regulation of the Internet as yet. Similarly, inclusion of advertisements of products like liquor and tobacco can be problematic. Drawing the line where the freedom of speech becomes obscenity could be another problem. However, new laws to regulate online journalism in particular and Internet as a whole are already on the anvil.

Best Online Resources for Writers and Web Content Developers

www.contentious.com includes a Resource Guide for content creators. This guide is an annotated link collection with references to lots of online articles, web sites, books, and other resources about content issues or the content industry. In addition, there is the online—writing e-mail discussion list. That list has attracted a wide variety of content creators, and related audiences.

Skills needed to succeed as an Online Writer

One must have browsed a Usenet newsgroup and e-mail discussion list. One must have sufficient knowledge of HTML for web page designing, Java script for uploading a page, frontpage, as mostly web pages are made on it, flash for adding animation and photoshop for putting up images.

Despite the obstacles of backwardness in attitude, digital divide, computer illiteracy, low bandwidth and high network traffic, online journalism is gaining momentum. It is revolutionizing the world of information. Today, with emergence of web logs, everyone is his or her own journalist. There has been enough democratization of information and, interpretative news has taken up good pace. Interpretative journalism has an immense potential in shaping the nation and taking the nation on news rails of development. The catch here is that journalists must know what not to write. It has provided enough space for public debate and discussions as every computer literate can participate. Convergence of print, audio and video has made it the most attractive media. Its user-friendly approach makes a mark on everyone. The best part of online journalism is that it is the fastest media world over. It can bridge communities and let the snow of isolation melt in moments. It is a universal media and transcends the boundaries of lands and people. It has enormous potential that is unfolding everyday.

The computer culture has already taken roots in the Indian newsrooms. The moving train of technologies is gaining speed and even district newspapers are adopting the new technology. The reach of internet among non-resident Indians all over the globe is tremendous. Internet journalism is therefore becoming a tool for opinion building. These days a young journalist must be acquainted with all aspects of news gathering, and web zines. Here are some of the examples of the original online editions of *India Today* and *The Times of India.*

Exercises

1. Define online journalism. How is online journalism different from traditional journalism?
2. Discuss the journalistic skills required for writing online.
3. What do you think are the advantages of online journalism?
4. What are the greatest obstacles and promises of online journalism?
5. Within online journalism, there can be interpretative journalism. Discuss the pros and cons of multiplicity of meanings a news item can attain.

bbc.co.uk
BBC Television
FIND A PROGRAMME
BBC News on TV and Radio
See what's on BBC TV tonight
Browse the A-Z index
The Inspector Lynley
ONE
TWO
THREE
FOUR
SCHEDULE
ABOUT BBC TV
TALK
MESSAGE B
DON'T MISS
BBC

expressindia
THE INDIAN EXPRESS GROUP

GROUP SITES
The Indian Express
The Financial Express
Latest News
Screen
Kashmir Live
Express Cricket
Lokasatta
Lokprabha
North American Edition (Print)

COLUMNISTS
The Indian Express
The Financial Express

CITY NEWSLINES
Choose City

SERVICES
Matrimonials
Find fun & romance! Click here!
HURRY NRIs! Citibank OFFER!
Low Airfares to India for March
Buy Certified Cars on Baazee!
Express Travel

INITIATIVES
Chandigarh War Memorial
Tell Them You Know

SUBSCRIPTIONS
Free Newsletter
Wireless Express

SYNDICATIONS
RSS Feeds

BIZ PUBLICATIONS
Select

Thursday, March 17, 2005 Net Edition

FLY@F1 350kmph Experience
Express Formula One: Full Coverage

Pakistan in India 2004-05

LATEST NEWS

Tears, anger greet Kanishka verdict: 'Oh my god, they will be punished later'

Rattan Kalsi emerged from the Air India courtroom with a look of shock on his face. The men accused of killing his daughter and 328 other people on Air India Flight 182 had been acquitted. (1309 hrs IST)

- Shocked families demand public inquiry
- Intelligence had warned of Kanishka bombing
- Canadian spy agency erased Kanishka tapes

AIR INDIA BOMBING
Kanishka mass-murder: Justice denied unacceptable

Clear motive to commit bombing but no evidence to support the theory. In short that was the stance of the Canadian judiciary that gave freedom back to accused. (1245 hrs IST)

- India-Pak Kolkata Test: Live Score

- **Pathan, Balaji pack off Pak openers**
- THE GREAT INDIAN DEBATE: Create more states
- **India may defy Bush to buy Iranian gas**
- SC allows Pappu Yadav to take oath as MP
- **Soren to meet Kalam, wants Munda ousted**
- Killer quake took India towards Indonesia
- Pak pitches for F-16s in talks with Rice
- **Kanishka: Victims' kin weep, accused smile**
- India, US hit snags over Iran, Pakistan
- Prime Minister to visit United States in July
- Tendulkar thrilled after joining 10,000-run-club
- Dravid delighted by opening day century
- **What next, Sachin Tendulkar!**

The Indian EXPRESS
March 17, 2005

- 20 yrs after Kanishka, both accused walk free
- Trapped in Sariska, poachers confess: We killed 10 tigers
- Energy, strategic talks next step in ties
- Musharraf will watch ODI in New Delhi on April 17: PMO
- PAGE ONE ANCHOR: Sting sequel has TV soap star running to cops

Select Sections

THE FINANCIAL EXPRESS
March 17, 2005

- Loss of face for India if Patents Ordinance lapses
- Drug cos cut output as trade offtake dips 25%
- India threatens to pull out of Iran pipeline...
- Race to 7,000: BSE Metal beats Sensex
- BOTTOMLINE: Operators see thaw through tourism

Select Section

EXPRESS SPECIALS

- **Time is running out for V.V.S. Laxman**

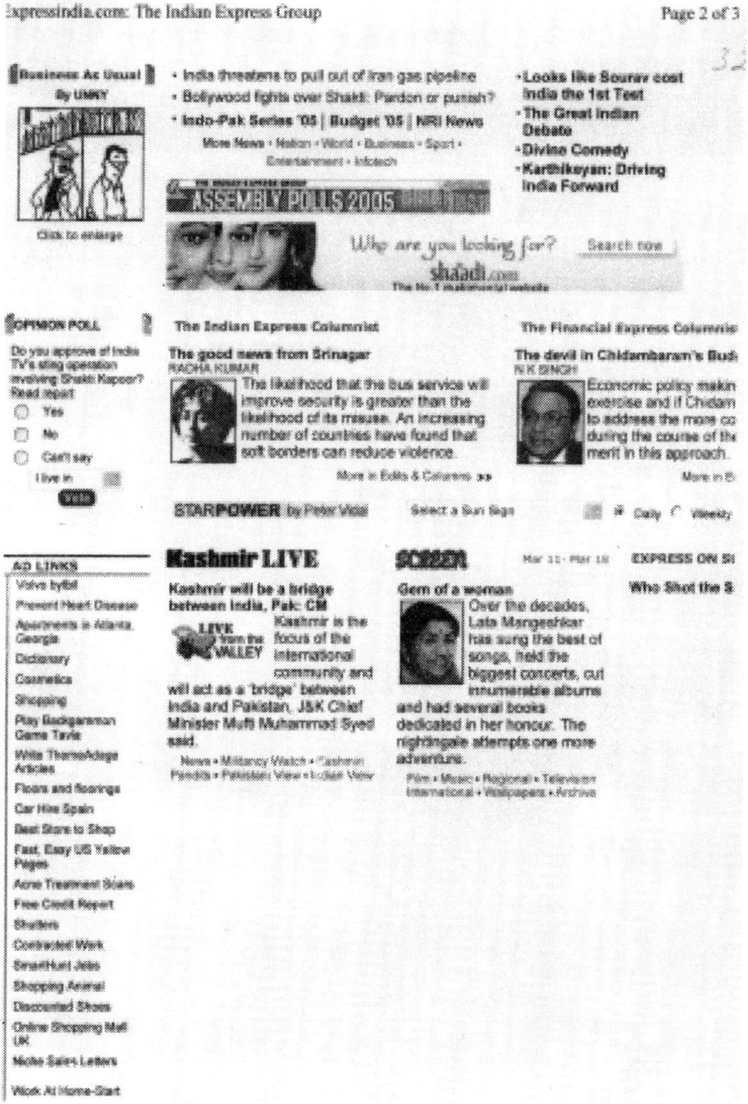

Expressindia.com: The Indian Express Group — Page 2 of 3

Business As Usual
By UNNY
Click to enlarge

- India threatens to pull out of Iran gas pipeline
- Bollywood fights over Shakti: Pardon or punish?
- **Indo-Pak Series '05 | Budget '05 | NRI News**

More News • Nation • World • Business • Sport • Entertainment • Infotech

ASSEMBLY POLLS 2005

Who are you looking for? Search now
shaadi.com

- **Looks like Sourav cost India the 1st Test**
- **The Great Indian Debate**
- **Divine Comedy**
- **Karthikeyan: Driving India Forward**

OPINION POLL
Do you approve of India TV's sting operation involving Shakti Kapoor? Read report
Yes
No
Can't say
I live in
Vote

The Indian Express Columnist
The good news from Srinagar
RADHA KUMAR
The likelihood that the bus service will improve security is greater than the likelihood of its misuse. An increasing number of countries have found that soft borders can reduce violence.
More in Edits & Columns »

The Financial Express Columnis
The devil in Chidambaram's Bud
N K SINGH
Economic policy makin exercise and if Chidam to address the more co during the course of th merit in this approach.
More in E

STARPOWER by Peter Vidal — Select a Sun Sign — Daily / Weekly

AD LINKS
Prevent Heart Disease
Apartments in Atlanta, Georgia
Dictionary
Cosmetics
Shopping
Floors and floorings
Car Hire Spain
Best Store to Shop
Fast, Easy US Yellow Pages
Acne Treatment Store
Free Credit Report
Shutters
Contracted Work
Shopping Animal
Discounted Shoes
Online Shopping Mall UK
Work At Home-Start

Kashmir LIVE
Kashmir will be a bridge between India, Pak: CM
LIVE from the VALLEY
Kashmir is the focus of the international community and will act as a 'bridge' between India and Pakistan, J&K Chief Minister Mufti Muhammad Syed said.
News • Militancy Watch • Kashmiri Pandits • Pakistani View • Indian View

SCREEN
Gem of a woman
Over the decades, Lata Mangeshkar has sung the best of songs, held the biggest concerts, cut innumerable albums and had several books dedicated in her honour. The nightingale attempts one more adventure.
Film • Music • Regional • Television International • Wallpapers • Archive

EXPRESS ON SI
Who Shot the S

Reader's Digest
17 March 2005
IN THIS MONTH'S ISSUE
CUSTOMER SERVICE
HAVE YOUR SAY
GIFT A SUBSCRIPTION
SUBSCRIBE NOW!
RENEW YOUR SUBSCRIPTION
INTERNATIONAL SITES
-- Select One --
FACE TO FACE WITH JOHN TRAVOLTA
Maybe Ben Franklin's early-to-bed, early-to-rise advice isn't for everyone. Travolta certainly is wealthy, and at 50, he still has his strapping on-screen good looks. And while wisdom is in the eye of the beholder, in person Travolta comes across as one of the happiest, least-tortured souls around...
John Travolta...
JOKE OF THE DAY
The settlement claim we were processing at our banks lacked some details. We wrote to the claimant to clarify if the deceased had died intestate. The reply came after some days. "He did not die in the estate, he died in hospital."
— — A. V. Menon, RD
More Laughs | Cartoon Capers
Submit a Joke
WORD POWER QUIZ
Where do you stand in world of words? Try our Word Power Challenge and we shall tell you! It is education and entertainment all in one!
Login
Subscribe for the Challenge
SUBMIT A JOKE
GATHER NAMES
GET US IN TOUCH WITH 14 FRIENDS
Reader's Digest
6 Golden Rules to Grow Your WEALTH
Germ-Proof Yourself
2005 MARCH
IN THIS MONTH'S ISSUE
FEATURES
Six ways to grow your personal wealth
The more control you have over your finances, the fewer money stresses you have. Here are six simple ways to take charge of your financial destiny.
Torture and terror in Riyadh
Tortured until he confessed to crimes he didn't commit, a Canadian survivor recounts his ordeal in a Saudi prison.
Germ-proof yourself
They are in the air we breathe and in the water we drink, and they cling to virtually every surface on the planet. Here are some common germ havens, along with

The Tribune
ONLINE EDITION

Thursday, March 17, 2005, Chandigarh, India
Updated at 3:00 am (IST)

NEWS AND VIEWS
- PUNJAB
- HARYANA
- JAMMU & KASHMIR
- HIMACHAL
- REGIONAL BRIEFS
- NATION
- OPINIONS
- MAILBAG
- BUSINESS
- SPORTS
- WORLD

THE TRIBUNE TSUNAMI RELIEF FUND

TSUNAMI HELPLINES
DEVASTATION
(in pictures)

VIDEOS

SPECIAL COVERAGE
- CHANDIGARH
- LUDHIANA
- JALANDHAR
- AMRITSAR
- DELHI

WEEKLY SPECIALS
- FORUM
- EDUCATION
- JOBS & CAREERS
- HEALTH & FITNESS
- SCIENCE & TECHNOLOGY
- SPORTS
- SOCIETY
- TRIBUNE CLASSIFIEDS

CLASSIFIED ADVTS
- BRIDES WANTED
- GROOMS WANTED
- OTHERS

US refuses to stop F-16 sale to Pak
- India ignores Rice objection on gas pipeline
- PM to visit US in July

New Delhi, March 16
India and the United States broke new grounds today in bilateral cooperation as Secretary of State Condoleezza Rice told the Indian leadership that an institutionalised mechanism of an 'energy dialogue' would be in place soon.

US Secretary of State Condoleezza Rice shakes hands with Foreign Minister Natwar Singh prior to a meeting at Hyderabad House in New Delhi on Wednesday. — Tribune photo by Mukesh Aggarwal

- IAF to get SU-30s on March 21
- Nation page: Rice meets Patiala students
- World page: US House resolution flays Modi's role

Sachin joins 10,000-run club
- Pervez to watch last one-dayer at Delhi

Sports page:
- Dravid's ton helps India recover
- Plenty of cricket left in me: Tendulkar

Sachin Tendulkar raises his bat to acknowledge the crowd after completing his 10,000 runs during the first day of the second India-Pakistan Test match in Kolkata on Wednesday. — Reuters

Kanishka case: both Malik, Bagri acquitted
Vancouver (British Columbia), March 16
Two Sikh activists were cleared today of involvement in the 1985 bombing of Air-India Flight 182 that killed 329 persons. A Canadian judge said

Search

CAST YOUR V...
Do you think th... closed the Taj c... under political ...
No
Yes
Can't Say
Vote
View Results
Suggest a Quest...
Send your comm...

NRIs & ...
Citibank

OTHER ...

Ripudaman Singh Malik and Ajaib Singh Bagri were not guilty of murder and conspiracy charges.

Judge's disclosure to be probed

New Delhi, March 16

Opposition led by the BJP today walked out of both Houses of Parliament over Supreme Court Justice S.N. Variava's revelations that attempts had been made to replace the trial judge in the fodder scam case against Railway Minister Laloo Prasad.

• Editorial: **Justice Variava's disclosure**

PM meets LS Speaker

New Delhi, March 16

In a bid to clear the air that differences had arisen between the executive and the legislature, Prime Minister Manmohan Singh took the initiative in meeting Lok Sabha Speaker Somnath Chatterjee here this morning over breakfast and put the record straight.

Moving to Canada?

Celebrating 20 years of NRI banking

Buses to Nankana Sahib this Baisakhi

Nankana Sahib (Pakistan), March 16

While Indian Punjab Chief Minister Amarinder Singh and Pakistan Punjab Chief Minister Pervaiz Elahi today laid the foundation stone of Baba Guru Nanak dual carriageway, the first lot of 10 buses carrying Sikh devotees from Amritsar to the historic town will ply on April 13, the Baisakhi.

Punjab Chief Minister Amarinder Singh performs the Sewa of Chaur Sahib at Gurdwara Janam Asthan Sri Guru Nanak Dev Ji at Nankana Sahib on Wednesday.

World page:

• **Pakistan's no to third party mediation**

• **Musharraf praises Indian hospitality**

• **Indian journalists fly in Pak army chopper**

• **Pak keen to restore Shiv Temple**

HOW TO PLACE ADVTS

Full coverage: India vs Pak 2005

Southasianmedia.net

Log in...Tribune ARCHIVE

HOROSCOPE

• WEEKLY

QUOTE OF THE DAY

— Condoleeza Rice

THE TRIBUNE MAGAZINES

On Sundays

Spectrum

On Saturdays

Saturday Extra

INDIANS NOT IN INDIA

TRIBUNE SPECIALS

• Turbans

• Athens 2004

EARLIER FEATURES

EARLIER TOP STORIES

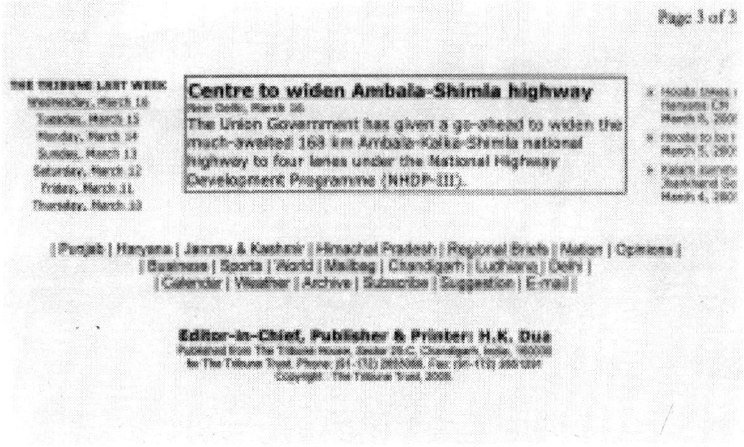

Page 3 of 3

THE TRIBUNE LAST WEEK
Wednesday, March 16
Tuesday, March 15
Monday, March 14
Sunday, March 13
Saturday, March 12
Friday, March 11
Thursday, March 10

Centre to widen Ambala-Shimla highway
New Delhi, March 16
The Union Government has given a go-ahead to widen the much-awaited 168 km Ambala-Kalka-Shimla national highway to four lanes under the National Highway Development Programme (NHDP-III).

Punjab	Haryana	Jammu & Kashmir	Himachal Pradesh	Regional Briefs	Nation	Opinions
Business	Sports	World	Mailbag	Chandigarh	Ludhiana	Delhi
Calendar	Weather	Archive	Subscribe	Suggestion	E-mail

Editor-in-Chief, Publisher & Printer: H.K. Dua
Published from The Tribune House, Sector 29-C, Chandigarh, India
for The Tribune Trust.
Copyright : The Tribune Trust, 2005.

INDIA TODAY
Good Housekeeping SUBSCRIBE NOW!
SUBSCRIBE
CURRENT ISSUE
ARCHIVE
LETTER FROM THE EDITOR-IN-CHIEF
MAIL OF THE WEEK
OFFTRACK
BODYLINE
EXPERT VIEW
YOUR WEEK
EYECATCHERS
COVER STORY: CONGRESS
DOUBLE TROUBLE
FULL STORY
WEB EXCLUSIVE FEATURES
A SCHOOL RESTORED
MORE WEB FEATURES
NATION: ELECTIONS
Wrong Numbers
STATES: HARYANA
On Lal Alert
AND SAVE

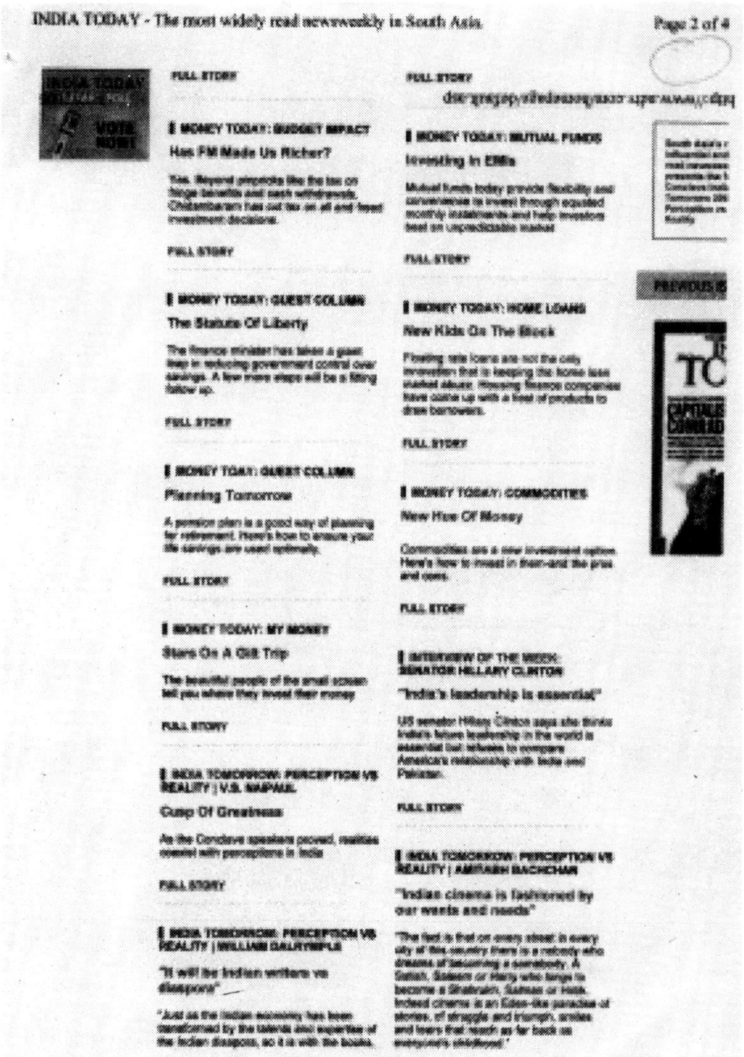
INDIA TODAY - The most widely read newsweekly in South Asia.
Page 2 of 4
FULL STORY
MONEY TODAY: BUDGET IMPACT
Has FM Made Us Richer?
FULL STORY
MONEY TODAY: MUTUAL FUNDS
FULL STORY
MONEY TODAY: GUEST COLUMN
The Statute Of Liberty
FULL STORY
MONEY TODAY: HOME LOANS
New Kids On The Block
FULL STORY
MONEY TODAY: GUEST COLUMN
Planning Tomorrow
FULL STORY
MONEY TODAY: COMMODITIES
New Hue Of Money
FULL STORY
MONEY TODAY: MY MONEY
Stars On A Gilt Trip
INTERVIEW OF THE WEEK: SENATOR HILLARY CLINTON
"India's leadership is essential"
FULL STORY
INDIA TOMORROW: PERCEPTION VS REALITY | V.S. NAIPAUL
Cusp Of Greatness
FULL STORY
INDIA TOMORROW: PERCEPTION VS REALITY | AMITABH BACHCHAN
"Indian cinema is fashioned by our wants and needs"
INDIA TOMORROW: PERCEPTION VS REALITY | WILLIAM DALRYMPLE
"It will be Indian writers vs diaspora"

HindustanTimes.com - The name India trusts for news Page 1 of 3

Uncertainitiesare most certain.
Get your Jeevan Saral policy today!

RUNS: 10
5th OVER

cash2

HindustanTimes.com

Pathan draws first blood, Pakistan 53 for one

A-1 verdict leaves many clueless

Hushed silence fell as judge pronounced the verdict, writes Gurmukh Singh.

Latest News »

More Stories »

Search

Quick Job Search

Go

Today in epaper

- My HT
- My Links
- HT Cricket
- HT Tabloid
- HT Classifieds
- Today's Headlines

Editions

News

On Edit Page

On Business Page

On Sport Page

Stamp duty rates get real: Slashed

Buying property in Delhi will be cheaper soon with state Govt deciding to reduce stamp duty, writes Amitabh Shukla.

How safe are baby toiletries?

Johnson & Johnson has been directed by the FDA to remove the word 'baby' from products meant for infants, writes Vijai B.

Other Top Stories »

'No pressure to change trial judge'

The SC judge clarified that there was no pressure on him to change the trial judge in the fodder scam.

Related Stories

Photos » Wildlife

Find Yo

HTTab

HTCri

HTNEX

http://www.hindustantimes.com/ 3/16/2005

HindustanTimes.com - The name India trusts for news Page 2 of 3

- India
- South Asia
- World
- Business
- New Economy
- Science & Tech
- Health
- Editorial
- Columnists
- Interviews
- Sport
- Cartoons
- Signposts
- Weather
- Web Exclusive
- Indians Abroad
- Pick of the day
- Week Scan
- Archives

- HT PACE
- Entertainment
- HT Specials

Gadgets

- Red Hot Lingerie on Auctions!
- Buy &Sell Cars....Best deals on Auctions!
- Red Hot Mobile Auctions

More

Interactives

- Crossword
- Photos
- Chat
- HT Blogs
- Have Your Say

Ad Links

against Wednesday's close of 6746.88.
Track the Sensex

Sex tourists turn to Brazil
Brazil has become the world's premier sex-tourism destination after tsunami wrecked Thailand.

US outsourcing Indian advocates
Legal outsourcing seems to be fast catching up in US, writes **Lalit K Jha.**
Full Coverage

More Stories »

- House panel calls AIIMS a failure
- 'Junior Nobel' eludes Indian Americans
- US wants India to scrap pipeline deal
- Best is in the West, let India wait!

Last 24 hours » Current Coverage

More Pictures

Other Photo Galleries

HT Specials »

Why do you pee in public?
What goes on in your mind when you unzip and 'let loose'? **Sunanda Kumar** examines.

Project Kashmir »

Armed with spades, not rifles
Troops in divided Kashmir are working to convert a mine-infested track into a peace road.

- India
- Technology

INFOTAINMENT Leisure | Music | Wheels | Books | Pets | Secret Corner

Music »

***Lord of the Rings* to take to stage as musical**
AR Rahman and Finnish group Varttina are composing music for the legend's stage debut.

Fashion & Style »

Fabrics of India, interpreted for world
Designers have given Indian fabrics a western touch to compete in the overseas market.

Relationships »

Brad and Jen can never be together again!
Despite rumours related to their reunion, the celeb couple reportedly have no such plans.

Quick Job Search

Keyword Go

Cinema

No more war films for JP Dutta

JP Dutta is back and plans to make a film for global audience.

Indians **Abroad**

Air-India to enhance American operations, improve services
Air-India is planning to boost operations by increasing frequency of flights and connecting new destinations.

- NRI News »
- Doing India Proud »

UK Edition

Indian cities low in rank
Mumbai, ranked 150th, is the top Indian metropolis in terms of quality of life followed by Bangalore and New Delhi.

- Asian Diaspora »
- UK News »

Web Exclusive »

http://www.hindustantimes.com/ 3/16/2005

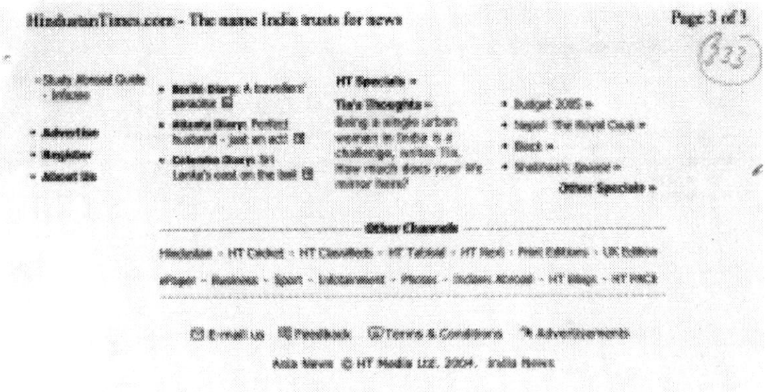

HindustanTimes.com - The name India trusts for news

Page 3 of 3

- Study Abroad Guide
- Infazoo

- Advertise
- Register
- About Us

- Berlin Diary: A travellers' paradise
- Atlanta Diary: Perfect husband - just an act!
- Colombo Diary: Sri Lanka's cost on the ball

HT Specials »

Tia's Thoughts »
Being a single urban woman in India is a challenge, writes Tia. How much does your life mirror hers?

- Budget 2005 »
- Nepal: The Royal Coup »
- Black »
- Shekhar's Space »

Other Specials »

Other Channels

Hindustan · HT Cricket · HT Classifieds · HT Tabloid · HT Next · Print Editions · UK Edition

ePaper · Business · Sport · Entertainment · Photos · Indians Abroad · HT Blogs · HT PACE

E-mail us · Feedback · Terms & Conditions · Advertisements

Asia News © HT Media Ltd. 2004. India News

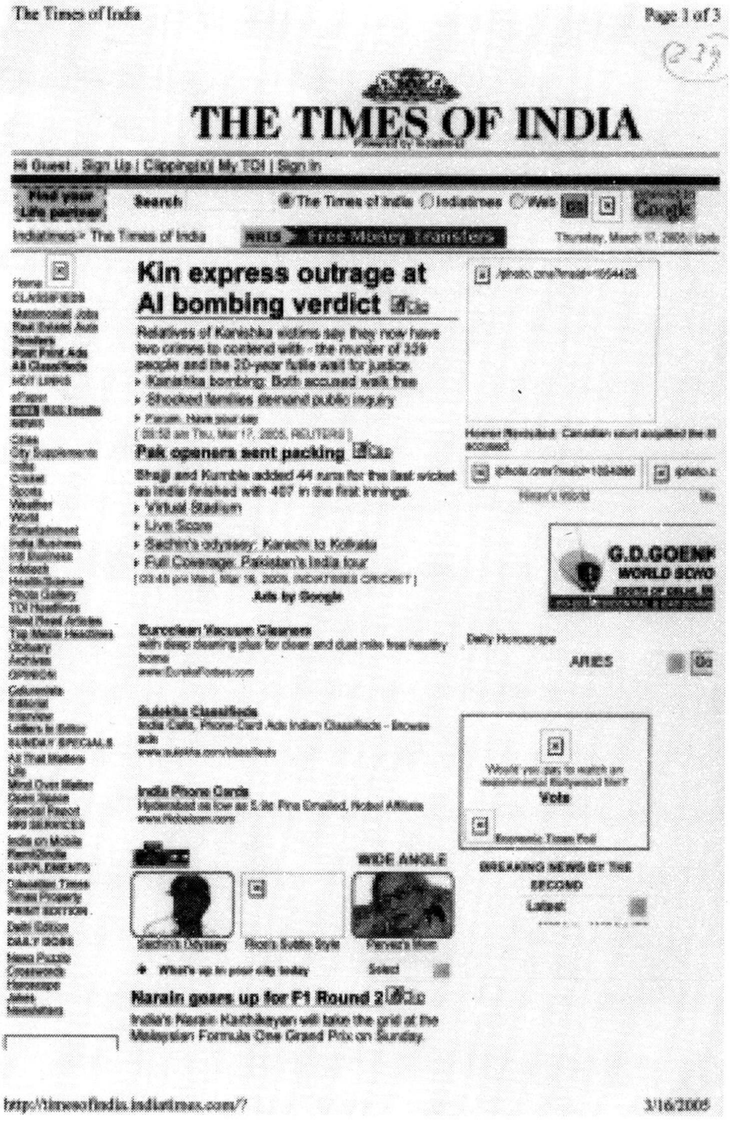
The Times of India
Page 1 of 3
THE TIMES OF INDIA
Hi Guest, Sign Up | Clipping(s) My TOI | Sign In
Find your Life partner
Search
The Times of India Indiatimes Web
Indiatimes» The Times of India
Free Money Transfers
Kin express outrage at AI bombing verdict
Relatives of Kanishka victims say they now have two crimes to contend with - the murder of 329 people and the 20-year futile wait for justice.
Kanishka bombing: Both accused walk free
Shocked families demand public inquiry
Pak openers sent packing
Balaji and Kumble added 44 runs for the last wicket as India finished with 407 in the first innings.
Virtual Stadium
Live Score
Sachin's odyssey: Karachi to Kolkata
Full Coverage: Pakistan's India tour
Ads by Google
Euroclean Vacuum Cleaners
Sulekha Classifieds
India Phone Cards
WIDE ANGLE
Narain gears up for F1 Round 2
India's Narain Karthikeyan will take the grid at the Malaysian Formula One Grand Prix on Sunday.
G.D.GOENK
WORLD SCHO
Daily Horoscope
ARIES
Vote
BREAKING NEWS BY THE SECOND
Latest
http://timesofindia.indiatimes.com/?
3/16/2005

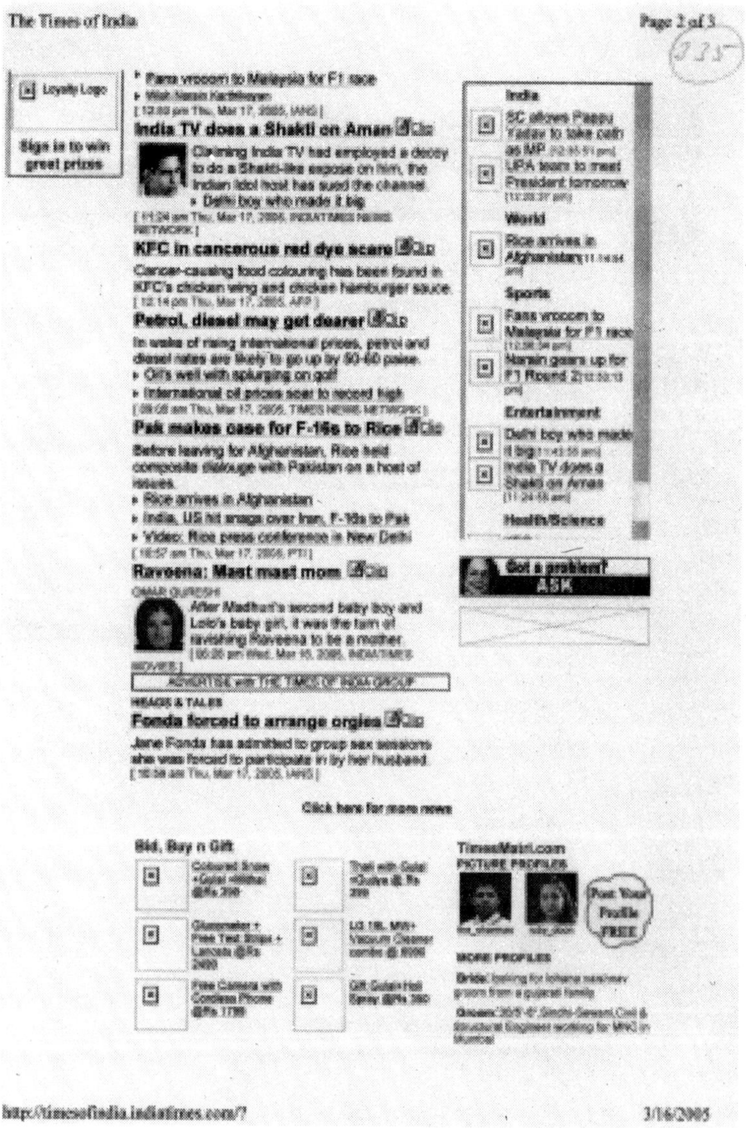

The Times of India Page 2 of 3

Loyalty Logo

Sign in to win great prizes

- Fans vrooom to Malaysia for F1 race

India TV does a Shakti on Aman

Claiming India TV had employed a decoy to do a Shakti-like expose on him, the Indian Idol host has sued the channel.

- Delhi boy who made it big

KFC in cancerous red dye scare

Cancer-causing food colouring has been found in KFC's chicken wing and chicken hamburger sauce.

Petrol, diesel may get dearer

In wake of rising international prices, petrol and diesel rates are likely to go up by 50-60 paise.

- Oil's well with splurging on golf
- International oil prices soar to record high

Pak makes case for F-16s to Rice

Before leaving for Afghanistan, Rice held composite dialouge with Pakistan on a host of issues.

- Rice arrives in Afghanistan
- India, US hit snags over Iran, F-16s to Pak
- Video: Rice press conference in New Delhi

Raveena: Mast mast mom

After Madhuri's second baby boy and Lolo's baby girl, it was the turn of ravishing Raveena to be a mother.

ADVERTISE with THE TIMES OF INDIA GROUP

HEADS & TALES

Fonda forced to arrange orgies

Jane Fonda has admitted to group sex sessions she was forced to participate in by her husband.

Click here for more news

India
- SC allows Pappu Yadav to take oath as MP
- UPA team to meet President tomorrow

World
- Rice arrives in Afghanistan

Sports
- Fans vrooom to Malaysia for F1 race
- Narain gears up for F1 Round 2

Entertainment
- Delhi boy who made it big
- India TV does a Shakti on Aman

Health/Science

Got a problem? ASK

Bid, Buy n Gift

TimesMatri.com

PICTURE PROFILES

Post Your Profile FREE

MORE PROFILES

http://timesofindia.indiatimes.com/? 3/16/2005

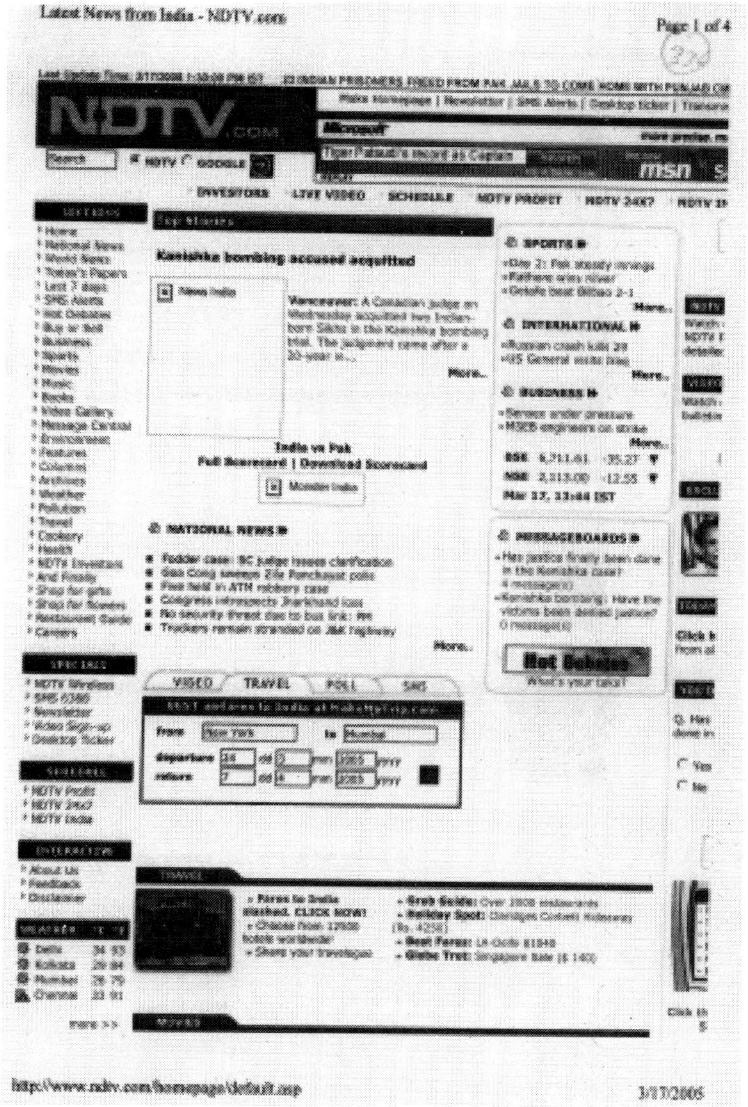
Latest News from India - NDTV.com
Page 1 of 4
NDTV.COM
INVESTORS
LIVE VIDEO
SCHEDULE
NDTV PROFIT
NDTV 24X7
Kanishka bombing accused acquitted
Vancouver: A Canadian judge on Wednesday acquitted two Indian-born Sikhs in the Kanishka bombing trial. The judgment came after a 20-year in...
More..
India vs Pak
Full Scorecard | Download Scorecard
NATIONAL NEWS
More..
SPORTS
INTERNATIONAL
BUSINESS
Mar 17, 13:44 IST
MESSAGEBOARDS
Hot Debates
What's your take?
VIDEO
TRAVEL
POLL
SMS
from
to
departure
return
http://www.ndtv.com/homepage/default.asp
3/17/2005

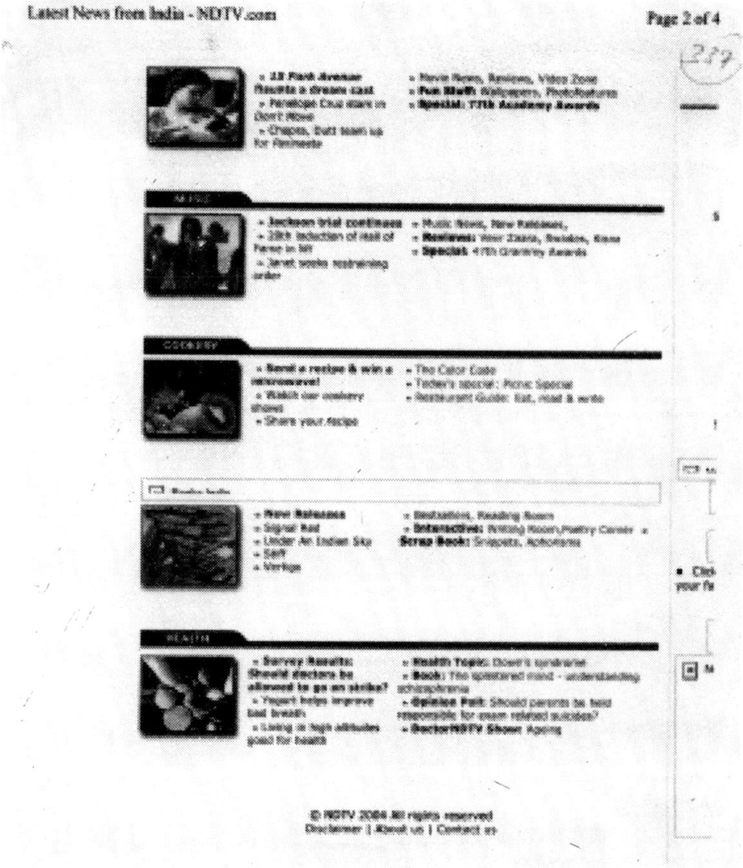

Latest News from India - NDTV.com | Page 2 of 4

- 13 Park Avenue flaunts a dream cast
- Penelope Cruz stars in Don't Move
- Chopra, Dutt team up for Parineeta
- Movie News, Reviews, Video Zone
- Fun Stuff: Wallpapers, Photofeatures
- Special: 77th Academy Awards

MUSIC

- Jackson trial continues
- 19th induction of Hall of Fame in NY
- Janet seeks restraining order
- Music News, New Releases,
- Special: 47th Grammy Awards

COOKERY

- Send a recipe & win a microwave!
- Watch our cookery shows
- Share your Recipe
- The Color Code
- Restaurant Guide: Eat, read & write

- New Releases
- Signal Red
- Under An Indian Sky
- Self
- Vertigo
- Interactive: Writing Room, Poetry Corner
- Scrap Book: Snippets, Aphorisms

HEALTH

- Survey Results: Should doctors be allowed to go on strike?
- Health Topic: Down's syndrome
- Opinion Poll: Should parents be held responsible for exam related suicides?
- DoctorNDTV Show: Ageing

© NDTV 2004 All rights reserved
Disclaimer | About us | Contact us

SECTION V

OPINION WRITING

18

WRITING FEATURES

Many Indian newspapers carry items which fall into the general heading of features but there seems some confusion about precisely what a feature really is. All too often the feature turns out to be a kind of second class news, written for no apparent reason, and differs from news only to the extent that it contains fewer hard facts.

Problems in definition

A young cub reporter who had proved himself to be capable writer of news stories was asked to try his hand at feature. Eager to succeed, the reporter set out to learn what a feature is, he was surprised to find that none of the vetern reporters and editors could offer a definition. The most helpful suggestion came from the city editor: "It is a catch hall. We have straight factual accounts on one hand; those are news stories. We have editorial reviews, and columns on the other hand; those are opinion pieces. Everything else we publish is feature material."

James Lewis, writer of *The Active Reporter* says that the feature is something which gives a new dimension to the news, which examines it, dissects it. The best type of feature is that which is topical, which is tied to the news.

The feature offers scope for real writing flair and the good feature-writer is the man able to sense what questions his readers are likely to be asking themselves about a particular piece of news. But he must present them with the best facts available and preferably, say where he got them. He, the writer, is comparatively unimportant except as a vehicle for presenting the new information. His personality and opinions should not get in the way of the feature. He is entitled to form an opinion in the feature and to draw a conclusion at the end of it, but it must be on the basis of the facts he has presented.

Metzler defined a good feature story is a creative work of art. It does not record reality so much as it offers an artful, but still factual, account of it, largely through the selection of facts by the writer and the interpretation placed upon the facts. The feature story never fictionalizes. It taps into some event or situation and weaves information into a coherent story designed both to entertain and to make a memorable point- a statement about reality. It could be, as here, a whimsical point or it could be serious. Often the feature will make a reader laugh or cry or say, "well, it could happen to anyone".

Success in feature writing depends largely on a writer's ability to see the significance of people's actions and to make sure the reader sees it, too. To do this effectively, the writer must have precise control over the content of the article. And that, in the end, may be the only possible definition of a feature story:

A feature story evolves when to make a point, the writer controls the facts—by selection, structure and interpretation—rather than the facts controlling the writer.

This places a big responsibility on the writer. Controlling the facts does not mean expressing opinions. It certainly does not mean fictionalizing. Nor does it imply a sinister omission or manipulation of facts in order to advocate a point of view or present a skewed view of reality. Rather it means trying to give a clearer view of reality as seen by a skilled and unbiased observer.

In nutshell the feature is not a snack to serve in place of a meal. It is a meal in itself. A feature which excites a reader's interest and then fails to answer his questions is a disaster.

Characteristics

A feature story, even if it can't be defined precisely, does have three distinguishing characteristics:

- It readily identifies with the reader, unusually on an informal or conversational basis. It covers topics carefully calculated to relate to most readers' concerns.
- It makes a point. Unlike the news story, the feature story must justify its existence to the reader. Sometimes in explicit terms, it says in so many words. Sometimes the point is implicit; the reader infers the point without having it spelled out.
- It is interestingly written. It is well-organized and to the point. It may cover a frivolous topic or a serious one, but even the serious

one is laden with humour, drama, suspense, irony—are literary characteristics that make a piece of writing come alive. This is done largely by showing people in action, thus demonstrating the humour, drama, and so on in their lives.

Mr. Brain Nicholas in his book, *Features with Flair*, has described features as the 'soul' of newspapers. A few important definitions are given below:

- The news story stops after it has presented facts or ideas. The feature story goes further. It explores the background, the birth and growth of the idea or event, provides a glance at future too. It conveys to the readers what are you, the writer or someone else, think about the idea or event. It has greater appeal to readers' imagination.
- Feature story is not just recitation of facts, but rather skillfully presentation of facts and associated ideas so as to spotlight that which is significant, but not apparent to the casual observer.
- A feature has its impact outside or beyond the realm of the straight news story's unvarnished who, what, when, where, why, how.
- The justification, strength, and the very identity of the feature lie in its presentation of the imagination, not in departing from or stretching truth but in piercing the peculiar and particular truths that strike people's curiosity, sympathy, skepticism, humour, and amazement.
- A feature is similar to a news story in that it gives the readers facts in an interesting form and is adapted to rapid reading. But it goes beyond those facts by amplifying them with study, research and interviews and to instruct, guide or entertain the readers who know about the subject as well as those who do not.
- It is a detailed presentation of some interesting subject in a popular form. It deals with the day's news, a timely or seasonal subject or any topic that appeals to a number of readers. Its purpose is to entertain, inform or to give practical guidance, i.e., to show to readers as to how to do something.
- The news story and feature articles are no doubt different, but they are not two widely separate types of writing.
- A feature is longer bits in newspapers—a piece of writing which explains, amplifies and interprets issues with study, research and interview.

- The exploration of facts—the purpose is to guide, instruct or entertain.
- In its broadest meaning, it is a material selected for presentation by a mass medium primarily because of some element other than the timeliness of its materials. The regency of the material is not the dominant characteristic. The peak of interest comes from one or other element.

In sum, the essence of a feature story is the drama of human endeavour. You show people, often ordinary people, striving to improve themselves, coping with troubles and obstacles, sometimes reaching beyond their grasp in quest of a worthwhile goal.

Feature and News Story

Though the two cannot be divided into any watertight compartments, still the feature has some distant characteristics as follows:

- News is an objective and factual account of events where the reporter sticks to facts and tries to answer, as far as possible the six basic questions—Who, What, Where, When, Why and How. The reporter weighs and evaluates the relative value of different ingredients in the story, and the most important of these are included in the lead. His purpose is to give facts or information of interest to the people. Feature on the other hand, goes much beyond the scope of the news story. It gives a new dimension to the news. It examines and dissects news and throws. It tries to explore the background, probes in depth an idea or the event. It is not just a narration of facts. The purpose is to both inform and entertain and also arouse curiosity, sympathy, humour and other feelings among the readers. A feature writer reacts to the people, situations, events and places, and provides a colourful background. This scope is much wider than news writing.
  Take for example a bus accident. A news item generally tries to answer what, when, where, who, why and how, another facts and details. The feature writer, on the other will go deeper into some aspects. For example, the reaction of the survivors and relatives to the accident, background of similar accident, loss of articles and behaviour of the community etc.
  If there is a hike in petrol prices, the news item gives the extent

of increase, the need for it and the possible consequences. A feature writer tries to find out the reaction of the car users, taxi drivers, transporters, so as to find out how they have affected in their day-to-day life. Even social effects due to increase in the cost of transportation can be an interesting subject for a feature writer.

- News story deals with recent and current events. It is like a dairy product, a perishable commodity. The speed is very important because it has to meet certain deadlines. This is not necessary in the case of features. A feature need not be only on a recent subject. The event might have taken place some time ago but it can still be a subject of a feature, if it is of interest to the readers.
- Brevity is the some of news writing. News story has not much scope for subsidiary or background material. Every word, counts in news writing. There is relatively more freedom to a feature writer in this matter. He can, to his requirements. Feature certainly occupies more space than an average news story.
- Feature and news story also differ in the style of writing. News story is generally written in inverted pyramid or purpose is to give a glimpse of an event, a factual account of the happening. It is a hurriedly written piece to meet certain deadlines. The lead or introduction in the news story attempts to present, as far as possible, all important facts. It has a certain set format and pattern. There is not much room for colour or ornamentation. The feature, on the other hand, follows an altogether different style. The feature writer has none freedom. He can freely react to situations, event and people with emotion and imagination. The feature can be written in colourful and fiction style depending on the feature writer communicates his thoughts in an effective, interesting and entertaining manner. He can develop his own style. Through informal style he can make readers as his partners.
- A reporter writing a news story does not give heading, title or sub-title. It is the function of the sub-editor. However, in news releases issued by the government or other organizations, the title and sub-title where necessary are inserted. The selection of the title and sub-title is definitely of greater importance in a feature. The title should sell the feature. It should capture the attention and arouse interest in the feature. Dull, weary and lengthy titles do not click with the readers. The title should carry off the feature, catch the reader's attention and the reader's eye.

However, care should be taken that it does not mislead the readers.

- The introduction of the lead in a feature need not be in summary format as in the news reporting. It may be simple direct beginning creating interest of the readers in the subject. The introduction may convey the central idea and also indicate the boundaries or limitations of the scope of the subject. One may start a feature with an anecdote, dialogue, interesting conversation, striking startling or interesting statement, but this should have a direct bearing on the subject matter.
- The style and length of the feature will also depend on the newspapers and periodicals for which the feature is written. The style will have to vary depending on the type of paper. Simple and clear writing without too many statistics or documentation will add to the value of the feature. Only well-known abbreviations should be used. A feature writer can make use of wider vocabulary than what is used in news writing. Similarly paragraph can also be longer than in the news story. Style may be literary, ornamental and colourful in a feature.
- A news story is limited to a single time and place. It is not always a complete story in itself. The presumption is that the reader is aware of earlier happenings on the subject. Feature, on the other hand, is a self-sufficient and self-contained piece.
- News is more or less common in all papers since the sources of news *i.e.* agency, broadcasts etc. are the same. The difference in news coverage in different papers lies on emphasis, extent of space and the slant. This is not necessarily in the case of features. In fact features give an individuality or distinctiveness to the newspapers.
- The purpose of the news story is to inform, educate and enlighten happenings. The feature, on the other hand, entertains, guides and instructs the readers.
- A reporter or a correspondent writing a news story does not generally put his name. The name is given only when the story is of some significance. Feature, on the other hand may be signed.
- While news stories are generally written in third person, features which are more in a nature of personal rapport may be written in first, second and third person.
- Most of the news go without illustrations. In features, photographs or illustrations are more or less a 'must'.

Feature and article

Though there are many similarities between feature and an article, yet each has a character and personality of its own. D.S.Mehta in his book *Mass communication and Journalism in India* has described the following characteristics of feature and an article.

There are many things common between a feature and an article, yet each has a character and personality of its own.

Both articles and features are non-news form of writing. They thrive on the quality of good prose. An article often acquires the character of a feature and a feature sometimes takes the characteristics of an article. It is not easy to draw a line. Each encroaches on other's territory.

An article is generally written on broad subjects, covering more than one aspect. In features, the subject-matter is specific, minute and narrow. Only one or two aspects are dealt with at a time. It deals with a single mood. The approach to the subject in the article is general while it is specific in the feature.

An article is an elaborate piece of composition, a product of mind, based on study and research. It is more scholarly and more serious in tone. It is generally well-documented. There are facts, figures and lot of statistics. The feature, on the other hand, is a product of heart, based on emotions, feelings and reactions of the writer to the people, places and events, and written in a much lighter vein. In features, facts and figures are not so essential.

In terms of length, an article can be lengthier than a feature. Again, besides information and educative material, an element of entertainment is generally there in a feature. It is not necessary for an article to provide entertainment or instruction.

While photographs, etc. are very essential in features, it is not so in the case of articles.

The style of writing an article is generally formal, more learned, heavy and sober. It can even survive dullness. The style in features is more informal, more colourful. Dullness is fatal to a feature. Features can dramatize, humanize an event or idea and provide joy and delight so as to make greater appeal to the readers.

In articles, an element of personal opinion is always there, as they are generally written by experts. The expert gives his views and conclusions after making a comprehensive study of the subject. In features, personal opinion is generally projected through others. The features may be written by the same person on a variety of subjects.

While an article has a conventional beginning, middle and end, the feature can begin and end even abruptly.

Classifying Features

Any classification of features is subject to debate. Features are so diverse that they are not easily divided and categorized. Almost any system of classification is certain to fail to take account of overlapping. Some features fit easily into more than one compartment. Nevertheless, these classifications will enable beginning writers to grasp the dimensions of the world of feature writing.

News features

As the title indicates, news features are tied directly to news events. This is a news story written in feature style. Instead of a straight, unvarnished account, it will use feature techniques, such as opening with an illustrative anecdote, even though the story's major purpose is to convey news, some news features are complete stories in themselves, carrying news story information in feature form. These features are connected to current events, and one gets ideas of these features from the news features. An interview with the parents of a local boy who has topped in an IAS examination is one example of a news feature.

Features which are not directly connected with news, but deal with subjects of continuing interest such as smoke-pollution, road safety, slums etc. are known as background features. These features may also be on anniversaries of battle, or birth or death of a person, or on hijacking of a plane, or on earthquakes etc. which can be linked with current events.

Features written on religious festivals, or on memory of God or Goddess fall in the category of mythological background features.

Comprehensive News features

This kind of story depicts trends and ongoing news issues rather than specific news events. It is better researched than most daily news stories because it comes from a wide variety of sources. It is usually more analytical and interpretive, it tries to depict not only what the news is but what it means.

The comprehensive news feature is the journalistic form that allows you to report the chicken pox rather than the individual pimples. The term really embraces a wide variety of journalistic practices. They go by such terms as depth reporting, investigative reporting, precision journalism, saturation reporting and interpretive reporting. Although each of these has a specific meaning, they all fall roughly broadly into this category. A comprehensive news feature is 'comprehensive' in that it draws from a wide variety of sources. It is 'news' in that it reports new things, some times—subtle trends. It is a 'feature' in its theme and structure, which are under tight control by the writer.

It differs from the simple feature described in three ways:

- It is usually longer and more complex.
- It is more newsy in conveying major trends and changes.
- It is more thoughtful in evaluating the meaning of the situation being conveyed. In short, it tries to convey the disease not the pimple.

To summarize, here are six basic characteristics of the comprehensive news feature:

- It is topical. If it doesn't relate to a specific news event, it at least deals with matters that concern large numbers of people.
- It identifies with the reader, not only in choice of topic but in readable style of writing.
- It explores the essence—the Why—of an issue or problem.
- It relies primarily on a reporter's ability to understand a problem or situation—often through open-minded and diligent research.
- It relies on a wide variety of sources.
- It makes a point.

All of this may sound intimidating to the student journalist. Nevertheless you can learn to write comprehensive news features first by studying them and then by starting with the elementary varieties.

Human interest Features

Human interest features are those that involve a reader emotionally, stimulating or depressing him, angering or amusing him, awakening sympathy or distaste. Many news stories and almost all feature stories have human interest elements, but the basic human interest stories are those that appeal almost solely to the emotions. The danger in writing human interest stories that awaken sympathy is that the writer is likely to allow himself to become sentimental.

Human interest features are now becoming very popular in India. One can get ideas of such features in a number of ways. Human interest features may be written on a day in the life of a common man, such as a constable, gardener, sweeper, beggar or a 90-years old man marrying the fifth time or a blind teacher taking a class or the problems of a housewife who manages to rear a family and go to school at the same time, make a readable feature not only for other housewives but for any person who can appreciate the situation. The emphasis in these features is on the unique views of life or an unusual occupation.

Interview features

Most feature writers spend most of their time conducting interviews. The facts they gather in interviewing may be shaped into stories that can be classified variously—interesting people, adventures, historical reminiscences, descriptive, how to do its, etc.—but all will be classified here as interview features. The problem for the writer in any case is to select from his notes the most interesting and important facts and observations, then to use his own intelligence, perception and writing ability to make them come alive.

Although most features are based on interviews, the special interview feature portrays a dialogue between a reporter and another person, often a public figure or celebrity. Sometimes it runs in question and answer format.

To produce a good feature, a writer should have sufficient material. He should have information that will enable him to describe interviews—her mannerisms, voice, laugh—so that the reader will be able to see as well as hear her. The most difficult problem is devising a lead that will capture reader's interest and also serve as a framework for the rest of the story.

Personality Sketch or Profile features

Another important type of features are biographical or personality features. Personality features are based on well-known persons and their achievements. In such features, the emphasis is on what has made the man great rather than cataloguing his achievements.

Personality features may be written not only on news-worthy

personalities or on great men who capture the imagination of people, but also on little known persons, such as a beggar who has become a millionaire. These are rag to riches stories which hold readers interest. These features are not biographical sketches. It is not necessary to tell the story from birth to death. It is sufficient to give just enough background of the person and his recent achievements. A feature writer need not give all details or deal with all aspects. The objective is to tell the readers about the qualities of the man, and how he has achieved the position of eminence.

Personality coverage can be both entertaining and educative. Details about Vajpayee's likes and dislikes, his political ideologies, bunched together with stray personal incidents can usefully be collected. Imagination comes into play in making use of such established data.

While a personality sketch is usually short and treats only one aspect of a personality, profile is longer, more detailed and psychologically deeper. It tries to depict what the individual is really like down deep. Let us look at the two features published in the newspapers. The following feature appeared in *The Indian Express* when Manmohan Singh became the 13th Prime Minister of India. This is how Manini Chatterjee delves into his life and career from his CV.

The Man

The PM who served seven PMs.

The Indian Express,
May 23, 2004.

The soft-spoken Sardar, self-effacing to a fault, has no independent base within the party and is described as a "political non-player." He derives power almost exclusively from the trust Sonia reposes in him.

Ever since she took over as party president in May 1998, Singh has been her most trusted advisor and pointsman—not just on questions of economic policy but also in dealing with politicians across the spectrum.

Be it drafting party documents or hammering out difficult alliances, Singh, in his quit way, was always on call. Unlike other members of Sonia's shifting inner circle, Singh was never regarded as a member of a "coterie."

But loyalty to Sonia is not the sole reason Singh made it to the top post. Long before Sonia was charmed by his clean image and sincerity, Singh had learnt to secure the trust and affection of his teachers and political masters. His humility, which conceals strongly held convictions and a pragmatic bent of mind, stems from his humble background.

Born in village Gah of Jhelum district on September 26, 1932, Singh lost his mother when he was just five months old and was brought up by his paternal grandmother. He studied in the village primary school and joined his father in Peshawar when he reached class VI.

Soon after his matriculation exam in March, 1947, the Partition riots broke out. His grandfather was killed but his grandmother and he managed to escape to India. He had to sit for the exams again—from a private school in Delhi's Chawri Bazar—and got a high first class and a university scholarship.

He started a pre-medicine course at Khalsa College, Amritsar, but his father had little money and asked him to join a commission agent's firm. He hated it and soon went back to studies—preferring maths and economics to medicine.

Although he came up the hard way, Singh does not have the usual arrogance of a "self-made man." In an interview to this reporter soon after he became finance minister in 1991, he recalled how much his teachers had helped him. M.R. Jain and S.K. Kalia taught him economics at Hindu College in Amritsar; S.B. Rangnekar at Panjab University, Chandigarh, "convinced me not to sit for the civil service exams and go to Cambridge to do an Economics tripos instead"; Joan Robinson, R.F. Kahn and Nicolas Kaldor at Cambridge, of whom Kaldor "influenced me the most."

His experience with government—with politicians more than bureaucrats—was equally rewarding. When he was still a student at Cambridge Kaldor wrote to his friend and then finance minister TT Krishnamachari, "TTK", as he was known: 'I have a student... ideally suited for the treasury."

On his return to India in 1957, TTK offered him the post of senior research officer in the Finance Ministry with a starting salary of Rs. 600. But Panjab University vice-chancellor A.C. Joshi, who had funded his scholarship, held him to his bond. "He said," Singh recalled, "this is just not on, this is a breach of trust and you must pay back all the money we spent on you with interest."

Singh didn't have the money and so stayed back to serve the university for three years.

But he was destined to join government. After completing a D.Phil from Nuffield College, Oxford, a spell with UNCTAD in New York, and a teaching stint at the Delhi School of Economics (DSE), he accepted the post of economic advisor to the Ministry of Foreign Trade in Indira Gandhi's government in 1971.

He had problems with senior officials and decided to quit and take an offer to head DSE. But Indira's principal secretary P.N. Haksar put his foot down and made him chief economic advisor to the Finance Ministry. In 1976, overruling objections from senior IAS officers, Indira appointed him secretary, economic affairs—a post he held through the Janata years.

Yet again, civil servants tried to get rid of him—pointing to his services to the government during the Emergency—but both Moraraji Desai and finance minister H.M. Patel stood by him. He had no problems with Charan Singh either.

When Indira Gandhi returned in 1980, she wanted him to take over a Planing Commission deputy chairman. He told her he couldn't because he was just 48, had neither inherited or married into money, didn't have savings, and the Rs 2,500 per month salary (for the cabinet-rank post) was too little to live on. Bureaucrats earned a lot more.

Indira Gandhi solved the problem soon enough. She made him member secretary of the Planning Commission so that he could do all the work in formulating the sixth Plan but didn't have to retire from the civil service.

The Babus objected once again. Indira silenced them with the riposte: "Is it written in the Constitution of India that there cannot be a member secretary to the Planning Commission?" Incidentally, N.D. Tiwari was then the deputy chairman and Pranab Mukherjee finance minister.

In 1985, after a term as RBI governor, he finally took over as deputy chairman, Planning Commission. Ironically, the one prime minister with whom Singh clearly did not share a great rapport was Rajiv Gandhi. Rajiv infamously ran down the Planing Commission as "a bunch of jokers" and Singh was critical of the 1985 budget.

But Singh has never gone on record about it, and only spoke of the cordial relations he shared with opposition chief ministers such as Jyoti Basu, Ramakrishna Hegde, and N.T.Rama Rao because "I did not politicise the planning process."

In 1987, he became chairman of the Geneva-based South Commission, returning to India at V.P.Singh's request to chair the prime minister's Economic Advisory Council. By the time he arrived, V.P.singh was no longer prime minister and Singh served Chandra Shekhar instead. When that government too fell in March 1991, he became UGC chairman.

Two months later, on June 21, he was sworn in as Narasimha Rao's finance minister.

As the man who changed the direction of India's economic trajectory and lent the term "Manmohanomics" to popular usage, Singh had earned his place in history. But the wheels of destiny never stop turning. Singh is now set to set more land marks—the first "apolitical" prime minister, the first Congress prime minister who is not the supreme leader of the party, and, who knows, perhaps the first leader of a Congress-led coalition to complete five years in office.

Which, for anyone who knows the byzantine politics of the Grand Old Party, may be a lot tougher than Atal Behari Vajpayee's record of leading a non-Congress coalition that lasted a full term.

How a rural boy became a top scientist

Teachers spotted talent and nurtured it

by Reeta Sharma
The Tribune,
February 7, 2004.

A village boy acquired wings by doing matriculation, first class first, in the joint Punjab and flew out with a promise of Rs. 117 in 1958. Today he is realizing his dream of setting up a Rs. 100 crore science city project. His long flight of 46 years is marked by overwhelming heights.

This person is Dr. Raghbir Singh Khandpur, who stepped out of Jandiala Guru in 1958 to join DAV College, Amritsar, to do B.Sc. His life is not only an eye-opener, but also worth a page in Punjab's history to motivate the coming generations.

"When I topped the matriculation examination, which was then held by Panjab University, I was totally ignorant of all the benefits that I was automatically entitled to. Even today my head bows in reverence to the teachers of those times, who played a crucial role in my life at that juncture. Since I came from a humble home, it was presumed, both by me and my family, that my education was over. So I appeared for a competitive examination for the post of railway mechanic and was selected. I was about to take up the job but for the role of teachers of the day.

"It was baffling for me that a team of teachers from DAV College, Amritsar, was sent by the then Principal, Prof. B.S.Behl, to ensure that I joined his college. It was this team, which motivated me to join the college.

They also informed me that I shall be getting much more that a mechanic's salary in the form of various scholarships that I was now entitled to. Nobody in Jandiala Guru knew that the Punjab Government gave Rs. 50 to the topper. Besides, Rs. 22 came from Panjab University as scholarship, Rs. 25 was paid by the DAV College management and Rs. 20 was given as the refugee student grant. The total amount that I was to receive was Rs. 117, which was then more than a clerk's salary. I was totally ignorant of this aspect. Thanks to the teachers, I ventured to do my B.Sc. and, once again, I topped in the university in 1962".

Principal Behl, once again, encouraged this brilliant boy saying that he was meant for the best institute of the country. That was the Indian Institute of Science (IIS), Bangalore. And, of course, his student did not let him down. He acquired the BE degree with distinction from the IIS in 1965. He was promptly taken in by the CSIO (Central Scientific Instruments Organisation).

For the next 24 years, he devoted himself to research at the CSIO and six of his inventions were patented. These were the foetal heart rate monitor, the photo-electric demodulator, the system for gas supply failure-alarm, the automatic temperature controller, the improved three way solenoid valve device for fluid direction control and management and the process of making an alcohol breath analyser and an apparatus by such process. Besides research, he has published seven books of which "Handbook of Modern Analytical Instruments" is considered to be the "Bible" in this field.

Later, Dr. Raghbir Singh Khandpur went to the Royal College of Surgeons, London for post-graduate research and training. His research and study tours also took him to Germany, France, the USA, China, Canada, Japan and Sweden. By 1971 he was posted as Senior Scientist at the CSIO, Regional Centre, Mumbai. Eventually he rose to the position of Director-General of CEDTI-Centre for Electronics Design and Technology, Ministry of Information Technology, New Delhi, in November, 1997.

His role as a scientist in the CSIO, will bear his stamp for many generations to come. He not only established the Medical Instrumentation Division, which is the most advanced centre of the country, but also created two CEDTI centres at Tezpur in Assam and Aizwal in Mizoram, during his tenure as Director General, CEDTI. He is also the founder-Director of CEDTI in Mohali. His dedication to his field of research and training is also reflected in his role as a consultant to various national and international organisations, including the UN, WHO, UNDP, UNDIO and the World Bank. He has received many honours and awards, including the Independence Day Award from the National Research and Development Corporation in 1989.

No wonder, the man who started his journey with Rs. 117 in 1958 was invited in May, 2002, to manage the Rs. 100 crore Pushpa Gujral Science City project in Kapurthala. In the agrarian society of Punjab, this is the biggest ever science project being established under the guidance of this self-made scientist, Dr. Raghbir Singh Khandpur. An unassuming and humble man, his dream now is to ensure that the Science City project should succeed in inculcating love for science in the minds of the primarily agrarian Punjabi youth.

When asked why Punjabi youth these days were chasing a materialistic life rather than knowledge and career, Dr. Khandpur turned pensive and replied with a rather heavy heart, "The blame should be shared by the parents and the teachers. While parents are no more inculcating any moral values in their children, the teachers, on the other hand, unfortunately are increasingly failing to perform their duties. The teachers of the day are merely doing their jobs with the aim and eyes on their salary alone".

To another query about the respect for scientists in the country, Dr. Khandpur said, "It is not just scientists, but almost every other professional, be it the doctor, the engineer, the teacher or the social researcher, all have been pushed to a secondary position by the bureaucracy of the country. In fact, the blame for the brain-drain too should be shared by the bureaucracy. The over whelming corruption in society is also one of the reasons why scientists or other researchers are neglected. The Indian society today is so obsessed with materialism that any research in science taking place in some dark corner is of no relevance to it.

Sidebar features

This is a feature story that accompanies a main news story. A story about a major flood or earthquake, may include such sidebars as an interview with a refugee family, a background story on what caused the flood or earthquake, or a colour piece on the work of rescue units—perhaps even a narrative account of a single dramatic rescue.

Geographical features

The geographical feature does not incorporate only topographical details, and details about climate and people. It can include exciting happenings or on adventure. A youth team from Rekong Peo or Pangi Valley explored the areas on route, experiencing adventures and taking risks can be an interesting geographical feature.

An example of Geographical feature is as follows:

The Lost World

Nilanjan Gupta
The Indian, Express,
March 23, 2004

"Don't go to Madagascar!" That is the only advice I receive in Mauritius when I reveal my plans to travel to the island off the east coast of Africa. Disembarking from my flight on Air Madagascar at Antananarivo—Tana, for short—and surrounded by 20 burly men, I begin to understand why. Thirty US dollars, the customs officer tells me, or could turn back and leave right then.

There are no half-measures in Madagascar. Disembarkation cards warn travellers against yellow fever, malaria and, believe it or not, circumcision. At night, shadowy, hooded figures straight out of Kafka stalk the streets of the city. There are whispers that disease walks among them. Catcalling prostitutes invite strangers to decent hotels that double up as brothels. The oppressive atmosphere of civil unrest hangs heavy in the dry air.

Daylight, and it could be another world, a world time forgot. A street named after Indira Gandhi, beautiful landmarks redolent with memories of Malaysia, Indonesia, Arabia, Europe—Madagascar was a France colony for more than 70 years—street life reminiscent of 1930s Europe, complete with bawdy cabarets, the Zoma, the world's largest open-air market, and the oxymoronic sight of a black man in a western suit sipping the over a French newspaper... could any other country yank together such opposites?

Madagascar is desperately poor—one US dollar is worth 6,575 Malagasy francs—but more than poverty, it is violence that is triggering an implosion in the country. A few months before I landed up, Tana mayor Marc Ravolomanana, a self-made millionaire, had had a violent showdown with Didier Ratsiraka, president for 20 years. Refusing to step down, Ratsiraka set up a parallel capital to Tana and claims the loyalty of half the army.

None of this concerns me, however, as I prepare for my excursion to beautiful Ambohimanga, the ancient tribal capital, 16 km from Tana.

The 'palace' is like nothing you'll ever encounter on the tourist trail. A 20-ft-high structure, its most striking feature is the four huge wooden breasts on the ceiling—a symbol of polygamy, I am told!

The floor of the house is stained with fresh blood, a sign that sacrifice survives. "A zebu (bull) was sacrificed here this morning for our ancestors," someone informs me helpfully.

Meanwhile, my money supplies are running low—alarmingly enough, foreigners are charged 35 times the local price—and since plastic doesn't work here, I am forced to abandon plans of visiting a wildlife reserve. Adventure, I decide, will have to come from other sources. And so, after my kind landlady does some smart-talking, I board a huge 10-wheeled Mercedes container truck being driven to the coastal resort to Morondava, 500 km. across the country.

It may have been novel for me, but the two drivers are obviously used to the idea. The room-sized truck is rigged out with two hammock beds. One is occupied by a laughing Indonesian woman—the girlfriend of the drivers, it later appears—who invites me to join her. Sex tourism is widespread here, never mind the huge billboards urging, 'Evitez la tourisme sexual (prevent sex tourism).'

As the truck rolls, my new friend—the tougher and more muscular of the two drivers—makes me cross my heart. But nothing could have saved me the shock of experiencing Africa first-hand. In a few hours, we traverse across mountains, plains, plateaus, deserts, fields and lakes. We stop for lunch at a roadside village, and I taste a herbal brew, similar to black tea, that is poured over rice and dry fish and acts as a coolant. We stop, also, for police roadblocks– marital law was imposed months ago- and to see a beautiful, large-eyed black woman sway to Soweto-style music amid a group of villagers.

As night falls, and with the roadblocks still a scary memory- there was every chance I would be hauled away—I realise I am in the safest place, high in the cabin of a huge truck with powerful headlights, driving through a beautiful, wild country. In added assurance, my driver-friend nods towards the Zulu spear that never leaves his side.

Travelling through the night—after a short break at a dhaba -type joint—we near the Mozambique channel and Morondava as dawn breaks. My trucker friends refuse any payment, asking only for a T-shirt. One tee less, I am two friends richer.

Near Morondava, I spot the giant baobab trees and an occasional ostrich farm, alongside the mini-Renault taxis wheezing their way past totem poles and bullock carts. On the coast itself, it's impossible to miss the ancient stoneworks, the dhows bobbing in the Indian Ocean—and Japanese tourists!

But again, I am waylaid by my own concerns—for I have a flight to catch the next morning, and less than 24 hours to make the 600 km journey back! A kind van driver agrees to take me back for half-fare, and soon, I am speeding through the awesome rural landscape—dotted with fortified mud hutments, proud tribesmen, disappearing forests, turtle-hunts—again.

For all the rush, though, I miss my flight to Mauritius. I spend the night at Ivato airport black commandos watching over me. My money has run out almost completely, but I can't resist spending my last few francs on some African musical instruments and ... err, a bar of Malagasy chocolate!

Madagascar is one of the poorest countries in the world, but it's also one of the most unspoilt. It's not as easy place to travel to, but the rewards, I promise, will last much longer than a chocolate bar.

Historical features

Many fact-filled articles dealing with local history can be developed with the assistance of community, historians, historical societies, and the files of every day newspapers. These feature stories serve a real need; while the public can find many books on state and national history, there are few sources outside of newspaper articles for presenting fascinating local history.

The historical feature is useful at certain time of the year. You can write a feature on the country's fight for independence or a personality linked with the national movement, to appear near January 26. If you wish to write on Vivekananda's birthday you can collect facts from his life story, include exciting incidents, perhaps contrast such happenings with something in the modern era.

An example of historical feature is as under:

The Annamalai University, which celebrates its Platinum Jubilee in 2004, has carved a niche for itself in the educational map of the country. This is how A.V. Raghunathan looks at the growth of the institution.

Setting High Standards,

The Hindu,
April 18, 2004.

Thanks to the visionary and philanthropist, Dr. Rajah Sir Annamalai Chettiar, the Annamalai University was established in the temple town of Chidambaram.

The University, which has celebrated many milestones in the field of education, will soon celebrate its Platinum Jubilee, the birth centenary of the second founder Pro-Chancellor Padma Bhushan Dr. Rajah Sir Muthiah Chettiar, and the Silver Jubilee of the Directorate of Distance Education.

The reputation of the institution bears testimony to the services rendered by the founder, Dr. Rajah Sir Annamalai Chettiar, who strove to uplift the rural populace through education, even in the pre-Independence era.

Initially, he founded Sri Minakshi College in 1920, which was later transformed into Annamalai University, in 1929 through passing of the Annamalai University Act. The buildings, hostels and playgrounds of the college served as the nucleus for the formation of the University. Its resources and infrastructure were further augmented by the donation of 300 acres and Rs. 20 lakhs by the founder.

Dr. Rajah Sri Annamalai Chettiar served as the first Pro-Chancellor of the University for two decades, and during his tenure, identified experts in various disciplines and induced them to head the respective departments.

Ever since, the University has carved a niche in the educational map of the country.

The torch was passed on to the founder's eldest son, Dr. Rajah Sir Muthiah Chettiar who took over as Pro-Chancellor in 1948.

He gave new dimensions and directions to the University and expanded the horizons of education by starting new departments of study, particularly agriculture, engineering and technology, commerce, business administration, dentistry and medicine.

Dr. Rajah Sir Muthiah Chettiar sowed the seeds for informal education by establishing the Directorate of Correspondence Courses and Continuing Education in 1979 with the objective of taking education to the doorsteps of the needy. The Directorate of Distance Education, as it is now known, has registered a spectacular growth, with 58 Study Centres under its purview, and over 2,60,000 students on its rolls.

Under the present Pro-Chancellor, Dr. M.A.M. Ramaswamy, who took over in 1984, the University has made rapid strides in all disciplines and grown exponentially.

The University now functions from an extensive area of 1,000 acres, with 48 departments of study, and more than 1,650 teaching staff, 3,950 administrative staff and a student strength of 13,846. In recognition of the quality education being imparted by the University, the National Assessment and Accreditation Council has accorded it the four-Star status.

The Rajah Muthiah Institute of Medical Sciences, comprising the 1050-bed teaching hospital, a dental college and a nursing department is equipped with the state-of-the-art equipment to render efficient health care services to the people particularly the rural poor. The Chettinad family has created an institution that spreads light in the spheres of education, health and social services.

Features on Pets/Calendar events/technical and scientific subjects/ hobbies

Stories involving pets that are unusual because of their breed or how they were trained invariably, produce readable 'human interest' features. The person who has a pet cat or other infrequently domesticated animal or who managed to train a monkey or bird to perform tricks can provide material for a feature.

Calendar events like 'New Year Day,' 'Valentine Day,' 'Children's Day,' Independence Day,' produce ample opportunities to develop features. A feature writer can interview Santa Claus at Christmas or list the resolutions that community leaders make for New Year Day. Almost every week there is an official designation ranging from 'Women's Day' to 'AIDS Day', and features can be tied into the serious or humorous aspects of these occasions.

Technical and scientific features explain in layman's language advances in science and medicines, technology or electronics. Such subjects are projected through features in simple language, so that even a layman can understand the significance of these changes.

Features on hobbies, particularly unusual hobbies, other's hobbies and how one has got interested in a particular hobby is yet another field for a feature writer. The hobbies of well-known retired people in different walks of life may be the interesting subjects of features.

Narrative features

Some observers see the narrative as another category of features, and in its pure form it probably is. It is like a short story, even though it treats material factually, it depicts events unfolding scene by scene, utilizing description, characterization and plot. However, the narrative is also a writing technique that can be used in any of the above categories of features. In such forms as anecdotes and case histories, narratives can be inserted into traditionally structured articles.

Service features

Service features tends to be thought of as 'utility' feature. The main emphasis is on 'how-to-do-it; features on leisure, education, fashion, food, home and garden, child care, family health, financial planning, physical fitness etc. come under this category. Such features are becoming increasingly popular as newspapers strive to get closer to the needs and interests of their readers.

EXCEL IN CBSE –PMT

Students must Strike a balance between Screening and Mains Examination While Preparing for the Entrance Test, Says Avinash Agarwal, Director of AIETS (Counselling cell)

The Times of India,
April 5, 2004.

The pattern for CBSE-PMT has been changed from this year. Negative marking has been increased from 25 percent to 33 percent, alloted time has been increased from 150 minutes to 180 minutes but the biggest change has been introduction of the subjective test. For the first time, the CBSE-PMT examination for admission into Bachelor of Medicine and Bachelor of Surgery or MBBS programme would be conducted at two levels—level I test will be a screening exam and will be objective in nature. Those who qualify the screening exam will only be eligible to appear in the mains examination. The mains examination would be subjective in nature. The gap between the objective which is on April 11 and subjective test which is on May 16 is a little over one month.

Subjective (Mains) and Objective (Screening) Test

In objective tests you are given four options which act as clues and help you to retrieve the knowledge whereas in subjective tests, you have to start thinking from stretch. So, a student requires clarity in fundamentals to tackle subjective questions.

In subjective tests, apart from knowledge of fundamentals what is equally important is to what extent you can reproduce the knowledge. And, the best technique to strengthen expression is by more and more practice.

Studying for the changed pattern

In the changed pattern, screening is only a qualifying exam. It is expected that about 10, 000 students would be short-listed based on their scores in screening exam. So, a very high score in screening exam does not give you any advantage. In order to succeed, the student has to excel in mains examination.

How to prepare for subjective test

The purpose of the subjective examination is to test your ability to think clearly and quickly, to organise relevant information in a coherent manner. For this you need absolute clarity of the subject. But it has been seen that normally students move directly to the formulae and start solving problems. The result, the moment the students faces an application-oriented problem based on the concept he gets struck. This is basically because of lack of proper knowledge of the subject. It is advised that student should follow following steps in order to have proper understanding of concepts and their applications :

- *Basic steps of learning any concept*
- *Understand the background of the concept.* ***Ask following questions :***
- *What is the concept all about?*
- *What does the concept say?*
- *Focus on significance of the concept.*
- *What are the exceptions to this concept?*
- *When and How to apply this concept?*
- *Follow the steps of derivation of the concept.*
- *Try to reproduce concept in your words.*
- *In case of any problem, read and understand the concept again.*
- *Understand the application method of the concept.*
- *Practice questions on the concept. Start from easy and gradually move to difficult ones.*
- *Diagnose the problems and take corrective measures.*

Other things to keep in mind

After mastering the concept and application methods, try to solve the questions on your own. In the beginning write down every step while solving question. Such students start solving the questions by missing the steps and adopting shortcuts. Remember solving the question completely without missing on any details helps in strengthening your understanding of the fundamentals. Always remember subjective exams require recall learning. Carefully figure out the major content areas to learn. Develop a pool of information for each topic. Answering words like 'why,' when,' 'where,' 'how,' 'key characteristics,' 'cause-effect,' and 'examples' for each topic will help to cover the critical information.

Steps in Writing Features

Getting ideas for features

Nobody ever called a news conference to announce a feature story. The first place to look for feature ideas is in the drama of everyday life. Especially look for situations in which ordinary people face extraordinary events. Look for features' story ideas in ordinary conversations. And most important, look for feature ideas inside your own head. It is in your mind that feature stories are discerned. They seldom merely "happen"; rather, they emerge from a writer's ability to see significance in everyday circumstances. Consider connections in events or circumstances that might at first glance seem to have nothing in common. In them a writer might recognize human drama that has meaning for other people.

Getting information

Once you have idea in mind the next step is getting information. This is important, you cannot cover up for lack of information by clever writing or fictionalizing. The success of your story depends on your ability to get significant and lively material. An orderly pattern for doing this comes in the following three steps:

See: See means starting with background reading of news clips and preliminary interviews. You have to get sufficient information to get a clear idea where the story is going—which leads to the second step.
Define: It means the point of the story has now become clear to you. You have gained the slice of the human condition that is to become the focal point of your story. Now your information gathering shifts into the third stage.
Illustrate: Illustrate means that you will find the quotations, the anecdotes, scenes, descriptions, and case histories that support your points. The task

is not forbidding; we do it everyday in conversation. A doctor who says that it has been a rough day in the emergency room may illustrate that point with graphic descriptions of some of the most interesting or bizarre cases.

Above all, a good feature story requires skill and empathy in asking questions. You are usually dealing with ordinary people, not newsmakers. Most of them have never been interviewed before. So the interviewer's job is to make the session seem like ordinary conversation—like friendly neighbours chatting. You'll find a formula for it. However, a University of Nevada professor, LaRue Gilleland, has devised a simple pattern for asking questions that seems uniquely suited to the quest-struggle-outcome nature of the feature story. He calls it GOSS, the letters representing Goals, Obstacles, Solutions, Start.

> *Goals.* What is the person or agency struggling to achieve?
> *Obstacles.* What stands in the way of achievement? What problems exist?
> *Solutions.* What is being done or proposed to surmount the obstacles?
> *Start.* How did it all begin? Understanding beginnings is often helpful in understanding fundamentals. Beginnings often make interesting anecdotal stories in themselves.

If your interviews focus on those elements, you can obtain the material for your feature stories. If you start by having the respondent identify goals, you will learn the direction of that individual's quest. Knowing the obstacles, and how those obstacles were overcome. Will give you the dynamic pattern of the appealing character struggling against obstacles to reach a worthwhile goal. Of course it's not that simple. To show the struggle, you must in your interviews press for graphic detail, particularly specific examples and anecdotes.

Getting anecdotes

You need anecdotes for your feature story, but when you ask for them your sources never can think of any. It is right, one solution may be to avoid stilted, formal kinds of interviews that kind where you have to ask for anecdotes.

Anecdotes are important to writers, for they have a unique ability to illustrate points that are hard to put across any other way. The anecdote, which by definition is a factual storiette that illustrates a point, gives drama to your writing. To a skilled interviewer, anecdotes are not hard to collect.

Following are the few suggestions which may help in your quest for anecdotes:

- Make clear at the start of an interview that you seek, illustrative stories. "I want to talk about your experiences." You might also add, "And what you have learned from them." Avoid using the term "anecdote". People tend to freeze up when pressured to produce one on demand.
- Keep the conversation informal, and tell stories yourself.
- Get anecdotal information via pre-interview research. Often you can get stories by interviewing family, colleagues, and friends of your subject. You can find stories by reading articles about a topic that you plan to discuss.
- Interview for "Crossroads" Fiction writers salt their stories with "Willy wonties": Crossroads where a character facts a crucial decision. Ask the business woman about crucial decisions she has had to make in her climb to success. To quite a dead-end job, perhaps. To fight a boss. To take on a project with a high risk of failure. To pursue a career instead of marriage. Everyone confronts such decisions. When you find an important one, you probe for enough detail to write an anecdotal narrative.
- Make sure you can recognize a good anecdote when you hear one. A newspaper writer, interviewed by a journalism student, reported that he had had the student laughing uproariously at accounts of his blunders as a beginning reporter. But when the reporter read the student's report of the interview he was amazed. Not one of his stories appeared. One good rule is, "Whenever you hear anything that makes you or others laugh, put it into your story, recounting it the same way you heard it. "Maybe you can make the reader laugh, too.

Getting Good Quotes

Like anecdotes, colorful quotations can add zest to your feature story. The quest for them starts with knowing the five variations of quotations commonly used in news and feature stories.

Direct quotations represent word for word what the speaker said, and they are enclosed in quotation marks. Some minor deviations from the exact wording are considered okay by most newspapers, provided the meaning is not changed.

Indirect Quotations represent what the speaker said and more or less the way it was said but with changes. Quotation marks are not used.

Paraphrased Quotations represents what the speaker said but are presented in the writer's words. No attempt is made to preserve the wording of the original statement.

Fragmentary Quotations are combinations of paraphrased and direct quotes. They are especially useful when the speaker has incorporated a few colourful words into an otherwise routine comment.

Dialogue is used when two, or more speakers are quoted in a conversational exchange, such as in a court trial. Dialogue often makes a news article more readable.

Structure of the Feature Story

The feature story offers considerable freedom to the writer, but a structural pattern does exist and should be learned. It is roughly equivalent to that of other forms of communication: a college theme, a speech, an essay. It starts with a central theme or central point. The theme is supported by factual data, quotes, ideas, observations, and so forth, that can be separated into the major supporting sections. The overall pattern of the feature, then, looks like this:

- An opening calculated to gain reader attention and interest, also to indicate what the article is about. Often it is an illustrative anecdote or a descriptive scene to set the stage.
- A general statement of theme in which you orient the reader specifically to what the article is about and perhaps what it means to the reader or how it ties in with some news event or trend. This orientation section some writers call it the "establishing section" or the "nut paragraph" may be brief or it may be explicit, taking several paragraphs.
- Two or more main supporting points for the theme. These are like topic headings for an essay or speech. They comprise the body of the article.
- Your ending should be strong. If your feature is well written, many readers will follow it all the way to the end. Do it with a colourful anecdote, a touch of humour, a worthy quotation, or a food-for-thought comment. Many endings try to tie together with the beginning, so that a question raised in the opening paragraph is answered to the reader's satisfaction in the end.

Although the above pattern fits most features (not always precisely), you will find exceptions. One exception is the narrative, the kind that reads like a short story, depicting a series of incidents involving a central character.

Be careful of narratives.

Like a short story, the non-fiction narrative must have a purpose. That purpose essentially is to make a statement about reality. To do this it must be more than a mere stretch of linear chronology. For instance, you could not tape-record a conversation in your living room, have it transcribed, and expect to publish it as either a short story or a non-fiction narrative. A non-fiction narrative, like a short story, must be a statement by the writer, shown through selection of detail, interpretation, and structure. It must have a central theme supported by documenting points, even if the points come within the narrative.

Exercises

1. How does a feature differs from a news story?
2. Considering the differences between news story writing and feature writing, what qualities a good feature writer have that are not necessarily shared by a good news reporter?
3. Features are said to be beyond reports, something more than them. Prepare a list of articles or proposed features, based on reports which you read in newspapers.
4. Classify the different kinds of feature.
5. What do you understand by feature? How does it differ from an article?
6. What are the points you will keep in mind while writing a feature?

19

EDITORIAL WRITING, BOOK REVIEW AND ART APPRECIATION

No newspaper or periodical is complete without its own articles, editorials, stories, special-subject columns and reviews. They are all opinion pieces. They may be written by member of its staff, received from casual contributors, or commissioned from others by the editor. They are to be distinguished from news stories given by its reporters. All of these need to have a high standard.

The ability to write well covers a vast sphere. It does not necessarily call for literary flourish, but demands material that conveys meaning to those who read it. For whatever purpose anything has to be written, its structure should be such that it conveys definite meaning. Since it involves mental activity, thinking is to be put to words that are written for someone else to read and comprehend.

In all human endeavour it has become important to be able to use written words purposefully, fruitfully and clearly. Language is the means of communicating with others. It is the unseen but definite link between the writer and the reader. Unless it is used effectively, it is futile having vast knowledge, a large vocabulary, and a keen desire to go through life cheerfully.

Though there are some differences—some of them subtle—in editorials, columns and critical reviews, there are some similarities also, let us consider these similarities first:

Opinion piece does not require any formula. The writer need not search desperately for the formula for an editorial, a column, or a critical review; because it does not exist.

Critical comments should be supported. Everyone knows that, in debate, one must give examples to prove a case; yet the most common weakness in opinion writing is the lack of illustrative examples. Too many writers only pronounce opinions. It is never good enough, however, only to state that a governmental or school policy, an actor, a book, a movie, or a ballet is good or bad. Tell why; offer examples. The drama critic who laments that the dialogue is limp, or cheers that it is lively, the editor writer who pontificates on the stupidity or wisdom of legislation—both are writing ineptly when they fail to support their contentions with examples. Not even the most respected editorial writer, columnist, or critic can convince his readers with bald opinion.

An opinion should be a reading experience. Writing opinion pieces in the lifeless form of most informational news stories is a lame excuse for interesting a reader. For effect, new phrases must be coined, sentences must be varied. The writer must demonstrate that he knows that one test of intelligence is the ability to make analogies—to show that this is like that, in a way that the reader who knows one will see the other.

This does not mean that the writer should make his piece a collection of literary pyrotechnics. Any phrase or idea that calls attention to itself and has become worn by years avoid it.

Criticism should begin where the writing begins, it should be woven at the end of a piece.

The word criticism does not imply slurs alone. One may criticize with praise. Perhaps most important, the writer may sneer and praise in a single piece and perhaps most often he should. Few works are entirely good or bad. One aspect will usually outweigh the other, but only in rare instances is there no opportunity to be both negative and positive in some degree. Mature writers often pull up collegiate writers for lack of balance.

An opinion piece must be knitted properly. Ideally, any piece of writing should consist of sentences and paragraphs that are so linked to one another that the perceptive reader has a distinct experience of following a connected line from the first sentence to the last. Most opinion pieces are so short that there is no excuse for a lack of unity. This can be achieved, however, only through careful organization and close attention to transitions which often require rewriting. One who is able to organize and polish his work in a single draft is usually saying little, or saying it poorly. Say something, and say it well. Revising, rewriting, reorganizing, polishing is often essential in producing the kind of work that can be described as all-of-a-piece.

Writing the Editorial

The editorial is the heart of a newspaper. It can make the difference between a publication's success or failure. All readers do not go through the opinion column. It is estimated that only 10 to 15 per cent take interest in it. But, it is claimed, all those who 'matter' read editorials. Although this cannot be really proved, the importance of editorials has to be accepted.

It has been said that the editorial expresses the paper's conscience, courage and convictions. In reality, it becomes the conscience, courage and convictions of the editor.

Who Writes Editorials

Editorials are written by staff members who are senior journalists and have established themselves as men whose opinion counts. They are expected to be abreast of almost all happenings and specialists in some spheres at least. They are written by a team of assistant editors who work under the guidance of the editor. The editor's policies weigh heavily and he decides the type of editorial it should be, its slant and the arguments to be presented.

Defining Editorial

It is the expression of an opinion in concise, logical terms, an interpretation of happenings to make their significance clear to the reader. It can be a combination of facts and opinion, for facts sometimes have to be given to justify opinion.

One of the best definition is offered by M. Lyle Spencer in his book *Editorial Writing*: "An editorial is an expression of fact and opinion in concise, logical, pleasing order for the sake of entertaining, of influencing opinion, or of interpreting significant news in such a way that its importance to the average reader will be clear."

There is a positive personal motivation in writing editorials. Although editorial writers remain anonymous in today's newspapers but their long association with journalism makes them known even without a by line.

Functions of the editorial writer

Editorial writers feel about public affairs and matters concerning people so strongly that they must express themselves. In doing so, they not only try to involve the reader with the issue discussed, but also perform a social role. It is essential for society that they should be allowed to become the conscious of the nation, and monitors of the government.

It has been accepted that editorial writers, in some cases, are the guardians of the freedom in democracy. In many parts of the world, criticism of public affairs spells danger for the opinion writer. It needs to be stressed that democracy can be measured only in terms of the freedom given to journalists.

Bearing this in mind, it would be evident that maturity and long experience in journalistic writing is necessary before such a role can be played. Specialization of study and depth in tackling various subjects are required. Continuous analysis of changing problems is to be encouraged.

Keeping all this in mind the editorial writer must consider his following functions :

- His function is to explain and analyse the news with reference to the prevailing situation.
- He fills in the background with regard to happenings about which people do not know much and suggests ways and means of keeping alive interests and actions regarding the subject.
- He suggests the possible course of action for those in authority as well as the common man.
- His editorials at times carry warnings about the likely results of doing or not doing something. They also call for the development of resources to fight some danger, or to support some cause.
- The editorial writer must present facts honestly, with everything in its proper context, and avoid distorting any situation. He is meant to guide the reader, not mislead him.
- His piece should not be written in order to exert personal influence or to seek favours for himself.

While he should always write according to his convictions, he must be ready to correct himself. A writer who is willing to review his own opinions and honestly expresses changes of view shows intellectual vitality, and keeps his writing alive.

An editorial is not necessarily critical or opinion-forming. Quite often it is simply that commendations have to be made. The activities of people in general and official agencies in particular are not necessarily so black that nothing is worthy of a good word. A newspaper can show a proper balance in its editorial column if it permits praise too?

The editorial should support every action that symbolises democratic principles. It must lend its strength to the freedom of all forms of expression. In doing so, it has to be clear and forthright. If it is to sound a note of caution, the editorial should be categorical and without reservation.

While fulfilling all these functions, the editorial must show an awareness of both sides of a question and not offer unnecessary backing to just one side of it.

These are all praiseworthy functions when they are practiced effectively, but the editorial writers themselves can be heard complaining that the editorial pages are down with a wasting disease. One of the best, Alan Barth of The Washington Post, commented, "Most newspapers were started by men who had something to say, but many of them are carried on today by men who merely have something to sell."

Rules for Editorial Writing

— Always use the pronoun "we" rather than "I", for an editorial. It is not the voice of an individual but of the newspaper itself, an institution.

— Always remember Thoreau"s dictum: "The one great rule of composition is to speak the truth."

Thoreau's principle was amplified extensively in 1949 by the National Conference of Editorial Writers in the adoption of a "Basic Statement of Principles":

Journalism in general, editorial writing in particular, is more than another way of making money. It is a profession devoted to the public welfare and to public service. The chief duty of its practitioners is to provide the information and guidance toward sound judgements which are essential to the healthy functioning of a democracy. Therefore the editorial writer owes it to his integrity and to that of his profession to observe the following injunctions:

— The editorial writer should present facts honestly and fully. It is dishonest and unworthy of him to base an editorial on half-truth. He should never consciously mislead a reader, distort a situation, or place any person in a false light.

— The editorial writer should draw objective conclusions from the stated facts, basing them upon the weight of evidence and upon his considered concept of the greatest good.

— The editorial writer should never be motivated by personal interest, nor use his influence to seek special favours for himself or others. He should hold himself above any possible taint of corruption, whatever its source.

— The editorial writer realizes that he is not infallible. Therefore, so far as it is in his power, he should give a voice to those who disagree with him in a public letters column and by other suitable devices.

— The editorial writer should regularly review his own conclusions in the light of all obtainable information. He should never hesitate to correct them should he find them to be based on previous misconceptions.

The editorial writer should have the courage of well-founded conviction and a democratic philosophy of life. He should never write or publish anything that goes against his conscience. Many editorial pages are the product of more than one mind, however, and sound collective judgement can be achieved only through sound individual judgements. Therefore, thoughtful individual opinions should be respected.

The editorial writer should support his colleagues in their adherence to the highest standards of professional integrity. "His reputation is their reputation, and theirs is his."

Some examples of editorial Writing are as under:

It's Censorship

By H.K. Dua

Over the years, the rigours of the Law of Contempt have prevented the Press and the people from examining the functioning of the judiciary.

The judiciary has also used the Law of Contempt as a shield against public scrutiny and criticism which are essential for its own health.

The Law of Contempt has particularly prevented the Press from reporting a few developments in the Punjab and Haryana High Court that are of vital public interest.

But now another development has taken place which is causing concern to the newspapers in Punjab and Haryana. We thought we should bring it to the notice of the people.

Several responsible newspapers in the region, including The Tribune, have received identical letters from an officer of the Punjab and Haryana High Court which seeks to place restrictions on them in doing their legitimate duty.

The letter written by Mr. M.M. Singh Bedi, Registrar (Judicial)-cum- Public Relations Officer of the Punjab and Haryana High Court, was received on the fax by the Tribune on April 7, 2004.

Mr. M.M.Singh Bedi's letter addressed to the Editor, The Tribune—which he describes as the High Court's Press communique—reads"

"It is understood that some news is going to be published in relation to the affairs of the High Court in the media. I am directed to issue a Press Communique to the Press (sic) that no news pertaining to the administrative affairs of the High Court should be published unless correctness of it is cross-checked from me."

The High Court's Press communique is brief and looks simple in language, but can have implications for the freedom the Press enjoys under the Constitution.

We do not know how Mr Bedi knew what stories the newspapers were likely to carry and what "the affairs" of the Punjab and Haryana High Court were that he was referring to.

Mr. Bedi also does not say under whose authority he has sent the missive to the newspapers. He merely says "he has been directed to" to do so, giving the impression that these are orders of the Punjab and Haryana High Court.

Inquiries made by us show that several judges are not aware of the letter to the newspaper or its contents. Some of them are as surprised as the recipients of this letter were.

Ordinarily, the Registrar (Judicial) functions under the authority of the Chief Justice of the High Court. As such we take it as an order of the Punjab and Haryana High Court.

But more than this, what is of concern to the Press is the High Court's intention behind issuing the Press communique.

Mr. Bedi says in the Press communique that "no news pertaining to the administrative affairs of the High Court should be published unless the correctness of it is cross-checked from me."

We, in The Tribune, and other newspapers are perhaps more concerned about accuracy of our news than Mr. Bedi. Most newspapers strive hard daily to check and counter-check facts before publishing news for the benefit of the public.

If it was just an advisory from Mr. Bedi, we might have taken it as a new-found keenness of the High Court's first-ever Public Relations Officer to show efficiency. But it is not so apparently.

What the High Court's ill-advised communique is trying to ensure is that the Press cannot publish a news about what is happening in the administrative side unless it is cleared by Mr. Bedi, who enjoys the officiating status of Registrar (Judicial)-cum-Public Relations Officer. It is fear of facts that seems to be the cause of the communique.

Essentially, a PRO, is supposed to be of help to the people and the Press, but the High Court's new officer has clearly been directed to assume the role of an authority which would have the power to pre-censor the reports and information which the newspapers are duty-bound to share with the readers on matters of pubic interest.

It is clear from the Press communique that the Punjab and Haryana High Court in its wisdom is trying to impose a kind of censorship—or a news clearing authority—for which it has no power under the Constitution. And nor we think it is proper for the Press to submit to it.

We in the Press will strive for accuracy and Professional values despite the High Court's directive and, if necessary, without the help of its Registrar (Judicial)-cum-Public Relations Officer.

—The Tribune
April 15, 2004

SAARC Pledge

But how to implement is the question

The 12th South Asian Association for Regional Cooperation (SAARC) session that ended at Islamabad on Tuesday was, perhaps, the most hyped in its 20-year history. This was bound to happen as it came in the midst of India and Pakistan making earnest efforts to normalise their bilateral relations through several confidence-building measures. This factor has played a major role in the successful conclusion of the session. For India, the major achievement is the signing of the Additional Protocol to the SAARC Convention on Combating Terrorism, which has been included in the Islamabad Declaration. It should help eliminate the monster of terrorism from the region.

With terrorism threatening peace and stability in South Asia, as also in the rest of the World, efforts to alleviate poverty through increased economic activity and other measures can hardly succeed. The problem, therefore, must get top priority. Terrorism has, in fact, been coming in the way of setting bilateral disputes too. The SAARC members must do everything possible to develop friendly relations among themselves for ensuring smooth implementation of the agreement on the South Asian Free Trade Area (SAFTA) and the social charter for promoting the welfare of the people in the region.

However, the implementation of the pledges made at Islamabad is easier said than done. Prime Minister Zafarullah Khan Jamali of Pakistan has said that his country will extend the necessary cooperation in fighting terrorism. But such assurances in the past were never fulfilled. In fact, cross-border militancy increased in the subcontinent after the signing of the 1987 Convention on Terrorism. The search for a barrier-free trade regime after the signing of the agreement on SAFTA should be easier now. The momentum to achieve this goal must be maintained for the ultimate cause of alleviating poverty in the region. Spurring economic activity, including trade, through the agency of SAARC is in the realm of possibility. After all, there has been considerable increase in the volume of regional trade after SAARC included this core subject in its agenda in 1995. Trade can help SAARC to deliver the goods in other areas too.

—The Tribune
January 7, 2004

In a stunning electoral verdict, the Bharatiya Janata Party (BJP) led National Democratic Alliance (NDA) was voted out of power on 13, May 2004 to pave the way for the return of the Congress party at the helm of the national affairs after eight years in wilderness. This is how the editorials in a different newspapers appeared.

Mr Vajpayee's high ground, Mrs. Gandhi's road ahead

—Shekhar Gupta

It's always so easy to tell loser what he did wrong. But you can't do that to Atal Behari Vajpayee. He packs just too much charm, old-world decency and dignity as also personal popularity and magisterial control over public opinion for you to raise questions like that about him. His party, and his strategists have so cruelly denied him the great trysts with destiny he had scripted if there was to be another term, peace with Pakistan, settlements with China and our own Nagas, even the National Highway programme. That he brought us so far down this road in such testing circumstances is by itself a compliment to one of our tallest leaders. Admiration for him, as young Rahul Gandhi so generously underlined in his post-victory chat with the media on Thursday, cuts across the political divide. It is rare to have a man approaching 80, after six decades in public life, with so many friends and so few enemies. So, let's not speak of him in the past tense. Vajpayee has to contribute even in this Parliament, as the leading voice of the Opposition as well as its most distinguished senior citizen.

The wise man will have his own take on how a leader with such wiped out so comprehensively? Rent-a-quote analysts and pseudo-socialists are out of the woodwork already. They call it the revenge of Bharat on India, the message from the poor to the feel-good classes and so on. The import of this election is more intricate than just that. If it was so simple, how come the greatest beneficiaries of feel-good economics, in South Bombay and New Delhi, the mall-multi-plex crowd in Gurgaon, have voted exactly the same way as the debt-strangled farmer in Vijayawada, the jobless graduate in Hazaribagh? This dramatic verdict is as much about anti-incumbency as about the rising expectations of our voter. As reform pulls more Indians above the poverty line, they are moving the bar of their expectations higher. From roti-kapada our makaan to bijli sadak-paani and then education, health, social dignity and security, quality of life issues. This voter is more unforgiving, demanding, tougher to fool. It would then require something extra-ordinary to blunt his almost compulsive rejection of the incumbent. Vajpayee had it in him to do so. There were times when he rose above his party in the national interest. A pity, the party failed to rise with him and when it went out seeking votes in his name, there was a disconnect. Vajpayee would, therefore, rue the few occasions he allowed pressures from the same party to hold back from what he knew to be morally correct. He stopped short of sacking Narendra Modi and was then forced into that suicidal alliance with Jayalalithaa.

This, however, is in the past. The reality of today and tomorrow is Sonia and her coalition. Even in this heady moment, she would know the meaning of carrying the faith-and-future of a billion people. She wasn't born among them. But she has adopted them as so many of them have accepted her. It's a formidable challenge. While she may do well to learn from her predecessor the art of managing a rainbow coalition, she also has to understand what denied him a place in history that should have been his for the asking. In the national interest, it is not good enough to rise above your party's interest most of the time. You have to do it all the time. The legacy of the family and the party she inherits is both mixed and complex. Her test lies in deciding how much of it to build on, how much to revamp—and how much to bury. The agenda is already formidable, form comforting the markets and writing the budget to picking up the thread with Pakistan and China, figuring out America, a complex world and India's place in it. There is no time to lose. For, if there's one thing Verdict 2004 tells us, it's this: the voter wants to see a better future, not tomorrow or the day after but today.

—Indian Express
May 14, 2004

Get real, Comrades!

Running a government is not like running a trade union. Time to learn from Comrade Deng

If words can destroy this was it. Comrades Bardhan and Yechury of the Left Front have between themselves helped wipe out several thousands crores of wealth of small and big investors with two sentences. One said the stock market can go to hell and the other said the disinvestment ministry will be closed down. The Sensex tumbled over 200 points. Forget what West Bengal Chief Minister Buddhadev Bhattacharya is doing. Forget the lessons CPM leaders may have learnt on their innumerable trips to China. Forget Jyoti Basu's voice of moderation. These guys are breathing old style commie fire. That was the message the markets took. So who'll pick up the tab now? Get real, Comrades. You are now in the real world.

First get real about Verdict 2004. The Congress and BJP share between themselves more than 50 per cent of the popular vote. Both parties have followed a set of economic policies over the past decade that the Left has relentlessly criticised. While the Congress and BJP have had differences on specifics, including on disinvestments, they have both in opposition supported economic bills brought forward by the other in government. Now comes the Left Front with no doubt an impressive surge in its popular vote, but one that is a fraction of the vote share of the Congress and BJP and one that is confined largely to Bengal and Kerala, with some picked up with the help of allies like the Congress in state like Andhra Prdesh. But so puffed up is the Left with its "parliamentary revolution" and a record of 64 MPs, that it thinks it has the mandate to run the entire country! This is the height of presumption. True, such self-importance is aided by the deal-making capabilities of CPM bossman Harkrishan Singh Surjeet. But merely because the likes of Mulayam Singh Yadav, Deve Gowda and Sharad Pawar have appointed Surjeet as their deal maker, does not mean that the Left tail can be presumptuous enough to wag the coalitional policy dog. That too before a common minimum programme has been worked out.

Perhaps some Left leaders think that giving loud and rhetorical speeches would mean no harm since the idea is to keep the comrades happy. But the impact of Bardhan's intemperate out-bursts and Yechury's partisan demand has been destructive for the stock market. Remember, if investors are scared away from India they can go elsewhere. The loss is not theirs but ours. Remember also that stock markets are here to stay. Even Shanghai has one. So there is no point in lecturing about finance capital and the wages of globalisation. This is the real world. A mere 64 MPs are not going to make globalised, market-friendly, capitalist India a Stanlinist cul-de-sac. So, rather than ask the markets to go to hell, it may be a better idea to find out how markets work and why people in power must talk in measured tones so as not to make them needlessly nervous, destroying people's wealth in the process. And, remember, "people in power" means you too, Comrades!

—The Indian Express
May 15, 2004

Right Choice, Baby

Nominated by Sonia, Manmohan will make excellent PM

Manmohan Singh, the man who steered India out of its worst economic crisis ever, will be the next Prime Minister of the country. We expect no major glitches—apart from the howls of some Congress netas anguished by the refusal of Sonia Gandhi to assume power—during his transition from Safdarjung Road to 7, Race Course Road, the PM's official residence. Congress's ally, the Left, which used to sneer at Singh by calling him 'McMohan' in the early days of reform, were the first to state that they had no reservations if he got the top job. All other allied parties have accepted him as well. There are many reasons why the good doctor is so widely accepted- and admired. First, he's a person of impeccable, personal integrity. Even the harshest critics of Singh's reform programme have never said anything nasty about the person implementing them. Two, he has always been a thorough professional, carrying out his mandate—whether it's teaching, advising government, running the RBI, making policy or simply setting the economic goal posts of an out-of-power Congress with best intentions. Three, he's a graceful person, not flashy or abrasive. That understated image hides a lot of resolve. Singh has always stood up for his convictions: Before he accepted the top job at the finance ministry, he wanted—and got—an assurance from prime minister Rao that he would work with no interference. Finally, singh is refreshingly free of dogma, facing up to reality and its compulsions with the clear analytical skills of a trained economist with years of professional experience behind him. This is what helped him move effortlessly from the Planning Commision in Geneva, to spearheading reforms that swapped state control for markets.

Suddenly, Manmohan Singh finds himself in the same situation as June 1991: Being asked by the leader of Congress to take over a huge assignment. Will he demand—as he did earlier—freedom from unnecessary interference? Will he get it? Sonia Gandhi has shown herself to be an exceptional leader, one who led her comatose party to electoral victory, was offered power and turned it down. In the process her stature has soared. Sonia Gandhi is no longer boss of a political party, not a minister or ever learning to look at with awe and admiration. Given that, Prime Minister Singh can expect the independence he needs to function efficiently. There can be moral guidance and—at least in the early days- support. But there won't be any remote control.

—The Times of India
May 20, 2004

WRITING THE COLUMN

Walter Lippman, who was probably the most distinguished "think- piece" columnist in the history of American journalism noted, "No doubt because I started life in the newspaper business as an editorial writer, I always think of a columnist as primarily a writer of signed editorials. There are differences, of course. But even if the two jobs are not identical twins, they are certainly near cousins."*

Lippman's chief concern as a columnist was public affairs, and it was not surprising he saw a close kinship between the kind of column he wrote and editorials, most of which were concerned with similar issues. In fact, many of the columns on public affairs—including most of those written by Lippmann, would fit comfortably into some newspapers in the space given over to editorials. In tone and substance some columns were indistinguishable from well-written editorials. The editorial—page editor only would find it necessary only to remove the bylines and substitute the editorial "We" for "I".

The column writer expresses his personal opinion on a subject in a column. The writer has a fixed style of writing, and he generally writes on fixed subjects and has fixed point of view. However, there are columns in a newspaper where other persons also contribute. Columns are on political, economic or cultural subjects or on sports, radio, films, books, humour etc. Generally, columnists write once a week though there is no fixed rule about its frequency. Many columns appear on the fixed day and on particular place.

* National Conference of Editorial Writers, Basic Statement of Principles, mimeograph, October 22, 1949.

Columns are so various that the bright young journalist who thinks he is developing a new one is almost certain to discover that his idea was not original. A single large syndicate may offer newspapers a number of columns on different subjects ranging from religion to gardening. In India number of syndicates are working which sell columns and features to newspapers on payment. Some columns are stimulatingly written, but, in general, expertise is presented in most specialized columns.

Some examples of column writings:

The Amarinder Diet

You can't be Serious

George? Hi, it's me, Amarinder. Must be about lunchtime there, I guess. Yeah, it's just after 11 here so the phone rates are half. What with the parliamentary election campaign on these days I'm trying to economise.

Naa-ah, nothing special. It's been tough the last couple days and I just felt like talking to some-one who understands. You must have read about the karsewa at our Golden Temple. Yeah ... huge mobilization, lot of potential. Unfortunately, due to some historical circumstances, my opposition party can get away with behaving like they own the place. They hogged karseva on Day One—I knew they would but I thought okay, I'll go in toward the end and sort of have the last laugh. My Intelligence guys told me it would carry on for a week. Man, talk about bad briefings.

People swarmed the place like ants on a biscuit. Okay, so on Wednesday I got a picture of me with a silver basin on my head in all the papers but everybody knew the last tola of mud had been scraped out of the sarovar three days previously. I just hope nobody finds out my flunkies went all the way to Chheherta to find some mud for my basin.

Then more bad luck. One of my rival party's two big cats went down with a heart attack just after karseva and copper it a week later. The old guy had also run the Golden Temple Managing Committee for 30 years. Strictly speaking it's not a political organisation. This dead lion was too valuable to let my opponents have him all to themselves. So I declared a state funeral, flags at half mast for five days, stuff for the widow ... and me and the missus did our best to look like the chief mourners. I couldn't do anything else; I had to cut in on the obsequies ... but given our complicated past I couldn't really pull it off either.

As if that weren't enough, the High Court quashed my liquor auctions and it's giving me grief over DSP appointments. I'm the one who's going to take a beating because of the stupidity of the Amritsar cops at Manawala kisan agitation and then I got more cop trouble over IPS cadre mismanagement. I hope I'm not boring you.

You know the last Congress chief minister to really have a solid grip here was Zail Singh. You're a bit like him. How? Let me put this as delicately as I can ... the biggest idiots in the world are those who think politicians need intellect. I guess that's why I'm calling you. I want your gut feeling this ... what should I do?

Start a war on terrorism? Hmmmmm .... there's a problem with that in my case. You see unless you count Ajit Singh Phoola, all the terrorists I have to deal with are in my own party. My deputy chief minister is doing her damnedest to scuttle my wife's campaign in Patiala. Manish Tiwari is not going to get out of Ludhiana alive if the local unit has its way and as far as I'm concerned Brar is a four-letter word.

The only handle I've got on any of them is I can threaten to come and campaign on their behalf. They'll do anything to avoid being seen with me. I told them that as soon as the high command finalises all the candidates, the campaign will pick up momentum and they said that's what happens when your're rolling downhill.

It's got so bad that a slimming parlour in Jalandhar is attracting customers with what they call the Amarinder Diet. The ad says: 'no matter what you do, you'll go on losing, losing, losing."

Okay, okay ... thanks a lot and good luck to you too. Talk to you again soon.

—Dona Suri
The Hindustan Times
April 4, 2004

Dil Jeet Lo

Funny, but Hindi film titles over the years have always managed to tap into the nation, and get the mood just right. However, this is the one time our film-makers have slipped up—leaving the prime ministerji to fill the gap. His advice to the boys currently playing in Pakistan is priceless. In fact it is so amazing that only a poet could have come up with it. Since cricket coaches and managers are not given to verse, their briefings to the team always remain at a mundane, pedestrian level (work on that swing, more spin, boys, more spin). It needed an Atalji to capture the asli sentiment of the Indo-Pak series. Instructed the PM: 'Dil Jeet Lo.' Simple, direct, emotional.

When I first heard it (out of context, I might add), I thought Atalji had sacked his ad agency and decided to become a copywriter himself. 'Dil Jeet Lo' is a far more powerful slogan than any of the tepid lines penned by the professionals. 'Garibi Hatao' has been a joke for decades. And 'India Shining' to me, sounds like a boot polish commercial. Enough has been written about the feel-good factor (which, to some, sounds alarmingly like a condom promotion). 'Dil Jeet Lo,' on the other hand, is fundamentally sound, to- the- point, and charmingly basic.

'Jeet' the word, has a straightforward, sentimental appeal. Everyone wants to win Everyone. Have you ever met a human being who says, "Hey, guess what, I want to lose!" It's all about winning—a war, an election, a match. 'Jeeto, India, Jeeto,' may sound a bit too childish, but it works!

So much for the neat slogan. Atalji should convince Team BJP that winning hearts is not at all that easy. Today's voter wants results and tangible benefits. A younger India was a naive India, where sentimentality ruled. Euphoria over its freshly-minted freedom made the voter slightly gooey with the thrill of it all—nobody knew what to expect or ask for. Today's voter is like a sharp investor looking for big returns. The heart may be in the right place, but so is the mind. To win this creature over, Atalji's Boys will need to unroll more than mere mush.

So far, the BJP strategists have thankfully not fallen for the line of least resistance and roped in bikini bimbos from Bollywood. That's one bobby-trap voters are not going to fall into no matter what the Congresswallas believe. Eye-candy is one thing, vote-magnets another. Sure, villagers will come and gawk. Men will ogle. Women will giggle. And the starlets will laugh all the way to the bank. But to convert dils into votes, it's going to take a lot more than parading assorted hotties at obscure rallies. Even an illiterate voter knows the difference between a beauty pageant/skin show and a campaign pitch.

Former cricket greats are talking about our boys choking in the finals and lacking that all-important killer instinct. Our captain is busy issuing smart quotable quotes about pulling the chain on the Rawalpindi Express. All this makes for great television and the media gobbles up each utterance greedily. But as the series (and the election campaign) heats up, we shall definitely remember Rajiv Gandhi's immortal words: "Hum jeetengey ya losengey" and chuckle a little, just to give ourselves a respite from the unbearable tension.

There is little difference between winning a local voter's dil and wooing the neighbour. If the attitude is honest, honourable and positive, anything is possible. As I write this, the Karachi One Day match has begun. A few hours from now we shall know whether India is still shining. And how good the feel good factor has been so far. Meanwhile, I sincerely hope and pray that after the Indo-Pak series, no film-maker will be inspired to remake an old tear-jerker titled, Dil diya, dard liya, I would rather wait for Dil ki Jeet. Or just plain Jeet, thank you.

The well known writer and journalist Mr. *Khushwant Singh* is also a popular columnist. His column, *with Malicē towards One and All* in the *Hindustan Times* and *This above All* is syndicated widely throughout the country.

Manmohan, my man!

—Khushwant Singh

When pondering over Sonia Gandhi's refusal to become PM and her choice of Manmohan Singh, we must bear a few things in mind. First, that the Congress owes its triumph over the BJP and its allies to Sonia. But for her whirlwind tour across the dusty heartland of Bharat, the outcome would almost certainly have been different. Only one who was 100 percent Indian could have carried the Indian masses with her.

The drubbing she gave to her opponents brought the worst aspects of their character in some of her detractors. Uma Bharti and Govindacharya played their naatak to the chavvani class (the cheapest four anna tickets in cinemas of yore). I did not expect any better of them. But I expected better behaviour from Sushma Swaraj whom I respect for her ability. Her histrionics were a great letdown. Did not she realise that by keeping Sonia Gandhi out of running for the post of PM, she was only strengthening the Congress? I also expected, Atal Bihari Vajpayee, as great a gentleman-statesman as India has known, to put an end to the nonsense. As in the past, he allowed his party-men to say nasty things and spoil his gentlemanly image.

I am, of course, delighted by Sonia's choice of Manmohan Singh to be the numero uno. We are all aware that he has no mass base. He had to be elected from Assam to enter the Rajya Sabha. Sooner or later he will have to find a constituency to elect him to the Lok Sabha. He is not a politician but a far-sighted administrator.

He has held many high positions – chief economic advisor, secretary, ministry of finance, governor of Reserve Bank, deputy chairman Planning Commission, chairman UGC, and finance minister. Before all that he had been a professor of econimics. And before that a topper in every class from school days to college in Oxford and Cambridge. He is essentially an academic of a professorial temperament.

It is difficult to fore-see what sort of PM he will make. There will be pressures from political parties and industrial houses. There will be favour seekers fawning over him to be made this or that. There will be sycophants, the worst enemies of everyone in power, who will keep filling his ears with flattery. From the little I know of him, he is not likely to succumb to any of them.

I have yet to meet another man who combined in him a brilliant mind with self-effacing modesty. I never heard him talk of himself or his achievements. Most of this comes from his religious upbringing. Over and over again the Gurbani emphasises that the worst enemy of every human is humain – 'I am' or the ego. One has to fight it with one's own will power. Humain deerag rog hai/Daaroo thi iss mahein (The ego is a foul disease, its cure is also in it.) Manmohan has no ego problems.

I have had some experience of his impeccable integrity when he stood for parliamentary elections from South Delhi. Despite my reservations against the Congress for its involvement in the 1984 killing of Sikhs, I went out of my way to support him. A couple of days before the polling, a relation of him came to see me and told me they had no money to hire buses or two wheelers to take voters to polling booths. I gave him some. A few days after the results were announced and Manmohan had lost, he rang me up and dropped in. He handed back the bagful of currency notes to me saying, "I didn't know you had given this, please take it back." How many Indian politicians today would do that?

There will be some fringe benefits in having Manmohan Singh as PM. It could take away some lingering bitterness of the experience of November 1984 from the mind of the Sikhs. It will forever silence communal minded Sikhs who accused the government for never trusting a Sikh to become a chief of the army staff. Now chiefs of army staff will be saluting a Sikh PM, as they did to the Sikh President Zail Singh. Incidentally both men owed their elevations to the Congress.

On the lighter side I look forward to a new brand of Sardarji jokes following Manmohan Singh's prime ministership. So far they have been the butt of humour as a simple-minded naïve community. Though Zail Singh himself was a man of great wit, his lack of sophistication was grist to the mill of Sardarji baiters. They will find it impossible to pick on Manmohan Singh as a Sardarji stereotype. All said and done, his promotion to the top position does fulfil the prophesy of the Gurus repeated at the end of every Sikh prayer: Raaj Karega Khalsa (The Khalsa shall rule.) Not with the kirpan though, but with a ball point pen.

Arresting conversation

Prisoner: *"Sir, please take this Rs. 1,000 and let me go."*
Inspector: *"But first tell me for what crime have you been arrested."*
Prisoner: *"For trying to bribe a police officer, sir."*
(Contributed by Rajeswari Singh, Delhi)

MIDDLE

A write-up that generally appears at the centre on the editorial page below the 'article' and above the 'letters to the editor' in a newspaper is known as 'middle'. It is so called in journalistic parlance because of its middle position between the two different types of opinion pieces on the same page.

The 'middle' is usually a humorous, entertaining and crisply written piece, a satire, an unusual experience or a personality sketch. It may either deal with an off-beat or a topical subject or attempt to expose or ridicule certain policy, programmer, activity or bring to public gaze some grievance or inconvenience. In all these cases, the 'middle' is written in lighter vein, so as to make it an interesting reading and provide entertainment to the readers.

The selection of topic, general approach, treatment, style, etc. followed in the 'middle' are akin to feature writing. Such compositions, as a rule, do not have much of statistics or documentation or scholarly or soberly treatment of the subject as is generally found in an article. It is also shorter in length as compared to an article. The language is simple but effective with small sentences. The focus or the thrust is always on specific aspect or on single point.

The success of the 'middle' lies in its holding the interest of the readers from the beginning to the end. 'Middle' is generally written by experienced people who have imagination and observation, and have developed necessary expertise by constant practice, over a period of time, in this type of writing. Some of the 'middles' as appeared in the newspapers are reproduced here.

Some examples of *Middle* are as under:

Fixing the 'Policket'!

by Vepa Rao

If India and Pakistan can play cricket for promoting cordial atmosphere, why not the BJP and the Congress in the present vitiated atmosphere of electioneering? My friend Dallabhai, a man who had made a fortune during natural calamities, was lit up with excitement. He roped me in as the sole umpire, since I had no political affiliations and diligently abstained from voting in Lok Sabha elections. He persuaded a retired judge to be the match Referee.

This cricket match had different rules. The batsmen wore pure white dresses. The body-line bowlers used colour-soaked balls. Strangely it's the bowlers who scored runs by getting past the opponents' bats and hitting them on the body or the white dress—bigger the dirty marks, more the runs. Batsmen got no runs but would be out like in ordinary matches to catches etc. Each side would play 30 overs.

This combo of politics and cricket was named "POLICKET", Dallabhai announced at the press conference.

Mr Narendra Modi was the natural choice as captain of the BJP team, while Mr Kapil Sibbal led the Congress team.

The latter won the toss but offered the choice to the former "as a goodwill gesture". The two hugged and garlanded each other. While each other, while spectators cheered their sportsman spirit lustily.

Modi chose to open the bowling. His balls rose sharply and hit the Congress batswoman on her white saree. He pulled out his cell phone and told a reporter: "Read the designs made by my orange balls—don't they look like a driver and a clerk? The Congress leaders are unfit for even these jobs".

Another batsman retaliated in the next over. He hit the ball hard at an old fielder's knee-joints. "Your old leaders who had betrayed the freedom movement should leave the field," he bellowed.

"Those of you wearing foreign dresses and wielding foreign bats should be out of the match" shouted Mr Modi and looked at me. I passed the buck to the Refree who decided that this argument came too late in this match.

I intervened to pacify all the parties concerned. Mr. Modi admitted that he had said it all "in the heat of the election campaign." A Congress batsman requested him not to behave like an "unbridled horse." They all smiled, hugged each other warmly and told the media about their mutual respect and their faith "in our great democracy." The ultimate winners in all this, they proclaimed, were the "intelligent and wonderful voters of this country."

A midnight knock woke me up. A seedy looking chap, Dallabhai's agent, handed me a packet: Sir, your commission in fixing the match..."

—The Tribune
April 15, 2004

The Politics of flinging things

Dilip D'Souza

In February 2001, this writer spent a week working in a Kutch village that was ravaged by the enormous Republic Day earthquake. It was a strange experience: Sad, because of the destruction and the numbering stories of tragedy, yet uplifting because of the commitment, enthusiasm and self-lessness of innumerable volunteers from all over the country. There were also several wrenching moments, and those came from watching how some relief efforts were being carried out.

On the highway in the flattened town of Bhachau, a large truck drove past, followed by a mob that was reaching, grasping, pleading as it ran. For on top were three men, flinging packets of Gluco biscuits overboard, causing already desperate victims of a calamity to snarl and fight over them. Over biscuits! In Shikarpur, a team on another truck was simply tossing old clothes into a sea of outstretched arms.

Not a thought given as to who got what, to the piles of discarded old clothes all over, to the meaning of this unfeeling act. After a few seconds of watching this, the degradation of the spectacle hit home. So I waded through the crowd, screaming at the team: "What are you doing?" They shrugged and went on tossing their stuff. At my shoulder, a man turned and said, "Why are you bothering? After this quake, we have become like animals."

Why these three-year-old memories? because of the news from Lucknow. A "birthday celebration" for BJP chieftain Lalji Tandon, a function to distribute saris to "poor" women. Without being there, it is easy to imagine the prevailing scene: The same sea of outstretched arms, like those at that Kutch village, saris flung at them instead of biscuits. Sure enough: The witnesses reported that the organisers "threw saris into the apporximately 5000—strong crowd of poor women crammed into a small park." Should we then be surprised at the resulting stampeded killing 22 women?

Why must people be treated this way? Earthquake victims, riot victims, even "poor" people? Pleading for and fighting over pitiful handouts, people turn into beggars, become animals. They get trampled to death. And yet, horrible as all this is, the truly ghastly aspect lies elsewhere: In those doing the handing out. They are applauded for apparently being well-meaning. Yet how destructive their attitude is of a thing like self-respect. How destructive of life?

The attitude that says you "serve the poor" by giving them stuff—too often, by throwing the stuff at them. The attitude that assumes victims of great calamities are, by definition, poor—and so need stuff flung at them. The attitude that presumes doing such things is good, and thus an appropriate way to mark a birthday. It's that attitude that killed the women in Lucknow.

We might have a fat catalogue of famous name cars for sale, or BPO operations mushrooming all over the country, or double-digit growth rates based on extrapolating from a monsoon-drenched quarter. All components of the India Shining we've heard so much about. But somewhere inside, each of us knows: Stand up anywhere and announce that you are distributing free saris—free anything, and you don't even need a birthday—and you will immediately attract a crowd. It will inevitably turn into a free-for-all. You can safely expect that some will be injured, some even killed.

And this will keep happening: as long as we have politicians arrogant enough to believe that their birthdays are best celebrated—their political prospects best improved—by distributing freebies. As long as they profess that this is service to the poor. As long as there are Indians desperate enough to stretch out hands. In the very act of gathering the "poor" and throwing things at them, whether in Bhachau or Lucknow, is an Indian reality; a commentary on the way we are. That reality shows up "India Shining" for the election gimmick it is, a slogan no less empty that "Garibi Hatao" was.

After all, it's been a generation since a prime minister used that last slogan to attract votes. The Lucknow tragedy tells us, if we needed to be told, that the garibi has by no means been hatao-ed. Remember that when you vote today, and in the next few days.

Chivalry is not yet dead

by Bhup Singh

It is the duty of the President's Military staff to organise and conduct all functions at Rashtrapati Bhavan, for which Standard Operating

Procedures (SOPs) are laid down and meticulously followed. Since the Military Secretary is always responsible to conduct the President, it devolves on his deputy to conduct the visiting Heads of States/ Governments and our own Prime Minister whenever anyone of them visits the Bhavan.

I received Mrs. Indira Gandhi near the President's study and she noticed that the Gianiji was already on his way to the State Room. She just took off, ran and overtook the President to be just in time to receive him at the venue. This sort of situation was a frequent happening as Gianiji would ask: "Time to ho gaya; Indiraji aaye ne kya"? (it's time for the function, has Indiraji come? and then he would say "Aapaan chalde haan" (let's go); without waiting for an answer.

"Please get some carpets put in the corridor; otherwise I am likely to break my bones running here", said Madam Prime Minister on one occasion. "Yes madam," I had replied, "We would not let you be hurt, even if you had a slip", which, I knew, was a distinct possibility with her pencil heels. She gave me a lingering look and smiled. She had a very canny smile to convey different things at different times. "Colonel; if I do slip, there is no way I escape hurting myself; as one cannot order it away even if one is in smart military uniform", she said.

"Aapaan chalde haan" (let's go) happened again within a fortnight. She was cheerful and smiling as I received her. She noticed Gianiji being escorted about 50 steps ahead of us and just about to enter the State Room. We just ran.

"Please ensure that I do not get hurt if I slip" was writ large on her face. Pencil heel slipped; and she was already half in the air when I grabbed her; and we both landed on the marble. She just missed hitting the side wall. Dazed, she got up first as I had not let her touch the marble at all; and then I got up. We quickly checked our clothes. Fortunately there was not a soul in the corridor in accordance with the SOP. "Please do not mention it to the President, he would be unnecessarily worried and I am perfectly fine: she said. "Yes of course, madam", I replied.

She apologised to the President for being late by two minutes. Function over; I escorted her back to the car, now, of course, walking slowly down the corridor. She did notice the round shaped carpets placed at three most slippery spots and smiled back. As we approached the car; she gave me a big pat—almost a hug—and shook me by the hand with a "thank you very much indeed", which left me perplexed and her PS and PSO both looking at me wonder-struck.

As she entered the car and asked for the extra cushions always carried for her by her PS; she turned to me and said; "Colonel, I am extremely happy to see that the chivalry is not yet dead". A broad smile was writ large on her majestic face, as I stood at attention bowing to her and she waved me a goodbye.

—The Tribune
May 22, 2004

Shape of Laloo trains to come

by Amar Chandel

Encouraged by the success of the kulhar experiment, Rail Mantri Laloo Prasad Yadav is believed to be toying with the idea of bringing about several other revolutionary changes.

Senior railway officials have been told to explore the possibility of removing all engines and pulling trains with the help of bullocks instead. This will give employment to thousand of bulls and their keepers. Fodder for the animals will be provided by the Rail Mantri himself.

To save precious foreign exchange, railway coaches will be made in Chapra with the help of mud and cow-dung. There will be no berths. Everyone will sit and sleep on the floor. Instead of the present capacity of 74, each of the 21st coaches will accommodate 740 passengers, plus 1,480 on the roof.

These coaches will be lit by diyas and lanterns, thus helping the cottage industry. Since there will be no ACs or fans, windows and doors will be dispensed with and passengers will enjoy invigorating fresh air. First class passengers will be provided manual ceiling pankhas with one end of the rope tied to their toes which they will operate themselves.

Pantries are also likely to undergo a change. Food will be cooked on chulhas and angithis. Everyone will eat daal, bhaat and gur laid out on banana leaves while sitting on the floor. Those desirous of fast food can cook their own khichri.

It is Rail Mantralaya's endeavour to provide all services in-house. Besides, mineral water, the department will also bottle mahuwa, taadi and bhang beverages.

To tackle the menace of ticketless travel in Lalooji's home state, all Biharis will be issued lifetime railway passes. Ticket checkers thus relieved will do social service at I Anne Marg.

The Railways will discontinue the publication of timetables. It is wasteful to spend so much money on them just because a handful of elite, educated people can calculate how much a train is running late.

An exercise is also on to find whether railway stations can be dispensed with altogether. Passengers will be free to pull chain wherever they have to get down or board a train, as is the custom in Bihar. This will fulfil Lalooji's dream of bringing trains to "aam Admis" doorstep.

Superfluous rail zones made by previous Railway Ministers will be abolished. The entire country will be divided into just two zones. Both will have headquarters in Patna – one at the house of Laloo Yadav and the other at that of Sadhu Yadav. Another successful Bihar model is sought to be tried out all over the country. Since the state has eradicated metalled roads, experiments are being carried out to find out whether it is at all necessary to run trains on tracks. Efforts are simultaneously made to identify persons to whom sleepers and girders thus freed can be sold as scrap.

To make sure that reforms are implemented promptly, the Rail Mantri will travel in trains incognito, disguised as Hema Malini.

LETTER TO THE EDITOR

The letter to the editor is a sort of feedback for the paper. In a letter to the editor, the individual expresses his personal opinion or grievance on a specific subject of his interest or offers a suggestion to overcome the difficulty. Letters to the editor may also pertain to petty complaints. Such letters can be effective if they deal with a specific point and advance logical arguments. They should not indulge in abuse or deal the subject-matter in a roundabout way. They are generally brief in length and are intended to make a point or counterpoint. In some cases, the letters are written in a very forceful style and make great impact on the readers.

A few examples of Letter to the Editor are as under:

Censorship is nothing but tyranny

In utter disbelief and stunned silence, we read H.K. Dua's front-page editorial "it's censorship" (April 15). While studying for the Bar at the Inns of Court School of Law in London in 1976, we had a Visiting Professor from Oxford to lecture us on Constitution. Comparing Constitution and Judiciary in the world, he commended the system that obtains in India. In particular, he cited the Supreme Court case pronounced by Justice Mehar Chand Mahajan. The very next day, Indira Gandhi declared Emergency. The Professor regretted the decision. There was no flood, famine or war. Raising his hands in despair, he declared

"God save India". Forget politics, we all know she did. Not only was the party in power routed but she lost her own seat in the elections.

Censorship is nothing but tyranny. It is enemy to freedom. It is quite extraordinary that a communique be addressed to a responsible daily like The Tribune in the mode and manner it allegedly has been done. Coming from the Punjab and Haryana High Court, claiming directions from the High Court, it indeed is a serious matter.

—Karam Chand
Barrister, Chandigarh
The Tribune
April 22,2004

If the Taj Mahal is the *seventh wonder of the world, our politicians and bureaucrats are the eighth. Constrained by the vote bank, they are doing nothing to protect the Taj from pollution. A concrete jungle in the name of development is an idea that is bound to create chaos. Instead of beautifying our heritage site and preventing its decay, they are complicating the matter. We cannot neglect the seventh wonder but let us try to change the eighth.*

—Neelam Bhatia, Delhi
India Today,
July 21,2003.

A grass-roots revolt

Andhra Pradesh's Assembly poll results prove the voters needn't be intellectuals to assess a government's performance or oust it. They have shown they cannot be taken for granted, or fooled by promises. Should their basic expectations not be met, they can teach a lesson to political rulers.

Naidu, the TDP's "IT-savvy CM" must have imagined that putting Hyderabad on the world map, honouring foreign dignitaries and IT-techies would get him the peoples admiration and get him re-elected. But, Andhra's people showed him the 'Exit'. The "hero of MNCs" ignored the plight of drought-hit farmers while his administration ignored basic rural needs and the common man. Naidu fails to read their pulse right.

True, Naidu did pioneer AP's IT revolution and did a competent job in pushing Hyderabad's industry, making the world notice the once-backward state. But people were unconvinced; the real sufferers during the TDP regime were farmers and youth.

Governments wanting to get re-elected in this age of "perform or perish" must meet peoples expectations.

—The Economic Times
May 14, 2004
S Krishna Kumar
By e-mail, May 1

Our Bahu After All

Why such noise over the foreign origin of Sonia Gandhi? Former Lok Sabha Speaker Sangma accepts her son Rahul but swears to resign if Sonia becomes the PM. The Prime Minister is keen to hold a debate on the issue of people of foreign origin itself. Kalpana Chawla marries a Frenchmen and achieves excellence in aeronautical engineering. We declare that she is the daughter of Punjab (and hence India). Agnes Xonxha Bojaxhieu comes from Skopje in Macedonia and serves the poorest of the poor in Kolkata. She is accepted as an Indian and respected as Mother Teresa. Sonia is an Indian citizen, though born in Italy, and yet she is dubbed a foreigner. Although, as a bahu, she has the right to vote, her political activities are under vicious attack lest she becomes the PM. Was sita not a foreigner in Ayodhya? As a bahu, she was thrown out to stay with Rishi Balmiki. Her fault was that she was a distrusted bahu. What kind of civil rights are we promoting in India against our bahus?

—Surjeet Singh, Mohali
The Times of India
April 7, 2004

Ayodhya

If we want to know how not to build a temple, we can take a lesson or two from the VHP. Its recent adventure in Ayodhya, seen clearly as an attempt to disrupt law and order, was easily foiled by a determined government in U.P. which took a "stern but tactful stand" with support from the Central government. There was hardly a ripple in the rest of India ("A flop show in Ayodhya," November 7).

For nearly a decade the VHP has been tilting at the windmill in the name of building a temple at the exact site where a mosque stood before it was torn down in full view of the media world-wide. The first lesson the VP can and ought to learn now is that there is no way it can built a temple on the basis of 'belligerent piety'. According to a section of orthodox and truly pious Hindus, Rama himself may not want a temple for Him to be built on a foundation drenched in blood. We are no more living in medieval times. The second lesson the VHP ought to learn is that there is no question of pursuing the legislative route "that will circumvent the judicial process"—to build a temple in a country with a secular Constitution. A secular government has nothing to do woth matters of individual faith. Ashok Singhal's rhetoric that "secularisation is the biggest enemy of the nation" has run out of steam.

What the VHP should do now is to deflate its ego, badly injured already, and await the verdict of the High Court. Alternatively, as the Prime Minister of India has suggested, it should come to terms with the minority community and seek as consensus, "a peaceful way through negotiations."

—Kangayam R. Rangaswamy
Winconsin, U.S.
Frontline
November 21, 2003

Verdict 2004

"Sir,—I refer to the editorial "The meaning of Verdict 2004" (May 14). The repeatedly disappointed yet patient common man of India has time and again clearly and decisively expressed what he wants from elected governments. The verdict in favour of the Left in many places is highly significant in the context of privatisation, globalisation and hitech policies of the Congress and the NDA Governments.

It is again unwisely being construed that the electorate has chosen the Congress alliance to 'rule' the country. One should not forget that the Congress lost in most of the States where it was 'ruling'. As rightly suggested in the editorial, the new Government should address the livelihood concerns of the people.

—K.V. Ramana Rao,
Hyderabad
The Hindu
May 15, 2004

ARTICLE

An article is an elaborate piece of composition written on some broad subject, well-documented, and expressed. Unlike features, the subject of the article is not very narrow, specific or minute. The article is generally written in sober style, and the subject-matter is treated in a scholarly manner. The general characteristics and difference between an article and a feature have been discussed in the chapter: Feature Writing.

A few examples of article:

The Left should have been kept out

By J.L. Gupta

Should the Congress have accepted the cooperation offered by the Communist parties? Or should the leftists have been left out? Whatever may have been the numerical options or even political compulsions, the Congress and its allies should not depend upon the people who have fought against them in the states of West Bengal and Kerala. They should not rely upon those who have shown reluctance to be a part of the government. But the leftists claim that they want to support from outside. Should the Congress and its allies, who claim to have fought on principle, succumb to the temptation and act on interest? I think not.

There are good reasons for the Congress to remain away from the communists. Forgetting the alphabetical proximity, the two have very little in common. The election manifestos of the two parties clearly show that there is no mutual admiration or respect. Ideologically they do not have much in common. And from a purely practical viewpoint, such a marriage of convenience is not likely to last for long. More than all this, it is not likely to promote the national interest.

The last few months had shown an upward trend in the share market. It was symbolic of economic advancement. The money was flowing into the Indian companies. From the native and foreign investors. This held promise of health and hope for the national economy. And as the leftists showed their inclination to support the Congress, a picture of uncertainty appeared and there was an unprecedented fall. The investors had lost substantially. The facts were reported in the media. The picture was of concern in all quarters. Yet, the leftists refused to keep quiet. If at all, they only added fuel to the fire by suggesting that there was manipulation. Are the coming events not casting a dark shadow? Can such an ally be an asset to the Congress or the nation?

Secondly, the performance of the Left leaves a lot to desire. There are two states in India where the Left has been in power. The states of West Bengal and Kerala. Let us see the situation in West Bengal first.

An acquaintance of mine was once posted in this state. After a few years we had met and talked. He narrated his experience. He said, "The state had all the industry. It could grow. But the people showed no willingness to work. They seem to believe that the rest of the country owes them a living. So the units have shifted or are going to do so. The state is suffering." Obviously, the policies and the style of functioning have been a red herring to the industrial advancement.

Then the state of Kerala. It has all that a man may ask for. Fertile land. Flora and Fauna. Cashew, coconut and coir. Forests. Rubber, Sea food, Spices, Forty two rivers irrigate its fields. The sea washes its shores. Sandalwood lends scent to its air. Its people have attained 100 percent literacy. They have controlled the growth in numbers. And yet, the state is poor. Very often, the treasury is unable to pay. Sometimes the salaries of the civil servants are released only when the funds are received from the Beverages (a euphemism for liquor) Corporation. They get food from the North. Vegetables from Tamil Nadu. Flowers from Karnataka. Thus, the people are dependant and not independent.

Why has such a situation arisen?

The reason is that the people have not been made to develop a work culture. The director does not give any direction. The labour does not labour. The manager does not manage. The laws have been interpreted liberally and implemented solely to please the poor. But they are not asked to do anything to help themselves. The result is that these people are conscious of their rights. Not the duties. Many may not even be aware of the fact that there is a chapter on 'Duties' in the Constitution of India.

If one looks at the two states from the heights in an aircraft, it is all green. On landing, one notices the bandh. The red flags. A large number of able-bodied men, walking together. Aimlessly. Shouting slogans. Wasting instead of working. And yet wanting everything. Truly red is an ominous colour. No doubt even blood is red. But the sight of it indicates intolerance. Even violence. Both are bad. For the individual as well as society. The red flag bears a hammer and sickle. And in political jargon, it is meant to represent the working class.

The society has progressed. Machine has helped man. To increase production and to decrease labour. Today the man need not wield the hammer and sickle. The machine does it. Yet we continue to accept the old symbol. It continues to cloud our perception. The leftists continue to live in the past and resist modernisation. They refuse to accept change. As a result we are living in poverty in the midst of plenty.

It is true that even the working of all the other states is not perfect. Yes! But two wrongs never make a right. Still more, it is also correct that the dignity of the individual is important. Every man must have enough to meet his needs. It is necessary. But we can get nothing without doing something. To do nothing is the sure way to be nothing. Therefore, it is imperative for us to develop a work culture. It is necessary to perform our duty to the best of our ability. Secondly, we have to control the wage bill. We must realise that if the entire amount collected as tax is paid as salary, nothing shall be left for development or expansion.

The claim that the leftist parties are working for the common good has not been proved to be true. The old concept has already changed beyond recognition in Russia and China. The Russian Union has broken. The China Wall has ceased to be a barrier. The Iron Gate has been opened. In India, we are still wedded to the old and archaic values. Despite the heavy wage bill our leftist brothers want more jobs. Are we trying to be more loyal to the king than the king himself?

Numerically, the Congress is the single largest party. Along with the allies, it is the largest group. Many others have unequivocal support. In the game of numbers, it is not imperative for the Congress to seek support from the communists. Once the dice falls in favour of the Congress, the pigeons on the rooftops shall flock to its aid. The numbers shall never be a problem. Thus, the party should stand on principle. It should not accept alms from those who can embarrass. It should form the government without the unwilling partners. If it succeeds, very well. If not, the people know what to do.

It is true that having alliances is the prerogative of the parties. Yet, it is clear that if progress is the objective, the leftists must be left out. Let them stay happy under the effect of their own opium. Let the malady be not afflicted upon the entire country. It cannot have a good or healthy effect.

The writer is a former Chief Justice of the Kerala High Court.

Creative leaders can change India

Vision and policies are a must

—A.P.J. Abdul Kalam

A knowledge society can be one of the foundations for the vision of a developed India. Knowledge has always been the prime mover of prosperity and power. The acquisition of knowledge has, therefore, been the thrust area throughout the world and sharing the experience of knowledge is a unique culture of our country.

India is endowed with natural and competitive advantages as also certain distinctive competencies. But these are scattered in isolated pockets and the awareness on these is inadequate. During the last century the world underwent a change from an agricultural society, where manual labour was the critical factor, to an industrial society where the management of technology, capital and labour provided the competitive advantage. Then the information age was born, last decade, with connectivity and software products driving the economy of a few nations.

In the 21st century a new society is emerging where knowledge is the primary production resource instead of capital and labour. Efficient utilisation of this existing knowledge can create comprehensive wealth for the nation and improve the quality of life—in the form of better health care facilities, education, infrastructure and other social indicators. The ability to create and maintain knowledge infrastructure, develop knowledge workers and enhance their productivity will be the key factors in deciding the prosperity of the knowledge society.

After 55 years of Independence (which was our First Vision), the aspirations are mounting that India should become a developed country—the Second Vision for the Nation. How can we prepare ourselves for achieving this Vision? To become a developed India, the essential needs are:

(a) India has to be economically and commercially powerful, at least to be one of the six top nations in terms of the size of the economy. Our target should be a GDP growth of 9-11% annually and that the people below the poverty line to be reduced to 10%.

(b) Near self-reliance in defence needs—of weapons and equipment—with no umbilical attachment to the world outside.

(c) India should have a right place in world forums.

Technology Vision 2020 is a pathway to realise this cherished goal. It consists of 17 technology packages in the core sectors. The task teams with nearly 500 experts of the country have worked for two years, deliberated the status of various branches of natonal development and generated 35 documents detailing the steps to be taken for creating wealth and the well-being of our people. "Technology" is the most vital key for achieving the goal.

We have identified five areas where India has a core competence for an integrated action: (1) Agriculture and food processing—we have to fix a target of 360 million tonnes of food and agricultural production (2) Education and health care—we have seen, based on the experience, that education and health care are inter-related (3) Information and communication technology (4) Reliable and quality electric power for all parts of the country (5) Critical technology and strategic industry.

These five areas are closely inter-related and lead to national food and economic security. A strong partnership among the R&D sector, the academia, industry and the community as a whole with the government departments will be essential to accomplish the vision.

India is a vast country with tremendous natural resources apart from qualified, talented human resources. I firmly believe that with such rich resource potential, our country, through appropriate policies and initiatives, can easily surpass any other in the field of economic development in the shortest time. All of us need to work together to make it happen. We shall certainly succeed.

We need balanced inter-sectoral and inter-regional development so as to ensure that the gulf between the rich and the not-so-rich is narrowed to the maximum. Our GDP has to double itself if we have to develop the way we want.

Economic development of the nation is a joint effort of the people's movement and governance. There was a time when one used to think that bringing about development was the main task of the government alone. In fact, I would go to the extent of saying that the government has to facilitate and monitor growth.

We all know that 70% of our population lives in rural areas and development of rural infrastructure cannot be viewed in isolation. In future, the development of urban infrastructure will further widen the urban-rural divide. Therefore, an integrated strategy is required and the villages have to be connected suitably to form urban areas. An example of this in PURA (Providing Urban Amenities in Rural Areas) that will bring rural wealth and prosperity. This model envisages a habitat designated to improve the quality of life in rural places and makes special suggestions to remove urban congestion also. Naturally, our most pressing urban problems are congestion removal, efficient supply of water and effective waste disposal in every locality.

Physical connectivity, electronic connectivity, knowledge connectivity and economic connectivity will make the cluster of villages with urban facilities. PURA will tremendously boost the economic development of the country. Industrialists and NGOs must come forward to adopt many PURAs.

What is needed for building a developed India? We have natural resources and we have human power. There are 700 million people below

35 years in the country's population. The nation needs young leaders who can command the change for transformation of India into a developed nation embedded with a knowledge society from now to 2020. The leaders are the creators of new organisations of excellence. Quality leaders are like magnets that will attract the best of persons to build the team for the organisation and give inspiring leadership even during failures of missions as they are not afraid of risks. I have seen and worked with creators of vision and missions. The vision ignites the minds and many missions emerge, with definite goals to achieve.

One of the important ingredients of success of the vision of transforming India into a developed nation by 2020 is the evolution of creative leaders. I am giving a connectivity between a developed India, economic prosperity, technology, production, productivity, employee role and management quality, all linked to the creative leader. Who is that creative leader.? What are the qualities of a creative leader? The creative leadership is exercising the task to change the traditional role from a commander to a coach, a manager to a mentor, a director to a delegator and from one who demands respect to one who facilitates self-respect. The higher the proportion of creative leaders in a nation, the higher the potential of success of visions like "developed India."

Reverence for life is indeed possible in the real sense if a philosophical thought of reverence can be transformed into actions by empowering various components of society. When a child is empowered by the parents as various phases of growth, he gets transformed into a responsible citizen. When a teacher is empowered with knowledge and experience, good young human beings with value systems emerge. When an individual or a team is empowered with technology, transformation to higher potential for achievement is assured. When a leader of any institution empowers his or her people, leaders are born who can change the nation in multiple areas. When women are empowered, society with stability gets assured. When the political leaders of a nation empower the people through visionary policies, prosperity is certain. When religions are empowered and become a spiritual force, peace and happiness will blossom in people's heart. Such an empowered stage will lead to the creation of enlightened citizens with a value system.

Here I suggest a solution by the evolution of enlightened human beings with a combination of education with a value system, religion graduation into spiritualism and visionary policies for prosperity. We should not allow any religion or any individual fanaticism to endanger our nation. The nation is very important compared to any individual or party or religion.

(This article is based on extracts from the Shri Dhirubhai Ambani Memorial Lecture delivered by the President of India in Mumbai on July 6. The Tribune, July 8, 2003)

Bill of rights and wrongs

—Rakesh Shukla

The removal of the inherent sexim and extending it to include men in the gender-neutral sounding. Jammu Kashmir Permanent Residents (Disqualification) Act, presently vociferously espoused by the National Conference, would disentitle the "father-son" duo of Farooq and Omar Abdullah from contesting elections or even voting!

The strong Indian women's movement seems to have had little impact on the inivisibilising of women as "people". In fact, Mehmooba Mufti, president of the PDP, herself a strong, visible woman and one of the only mainstream politicians who speaks out against army excesses and champions human rights, appears to be a classic example of internalising partriarchal values in her categorical support for the bill.

In any case, it does appear puzzling the J&K autonomy should sink or swim on the plank of the state government's passing a legislation discriminatory to women.

At one time managements of minority institutions took the plea that scales of pay and allowances, pension, gratuity, medical facilities, provident fund for employees could not be made as legislations prescribing the same would constitute an encroachment on the fundamental right guaranteed to minorities to establish and administer educational institutions under Article 30 (1) of the Constitution. In 1986 in the Frank Anthony School case, the apex court dismissed the plea and took the view that these laws in no way dilute the minority status or affect the preservation of the distinct culture of any section of society.

Denial of equality and discrimination on the ground of gender under the cloak of J&K autonomy seems akin to the logic put forward by the minority institutions.

The Supreme Court had occasion to deal with gender discriminatory inheritance laws in a community in 1996. Madhu Kishwar had challenged provisions of the Chottanagpur Tenancy Act 1908, under which land and property rights were inheritable only by the descendants in the male line among the indigenous communities of Jharkhand. The case had a chequered career. First filed in 1986, it was urged that excluding tribal women from inheritance of land or property belonging to father, husbands or mother and conferment of the right to inheritance to the male heirs or lineal descendants being founded solely on sex was discriminatory and violative of the rights to equality and life—that tribal women toil, share with men equally the daily sweat, troubles and tribulations in agricultural operations, and the denial of rights was unjust and illegal.

The case was adjourned with the understanding that the government would examine the desirability of amending the law to give equal inheritance rights to women. However, the tribal advisory board constitutes took the view that granting the right to women would "enlarge the threat of alienation of tribal land in the hands of non-tribals". The case was finally argued and decided in 1996.

The majority judgement upheld the provisions. However, on the ground of right to livelihood being part of right to life, it held that the immediate female relatives of the last male tenant could hold the land as long as they remain dependent on it for earning their livelihood, for otherwise it would render them destitute. The exclusive right of male succession remained in suspended animation till the female descendant's right to livelihood remained valid.

The dissenting minority judgement of Justice K. Ramaswamy held that customs and mores must undergo changes with the march of time. The denial of agency and the view that women are given to being entrapped by wily men was firmly rejected. The threat of alienation to non-tribals was held to be adequately safeguarded against by other laws requiring permission before transfer of any tribal land to non-tribals. The judgement held that Scheduled Tribe women would succeed to the estate of their parent, brother, husband and inherit the property with equal share with the male heirs.

Judicial history is replete with illustrations where the dissenting minority view of a judge has proved to be more enduring and in tune with justice, equity and good conscience.

—The Indian Express
March 17, 2004

REVIEWS AND CRITICISM

"Critic and author bear the same relationship as the knife and the throat." Some of the sharp antagonisms have developed between authors and those who criticize their work.

There was a time when many newspaper reviewers considered themselves specialized reporters. They sharpened their pencils, gathered swatches of copy paper and went off to plays and movies much as their colleagues went out to cover the police beat. They reported what happened on the stage and screen and recorded the reactions of the audiences. The book reviewers simply sketched the plot.

Those were the days of 'reportorial rewriting." Now, however, almost any newspaper of consequence features 'critical reviewing'. In fact, the words review and criticism are synonymous in journalism.

Successful reviewing of books, art exhibitions, films and drama and radio and television programmes calls for an expertise in journalistic writing which is different from all other forms. It is not necessarily practiced by regular staff members. Seasoned critics, analysts and specialists in various fields of reviewing contribute to newspapers by a regular arrangement.*

Senior staffers do some reviewing, but there is seldom full-time critic employed by any publication. Even film reviewers who are on the regular roll of a publication are called upon for other writing and general journalistic work. It is considered expensive to have men only to review films or write critical analyses of books, radio, television etc. Moreover, this can cause monotony in style and limitation of ideas.

The critics write reviews on a variety of subjects such as books, plays, films, television and radio programmes, etc. While writing reviews, the critics should keep in mind that they are not writing for themselves, but are addressing the readers. Any attempt, therefore, to project too much of the critic's own viewpoint, or to criticize the work for the sake of criticism, or for the sake of controversy would not enhance the value of the writing. The effort should be to find out something 'good' in everything.

The work to be reviewed should be adjudged in proper perspective, i.e., the level of readers or audience for whom it is meant. The review should have two major elements—explain or describe and assess or evaluate the work. One salutary principle is that one should not write anything about a person, which one would be ashamed to tell him to his face. The pen should be used with great care.

The critic need not be a practising expert in a particular field, but he should have sufficient background knowledge of the subject. The reviewer is free to give his own assessment, opinion and judgement about the work, provided it is not based on untruth or malice; at the same time he should not become annoyed, if the people do not agree or accept his viewpoint.

---

* Reviews and criticism are based on book Professional Journalism by Patanjali Sethi, Bombay-Orient Longman, pp. 145-152.

How does an outsider become a Reviewer?

Possession of knowledge and ability to access count. If you are an authority on economics, you could get a chance to review books on the subject. Still, you have to be able to write in a readable and acceptable manner. An art critic is given importance provided he knows about art, has kept in touch with developments and trends, and can express himself clearly.

Guiding Readers

It has to be stressed that a review is meant to guide readers. Undoubtedly, some critics view things as perfectionists and what they write can hardly give any guidance. They review, or seem to, only for other critics. Nevertheless, even these can be helpful once their point of view is understood and style accepted.

Generally, it should be asked, "Does it help the readers?" Of course, the answer must be in the affirmative. It is also necessary to ensure that the review is of good standard that will help the publication. This implies responsibility and objectivity in views, and maturity of expression.

Busy staff members, usually reporters, half-baked critics and over enthusiastic writers wishing to get into print usually prepare what can best be described as a 'reporting-review.' It is basically a report of the subject-matter of the thing under review with a few comments thrown in.

A newspaper which either cannot afford to have specialised critics or does not have the space to be allotted separately to reviews, prints this type of review. By the very nature of its structure, as well as the fact that it is written by a non-specialist, it is not a true review. Basically, it consists of reporting the plot of a play or the film seen and presenting personal and/or audience reactions. In art, such a review refers to the reactions. In the case of books, the subject matter is sketched briefly and a few general comments are made. Somewhat the same pattern prevails with regard to other subjects.

A critical review is necessarily a judgement by one who knows the subject. In it, basic information has to be supplied by the critic. Moreover, the review must stand alone on the merits of the assessment made by a knowledgeable critic. An acceptable review of this type is not completely devoid of a few sentences of reportage and information, but critical analysis is its main function.

Although it stands on its own merits, a good review is not a thing by itself. Analogies must be brought in because the subject has to be studied in the context of existing standards. This means that the review incorporates references to other films, exhibitions, or books either by others or the same person. Giving examples also helps to bring out contrasts which sharpen the comments and result in clear understanding of the thing reviewed.

Busy critics tend to rust or get bored with their job. Day in, day out, they produce the same type of writing. They become addicted to certain phrases and depend on cliches. This happens particularly in art reviews. Brush work becomes either 'bold' or 'timid', the conception is 'uncertain; or 'masterly'. Ample use is made of the following terms: Colourful expression, painting in mood, mature project, growing maturity, depth and colour, vibrant hues, departure from convention. Unfortunately, the critic cannot depart from his own conventional reviews if he sticks to stereotyped forms.

Avoiding Vagueness

At the same time, care has to be taken to avoid vagueness. Critics have a tendency to prove their knowledge by using words which come to them easily and yet do not convey the exact meaning. Often it becomes a matter of what you can not understand must be 'good' or 'anything that goes over your head is impressive'. There is also vagueness of another type. But what do these words actually mean? Adequate for whom? Tolerable in what way? Good or bad in what sense? Do they respond to a sense of judgement? Generalizations like these may be adequate to the needs of the critic, but his writing can hardly be called tolerable for the reader.

In this context, it is essential to remember that a critic has to try and paint a picture of what he has seen. A review depends on the judgement, organization, contrast, visual pictures, natural ending, and significance of what you are saying. Examples to prove your statement are helpful.

As you cannot tell much and saying too little leaves the review incomplete, what do you do? It is easy enough to say that practice makes it possible to say just enough. Yet it is essential to highlight factors pertaining to different reviews.

Book Reviews

Reviews are classified according to their size. This is determined by the space allotted in a publication, as well as the subject-matter and nature of a book that interests the editor. The importance or popularity of the author are also considered.

Not all books received by a publication are reviewed. A small number are selected, but courtesy demands that others not being reviewed must be mentioned. They are listed under the headline: 'Books Received.'

How to do?

The small review is generally of three to five paragraphs. The contents are treated with greater detail in a separate section of the review. Details of the publisher, background and language structure are given. The critic has a chance to give his own assessment.

The detailed study is normally among the largest reviews. Every aspect is carefully analysed. The motivation of the author, his ability to convey a philosophy or an idea and his style are studied. All relevant information about the books is given. On rare occasions a book is analysed thoroughly.

With man's growing interest in ever-increasing spheres of activity, the classification of books into categories is undergoing a change. The main groups into which books are divided are: Fiction, politics, philosophy, religion, sociology, social welfare and anthropology, science, adventure and economics.

For general subjects it is not always that a specialist is needed. Most people can review fiction. The reviewer has to remember that while he is pertinent in his comments, they should not hurt the author. Abstract views and vague expressions must be avoided, and the review must be clear enough to guide readers. The tendency to be stuffy and difficult can be compelling with critics, but is dangerous. An honest critic will take his own time and not be bullied into giving reviews unless he has read the book and analysed it to his own satisfaction.

Some reviewers analyse the book by just reading the details on the jacket or cover, glance at the beginning of the story and have a look at the middle and the end. It is somewhat like a woman who said that she always read the middle of a novel first. Her reason: 'That makes me wonder how it began and get excited about how it will end. That makes life interesting, doesn't it !'

Sometime when a book is written by a known author, the editor feels compelled to feature a review of it even if there is no one who can study it in detail. Or it is reviewed hurriedly, purely to complete a formality. Any review presented after this is a complete deception.

While reviewing the book, keep a slip of paper with you so that you can jot down words, phrases and pertinent points when they occur to you. Against each of these, you must write the page number so that later when you write the review you can check the context in which you have made your comments. It is useful to keep ready a few quotations from the book. They can help you to justify your comments.

Decide on your introductory and closing remarks on the basis of the total impression that you have obtained about the book. Rearrange the points and then write the review. Some examples of book review are as under:

The Namesake

By Jhumpa Lahiri
Flamingo
Price Rs. 386

In her debut novel of accident and happenstance, Jhumpa Lahiri revisits the themes that propelled her nine Pulitzer Prize winning short stories in Interpreter of maladies. The episodic inquiry has given way to a gentle-paced, two-generational narrative. The dark corners left tantalising unlit in those tales have now been meticulously mapped. The abrupt folds in those narratives have been ironed out, the devotion to drama has evened out into a diarist's preoccupation with minutiae.

In this disappointing novel of immigration and adjustment, a young man's unease about his given names provides a peg for Lahiri to chronicle the process of balancing ancestral loyalties and new engagements. Gogol was never meant to sally forth into childhood named after a dead Russian writer. When he was born to Ashoke and Ashima Ganguli, both newly moved to Boston from Calcutta, he a graduate student at MIT, she a homesick housewife, a name had already been chosen for him. Ashima's grandmother had herself made a rare trip out of her Bengal home to airmail the chosen name. But the letter never arrived in Boston, a sudden stroke rendered the old lady incoherent, and the little one had to be temporarily christened after Ashoke's favourite writer.

Predictably, when Gogol is given a "good name"—Nikhil, from Nikolai—he rebels, and Gogol he stays. Till he enters university and the odd shape of his name embarrasses him and the Indian resonance of Nikhil provides a comforting introduction into a more multicultural environment.

The name Gogol, however, has a longer back story. It recalls Ashoke's brush with death during a train journey at the age of 22. A collection of Gogol's short stories had kept him upright and awake and thus marked for survival in brutal rail accident. This second life gave him courage to imagine life beyond India, to aspire to higher education and professorhood in an American university.

For Ashima, the compensations are meagre. Instead, as she tends her suburban quarter-acre home, her days and years are punctuated with tidings of death from India and with preparation of Bengali delicacies to tide over pangs of nostalgia. Her heart is so resolutely oceans away that it will take three decades of an uneventful life in this seemingly strange land for her to acknowledge that equilibrium lies in dividing time between America and India.

Gogol's passage to a semblance of equilibrium is rather different. He is more adept at adjusting to his American life than to his Indian inheritance. In fact, as he meanders through a relationship with a Waspish art editor, someone remarks that he could even be Italian. No, the American part is easy, it is the return to his family, to his roots, that is more tumultuous.

Lahiri is extremely graceful as she nurtures her characters in circumstances that are at once familiar and alien. She has enough poise and confidence to allow them to venture into terrain that may not have been part of her original map. In doing so, The Namesake becomes more than a mere immigrant's tale. If it is the immigrant's burden to forever strive towards an equilibrium between the inherited and the acquired, it is also a task that falls upon the rest of us as we negotiate our way through rapid social change.

It is unfortunate, then, that her central plot does not quite click. As Gogol becomes Nikhil, and then Gogol/Nikhil, Lahiri's attempt to sue the Indian custom of "pet names" and "good names" as a springboard to dive into the world of transplanted Indians is rather weak. It fails to thread an entire novel and a cluster of life stories together.

Mini Kapoor
The Indian Express
September 21, 2003

India Down the Pages

The Times Group Since 1838
Times Group
Price: Not Mentioned
Pages: 148

Seth Ram Kishen Dalmia bought Bennett Coleman & Co., publishers of ***The Times of India*** *and its other publications, in 1947. He* *wanted to have a subservient press to propagate his brand of Hinduism with cow protection and vegetarianism as top priorities. He hated Nehru's agnostic socialism; in return Nehru hated his guts. I had a very brief meeting with Seth Dalmia. I had applied for the post of editor of* ***The Illustrated Weekly.*** *he asked me one question: "Do you know Sanskrit?" I replied, "No, Sir, I don't". He dismissed me curtly: "Go and learn Sanskrit, then come to me." I got the job 20 years later, without a word added to my Sanskrit vocabulary.*

If Dalmia had his way, Bennett Coleman's publications would be devoted to propagating his brand of Hindutva. Fortunately he got into severe financial trouble and had to give the publishing house to his son-in-law Shanti Prasad Jain, husband of his eldest daughter through Rama, the first of his six wives. It was Shanti and more his son Ashok who put Bennett Coleman back on its feet. Today Ashok's widow Indu and her two sons Samir and Vineet run the company. The driving force behind its spectacular success as India's leading group of newspapers is Samir.

It took over as editor of Illustrated Weekly in 1969 and held the post for nine long years. I got an insider's view of the organisation. It ran like a well-oiled machine. Editors were well-paid, provided a house allowance, a new car and fringe benefits. We sat in red swivel chairs, served tea and coffee and a sumptuous vegetarian lunch. We were given a key each to open doors of lavatories reserved for editors. To have a pissoir of one's own was the ultimate in editorial prestige.

I was fortunate in being left to reshape the Weekly. The Jains had been divested of control of the company for some financial hanky-panky. A benevolent retired Justice K.T. Desai was officiating chairman. An able and non-interfering Ram Tarneja was general manager. I lasted out till the company was restored to the Jains.

The Times groups has every reason to crow over its achievements. There are newspapers which enjoy more credibility and provide better reading. But the Times reigns supreme. The credit goes largely to Samir. He sensed that if print had to survive TV, it had to radically alter its content. While a weekly relies heavily on the personality of its editor, a daily does not. Three-fourths of its content is taken from the wires or foreign agencies (strip cartoons and crosswords, for example); the rest comprises correspondents' reports and readers' contributions, leaving the editor and his deputies a third or even less of the editorial page to comment on world and national events. Not many people read editorials. The Times' first Indian editor Frank Moraes was much respected for his forthrightness but not much read. His successor N.J. Nanporia was neither admired nor read. Sham Lal was lauded for his erudition but few people read more than his opening paras. Likewise Girilal Jain, regarded as a perceptive political analyst and the first protagonist of Hindutva, had few takers. His successor Dileep Padgaonkar failed to convince his proprietors that "next to the prime minister he was doing the second most important job in India".

So we have the ironic situation that while we can name editors of other dailies, no one knows the name of the editor of the most widely circulated paper in the country. Samir Jain (rightly?) concluded that editors were dispensable. From his great grandfather he has inherited the uncanny gift of making money: the Times has become a major money-spinner. The trinity who run it know what is and what is not dispensable. R.K. Laxman is not dispensable (he is worth three editors). God and religion are not dispensable: so we have articles on god, yoga, meditation and quotes from the scriptures. Scantily clad starlets are not dispensable: male readers need some titillation every morning. Books and book reviews are as dispensable as editors. That is the secret behind the longevity of the old lady of Bori Bunder. Also periodical injection of life-giving drugs by the Jain trinity. A reasonable way of discovering this secret is to compare its Sunday supplements with those of other national dailies. It has a string of contributors who command readerships of their own.

The one lasting contribution Bennett Coleman has made to Indian journalism is to cut to size editors who had grandiose notions about their positions. The roll of honour of those unceremoniously shown the door includes Frank Moraes, Girilal Jain, A.S. Raman, Kamleshwar, Inder Malhotra, Prem Shankar Jha, Dom Moraes and Dileep Padgaonkar. I don't feel too bad being named among them.

Khushwant Singh
Outlook
July 21, 2003

Mila in Love

By Dina Mehta
Penguin India
Price Rs. 295

There is something about madness and mothers. It's a recurring motif in literature, as obdurate as incurable madness. Years ago in his autobiographical ***My Son's Father, Dom Moraes's*** *showed his beautiful, talented mother going slowly mad. Recently Hiro Boga's Shahnaz had*

Dilnaz, a genius mathematician and a reluctant mother who descends into manic depression.

Fellow-Parsi and Mumbai resident Dina Mehta has followed it up with her latest novel Mila in Love.

It's a story told by Sharmila, or the abridged Mila, of life, falling in love and staying in love. It could be the story of any upper-crust Mumbai girl except that there are a series of complications here. Mila's mother is sent off to serene Panchgani to recover from depression. Her father finds an almost instant replacement in his efficient secretary and merry widow Gita. But the mother returns. And the madness returns.

Then there is the love interest. Rayhaan, a Parsi-Punjabi hunk, whose looks belie purist arguments, reaffirming that crossbreeds get the best of both worlds. Rayhaan is infatuated by the mother, and the daughter by him.

In the complicated net of relationships, Mehta shows that the victims and persecutors in society are often all within our family. Mila's maternal grandmother is an ogre as mother-in-law. She is no TV serial character. She is neither part of the new age brigade spouting faux sentiments of daughter-in-laws are daughters, nor is she member of the Machiavellian club. She simply believes her son's wife is meant to be ill treated. And Mila's aunt, after years of carrying the cross, shrugs it off in one supreme effort. The sheer effort appears to have exhausted her and she returns home. Why did she give up the fight? What makes women like her stay with misery?

Mehta earlier explored a women-centric theme in a play, ***Brides Are Not for Burning.*** *It won first prize in a* ***BBC*** *competition. Her first novel* ***And Some take a Lover*** *focussed on the divided loyalties of a Parsi family during the Quit India movement.*

Through its passing observations and references, Mehta's new novel catches snatches of life in a metro that's constantly changing but never really changing. Minis may have replaced saris at parties but the pleats of traditional thinking are tucked firmly in place. So there's Mila's friend Ritu whose giving birth to a daughter is almost a community crisis, the only grace being that this was the first child. And of course there's always that spiritual Hindu's material consolation, girls are Lakshmi.

And the observations cut across community lines. At the wedding of her Parsi friend Baimai, Mila sees the banality of society weddings. "The festooned garden, the lights ... the women wearing their ransoms on their bosoms ... all the riot of expense, waste." Baimai's family is also living the ultimate Parsi nightmare: their son wants to marry a non-Parsi, a dark Goan Catholic.

The novel ends with Mila's childhood dream coming true. Rayhaan, now a famous author, finally reciprocates her love. Mila's brother too finds love in a convenient arrangement. Choosing an arranged match over his girl-friend, Vikram is your average well-brought up professional, a modern guy whose liberal thinking comes a far second to pragmatism.

***Mila in Love** is a racy novel that mixes a personal story with vaguely disturbing contemporary takes.*

Devyani Onial
Indian Express
August 17, 2003

Art Reviews

Art reviews are of numerous varieties. They can be superficial, knowledgeable, thought-provoking, perfectionist, discouraging or encouraging to the artist. Much depends on the actual work under review. It is best to let your perfectionism stand in the way of a good review.

Factors which influence the critic are the artist and his background, hand-outs and publicity material, opinions of other critics and, sometimes, the herd instinct which a critic follows because he does not have enough knowledge of the medium. It is interesting to note that a painting hung upside down in an European exhibition was once acclaimed by judges and received a prize. Not too long ago, a group of critics were divided about their quality, none of them found much fault with them. Some acclaimed them as showing talent. There were articles about the paintings. Later, it was discovered that they were the work of a frenzied ape wielding a brush over the canvas held by his master!

All this means that for an honest critic, knowledge of art, and developments in the world of art, and awareness of styles and modes of expression are essential. Only then can there be honesty of approach and expression. Yet a critic who is aware of all these is likely to use pompous phrases to display his knowledge. Moralising and pontification have to be avoided because they only destroy a good review.

A film review serves the reader, the newspaper and sometimes the producer. As in other cases, the critic has to be an expert. He must be fully aware of film techniques, styles and expression. Besides these, he must have sharp faculties, knowledge of art and culture and should be able to write objectively.

It is not easy to see day in day out and continue to write good reviews about them. Owing to the variable quality of films from almost moronic expressions to highly sophisticated presentations, a part of the drabness rubs off on the viewer. A critic should be willing to see a large number of films as a duty, even if these is no pleasure in seeing them.

Normally, press shows are held earlier than the release of the film. Hindi films sometimes do not have press shows as the critic is invited on the first day of the release. Influence is exerted through more than courteous treatment of the critic at such shows. He is flooded with publicity material and sometimes the director or the producer sits with him to clarify doubts.

Although it is not possible to write much while seeing the picture, it is a good practice to have a few sheets of blank paper with you, each meant for a different aspect of the film. On these, essential words can be jotted down to guide the critic later on. The basic details about the stars, story and technical aspects can be obtained from the publicity data supplied. Thereafter, shifting and re-arranging is done and the review is written.

The style of film reviews has undergone a great change. Honest reviewers these days make detailed references to the story-content. Mostly, details of the technical aspect of the film are presented satirically with the story. There are no separate parts of the review for different technical aspects. The conventional style goes like this:

Introductory remarks, story-content, acting details, technical qualities and summing up.

It is not always that film reviews are objective. In some newspapers, they are written by publicists posing as journalists. This happens because such newspapers are afraid of endangering their chances to obtaining advertisements. So, reviews which are more like blurbs and puff paragraphs are included. Some of the film reviews are as follows:

Stage Reviews

Stage reviews follow basically the same pattern as film reviews. Only, in this case, the critic devotes definite attention to the development of the theme. Analysis is made on the basis of awareness that actors on the stage cannot appear for re-shooting as happens in films. This means that greater acting talent is called for.

The characters have to be on stage and the audience has to remain in the auditorium; this is the basic difference between the stage and film. For a play, there are no mid-shots or close-ups; they are all long-shots.

Audience participation is brought about in a stage performance;

this inevitably influences the critic. A reviewer has to bear all these factors in mind in order to be fair in his comments.

While sight and sound are used in films and the stage, in the case of the radio only hearing is involved. The total effect is limited. The spoken words, and sound structure of the programmer are given importance. The slightest gap on the radio appears a long one primarily because no characters are seen whose action can cover the gap. Clarity of voice and sharpness of sound effects are the most essential characteristic. The listener's imagination is needed much more than in the case of films and the stage.

A reviewer has to keep in mind the limitations and conceptual use of the radio medium. His analysis has to incorporate all the elements stated.

Exercises

1. Write an editorial on Congress President Sonia's visit to Shimla on 7-9 July, 2003.
2. Clip editorials from three national dailies on the same topic. Find the similarities, differences and slant among them.
3. At times basic news is converted into an 'editorial' by just adding a few comments. Using this method, make some 'editorials.'
4. Which book has influenced you most? Write a short review.
5. Write a review of a widely known book, then compare it to a noted critic's review of the same book. Are there significant differences?
6. Select film reviews which you think are vague and not of practical value to the reader. Rewrite them as they should be.

SECTION VI

ETHICS AND PRESS LAWS

20

MEDIA ETHICS AND PROFESSIONALISM

Ethics refers to the values system by which a person determines what is right or wrong, fair or unfair, just or unjust. It is expressed through moral behaviours in specific situations. An individual's conduct is measured not only against his or her conscience but also against some norm of acceptability that has been societally, professionally, or organizationally determined.

Ethical philosophies

A person's philosophical orientation can also determine how he or she acts in a specific situation. Philosophers say the three basic value orientation are:

1. Absolutist ethics
2. Antinomian or existentialist ethics
3. Situation ethics

Absolutist ethics

Absolutism holds that there is a fixed set of principles or laws, from which there should be no deviation. They believe every decision is either 'wrong' regardless of the consequences. For them if it is wrong to lie, it always is wrong to lie. If a murderer asks where his intended victim is the absolutist could not lie to save a life. If the action is right, it does not matter whether a friend is killed. The consequences are irrelevant.

The absolutist Journalist is concerned only with whether an event is newsworthy. If it is interesting, timely, significant or important, it is to be reported, regardless of the consequences.

The philosophy is attractive to some journalist because it assumes the need for full disclosure. Nothing newsworthy ever is withheld from the public. In the end, these journalists believe, publishing without fear of the consequences or without favour for one group's interests over another is the highest ethical principle.

Antinomian or existentialist ethics

Antimonianism reject all rules and, in effect, all ethics. The term antinomian means against law. The antinomian has neither a predetermined standard of conduct nor moral rules. Their choices are made without a prescribed value system, decides on the basis of immediate rational choice. Actions in any situation is spontaneous and unpredictable.

Antimonian journalists are not concerned with motives, consequences or obligations. That does not mean that they would always lie, cheat or steal. Antimonian journalists might pose as someone other than a journalist in an attempt to gather information. On some occasions, they would not be bothered by doing it. To them every situation is different. There are no principles that can guide decision making. They have faith in them ability to extemporize in any situation. No preparation is required.

While the concept of absolutism is attractive to many journalists, few choose antinomianism. Most mainstream journalists reject it because it is not only antiethical to their upbringing but also inconsistent with a responsible press. The principle that the press has a responsibility to the reader implies a concern for the consequences that antinomians do not have.

Situation ethics

Between the two extremes of antinomianism and absolutism lies a third philosophy, *i.e.* situation ethics. Unlike anti-nomianism, situationism does not hold that everything is relative. Their decisions are based on what would cause the least harm or most good.

The situationist knows, understands and accepts the ethical maxims of the community and its heritage and weighs them carefully before making a decision. For example, a situationist most likely believes that lying is unethical. But if a murderer asks where his intended victim is, a situationist would lie to save a life.

- In the broad sense, for the person holding to situation ethics, people always come first. In every ethical dilemma, they always do what is best for people. Sometimes this takes the form of utilitarianism. They act in a way that is good for the largest number of people. Sometimes this means that they must act to benefit the most people in the long run. Unlike the absolutist, the situationist is always concerned with the human consequences.

Making an ethical decision is often not an easy matter for the situationist. Yet most situationists hold that what is clearly unethical is not to decide, not to decide is to make a decision.

Ethical Dilemmas

Ethical problems tend to came in the following categories:

- Payola
- Plagiarism
- Conflict of interest
- Withholding information
- Deceit
- Invasion of Privacy

Payola

The term is used when money or gifts are given in expectations of favourable coverage from journalists. Gifts, sometimes even outright cash payments, are common in the news business. During the past few years, and more so in the recent past, the lowering of ethical values in the media have been widely reported. The pernicious practice of accepting envelopes containing gift coupons or hard cash by the press reporters in India at the press conferences where new issues are launched has been widely commented upon. In Tamil Nadu, for example, this practice is euphemistically referred to as 'envelope journalism'. In the context, Richard Scaffer observes:

Envelope journalism diminishes the self esteem of journalists who practice it, and likewise diminishes credibility of the press itself. Corruption among journalists is very difficult to document. Everyone suspects that it is rampant, but no one wants to admit to practising it. Publishers, it is evident, are often in collusion with corrupt journalists, particularly when they tacitly encourage envelope journalism by paying journalists wages they can barely survive on, knowing these journalists will be forced to find creatively unethical means to augment their salary by prostituting themselves professionally.

Another dimension to the ethics issue is related to 'cheque book journalism'. Where the reporters are hired or they sell the story to the highest bidding publication. As it happened in the case of Veerapan, smuggler. The Tamil periodical claimed that it had hired the reporter to cover this story but the reporter denied. But when he sold the story to the English fortnightly, it became an issue. Complaints were made to the Press Council of India. The Press Council dismissed the complaint of the Tamil periodical. But the truth never came out. The question arises, Are reporters who do not pay their own way being bought? A good many persons inside and outside the press think that either they are being bought or they may give readers the impression they are. The appearance of impropriety may be as damaging as actual impropriety.

Sports promoters attract reporters from around the country to their events. Reporters justify the trip by writing stories. Airlines inaugurating flights often invite media representatives to take the first flight free in order to seek favourable coverage in the travel or business sections of the media. And if the reporter has taken the flight another story extolling the virtues of visiting Lakshadeep or Kathmandu. Television critics are invited to the premiere shows, interviews and parties with the stars. The networks offer to pay all expenses of the reporters and in lieu want reviews to be favourable, but mainly they want publicity. Their preview week for the critics guarantees stories in paper around the nation.

Issues involved

- Do reporters who accept free tickets or accommodations write more favourably about a subject than they would if the newspaper paid the expenses?
- When promoters are paying the way, are stories written that otherwise would not be?
- Does the public believe that a reporter is compromised by accepting envelops, free gifts or travel?

These are some of the issues, which should be addressed by the industry while it is by no means unanimous in its opinion, the industry is in general agreement that the press should avoid gifts and free travel. The issue that remains unresolved is whether there is a cut off point. Is credibility impaired by a cup of tea or coffee, a free meal or travel? Can journalists dashing about to cover a national political convention stop at a booth run by a special interest group to grab a free snack?

Such type of favouritisms should be discouraged by the industry. In many cases the decisions about whether to accept gifts, tickets or trips is taken out of the reporter's hands. Many newspapers have given their travel editors larger budgets instead of permitting them to accept free trips from airlines and travel agencies. Some news organizations will estimate the cost of meals or travel and reimburse the host organization.

Plagiarism

Plagiarism is the taking of another's words and representing them as their own. In other words using or passing off the writings or ideas of another as one's own without crediting the source. It is not only unethical, it is illegal.

"The practice, increasingly indulge in by some newspapers of lifting news from other newspapers and publishing them subsequently as their own. This malpractice may not be amenable to wholesale prevention or actionable as a breach of copyright, because news once published becomes public property. To remove its unethicality, the 'lifting newspaper must duly acknowledge the source of the report at the beginning or at the end of the news. However, the position of feature articles is different from 'news'. Feature articles shall not be lifted without permission/proper acknowledgement." (Sarkaria, 1995).

However, differentiating between plagiarism and research is often difficult. Events in a news story cannot be copyrighted, but the specific account of the event can. Journalist can rewrite the article without violating the law. A survey was conducted by the Ethics committee of the American Society of Newspaper Editors in USA in 1986 on 225 editors. The survey revealed that one out of six editors reported that they had encountered plagiarism in the last three years in their newspapers. In India this practice is very common. Reporters consciously or unconsciously, deal with many situations that could involve plagiarism. Roy Peter Clark, who edited the book of winning entries listed plagiarism in the following manners:

Taking material verbatim from the newspaper library

Even when the material is from your own newspaper, it is still someone else's work. Putting the material in your own words or attributing it is plagiarism.

Using material from other publication

Electronic data bases are available in abundance. It becomes even more difficult to detect plagiarism with the multitude of sources available to the reporter. Reporters who do not clearly indicate the source of their information take the risk of using material.

Using material verbatim from the news agencies

It is fairly common for newspapers to take material from the news agencies, add a few lines or paragraphs of local information and publish the story as the work of the newspaper or under a byline, Even though it is common, it is not right.

Using news releases verbatim

This is a shadowy area because the companies and individuals who send the releases are delighted to see them published. Most newspapers, however, rewrite them. But many reporters send these stories verbatim to the paper under a byline which is unethical. If they send under a byline, the stories should be substantially the reporter's work. Except for quotes the stories should not include verbatim reproductions of portions of the release. If a release is used verbatim, the source should be credited.

Using the work of fellow reporters

Often more than one reporter is assigned to a story, so it is a collective effort of many reporters, but the article will appear under one byline which is unethical. But now the work of others is credited in a note at the end of the story. For example, contributed by: Kunal, Medhavi and Siddharth.

Using old stories over again

Some reporters and columnists use stories or columns they had done years earlier without attribution. This is unethical. The publication in which the original version appeared has a stake in that story, and the readers have a right to know that they are reading recycled material.

No one approves of plagiarism still, there is considerable argument about what constitutes. As in many other shadowy ethical areas, however, most of the problems are avoided when reporters and editors think first. More plagiarism is committed unconsciously than knowingly.

Conflict of Interest

Conflict of interest is closely related to Payola. In Payola a reporter actually receives some material benefits but in conflict of interest the benefits are intangible. This intangible benefits raises many questions: Do the reporters have the opportunity to forward the causes of organizations to which they belong? Do reporters' allegiances interfere with their ability to be objective? Can a member of either the Congress or B.J.P party cover the political beat? Can religious editors objectively report on developments in their own institutions? Can a reporter objectively cover the school board if another reporter, an editor or a publisher is a member?

Some of the conflicts do involve material benefits. Can a financial reporter objectively report on a company in which he or she owns stocks? Should a financial or business writer use inside knowledge to buy stocks, bonds or commodities? Can a sports reporter who is given extra tickets to sell or distributes to friends objectively report in a team?

Sometimes the conflict arises because the reporters are serving themselves or the paper instead of the readers. This occurs when a reporter elects to do a story or a series that may have little interest or importance for readers but that would be a good entry for a journalism contest. Many trade associations give substantial cash awards for stories about their special interests, ranging from food and furniture to cigars and cars.

A conflict can arise, when a journalist holds a second job. Most newspapers have written policies on the subject, and few allows reporters to work for a competitor or to do work that conflicts with their primary job. Reporters have to require prior approval for any outside activity.

A more troublesome conflict arises over a reporter's or editor's spouse working on volunteering for certain activities. Many newspapers do not permit its editorial employees to make editorial decisions about people they are related to by blood or marriage.

Finally, the conflict may arise, because of newspaper or management entanglements in the community. What is the newspaper's position with respect to, FICCI if the publisher is its president? How does the paper treat an institution when the editor is a member of the board of directors? Can a reporter cover the issue objectively if his own child is studying in that school? In such circumstances would the public perceive the coverage to be unbiased?

Withholding Information

A fourth category of ethical questions involves both reporters and editors, who must make decisions about withholding information. A reporter decides daily about what will and will not be included in a story. Most of the decisions will be based on criteria of news value; if the news is timely, interesting and important, it should be reported. But there are times when other factors will influence the decision.

To what extent does the public have a need to know about an individual's private life? Does the public need to know details of the sexual entanglements of public officials? Is the inclusion of the addresses of elderly robbery victims who live alone an inducement for others to victimize them? Is it ethical to report if a minister is killed in a car accident and a dozen girlie magazines are found in his car. To what extent it was ethical to intrude the private lives of Bill Clinton—Monica Lewinsky case.

A commonly accepted practice among both print and broadcast journalists is to withhold the names of sexual-assault victims because there is a perceived social stigma attached to being a rape victim. Those who argue that the names should be printed say that the female can unjustly accuse a male without suffering the consequences of public scrutiny, that the social stigma of being a rape victim will never fade until the media start handling it as they do other crime news and that withholding those names makes the media vulnerable to pressure to withhold names in other news. For the moment, at least, those who withhold the names are clearly in the majority.

Photography is another area of information that is being scrutinized more carefully these days. The most dramatic, shots of tragedies, fires, crimes, rescues and accidents are no longer published routinely. That is because more and more, readers are saying that they find them offensive. Because pictures are so powerful, they have impact beyond words, therefore, they must be handled carefully. Now the question arises is it ethical to show the face of a dead person or to show grieving relatives or to show death? Editors have found that proximity is an important consideration. Readers are more apt to accept pictures that show the faces of dead people if they are not local. A picture of a body under blanket is much less offensive than one not covered, even if readers can't see the face. The larger dramatic pictures are displayed, the more likely it is that some readers are going to believe the newspaper is sensationalizing the story.

Despite all this, few editors withhold pictures or film merely because some readers or viewers might object. The important thing is to know when and why they will object. Then if the decision is to print or broadcast, the editors can be prepared to answer the criticism with arguments considered before the decision was made rather than in hindsight. Several survey's results indicate that most editors are situationists. They are concerned about the consequences of their acts. While this concern helps them decide when, and whether to withhold information, in the industry there still is a tradition of fierce independence and loyalty to the reader.

Deceit

This category of ethical questions involves reporting techniques that might deceive readers, sources or those under investigation. Some of these practices, are anathema to nearly everyone, others are more debatable, and still others may be illegal and yet be ethical.

Some journalistic techniques can deceive readers which make them believe that a story is accurate and fair. One such practice involves picking up quotes from newspaper clippings and recycling them as if they were timely and presented in the right context. Another involves reporting charges against an individual without giving adequate opportunity for reply in the same article. A third is the subtle use of words to colour a story such as 'claims' for 'says' and 'demands' for 'asks'. And still another involves the subtle practice of ignoring news when it might be considered damaging to a newspaper's editorial or advertising interests.

The undesirability of some other techniques is not so clear cut. Lying, surprisingly enough, is one. If it is wrong to lie, then the absolutists never would conceal their identity to gather information. The situationist, however would balance the information to be gained against the deceit involved.

Frequently, reporters are requested to conceal not their own identities but those of their sources. News columns and broadcasts are sprinkled with references such as 'highly placed sources', 'government officials', and 'sources close to the Prime Minister'. These descriptions are often code words understood by other journalists but usually not known to the reader.

Widespread use of anonymous sources may be necessary when covering volatile diplomatic issues and exposing management or crime in public offices. But it is not necessary in all of these instances, and the practice is subject to abuse. Politicians and private parties alike use anonymity to destroy other people's reputations, to test public opinion on new programmes and to advance special interests. Reporters who allow themselves to be used by sources who have no legitimate reason for anonymity, damage the credibility of their publications. Even when the reporters decide that the requests are legitimate, they are obliged to double check the accuracy of the information given. Verification is absolutely necessary.

Reporters use many techniques they would consider unethical in a given situation, may be justifiable. They have led sources to believe they knew more than they really did in order to force more information into the open. Much of the consumer reporting involves the reporter acting in the role of the consumer. Ashwini Sarin, a senior journalist got him arrested to expose the conditions prevalent in the Tihar Jail. He also purchased a lady named 'Kamla' by pretending to be one of the buyer in order to expose women trade in Madhya Pradesh. Such stories would be impossible to cover if reporters identified themselves.

Rationale for certain kinds of Deceit

It would have been much simple if gathering information were a matter of asking questions and obtaining responses. But what the investigative reporters wants is more technical, more valuable and more protected than ever. The records that reporters need to investigate government officials are locked in safes or stored in computers. People who fear for their jobs are afraid to talk to reporters. Some documents are shredded to destroy evidence, while others are classified to avoid embarrassment rather than to protect national security. Many journalists believe that these extraordinary problems require extraordinary measures. That is why some journalists are willing to deceive people in some situations. That is why some journalists are willing to accept stolen documents in some situations. But just as most journalists believe that if they must err, they should err on the side of publication rather than suppression. Some journalists also believe that they should try for every legal and unquestionable means of gathering information before considering more dubious techniques.

Absolutist reporters cannot operate successfully in today's society. The information they need often is not available by conventional means. Situationists are more successful because they balance the good to be gained against the transgression to be committed. It is a fine line that situationists must draw. Journalists not deeply committed to a set of ethical principles will too easily and too often forget those principles in the heat of the hunt for information. As a journalist one must be prepared to defend the ethical against the unethical, sometimes against its own employer. And must also be prepared ultimately to give up job to defend principles.

Invasion of privacy

The public generally feel that journalists too often simply run over people's private lives. For that reason and others, public confidence and respect for the press is relatively low. The perception that journalists peek in windows, crowd around private citizens who have been thrust into the public limelight and intrude into private spaces in pursuit of a story is based partly on fact and partly on fiction. Movies and television shows often portray the press as uncaring, insensitive, unthinking members of a pack whose only concern is to get the story.

Invasion of privacy is a violation of a person's right to be left alone. A reporter may be under invasion of privacy suit under the following circumstances:

1. When a reporter physically intrude into a private area to get a story picture.
2. When a reporter publishes a story or photograph about someone that is false but not defamatory.
3. When a reporter discloses something about an individual's private affairs that is true but also is offensive to individuals of ordinary sensibilities.
4. When a reporter uses someone's name or picture in an advertisement or for similar purposes of trade.

The term 'privacy' has been coined by Thomas Cooley, the American scholar who defined it simply as a right to be let alone. Since then some aspects of the right of the individual to be free from and protected against highly offensive publicity, concerning private life, affairs and activities, which do not impinge upon public interest, has been recognized in several countries. Legal relief for invasion of privacy is achieved through an action for the public disclosure of private facts, the publicity of which is not 'newsworthy,' i.e. not of legitimate public concern.

Intrusion or invasion on the privacy of individuals is not permissible unless out weighed by genuine overriding public interest not being a prurient or morbid curiously. The right to privacy is implicit in the right to life and liberty guaranteed to the citizens of this country by Article 21. A Citizen has a right to safeguard the privacy of his own, his family, marriage, procreation, motherhood, child-bearing and education and other matters. None can publish anything concerning the above matters without his consent—whether truthful or otherwise and whether laudatory or critical if he does so, he would be violating the right to privacy of the person concerned and would be liable in an action for damages. Position may- however, be different, if a person voluntarily thrust himself into controversy or voluntarily invites or raises a controversy.

Article 12 of the Universal Declaration of Human Rights made by the International Convention on Human Rights 1948 (ratified in 1978) proclaims.

No one should be subjected to arbitrary interference with his privacy, family, home or correspondence, nor to attacks upon his honour and reputation. Everyone has the right to the protection of the law against such interference or attacks.

Article 8 of the European Convention on Human Rights guarantees the right of privacy, against *the government*, thus:

Everyone has the right to respect for his private and family life, his home and his correspondence. There shall be no interference by a public authority with the exercise of this right except such as is in accordance with the law and is necessary in a democratic society in the interests of national security, public safety or the economic well-being of the country, for the prevention of disorder or crime, for the protection of health or morals or for the protection of the rights and freedom of others.

It is true that the people's right to know and freedom of the press to impart information about the working of the Government and its functionaries, are facts of the fundamental guarantee enshrined in Article 19 (i) (a) of the Constitution, but the said right is an essential ingredient of personal liberty. It further follows, if there is a clash between the public official's privacy and the public's right to know about his personal affairs and traits of character impinging upon or having a bearing on the due discharge of his official duties, the former must yield to the latter. However, it is equally obvious that in matters of personal privacy which are not relevant to the discharge of his official duties, the public official enjoys the same protection as any other citizen.*

Rationale of privacy

The rationale of privacy has been aptly summed up by the eminent jurist, Soli Sorabjee:

Human beings need to preserve their individuality to enable them to lead their lives with dignity which becomes difficult if intimate details

* R.S. Sarkaria, A Guide to Journalistic Ethics, Press Council of India, New Delhi, 1995.

of a person's life, his or her innermost thoughts, fears and desires are exposed to public gaze. Hence, individuals require protection from surveillance by the state and its minions as also freedom from ruthless intrusion into their personal affairs by the all prying eye of the public and the Press. The essence of privacy lies in an individual's right to be let alone, "the most comprehensive of rights and the right most valued by civilized men."

If the media continue to exhibit such responsibility, public trust and confidence in the institution may grow. However, decisions to withhold information to protect someone's privacy are not made without cost. Every time it is done, the media get requests from others who want to be treated the same way. The extreme result of that type of policy is a nameless and faceless news report.

The courts usually protect the press against invasion of privacy suits when it is reporting matters of legitimate public interest. There are exceptions. One is, when a reporter invades someone's privacy by entering private property to get a story. One cannot trespass an private property to get a story or take a picture even if it is newsworthy. The courts will not protect when a reporter is a trespasser. Two, the court will also not protect if a reporter invades someone's privacy out of carelessness. For example, a legal problem arises if a picture or information from a story about a pedestrian struck by a careless driver is used again in connection with a story, say, about careless pedestrians. The pedestrian who was hit could file a lawsuit charging either label or invasion of privacy because the case may involve some damage to reputation. If it were the driver rather than the pedestrian who had been careless in the original incident, reporter's later story is also false.

The courts say that in order for privacy to be invaded there must be a morbid and sensational prying into private lives. Merely being the subject of an unflattering and embarrassing article is not enough.

The Media Response

The journalist's commitment to ethical practices is not a new one. For generations, journalism has been practiced by honourable people who have gone to jail, lost their jobs and suffered numerous other hardships in defense of their principles.

Journalism requires a commitment to truth, a sympathy for the public interest and willingness to shun personal aggrandizement. But the journalist's ethical code is voluntary. As such, it has to be accepted on a personal, intellectual and moral basis. There are no licenses to be withdrawn as in the case of medical, and accounting progressions. And that is as should be, not only because a free press requires freedom from licensing, but also because ethical behaviour cannot be legislated.

No codes, whether mandatory or voluntary, can anticipate all situations. Even laws are constantly revised to accommodate omissions and changing social norms, codes are adequate guidelines. Journalists must draw upon their own moral codes to provide specific answers to the complex questions faced in their daily work.

In India, the Press Council of India (PCI) has been mandated to build up a code of conduct for journalists in accordance with high professional standard. The PCI has brought out an updated and succinct compilation of principles of journalistic ethics, sorted out from the adjudications of the council and the guidelines issued from time to time.

The guidelines framed by PCI for guidance of journalists are given in the Annexure I.

Exercises

1. You learn that the daughter of an industrialists has been kidnapped. The family has not been contacted by the kidnappers, and police officials ask you to keep the matter secret for fear the abductors might panic and injure the child. Describe how the absolutist, the antinomian and the situationist would react to the police request and what their reasons would be to justify their decision.
2. Is there an ethical difference between receiving a bottle of liquor and receiving a round trip airline ticket from India to Australia from a news source? Explain your answer, and identify the philosophical category (absolulist situationist or antinomian) that your response fits.
3. A Woman bank teller thwarts a robbery by alert thinking; the would-be robbers escape. The bank manager, fearing the woman or her family might suffer reprisals, urges you to omit any identification in your story. Would you :
   (a) Follow your usual style of carrying full name, age and address?
   (b) Use only her name but no address?
   (c) Omit her name and describe her only as a "teller"?

Justify your response.

21

PRESS LAWS

"If you write that, I'll sue."*

That threat can be intimidating to the young reporter who hears it for the first time. Those with a bit more experience will have encountered the situation many times. In either case, such a threat should not be taken lightly. It is quite possible that the person making it is both serious about the threat and accurate in insisting that your information is incorrect. If you are wrong, both you and your newspaper could suffer.

Reporters, who know their stories are accurate, are never intimidated by such threats. If what you write is true, and you can prove it, you have little to fear when threats of lawsuits are tossed about. The laws that pertain to libel, invasion of privacy and protection of sources are among the many you should know about. In an era when people increasingly turn to the courts to solve their problems, it makes sense to have an understanding of your rights as a journalist to gather and write the news.

Fact Reporting

Fact reporting is the surest way to keep you and your paper out of the courts. So the key to avoiding legal problems is accurate, fair minded and factual reporting. The important ethical principles of reporting can be summarized in four words, as suggested by veteran newsman and former professor, Dean F. Rea: These are—Fairness, Accuracy, Completeness and Temperance.

Fairness means that you will be honest and aboveboard, that you will not engage in trickery or deceit. It means you will not accuse (or quote someone else as accusing) a person of wrongdoing without evidence and without giving the person a chance to respond or explain. It means that your reporting will contain no personal bias. Granted, everyone has

---

* Brian S. Brooks, et. al, *News Reporting and Writing,* New York: St. Martin's Press, 1988, p. 441.

personal opinions, but a good reporter can rise above personal leanings. Be tolerant and open-minded. You certainly don't have to agree with everything you quote people as saying. By allowing people to say what they really think and feel, you depict a broader, more varied world—also a more interesting world, difference of opinion is not only what makes horse races, but also adds colour and zest to the reporter's professional life.

Accuracy being accurate is not easy. It requires you to take great pains to be correct in every detail, checking and double-checking the small details as well as the large concepts. Names, addresses, ages—these are where mistakes most frequently happen. If you can't even spell a person's name right (when you have city directories, telephone books, and other sources available), can your reporting of other facts and ideas really be trusted?

Accuracy is more than just factual details, however, "Balance" is also essential. Your account of, say, executive council meeting could conceivably be accurate in the details you chose to report, but dreadfully inaccurate if you chose to report only one side of a controversy and not the other.

Completeness your story should include not only a balanced account but a complete one which means taking special pains to get the other side of the story. It means seeking replies from those whose good name might be ruffled in the heat of discussion in the executive council.

Temperance does not apply here to abstinence from alcohol or drugs, though that's good advice to follow while on the job. Rather, the term means restraint, in common sense. It means not going off the deep end. It means good taste. It means avoiding the pitfalls of sensationalism such as elevating petty gossip to banner headline status or blowing minor details grotesquely out of perspective.

These four principles are the benchmarks of good reporting. On the whole they go beyond what the law requires. With these principles in mind, let's look the major legal considerations one by one. They are : (1) libel, (2) invasion of privacy, (3) access to open meeting and public records, (4) protection of sources, and (5) copyright.

Libel

Libel is the foremost hazard in day-to-day reporting. Libel is defined as defamation in writing as opposed to defamation by the spoken work (slander). However defamation that comes from broadcast news is considered libel rather than slander.

The term *defamation* means an untrue and unprivileged statement that tends to hold a person up to public contempt, ridicule, or hatred, or to injure a person's reputation, or to cause a person to be shunned or avoided, or to injure personal business or professional pursuits.

A person who claims to have been defamed may bring a civil lawsuit into the court. Upon winning the suit the defamed person may collect monetary damages running into thousands of rupees.

So it's important to avoid lawsuits in the first place. Step one is to recognize libel when you see it. Suspect libel whenever someone or some agency accuses of any kind of wrongdoing, such as a crime or a moral indiscretion. Some statements are so recklessly extravagant that they should ring alarm bells the moment you hear them. For example it's dangerous to call (or quote someone as calling) a person any of these terms :

Adulterer, murderer, cheat, blackmailer, racist, embezzler, gangster, and a host of similar terms.

All of these are so reckless that a journalist ought to recognize them immediately. As noted, quoting another person's libelous statement does not protect you from liability.

Someone suing you for libel must establish four elements : *defamation, publication, identification,* and *fault.*

Defamation has already been defined as an injurious statement about another person or agency.

Publication means the defamation has been disseminated to other people.

Identification means that the person or group bringing the suit must be specifically identified. This does not always mean the defamed party must be named. To refer to "a certain butcher on Park Street in Kolkatta who sells adulterated meat" is cause for action if only one butcher operates on Park Street. If two butchers operated there, you might even be sued by both because the innocent butcher may have suffered injury as well as your intended target. however, statements like "all politicians are crooks" are so vague as to preclude libel actions.

Fault means that the defendant—the reporter and the paper—has done something wrong which brought about the libel: what the law calls "negligence." States vary in the way they define negligence, but in general it boils down to this question: Did the reporter exercise a reasonable care collecting and writing the information?

This "simple negligence" applies to libel suits brought by private citizens. A different standard applies to public officials and what the courts call "public figures." They must prove "malice," which is a higher level of negligence. The legal definition of malice is that the reporter or paper either knew the information was false or acted with "reckless disregard" to whether it was true or not.

The significance of this is that juries tend to decide against the media, but that higher ("appellate") courts, looking at the finer nuances of media law, tend to overturn the jury decision. It's small solace to media to win the case ultimately in the appellate courts, however, because of the enormous expenses involved in defending a case.

Libel suit defences

There are three traditional defences against libel: truth, privilege, and fair comment and criticism. Two other constitutional defences—the actual malice and negligence tests—are commonly used in more limited circumstances.

Truth: It is, of cource, a defense against libel, but it may not be as solid a defence as you think. Knowing something to be true and proving it in court are two different things. You must have documentary proof or a string of witnesses willing to testify in court before you are on safe ground. This means that a reporter, particularly an investigative reporter, must know the rules of evidence just about as well as a prosecuting attorney before proceeding to publish.

While you must always strive for absolute truth in all of your stories, the courts will settle for what is known as 'substantial truth' in most cases. This means that you must be able to prove the essential elements of all you write.

Privilege: In addition to truth, the courts traditionally have allowed another defence against libel: privilege. Privilege is based on the principle that public debate on pubic issues should be uninhibited, even "robust and wide open", to use the words of one jurist. This defence applies when you are covering any of the three branches of government. The courts allow legislators, judges and government executives the absolute privilege to say anything—true or false—when acting in their official capacities. The rationale is that the public interest is served when an official is allowed to speak freely and fearlessly about making laws, carrying them out or punishing those who do not obey them. Similarly, a party in a judicial proceedings, such as an attorney or judge is absolutely privileged to say or publish false and even defamatory information about another person during that proceeding.

As a reporter you do have a conditional or qualified privilege to report what public officials say your privilege is conditional upon your report's being full, fair and accurate coverage of the court session, the legislative session or the Prime Minister's press conference, even if any one of those includes defamatory statements.

You can quote anything the Prime Minister of India says without fear of losing a libel suit. But there are many other levels of executives at all levels of government, national, state and local. Mayors of small towns, for instance, often hold part time positions. They are absolutely protected from libel suits, and you are conditionally privileged to report on what those officials say when they are acting in their official capacities. The problem arises when the mayor says something defamatory when not acting in an official capacity.

Fair Comment and Criticism: "Fair comment and criticism", is the term applied to an honest expression of opinion on a matter of public concern. The opinion may be vigorous, even satirical or sarcastic, but it must be based on facts correctly stated. It must concern itself with the public aspects of the work, which is to say that you may pass judgement on the literary merits of an author's but not his or her private morals.

A mis-statement of fact, of course, would be treated like any other libel case. You can voice the opinion that the author's work is "dull, worthless, trashy, unworthy of thinking men and women," and so forth, but if you add that the author plagiarized the work, you'd better by prepared to prove it. Similarly, you must avoid questioning the artist's motives with remarks like, "He's obviously a racist or he wouldn't have written such trash."

The Actual Malice and Negligence tests

The term "malice" does not carry the usual meaning of "ill will", but refers to the publication of statements known to be false or with "reckless disregard" of their possible falsity. To prove malice the public official or public figure who brings the suit must show "sufficient evidence" to permit the conclusion that in fact the defendant entertained serious doubts as to the truth of the publication.

Assume you were told that years ago your town's mayor had been involved in a bootlegging operation. Your source was a friend of the mayor who knew him 20 years ago in Lucknow. You print the story. After it is published you find it was not the mayor but his brother who was the bootlegger. The mayor sues. You are in trouble. You must try to convince the court that you should have been to trust your source and that you did not act with "actual malice." If the source had given you many stories in the past, you might be able to convince the court that you had good reason to believe what you were told. You also would have to show what else you did or failed to do before you printed the story. Did you call anyone in Lucknow to check? Did you talk to the mayor'. Did you try other ways to verify the information? All these questions will be asked as the court tries to decide whether you recklessly regarded the truth.

Usually a reporter who has tried diligently to do all possible research for a story will be able to meet the actual malice test and win a libel action. The key is verification: checking the information with as many sources as possible.

In order to bring a successful libel suit, "fault" must be proved. Fault comes at two levels: "Simple negligence" by the media defendant in the case of a private person, "actual malice" in the case of a public official or figure. Here you must understand that a "public official" is one who occupies that public office and the "public figure" is one who does not hold public office but is prominent enough to be public figure among the public eye. For instance, a doctor who runs private medical practice but is so concerned about iodine deficiency that he has made many public speeches. He has become a public figure because he has thrust himself to the forefront of the iodine deficiency controversy.

So the fault requirement has become a standard defence as the defendant tries to prove that he or she was not negligent in a suit filed by a private person or that no actual malice occurred in a suit filed by a public official or figure.

Punishment Section 500 IPC prescribes the punishment for defamation. The section reads as follows:

"Whosoever defames another shall be punished with simple imprisonment for a term which may extend to two years, or with fine or with both." Punishment for a journalist may be severe in view of the fact that the defamatory statement gets wide publicity.

Invasion of Privacy

Privacy is not the day-to-day problem that libel is, but it has its own peculiarity largely because it's vague area of law. In general, the law of privacy boils down to the right of citizen to be left alone. The more a person is in the limelight—celebrities and public official particularly—the more privacy one surrenders. Even celebrities and public officials are entitled to protect some private facts of their lives.

Privacy law generally comes in four categories:

Appropriation: You cannot appropriate another person's name for commercial gain. You cannot use a name or photo of a person celebrated or not, in an advertisement without that person's permission.

Intrusion: You cannot intrude unreasonably on another person's seclusion. This precludes electronic eavesdropping or going to unreasonable lengths to photograph a person in seclusion, such as using a helicopter and a telephoto lens to get a picture of the mayor sunbathing nude in secluded backyard. Similarly, you cannot trespass on private property in quest for information, such as following the police or fire-fighter into a private home to photograph a crime or fire scene. You cannot give false identity to gain access to a private area. However, a person gives up the right to privacy when going into public zone: the streets, sidewalks, parks, public auditoriums.

False light: You may not cast a person in a false light such as ascribed views he or she does not hold, or describing the person as having done thing the person has, in fact, not done. This is true even if the description is highly laudatory.

The Saturday Evening Post published a photo of a child almost struck down by a careless motorist to illustrate an article titled. "They Asked to be Killed." The court held that the photo falsely depicted the child as a careless pedestrian. False light cases are becoming increasingly important as writers experiment with "new journalism" or "literary journalism," which means using the methods of fiction to depict factual materials. To some careless or unscrupulous writers, however, it means "fictionalizing": creating fictitious events and dialogue of conversations involving real people without a scrap of evidence that these things even occurred. Celebrities, long the target of careless and distorted reporting, have been striking back at the gossip papers, and juries are sympathetic to the celebrities.

Embarrassing facts: Use caution when writing about a person's private life, particularly when revealing embarrassing or unduly intimate facts. This is an unpredictable area of privacy law. Consider the following examples: (1) You write about a former child prodigy years later, depicting the highly idiosyncratic lifestyle of a person attempting to live in seclusion. (2) You write about a well-known athlete, going beyond the public side of his character and delving deeply into his private life. (3) You depict, years later, the earlier activities of a former prostitute involved in a sensational murder trial who has since assumed the identity of a respectable matron, putting her past life behind her. (4) You use without permission a photo of a woman emerging from a carnival fun house, her skirt blown above her waist by a jet of air. (5) You write about a person who had committed a crime years earlier but has since been living exemplary life following his release from prison.

Though these are the actual cases but the variety of ruling suggests the need for caution in dealing with truthful but potentially embarrassing details of a person's private life.

Defences

Unlike libel cases, truth is not always a defence in privacy cases. Your account may be totally factual and true and yet be subject to privacy litigation. Two level of defences are commonly used in privacy suits.

Newsworthiness: This is the defence particularly suited for litigation of Category 4, depicting of intimate facts. This means the information provided is truly a news event or concerns a person, particularly a famous person, in whom the public has a legitimate interest. By and large this includes people who were once infamous in the public eye, and have since retired to oblivion. Legal definitions of newsworthiness tend to be even more vague than our own journalistic definitions.

Consent: Clearly you need consent—usually in writing—to use someone's name or likeness to be used for commercial gain. Consent, however, is not required for news reports or news photos dealing with public activities such as public meetings or automobile accidents on the motorist needs no consent for publication in the newspaper where it originally appeared because it was a newsworthy incident. It was only when its use in the *Saturday Evening Post* cast the child in a false light that the absence of consent was meaningful.

"Implied consent" can also be a defence in cases where revealing facts are published in, say, a newspaper interview. If the person has invited you to her home, agreed to be interviewed, and spoke candidly about her personal life while you took notes, raised no objection to their possible publication, then she has *implied* consent so long as the proposed story was not misrepresented and is a balanced account of the interview.

"False light" suit defences are to prove the truth of the published statement and to show the absence of actual malice—knowledge of falsity.

"Intrusion" suits—the telephoto shots of the nude mayor in the backyard is also hard to defend other than to convince the court that the activities complained of do not constitute "intrusion." Failing that no legal defence exists for intrusion.

Access to Information

The compelling function of the press is that it shall supply information on all matters which may be of interest to the community provided that the information is accurate and fair. The community wants information not only of tangible facts happening round the corner, but of facts and opinions from all parts of the world. It is not satisfied in knowing merely that a Minister was removed from office, but even more interested in why he was removed and what is the truth behind the scene.

With the increasing complexity and diversity of world—wide socio-economic relations, you can no longer rely merely on his own or directly verifiable sources of information, but must collect it from diverse sources.

To do your job, however, you must have access to the machinations of government: the meetings, the paperwork, the decisions, the records.

Not everyone agrees with that principle, of course. Some secretive bureaucrats insist that it is in the public interest to make decisions in private and announce them (if at all) after everything has been concluded. This limits public knowledge and debate on an issue, thus severely crippling the concept of self-government. For that reason, such secrecy is illegal in most governmental jurisdictions in the State legislations and court decisions have generally opposed the view that secrecy is in the public interest.

Protection of Sources

Another area you must know about is your ability—or inability—to protect your sources and notes. The problem may arise in various situations. A grand jury that is investigating a murder may ask you to reveal the source of a story you wrote about the murder. You may be asked to testify at a criminal or a civil trial. Or the police may obtain a warrant to search the news room, including your desk.

The conflict here is between a reporter's need to protect sources of information and the duty of every citizen to testify to help the courts determine justice. By the nature of your work as a reporter, you will be at the scene of events that are important and newsworthy. Anyone wanting the facts about an event can subpoena you to bring in all the details. Journalists usually resist. They work for their newspaper, radio or television station, not a law enforcement agency. Their ability to gather information would be compromised if the sources knew that their identities or their information would go to the police.

The only way to avoid such confrontation with the courts is not to promise a source you will keep his or her name confidential.

Copyright

The copyright Act, 1957 provides the author with protection against unfair appropriation of his or her work.

The law is too complex to treat here except to explore briefly the one aspect of copyright that is of concern to most reporters: How much, if may, can a reporter quote from copyrighted material without permission of the copyright holder.

The answer is not simple. A "fair use doctrine" has emerged from court decisions over the years that suggests that a small amount of quotation from copyrighted materials is permissible in the interests of a free flow of ideas.

In determining 'fair use' following factors are taken into consideration :

- Is the use for commercial or nonprofit purposes?
- What is the nature of the copyrighted work?
- How much is being used?
- Will the use damage the salability of the original?

The following guidelines, however, might help you in deciding how much to quote without asking permission, assuming you are using copyrighted material in a local newspaper of general circulation :

- In factual articles depicting a situation of public interest, quote not more than 5 percent of an article or essay, or upto 200 words, whichever is less (For example, use not more than 75 words of a 1,500—word essay.)
- Do not quote from poems or song, lyrics without permission.
- Be wary of quoting from purely "literary" works such as novels, short stories, and plays. Have reasonable justification for use of the excerpts.
- Do not reproduce photos, works of art, or statistical tables without permission.
- Have a noble reason for using a quote: public interest, public welfare, public health and safety, the education of the young, and so forth. The more public interest that can be shown, the safer it is to use the material without permission.

- Remember that only the arrangement of words—not the facts themselves—are copyrightable. Therefore, facts contained in a copyrighted news story can be sued, though they should be confirmed by your own independent research (never trust another publication to have the facts straight.)
- Always ask permission when quoting from private letters unless they were obviously intended for publication (such as a letter to the editor). Common law protects unpublished materials, and even a snippet of such a letter must not be used without the permission of the author. (Common law is more strict in this matter than statutory copyright.) You must obtain permission from the *sender,* not the receiver.
- Always credit fully the source of the quotation.
- If in doubt about any of the above considerations, get permission. It's seldom refused when small amounts of quotation are involved, because local newspaper reproduction seldom offers commercial competition to a copyrighted work. Indeed, it may even enhance sales.

Apart from the above major legal considerations, the journalist should also be familiar with some of the following laws and Acts and Press Organisations.

Contempt of Courts Act, 1971

The Act of 1971, for the first time, gives a complete definition of the expression 'contempt of court' in section 2 by codifying the result of judicial decisions. Clause (a) of section 2 states that there are two categories of contempt under the Act : (i) Civil contempt and (ii) Criminal contempt.

Wilful disobedience to any judgement, decree, direction, order, writ or other process of a court or wilful breach of an undertaking given to a court constitutes 'civil contempt' under Clause (b) of Section 2.

Any publication which interferes with or undermines the administration of justice or has a tendency to do so constitutes 'criminal contempt' under Clause (c) of Section 2: and this the category to which the Press generally becomes answerable.The definition in Clause (c) of Section 2 is in the following terms :

Criminal contempt means the publication (where by words, spoken or written, or by signs, or by visible representations, or otherwise) of any matter or the doing of any other act whatsoever which:

(i) scandalises or tend to scandalise or lowers or tend to lower the authority of any court, or
(ii) prejudices or interferes or tends to interfere with the due course of any judicial proceedings, or
(iii) interferes or tends to interfere with, or obstructs or tends to obstruct, the administration of justice in any other manner.

Publication of any thing which tends to create in the minds of people an apprehension about the integrity, ability or fairness of a judge or which tends to deter litigants from complete reliance upon the court's administration of justice, amounts to contempt. Similarly, a publication which is likely to cause embarrassment in the judge's mind to the discharge of his official duty is a contempt of court. But if it is proved that the concerned writing would undermine the prestige or authority of the court or public confidence in the administration of justice by it, then it is contempt even if the vilificatory criticism relates to the judge's non-judicial functions like the functions of an administration judge. Imputation of improper motives in deciding a case is obviously a contempt of court.The press does have the right which is also its professional function,to criticise and advocate.

Publication of reports of crime is a regular feature of the news. Such items are clearly matters of public interest. But it is also clear that a trial for the commission of these crimes will probably follow sooner or later. A report of the crime may, however, accurate it attempts to be, contain a statement of fact which is likely to hotly disputed at trial. It may be a question of identity or of some small detail on which a criminal trial can sometimes turn. In order to compile a report it is usually necessary to interview witnesses who may later be witnessed at the trial. The reporter may be able to obtain a very full account of what occurred and be in a position to publish a considerable amount of what would later become evidence at the trial. But there are dangers in their publication, particularly where the circumstances of a crime seem to lay suspicion upon a particular person. Even the publications of photograph of an accused is a question of extreme delicacy as in many criminal trials identification of an accused person is a vitally important issue. A witness, unable to form a mental picture of the accused might quite honestly derive such a picture of the person whose photograph he has seen in the newspaper. Such a publication may cast doubt on the prosecution's identification evidence or jeopardise the accused. Either way it is undesirable. On the other hand, photographs of wanted men are sometimes published at the request of police either to assist in their apprehension or to warn the public against them, or both. It must, therefore, necessarily be a question of fact and circumstances whether a publication in any particular case offends against the law.

Journalists sometimes investigate suspected crimes, malpractices and abuses and accumulate evidence. Publication of such material is often in the public interest and also helps in boosting the circulation of the newspaper. The law of contempt does not hinder publication of such accumulated evidence before the accused are arrested and charged. But when once judicial proceedings are set in motion, the press should not publish the evidence. When a person is being tried for an offence, if the press has evidence that some other person is guilty of the crime, propriety would demand that the evidence in the possession of the press be placed before the court. By adopting such a course it will get the credit for its investigative effort though the advantage of increased circulation through publication exclusively in its column would be lost.

However, the power to punish for scandalising the court, is to be used sparingly and in defence to the administration of justice only. It can not be used for vindicating personal insult to the judge. Bonafide criticism that is fair and reasonable criticism of a judicial act in the interest of public good does not amount to contempt. But if improper motives are attributed to the judges then it ceases to be bonafide. A judgement can be criticised as erroneous but dishonesty on the part of the judge in delivering the judgement can not be alleged. If a statement is likely to prejudice or interfere with the due course of justice, then the truthfulness of the facts on which it is based, is no defence. Trial by the newspapers has been considered by courts as interferences with the proper administration of justice in pending cases.

However, punishment can be awarded for interference with the due course of justice only if the interference is substantial. Similarly, a person will not be guilty of contempt of court for innocent publication of distribution during the pendency of civil or criminal proceedings of a matter which would otherwise deem to constitute contempt.

Limitations of Contempt of court

- Innocent publication and distribution of matter which falls under any of the categories of contempt under the Act.
- Fair and accurate report of judicial proceedings; publication of

a fair and accurate report of a pending judicial proceeding is protected under Section 4 provided it is not prohibited under Section 7. Section 7 prohibits such publication where it is prohibited by a statute or by the court on certain grounds, such as security of the State, public order and the like.

- Fair criticism of judicial act, publication of fair criticism of a judicial act including a judicial decision is also protected under Section 5 because the public has an interest in the proper administration of justice. Judges and courts are likely to open to criticism and if reasonable argument is offered against any judicial act as contrary to law or public good, such criticism is protected and will not amount to contempt. The plea of fair comment on a judgement can not be availed of if the comment is made before the case is heard and finally decided. Under explanation (a) to Section 3, a case can not be said to have been finally decided until the period of limitation for preferring appeal or revision against the decision commented upon has expired or, if appeal or revision has been filed, the appeal and revision, too, has been heard and finally decided.
- Bonafide complaint concerning the presiding officer of any subordinate court is not contempt of court.

Many written words may be both contempt and defamation. To describe a judge in his judicial capacity as a swindler is contempt of court as well as defamation.

Under Section 129 and 215 Criminal Procedure Code, Supreme Court, High Courts and Lower Courts have been given the powers to punish any institution, an organisation, a person or any government officer for contempt of court.

Punishment

In case of civil contempt, the contemptor cannot be sent even to simple imprisonment. He can be detained in a civil prison for not more than six months, normally a fine would be considered sufficient to meet the ends of justice.

In case of criminal contempt, a contemptor can be punished with simple imprisonment only for a term expanding up to six months or with a fine upto two thousand rupees or with both. If he makes a satisfactory apology, the accused may be discharged or the punishment awarded may be remitted.

The time limit for action for contempt of court is one year from the date on which the contempt is alleged to have committed.

The Working Journalists and Other Newspaper Employees (Conditions of Service) and Miscellaneous Provisions Act, 1955

This Act regulates certain conditions of service of working journalists and other persons employed in newspaper establishments.

The First Press Commission found that the emoluments received by the journalists were on the whole unsatisfactory. It could not undertake a detailed investigation for fixing scales of pay for different categories of employees. But it recognised the necessity for fixing a minimum wage for the journalist employees and made recommendations relating to the minimum wages paid to them. In 1955, The Working Journalists (Conditions of Service) Miscellaneous Provisions Act was enacted and the Industrial Disputes Act, 1947 was made applicable to working journalists also. With the successive revisions of pay scales through Wage Boards, neutralisation of the rise in the cost of living and provision of security of service, the terms and conditions of service of newspaper employees have considerably improved. Some important provisions of the Act are:

(i) The provisions applicable to workmen under the Industrial Disputes Act, 1947 shall apply to working journalists.

(ii) The working journalists, who have been in continuous service for at least three years in newspaper establishment are entitled for gratuity equivalent to fifteen days average pay for every completed year of service or any part thereof in excess of six months on termination, retirement, resignation or death as per Section 3.

(iii) No working journalist shall be required to work for more than one hundred and forty four hours during any period of four consecutive weeks, exclusive of the time for meals. Every working journalist shall be allowed during any period of seven consecutive days rest for a period of not less than twenty four hours inclusive of the period between 10 P.M. and 6 A.M.

(iv) Every working journalist shall be entitled to earned leave on full wages for not less than one eleventh of the period spent on duty and leave on medical certificate on one -half of the wages for not less than one- eighteenth period of the service.

(v) A Wage Board shall be constituted by the Central Government for fixing and revising of rates of wages of working journalists. The Wage Board shall consist of :

(a) Two representatives of newspaper employees;
(b) Two representatives of working journalists ;and
(c) Three independent persons, one of whom shall be a person who is or has been a judge of a High Court or the Supreme Court and who shall be appointed by the Government as its Chairman.

The Section 12 of the Act empowers the Central Government to enforce recommendations of the Wage Board and make modifications in the recommendations, if necessary.

(vi) The Central Government can fix interim rates of wages in consultation with the Wage Board under Section 13-A.

(vii) A Wage Board shall be constituted by the Central Government for fixing or revising rates of wages in respect of non-journalist newspaper employees (Section 13-B). It shall consist of :

(a) Two representatives of newspaper employees;
(b) Two representatives of non-journalist newspaper employees;
(c) Three independent persons, one of whom shall be a person who is or has been a judge of a High Court or the Supreme Court and who shall be appointed by the government as its Chairman.

(viii) Provisions of the following Acts shall apply in every newspaper establishment employing twenty or more employees:

(a) Industrial Employment (Standing Orders) Act, 1946.
(b) The Employees Provident Fund Act, 1952.

(ix) If any employer contravenes any of the provisions of this Act, he shall be punishable with fine which may extend to two hundred rupees. If the offence is committed for second time, the fine may extend to five hundred rupees.

Contempt of Legislature

Privileges are certain fundamental rights of each House which are generally accepted as necessary for the exercise of its constitutional functions.

Article 105 and 194 of the Constitution provide for Parliament and State Legislatures the powers, privileges and the immunities they have.

Clause (2) confers immunity to publication of proceedings, papers etc., of a House only when the publication is made by or under the authority of that House. The implication is that even a true newspaper report of proceedings of a House is not protected under this clause.

Clause (3) as it originally stood stated that in all those respects not covered by these provisions, the powers, the privileges, and immunities of Parliament and State Legislatures, until defined by law, shall be those of the House of Commons of the Parliament of the United Kingdom as existing at the time of commencement of the Constitution.The forty fourth amendment of the Constitution made verbal changes in this clause omitting the reference to the House of Commons, but the substance of the clause remains the same. Thus the position is that if one were to ask what are the privileges of Parliament and State Legislatures in India other than those specified in Article 105 and 194, the answer is that they are the same as those of the House of Commons as existing on 26th January 1950.

The First Press Commission recommended that both Parliament and State Legislatures should define by legislation the precise powers, privileges and immunities which they possess in regard to contempt and the procedure for enforcing them. This question has been a matter of public debate over the years and several arguments have been propounded for and against codification of privileges. The main argument against codification of privileges which has weighed with the Parliament and State Legislatures appears to be that once codification is done by law, such a law would automatically become subject to all the fundamental rights guaranteed in part III of the Constitution and the matter would become justiciable, conferring powers on the courts to adjudicate on questions of privilege thereby lowering their dignity. It has been said that codification of privileges would expose Parliament and State Legislatures "to an alien body" viz., the judiciary. Second Press Commission stated that the judiciary which is as much a creature of the Constitution as the Parliament or State Legislature is not an alien body under the scheme of our Constitution. In fact, laws enacted by Parliament and State Legislatures are, on occasion, being struck down by the courts when warranted by the constitutional provisions and on that account it can not be said that the dignity of Parliament or the Legislature suffers. Similarly, the judges of the highest court of the land are appointed by the executive and for that reason one can not say that their independence or prestige is affected. They viewed that from the point of view of freedom of the Press it is essential that the privileges of Parliament and State Legislatures should be codified as early as possible. A journalist or editor can be punished with imprisonment or administered a warning , admonition and reprimand for the breach of privilege of the House. His privileges like facilities to enter the precincts of the House and cover its proceedings can be withdrawn. He can be asked to publish an apology. However, no fines are imposed .

Contempt has a wider sweep than breach of privilege. Contempt can be committed by an act or utterance which undermines the dignity of the House even without violating any particular privilege of the Legislature.

But it is not a breach of privilege to publish without malice a substantially true report of the proceedings of the House even if it is defamatory, seditious or obscene in nature. No civil or criminal proceedings can be launched in a court of law for publication of such a report even if it offends the law relating to official secrets, defamation, sedition, obscenity or other offences under the IPC.

The Legislature in India has not enacted any law codifying its privileges, mainly because any such law will be subject to a judicial review in respect of the citizens, fundamental rights, but the action has been taken in use of inaccurate, distorted, unfair, wilful or mendacious rendering of the proceedings. Now there is a strong demand by the Press .

The Official Secrets Act, 1923

This act was enacted by the Britishers during the British rule. Some amendments have been made after independence but now there is a strong public opinion by the Press Council, Press Commission and Journalistic Associations to revise the whole Act because this Act is very hard and strict. It extends to the whole of India and applies also to the government servants and the citizens of India living outside India.

The Official Secrets Act, 1923 is a comprehensive document relating to official secrets and defines a number of offences. The Act is aimed at maintaining the security of the State against leakage of information, sabotage and the like. It consolidates law relating to the official secrets. It deals with two kinds of offence:

(i) Spying (Section 3 and 4)
(ii) Wrongful information of any other secret official code or password or any sketch, plan, article, model, note, document or information (Section 5).

Under Section 3 of the Act , it is an offence if any person for any purpose prejudicial to the safety or interest of the State.

(a) approaches, inspects , passes over or in the vicinity of or enters any prohibited place; or
(b) makes any sketch, plan, model or note which is calculated to be or might be or is intended to be directly or indirectly useful to enemy; or
(c) obtains, collects, records or publishes or communicates to any other person any other sketch, plan, model, article or note or other document or information which is calculated to be or might be or is intended to be directly or indirectly useful to an enemy.

Punishment for spying in relation to the country's defence is up to 14 years. It is not necessary to show that the accused person is guilty of any particular act tending to show a purpose prejudicial to the safety or interest of the State, and not withstanding that no such act is proved against him, he may be convicted, if, from the circumstances of the case or his conduct or his known character is proved, it appears that his purpose was a purpose prejudicial to the safety or interest of the State.

Under Section 5 of the Act, it is an offence if any person having in his possession or control any secret official code, or password or any sketch, plan, model, article or note, document or information which relates to or is used in a prohibited place or relates to anything of such a place, or which has been made or obtained in contravention of this Act or which has been entrusted in confidence to him by person holding government office, wilfully communicates the same to any person other than a person to whom he is authorised to communicate or it is his duty to communicate. It is also an offence under the same section.

— if any person voluntarily receives any secret information,

— person having in possession or in control any authorised information,
— retaining information without any authority,
— use of information in possession of government officers to help a foreign power,
— communication with foreign agents,
— if the person fails to take a reasonable care of secret information,
— incitement to commission of offence is also an offence.

Under this Act, it is the duty of every citizen to give information regarding commission of offence by any other person. Every citizen is requested to attend courts to testify. This section prescribes punishment with imprisonment upto five years or fine or both.

Under the provision of this Act, any publication by a newspaper of an official secret, whether in the form of note, document, code or password, sketch, plan or model, makes not only the correspondent, editor, printer and publisher liable to punishment but also every director and officer of the company or corporation with whose knowledge and consent the offence was committed becomes guilty of a like offence.

In India, it has been widely demanded that Section 5 of the Official Secrets Act which prohibits free reporting should be done away with. Press Commission and the Press Council of India also favoured the same opinion. The Council asked for the repeal of the Official Secrets Act,1923 *in toto* and to enact a new legislation which may be called Freedom of Information Act. Exceptions or permissible restrictions to this freedom may be specified in the proposed Act.

The Press and Registration of Books Act, 1867

This is the oldest of the existing Press Laws. It has been amended a number of times after independence. The provision of the part VA relating to registration of newspapers and the creation of the office of Press Registrar were inserted by the amending Act in 1955.

The word 'newspaper' has been defined in sub-section (1) of Section 1 to mean "any printed periodical work containing public news or comments on public news". Therefore, the definition comprehends not only daily newspapers but also news magazines of all periodicities under one category. The publication of a newspaper commences only after the making of a declaration under Section 5(2) and its authentication under Section 6 as laid down in Section 5(2c). This being so, the Magistrate authenticating the declaration can not ascertain the contents of the publication to make sure that it falls within the definition of 'newspaper'. However, under section 8 B(iv), the Press Registrar can make an application before the Magistrate for cancellation of the declaration in respect of a newspaper.

Registration

Under this Act, the intending printer/publisher has to appear in person or through an authorized agent before a specified Magistrate, and make a declaration that he is the printer/publication incharge/publisher of the newspaper and indicate therein the language and periodicity, the title of the newspaper and also a precise account of the premises where the printing or publication is to be conducted. Then the Magistrate has to write to the Press Registrar to ascertain whether the title proposed for the intended newspaper is free or is the same as or similar to that of any other newspaper published either in the same language or in the same state. The Press Registrar has to give a reply after verification of his records. On receiving clearance from the Press Registrar, the Magistrate has to authenticate the declaration and send copies thereof to the intending printer/publisher and the Press Registrar. After receipt of the authenticated declaration, the Press Registration has to issue a certificate of Registration. In view of the registration, Second Press Commission recommended that 'there is no need for personal appearance before the Magistrate for this purpose. After sending the declaration and the affidavit regarding the title the publisher should be free to commence the publication."

Press Organisations

Registrar of Newspapers for India

The office of the Registrar of Newspapers for India (RNI) also commonly known as the Press Registrar was created on 1st July, 1956, pursuant to a recommendation of the First Press Commission by amendment of the Press and Registration of Books Act, 1867.

Functions

It functions as a central government body responsible for the completion of a register giving particulars like ownership and circulation of all newspapers published in India.

As per the provisions of the Press and Registration of Books (PRB) Act, 1867 and rules under it, the Registrar of Newspapers for India is required, *inter alia* to submit an Annual Report to the Government of the status of newspapers before 30 September every year.

It overseas the allocation of titles, newsprint and certificate for the import of printing and allied machinery required by newspaper establishments and also sees to the enforcement of the provisions of the Press and Registration of Books Act, and has the authority to inspect newspaper records and documents. The RNI frequently carries out checks to find out whether the newspapers registered with it are published regularly and also whether circulation figures claimed by the newspapers are credible. It is duty of the Press Registrar to register all newspapers published in the country, to issue certificate of registration to them, to maintain the particular rating to them in a register and to submit it to the Central Government an annual report containing a summary by the information obtained by him during the previous year in respect of newspapers in the country. These annual reports entitled "Press in India" contain valuable information and statistics relating to the press.

The Press Registrar requires information about circulation figures to ensure that :

- the newsprint used is in proportion with the circulation figures,
- the printing capacity is in proportion with the circulation figures,
- the newsprint waste is normal,
- the payment of newsprint has been made in accordance with rules, and
- the details (paging, printing and circulation dates. etc.) pertaining to number of supplements printed in advance are correct.

Audit Bureau of Circulation (ABC)

ABC is an independent, self-financing and private body charged with the responsibility of conducting regular audit of the 'net circulation of newspapers' and issues certificates of Net Paid Circulation every six months. It has a very high reputation of reliability and impartiality and is, therefore, quoted with authority.

Need

During the early 1900's with the growth of mass advertising, some newspapers and magazine publishers began inflating the number of readers for their publications in order to at least get more revenue from advertisers. In an effort to check this deceptive practice, advertisers and publishers joined together to form the ABC in 1914. The organisation's purpose was to establish ground rules for counting circulation, to make sure that the rules were enforced, and to provide verified reports of circulation date. In India it came into existence in 1948.

Objectives

- To issue standardised statements of the circulation of members,
- To verify the figures shown in these statements by auditor's examination of necessary records,
- To disseminate circulation date for the benefit of advertisers, advertising agencies and newspaper publication.

What does ABC consider?

It considers the following :

- Whether the changes in the supply desired by agents have been done timely or not,
- Whether the supply is in accordance with the demand of agents or not,
- Whether payment is received from the agents in time or not,
- Action taken by the circulation department on the complaints of agents,
- The timeliness of payment made to the different modes of transport used for supplying newspapers,
- The agreements made with the dealers/agents,
- The preparation of the newsprint used and the circulation.

Functions

The ABC functions in the following manner :

Publishers keep detailed records of circulation data. In the case of a newspaper, these records would include such information as the number of copies delivered by carriers, the number of papers sold over the counter and the number delivered by mail. Twice a year, publishers file a circulation statement with the ABC which the ABC in turn disseminates to the clients. Once in every year, the ABC audits publications to verify that the figures that have been reported are accurate. An ABC representative visits the publication and is free to examine records and files that contain data on press runs, invoices for newsprint and transcripts of circulation records.

ABC report helps the advertisers as well as the newspaper. From the verified facts, the advertisers can draw their conclusion and prepare advertising plans. Newspapers are also benefited by the ABC report. Firstly, they gain respect and confidence of advertisers. Secondly, on the basis of the report, they can peep into their own activities and programmes and make a modest review of the progress made by the newspaper. Thirdly, the report is an evidence of the newspaper's worth.

*Press Information Bureau**

The Press Information Bureau (PIB) is the nodal agency of the Government of India to disseminate information to the print and electronic media on government policies, programmes , interactive and achievements. Functioning as an interface between the Government and the media , the PIB also provides feedback to the Government with people's reaction as reflected in the media, with its eight Regional Office and 35 Branch Office and Information Centres, that disseminates information though different modes of communication, such as press releases, press notes, feature articles, backgrounders, briefings, interviews, press conferences and press tours, etc. The information material released in Hindi, Urdu and 13 other regional languages reaches about 8,400 newspapers and media organisations according to *India* 2005.

The bureau at headquarters has a team of officers (Departmental Publicity Officers) who are attached to various ministries and departments for the purpose of assisting them in disseminating information to the media through press releases and press conferences etc. and advice on all matters pertaining to publicity activities. They also provide feedback to their respective ministries and departments. As part of the Special services, the Feedback cell in the PIB prepares a daily digest and special digests based on news stories and editorials from national as well as regional dailies and periodicals. The feature unit of the Special services of the Bureau provides backgrounders, updates, features and graphics. These are circulated in the national network and also sent to the Regional and

* India 2005, Publications Division, New Delhi: Ministry of I&B.

Branch offices for translation and circulation to the local press. PIB arranges photo coverage of Government activities and the photographs are supplied to dailies and periodicals published in English and other Indian languages all over the country.

The PIB website (www.pib.nic.in) is becoming more and more popular with the media. The website was reviewed and a new comprehensive facility for database search on PIB's publicity material was added. This website was updated every hour. The Bureau is linked with all regional and Branch offices over computer network to facilitate fast feeding on dissemination of information. The Bureau is connected to 26 regional centres by video conferencing system to enable media persons at regional centres participate in press conferences in New Delhi and in other parts of the country. The bureau organised multiple video conferencing between its headquarters and Regional/Branch Offices. The Bureau provided with computer and internet facilities to all Departmental Offices and Sections. Computer training was given to all its officers and staff. One additional computer and printer was given to all Branch offices during the year because of increased use of computers and increased workload. All regional and Branch Offices have been put on internet/ mail with ISD connections. At PIB Delhi news services such as UNI/PTI ticker on network, full page newspaper, electronic library were added during the year.

PIB provides accreditation to media representatives including foreign media to facilitate them to have easy access to information from Government services. Apart from regular accreditation, PIB also grants more than 500 temporary accreditation every year to foreign media persons who visit India for a short period.

Press Council of India

The Press Council of India has been established for the purpose of preserving the freedom of the press and of maintaining and improving the standard of newspapers and news agencies in India. The Chairman of the Council is by convention, a retired judge of the Supreme Court of India. He is nominated by a committee consisting of the Chairman of Rajya Sabha, Speaker of Lok Sabha and one elected representative of Council members. The Council has 28 members- 20 from the newspaper world, five are members of Parliament (three nominated by the Speaker of the Lok Sabha and two by the Chairman of the Rajya Sabha) and remaining three are nominated by the Sahitya Academy, the Bar Council of India and the University Grants Commission. The Council is reconstituted every three years. The Council has its own source of revenue in that it collects levy from the registered newspapers and news agencies. It also receives grant-in-aid from the Central Government for performing its functions.

As an autonomous quasi-judicial body, the aims of the Council is to administer ethics and to inculcate principles of self regulation among the press. It also keeps under review any development likely to interfere with the freedom of the press. The Council discharges its functions primarily through adjudication on complaint cases received by it, either against the press for violation of journalistic ethics or by the press for interference with its freedom, where the council is satisfied during the inquiry that a newspaper or a news agency has offended against the standards of journalistic ethics or public taste or that an editor or a professional journalist has committed a professional misconduct, the Council may warn, admonish or censure them or disapprove their conduct. The Council is also empowered to make such observations as it may think fit in respect of the conduct of any authority, including Government for interfering with the freedom of the press. The decisions of the Council are final and cannot be questioned in any court of law.

M V Kamath, in his book, *The Journalists Handbook,* says : *The Council, it is important to remember, is NOT a court of law. It is a court of honour. Its verdicts are not judicial pronouncements. Therefore, there is no question of punishment imposed on an offending journalist or newspaper. The Council cannot award damages to the aggrieved party.* As Mudholkar puts it : *The only weapon in its armoury is moral authority. The sole strength of the Council lies in its appeal to conscience.*

Mr Justice K Jayachandra Reddy has been appointed as new Chairman of Press Council for a three year term with effect from 8 August 2001 to 7 August 2004 upon expiry of the term of Justice P B Sawant on 7 August 2001.

During 2001-02, the Press Council of India received 1,250 complaints of which 390 were filed by the press and 860 were against the press, 523 cases were already pending. Of these the Council adjudicated 130 cases. 1,045 cases were dismissed by the Council at the preliminary stage for lack of sufficient grounds for inquiry. The Council has disposed of 1,175 matters during 2001-02. Press Council Act 1978, also empowers the Council *suo moto* studies on various matters that have bearing on the freedom of the press and its standards.

Exercises

1. It is said that newspapers run libelous material every day. From a recent issue of newspaper, find articles that you think contain potentially libelous statement. Look for it in accounts of arrests, police activities, court proceedings, and deliberations of major public officials and public bodies. Write a report discussing what legal risk the paper took in publishing the material, what precautions it might have taken, and what defences it might offer. Should a legal action be taken against it? Clip the articles and attach them to this report.
2. Your photographer enters a house without permission and takes a picture of the sale of illegal drugs. Discuss the issues raised by these events and state whether you would publish the picture. Why or Why not.
3. "Defamation is viewed much more seriously in the Western Worlds than in India"—Comment.
4. Describe the kinds of contempts under the Contempt of Courts Act, 1971.
5. How best are the interests of a working journalist protected by the law in our country?
6. Discuss the main features of the Working Journalists and Other Newspaper Employees (Conditions of Service) and Miscellaneous Provisions Act, 1955.
7. "The best people to make laws for the press are journalists themselves"—Comment.
8. Discuss the need for codifying parliamentary privileges.
9. What do you understand by the term Contempt of Legislature?
10. What are the basic provisions of 'Official Secrets Act.'
11. Do you think that the Official Secrets Act come in the way of journalistic pursuit?
12. Discuss the procedure to be followed in getting the newspaper registered with the Press and Registration of Books Act, 1867.
13. Describe the functions of Registrar of Newspapers for India.
14. Why Audit Bureau of Circulation is needed? How does it function?
15. Discuss the role of the Press Information Bureau (PIB).
16. Do you think the Press Council should be given powers to prosecute the media and media persons? Give reasons in support of your answer.
17. Can the Press Council effectively curb scurrilous writing in Indian press. Comment.

SECTION VII

BROADCAST NEWS

22

WRITING NEWS FOR BROADCAST

Writing for broadcast news is a relatively new profession. Few people heard the first radio newscasts and few would have watched the first news items broadcast over experimental television. Today large number of people say that television is major source of their news. Large number of studies have been carried out regarding whether newspapers or television is the most credible news source. Of course, broadcast media are not always present to record the news while it is happening. Much of the time broadcast journalists must write and report news after it has occurred.

Broadcasting news has a simple objective. This is to capture the essential ingredients of a story and explain them in a straight forward, simple language that can be easily understood when heard over the air.

Selecting and writing news for television and radio is slightly different from selecting and writing news for newspapers. The differences arise primarily from the technology involved in print and in the electronic media. We will explore these differences here as we discuss news reporting and writing for the broadcast media.

Criteria for Selecting Broadcast News

The criteria for selecting broadcast news is the same as for the print media vis-a-vis impact, proximity, timeliness, prominence, novelty and conflict etc. All of these criteria apply to the selection of broadcast news. But there are three major differences between print and broadcast news selection which are as under:

Timeliness

Broadcast news writers give more emphasis on 'timeliness.' "When" is very important. It often determines whether a news item will be used in a newscast. The breaking story receives top priority. If an event is significant enough, regular programming can be interrupted. The broadcast media are the 'now' media. This sense of immediacy influences everything in broadcast news, from what is reported to how it is reported. Even when television and radio air documentaries or in-depth segments, they try to infuse a sense of urgency a strong feeling of the present, an emphasis on what is happening now.

Information

Broadcasters are generally more concerned with information than with explanation. Because air time is so precious, broadcast news emphasizes more on 'what' and 'where' than on 'why' or 'how'. Most stories are told in 20 to 30 seconds; rarely does a story run longer than two minutes. A minute of news read contains only 15 lines of copy, or about 150 words. Although broadcast news writers may never assume that their audience knows anything about a story they may often have to assume that listeners or viewers will turn to their newspapers for further background and detail.

Audio or Visual Impact

A third difference between broadcast and print news results from the technology involved. Some news is selected for radio because a reporter has recorded an on the scene audio report. Some news is selected for television because it is visually appealing. For this reason news of accidents or of fires that may get attention only in the records column of the newspaper may get important play on a television news cast. If a television crew returns with good pictures of an event, that event may be part of the next newscast, regardless of its significance. Of course this is not always the case.

Writing Broadcast News

Broadcast writing emphasizes certain characteristics that newspaper writing does not, and story structure may also vary. Some of the characteristics are as under:

Immediacy

Avoid the past tense as often as you can. Present tense shows immediacy. 'Say' is better than 'said.' Of course, to be accurate, the past tense is sometimes necessary, then use present perfect tense whenever possible because it points up immediacy. The clause ' the environment as a whole has deteriorated' written in the present perfect tense, also has the advantage of sounding natural and conversational.

Sometimes the sense of immediacy is underscored by adding the time element. You might say 'just minutes ago' or on a morning newscast, 'this morning'. If there is no danger of inaccuracy, reference to time can be omitted.

The best way to avoid past tense is to avoid yesterday's story. You can do that by bringing yesterday's story up to date. By leading with a new development or a new fact, you may be able to use the present tense. Remember, radio and television are 'live'. Your copy must sound that way.

Conversational Style

Write the way you talk is good advice for most kinds of writing; it is imperative for broadcast writing. 'Read your copy aloud' is good advice for most kinds of writing; for broadcast writing 'that' is used more often than 'which'. It is more conversational. And broadcast style is the style of conversational. It is simple and informal. The key is to remember that you are talking to people. Tell them what just happened. Tell them what you just saw or heard.

Write so that your copy sounds good. Use simple, short sentences, written with transitive verbs in the active voice. Try to avoid forms of the verb to be, is, are, was, were – for they are the weakest of all verbs. People rarely use verbs in the passive voice when they talk; it usually sounds cumbersome and awkward.

Writing the conversational style does not mean that you may use slang or that you should write ungrammatically. Nor should you use vulgar or off colour expressions. Remember that your audience is composed of people of all ages and sensitivities. The broadcast media have been given credit for raising the level of properly spoken English. While writing for broadcast, use these words with caution because any one of them could lead to accusations of libel.

Admit,	confess,	atheist,	
blackmail,	bribe,	bribery,	
communist,	defraud,	fraud,	
illegitimate,	incompetent,	suicide,	swindle

Tight Phrasing

Although actual conversational English tends to be wordy, you must learn to write in a conversational style without being wordy. That means you must condense. Tight phrasing is the most common injunction heard in a broadcast newsroom. You must tell your stories in the fewest possible words. It means as one news director has said, "boiling down a flood of information into a concise meaningful trickle". To do this expertly requires judgement. You must choose -select out- from your notes, or from the wire story, or both, what is essential. You must recognize what is basic, what gives the story meaning. And you must know what words to use in order to be succinct. Cut down on adjectives and adverbs. Eliminate the passive voice. Use strong active verbs. Make every word count.

In tight writing, you are selecting what to report. That is why, as a news writer, you are an editor too, with all the responsibility that editorship entails. The amount of background information which can be included in any news story is limited. In broadcast news there is not the room- time for background that exist in print journalism. When a story has been in the news for days, even weeks, it is assumed that the listener knows the background. Only the latest developments in these so – called "running" stories are reported. The cut off date for providing such background information is, inevitably, arbitrary. You decide one day, in reporting the story, that by this time the basic facts are generally known. You must, in your judgement, be quite sure of this. There's no use reporting the story if you leave out to the background that enables the listener to know what the story really is all about.

Strive always for clarity. Simplicity of language and clarity, which come from clear thinking, go hand in hand. *Bill Small,* the broadcast veteran who teaches at Fordham, says, "Good television journalism presents news in the most attractive and lucid form yet devised by man". In TV, the attractiveness and lucidity depend on the use made of words and pictures. In radio, they depend on the use made of words alone. And neither sentences, nor visual sequences can be long drawn out, discursive, or diffuse. In both media, tight editing applies.

Unlike the reader, viewers and listeners can't go back over the copy. They see or hear it only once, and their attention waxes and wanes. So, you must try harder to be clear and precise. All of the emphasis on condensing and writing tightly is useless if the message is not understood. Better not to report at all than to fill air time with messages that have no meaning.

Clarity demands that you write simply, in short sentences filled with nickel -and -dime words. Don't look for synonyms. Don't be afraid to repeat words or phrases. Oral communication needs reinforcement. Avoid foreign words and phrases.

Avoid phrases like "the former" and "the latter". Repeat the proper names in the story rather than using pronouns. The listener can easily forget the name of the person to whom the pronoun refers.

When you are tempted to write a dependent clause in a sentence, make it an independent clause instead. Keep the subject close to the verb. Close the gap between the doer and the activity. Look at this news item:

A man flagged down a Highway Patrol officer near Pooh in Kinnaur district, today and told him a convict was hiding in his house. The prisoner one of five who escaped from Tihar jail on Saturday, surrendered peacefully.

The second sentence contains 10 words between the subject 'prisoner' and the verb 'surrendered'. By the time the broadcaster reaches the verb, many listeners will have forgotten what the subject was. The story is easier to understand this way:

A man flagged down a Highway Patrol officer near Pooh in Kinnaur district, today and told him a convict was hiding in his house. The prisoner surrendered peacefully. He's one of the five who escaped from the Tihar jail on Saturday.

The third sentence is still a complex sentence, but it is easily understood. The complex sentence is often just that—complex—only more so in oral communication.

Clarity also requires that you resist a clever turn of phrase. Although viewers and listeners probably are intelligent enough to understand it, they simply will not have the time. A good figure of speech takes time to savor. If listeners pause to savor it (presuming they grasped it in the first place), they will not hear what follows. Clever columnists often fail as radio commentators. Too often the listener asks, "What did he say?"

Generally though, literary speech is undesirable. Even more dangerous than figures of speech are numerical figures. Don't barrage the listener with a series of numbers. If you must use statistics, break them down so that they are understandable. It is better to say, for example, that one out of 10 Indians reads newspapers than to say 10 crores read newspapers in India,

Remember that you are writing for the benefit of your listeners. You serve them best by emphasizing immediacy and by writing conversationally, tightly and clearly

Story Structure

Now that we know the characteristics of broadcast writing, let's examine the story structure. Writers must craft broadcast leads somewhat differently from print leads. They must also construct special introductions and conclusions to filmed or recorded segments and synchronize their words with taped segments.

Writing the Broadcast Lead

Both newspaper and broadcast reporters must attract the attention of their audience. But when you write for broadcast, you may need to attract attention differently.

One way to do this is by preparing your audience for what is to come. You cue the listeners to make sure they are tuned in. In effect, you are saying, "Now listen to this." You introduce the story with a general statement, something that will pique the interest of the audience, and then go to the specific. For example:

General Statement: Things are far from settled for DAV School teachers strike.
Specifcs: School officials and union representatives reached no agreement yesterday. They will not meet again for at least a week.

"Cuing in" is only one method of opening a broadcast story. Other leads go immediately into the what and the who, the where and the when. In broadcast news the what is most important, followed by who did the what. The time and the place may be included in the lead, but seldom is the why or the how. If time permits, the why and the how may come later in the story, but often they are omitted.

The first words of the leads are most important. Don't keep the listener guessing as to what the story is about. Don't begin with a dependent clause as in this example:

Despite continued objections from the teachers, toilet near the classroom is under construction.

The opening words are meaningless without what comes later. The listener may not know what you are talking about. A better way to introduce this story is:

The toilet near the classroom is under construction – despite continued objections from the teachers.

As you do in a lead for a newspaper story be sure to identify an unfamiliar name, by introducing a person, you prepare listeners for the name that they otherwise may miss.

Don't mislead. The opening words must set the proper tone and mood for the story. Attract attention, by don't tease. Answer questions, but don't ask them. Question leads are for commercials. Lead the listener into your story.

Writing Lead-ins and Wrap-ups

Broadcast journalists must learn how to write a different kind of lead, called the lead-in, that introduces a filmed or recorded excerpt from a news source or from another reporter. The functions of a lead-in are to set the scene by briefly telling the where, the when and sometimes the what, and to identify the source or reporter. Here's an example:

In Shimla today, the mood was jubilant and hopeful Anil Khimta reports.

Lead-in should generate interest. Sometimes several sentences are used to provide background as in the following:

We will all be getting the official word this morning on how much less our rupees bought last month. The consumer price index for October is expected to show another sharp rise in retail prices. The rate of inflation was two percent in August and two point five percent in September there is more on our inflation woes from Sanjeev.

Be careful not to include in the lead-in what is in the story. Just as a headline should not be stolen from a lead of a newspaper story, the lead-in should not use the opening words of the correspondent. The writer must know the contents of the taped report in order to write a proper lead-in.

After the recorded report, you may want to wrap up the story before going on to the next item. This is especially important in radio copy since there are no visuals to identify the person just heard.

If the story reported by *Mukesh Rajput* was about a meeting to settle a strike, you might wrap up his report by adding information:

Rajput reports negotiations will resume tomorrow.

A wrap up such as this gives your story an ending and clearly separates it from the next story.

An example for a TV news script is given below:

Date:
Slug: Twin murder at Jakhoo Hill
Report: Pratibha Chauhan

Dur:
TC in:
TC out:

Anchor Lead–in: The capital city of Shimla was once again jolted this morning as the news of the murder of a couple in a posh locality of the city spread. The murder was reported to the police in the early hours by their servant.

V/O1

	Dur: 29 TC in: TC out:
Various of the murdered couple	This couple was brutally murdered last night by unidentified persons while
Various of the ransacked house	they were still asleep in their house. The palatial bungalow
Blood soaked bed-sheets pool of blood on the floor and the walls of the bedroom	of the murdered couple situated on the Jakhoo Hill was completely ransacked by the miscreants. As per the available information, the deceased man and his wife were alone at their house at the time of the incident as their only son was out for holidays with his friends. The servant of the house informed the police about the murder in the wee hours of the morning.

S/B.
DUR: 18 SECS
TC in:
TC out:
Lal Chand
Servant

I went in their room to serve bed tea at about 5:00 A.M. When I entered the room I saw bibiji lying on the bed with blood all over her. I got scared. When I moved forward I saw saahabji lying on the floor in a pool of blood. Then I panicked and called the police.

	V/O2: Dur: 17secs TC in: TC out:
Various of the bedroom window Police personnel examining the scene of the crime various of the house Servant along with Investigating officer	According to the police investigations, the murderers seem to have entered the house with the motive of burglary. They broke into the house through the bed-room window and struck the couple by a blunt object on the head. The police are interrogating all suspects including the servant who informed them

S/B
Dur: 16 secs
TC in:
TC out:
Krishan Singh
SSP

It seems to be the handiwork of the same gang has struck at three other places in the city over the past week. We stepped up the night patrol in the city. We advise the people to properly lock the doors from the inside at night.

V/O3: 9 secs
Dur:
TC in:
TC out:

LS of the house neighbours of the couple gathered Outside the house	However, the SSP's advice is expected to do little tomitigate the insecurity of these people. For even the locked doors and windows can't keep out the fear.

Writing for Videotape

Writing for a videotaped report really begins with the selection of the subject and how it is to be videotaped. The writing continues through the editing and selection process. And always, it is done with the pictures clearly in mind.

Words and pictures must be complementary, never interfering with each other. Neither should the words and pictures ignore each other. Your first responsibility is to relate the words to the pictures. If you do not, viewers will not get the message because they will be spending their time wondering what the pictures are about.

At the beginning of a scene or when a scene changes you must tell the viewer where you are or what is happening. Once you are into the scene, the script may be more general and less closely tied to the pictures. For example, if the report concerns the continuation of a steel strike and the opening scene shows picketers outside the plant you can explain the film by saying :

Union members are still picketing Jindal steel today as the steel strike enters its fourth week. Viewers now know two things that are not obvious in the film ; who is picketing and where. If the scene should switch to people sitting around a table negotiating, you must again set the scene:

Meanwhile, company officials and union leaders are continuing their meetings— apparently without success.

Once you have related the words to the pictures, you may go on to tell other details of the strike. You are expected to provide information not contained in the pictures themselves. In other words, you must not only comment on the film, but complete it. Part of completing it is to give the report a wrap-up or a strong ending. Don't be cute and don't be obvious, but give the story an ending. The ending for the steel strike story might be:

Experts agree on one sure result of the strike—steel prices will rise again.

Preparing Broadcast Copy

Preparing copy to be read by a newscaster is different from preparing it for a typesetter. Your goal is to make the copy easy for the newscaster to read and easy for the audience to understand. What follows will help you accomplish those two goals.

Format

Most broadcast news editors want triple-spaced copy. Leave two to three inches on the top of the page and one to two inches on the bottom. For radio copy, set your typewriter so that you have 70 characters to a line. Each line will average about 10 words, and the newscaster will average 15 lines per minute. Some stations require you to start each story on a separate piece of paper. That way, the order of the stories can be rearranged, or stories can be added or dropped easily. If a story goes more than one page, write "MORE" in parentheses at the bottom of the page.

Television copy is written on the right half of the page in a 40-character line. Each line will average about six words , and the newscaster will average about 25 lines per minute. The left side of the copy is used for radio or video information. This information, which is not to be read by the newscaster, is usually typed in all caps. The copy that is read is generally in upper and lower case. In television copy the stories are numbered, and each story is on a separate page. If a story goes more than one page, write, "MORE" in parentheses at the bottom of the page.

Do not hyphenate words, and be sure to end page with a complete sentence or, if possible, with a complete paragraph. If the next page should be missing in the middle of a broadcast, the newscaster can end, at least, with a complete sentence or paragraph.

At many stations copy is prepared for a video prompter, a mechanical or electronic device that projects the copy next to the lens so that newscasters can read it while appearing to look straight into the lens. Copy for the video prompter is often typed down a column in the middle of the page.

Date the first page of your script, and type your last name in the upper left hand corner of every page. Stations vary regarding these directions. The local news director determines the slug for a story and its placement. Some directors insist that the slug contain the time of the broadcast. If a story continues to a second page, write under the slug first add, or second add, or page 2, page 3, and so forth. Here is an example of writing television news script.

Names and titles

In broadcast style unlike that followed by newspapers, well known names even on first preference, are not given in full. You may say Governor Kokje of Himachal Pradesh. Middle initials should not be used unless they are a natural part of someone's name (Sharma, Bal K.) or unless they are necessary to distinguish two people with the same first and last names.

Titles should always precede names so that listeners are better prepared to hear the name. When you use titles, the first name and middle initials may be omitted. For example, broadcasters would say President Kalam. Newspapers write out names like Himachal Governor, Mr. V.S. Kokje. In broadcast, use either the first name or the nickname but not both.

Pronunciation

The writer's job is to help the person who reads the news, pronounce the names of people and places correctly. To do this, you should write out difficult names phonetically in parentheses. Many individual stations have handbooks of their own. You may have to look up difficult names in unabridged dictionaries. If you don't find the name there, use your telephone, call the person's office. Never assume. Never try to figure it out. Find out.

Abbreviations

Generally, you should not use abbreviations in broadcast copy. It is easier to read a word written out than to read its abbreviations. Do not abbreviate the names of states, countries, months, days of the week or military titles. There are exceptions, and when you use them, use hyphens instead of periods because the final period in the abbreviation may be misread as the end of a sentence.

You may abbreviate U-S when used as adjective, and the Dr., Mr., Mrs. and Ms. a.m. and p.m. Hyphens are not used for acronyms such as IAS and HCS which are pronounced as one word.

Symbols and Numbers

Do not use symbols in broadcast copy because a broadcaster can read a word more easily than he or she can remember a symbol. Such symbols as the dollar sign ($) and the percent sign (%) are never used. Don't even use the abbreviation for number (no.)

Numbers can be a problem for both the announcer and the listener. As in newspaper style, write out numbers one through nine. But write out eleven, too, because 11 might not be easily recognized as a number. Use figures for 10, and from 12 to 999. The eye can easily take in a three digit number, but write out the words thousand, million and billion. Hence, 3,800,000 becomes three million, 800 thousand. Write out fractions (two and a half million dollars) and decimal points (three point two percent).

Some stations have exceptions. Figures often are used when giving the time (3:20 a.m.) sports scores and statistics (The score was 5 to 2). Ordinarily, you may round off big numbers. Thus 48 point 3 percent should be written nearly half." But don't say "more than one hundred" if 104 people died in an earthquake.

Use st, nd, rd, and th after dates: August 1st, September 2nd, October 3rd and November 4th. Make the year easy to pronounce: June 9th, 2004.

Quotations and Attributions

Most broadcast news writers rarely use quotation marks. Because it is difficult and awkward to indicate to the listeners which words are being quoted, use indirect quotes or a paraphrase instead.

If it is important that listeners know the exact words of a quotation (as when the quoted words are startling, uncomplimentary or possibly libelous), the quote may be introduced by saying "in his own words", "with these words," "What she called," or "she put it this way." Most writers prefer to avoid the formal 'quote' and 'unquote' though 'quote' is used more than 'unquote'. Note the following example:

In Singh's words quote, "there is no way to undo the harm done"

If you must use a direct quotation, the attribution always should precede the quotation. Because listeners cannot see the quotation marks, they would have no way of knowing the words are a direct quote. If by chance the words were recognized as a quote, listeners would have no idea who is saying them. For the same reason, the attribution must always precede the indirect quote.

And if you must use a direct quotation keep it short. If the quote is long and it is important to use it, you should use a tape of the person saying it. However, if you are compelled to use a quote of more than a sentence in your copy, break it up with phrases like, "Singh went on to say".

Punctuation

In broadcast copy, less punctuation is good punctuation. The one exception is the comma. Commas help the reader pause at appropriate places. Use commas, for example, after introductory phrases referring to time and place, as in the following:

In Shimla, two youngsters from Delhi died when their car overturned and caught fire.

Last week, vegetable prices had reached an all-time high.

Sometimes three periods are used in place of the comma.Periods also take the place of the parentheses and of the semi-colon. They indicate a pause and are more easily visible. The same is true of the dash—typed as two hyphens.

The only punctuation marks you need are the period, comma, question mark, dash, hyphen and, rarely, quotation marks. To make the words easier to read, use the hyphen in some words, even when the dictionary does not have it: anti-discrimination, co-operation, non-aggression.

Correcting copy

Do not use the copy- editing marks you learned for editing newspaper copy. If a word has an error in it, cross out the word and write the corrected word above it.

And of course, always make your corrections neatly and clearly. Stations may vary in the writing style and in the preparation of copy.

Exercises

1. Watch evening television newscast. Make a simple list of the news stories. Then try to find out those stories in the next morning's newspaper and compare the coverage.
2. Read a copy of a current newspaper. Then write a five minute newscast paying special attention to lead –ins and wrap-ups.
3. Rewrite any UNI, PTI newspaper story in broadcast- writings.

SECTION VIII

WIRE STYLE

23

NEWS AGENCIES

Definition

A news agency, according to UNESCO, is "an undertaking of which the principal objective, whatever its legal form, *is to gather news and news material of which the sole purpose is to express or present facts, and to distribute this to a group of news enterprises, and in exceptional circumstances to private individuals with a view to providing them with as complete and impartial a news service as possible against payment, and under conditions compatible with business laws and usage."*

Hence news agencies were classically defined as 'wholesale' media, gathering news for the purpose of distributing it to other—'retail'—media, mainly newspapers and broadcasters, who packaged news agency news for their own distinctive readers and audiences. Until recently, news agencies did not have a direct access to an audience consisting of individuals; their services were mediated through their subscribers. This classic definition of news agencies still holds true in good measure, but now needs to be extended and re-contextualized. In addition to their traditional 'wholesale' role, news agencies have become increasingly important as 'retail' sources of information not only for media but also for individual citizens. This has been in evidence for some time in the provision of financial news services for financial institutions, brokers, exchange agencies etc., but is every day more in evidence in the provision of general news through the Internet. However, even on the Internet, clients typically access news agency news through secondary, or 'retail' agents consisting of general interest (e.g. Yahoo!) and corporate web sites, the websites of newspapers and television stations or through Internet portals such as Netscape.

The result is that increasingly the news agencies are thinking of their markets in terms not of media clients but of large numbers of individual news consumers. Associated Press established The Wire, an on-line news service accessible through the sites of AP member media, in 1996, and began offering on-line access to its Photo Archive in 1997. Despite all these changes in communication technology and media markets, most news agencies still perform their traditional role as wholesalers of news for media. The times for news agencies are rapidly changing. What will happen to them in the future is not certain.

Origins of global news system

News agencies can be said to have been among the first highly visible manifestations of 'globalization' in the nineteenth century, a process of the interlinking of different national economics through the activities of transnational economic and financial trade. However, the agencies (especially at national level) have also been important symbols of national identity as well as contributing to the development of the nation-state by rationalizing the national organization of news collection and dissemination.

The French agency Havas (predecessor to AFP), founded in 1832, is considered by many scholars to be the world's first news agency. It started by translating items from domestic and foreign newspapers. In the beginning it was a private firm owned by a former banker, Charles Havas. The Associated Press was founded in New York as a press cooperative in 1848. A second major agency in Europe, the German Wolff, was founded in 1849.

The USA became the only country to have two global agencies in the world's news market (indeed, for several decades there were three, including Hearst's International News Service). The other two Western agencies that now dominate the global print news market are the French Agence France-Presse (AFP, founded in 1944 as a direct successor of Havas) and Reuters.

The 'Global' News Agencies

News agency identity has a variety of geographical markets. They gather news independently from most countries of the world and see it to its clients in most countries, each of these has a long established national identity. Most celebrated global print news agencies are AFP, AP and Reuters. Of these big three news agencies, Reuters has become spectacularly wealthy as a result of a 1970s redirection of core business towards computer used information and transaction services for financial markets. The other two major agencies, AP and AFP, control substantial worldwide human resource and communication assets; but they do not typically generate substantial revenues in excess of operating expenditures, nor have they been constituted for that purpose. Both these agencies derive the largest share of their revenues from their domestic markets.

REUTERS

The first Reuters' Bureau was opened at Royal Exchange, London, in 1851. In 1865 it was formed into a company with a nominal capital of £ 250,000 in 10,000 shares of £ 25 each.

Reuters Economic Service is the largest International Commerce and business news service. It is today a commercial company quoted on the London Stock Exchange. In 1999, it earned total revenue of $ 5049 million and had net assets of $ 13,827 million. It is listed as one of the leading UK companies and is one of the world's largest media enterprises.

Reuters is the largest international multi-media news agency, reporting extensively from around the world on topics ranging from financial markets to general and political news. More than 90% Reuters revenue comes from Reuters financial service business. Some Reuters coverage, including pictures and video, is of wars or conflicts during which all sides are actively promoting their positions and arguments. The world relies on Reuters journalists to provide accurate, clearly sourced accounts of events as they occur, wherever they occur, so that individuals, organizations and governments can make their own decisions based on the facts.

ASSOCIATED PRESS OF AMERICA

The Associated Press (AP) was founded in 1848.

AP is a co-operative, non-profit making co-operation and its entire source of revenue is subscription by members. AP is the only agency which has laid down in its rules that it should not enter into any binding deals with any Government or Government institutions, for fear of having its services utilized for propaganda purposes. Control of AP vested solely in its members. Control of the Associated Press is exercised through a Board of Directors elected by the regular members at the annual meeting. A Director's full term is three years; the by-laws provide that he can be elected for two more full terms. AP gives the same type of service to its members in America and abroad. Its agreements with foreign competitors are noteworthy. AP makes available to Reuters' its news at New York; Reuters' make it available at London but neither AP nor Reuters has access to the other's international file; in the international field they are competitors. Similar arrangements also exist between AP and AFP.

It also has a strong digital phone network offering 1000 photos a day worldwide, and a 24-hour continuously updated on-line news service (The Wire) which is available to subscribing newspaper or broadcast members to incorporate into their own websites (There were 450 such subscribers in 2000). This includes international and national, but not state news.

AGENCE FRANCE PRESSE (AFP)

AFP was founded in 1835, under the name of Agence Havas in Paris. Since its establishment Havas experimented a lot to place it on a sound footing. In 1857 Havas signed a contract for distribution of news with the Associated Press of America. Contracts with Wolff and Reuters were signed earlier. In 1946, the French Government bought up the assets and equipment of the Agency's information branch in order to set up a propaganda office. This Office Francais d' Information (OFI), was later taken over by the Germans and turned into AFIP- a branch of the Nazi agency DNB. To counter this, AFI (Agence Francais Independent) was started in London in 1940. In occupied France an agency called AIO was functioning and another independent agency called France Libre preserved the tradition by supplying news to the resistance movement. All these agencies were amalgamated to form the present AFP which is a public body now. Its Director General is appointed by the French Government which also makes an annual grant, fixed in the budget for services taken by the Government.

Recent Strides

The AFP website in August 2000 claimed that the agency had bureaus in 165 countries, and employed a full-time staff of 2000 of whom 950-1200 were journalists and 150-200 were news photographers (the numbers vary between AFP's French-language and English-language websites) augmented by a network of 2000 freelancers or stringers. Revenue in 1998 was $228 million, although the profit-turnover ratio was zero. AFP also offers photo and television. The agency distributes 2 million words, 250 photos and 80 graphics each day in six languages (French, English,

Spanish, German, Arabic, and Portuguese) and claims to serve a total of 10,000 media clients either directly or through national agencies.

Conclusion

These brief company reviews reveal a number of distinctive features. One is the phenomenal growth of the financial information and transaction market, and the pre-eminent role within it of Reuters. Apart from Reuters, the main players are US companies. With the decline of UPI (once considered a member of the "Big Four'), which in 2000 was sold to the News World Communications, owners of The Washington Times, the number of major players in the traditional general news agency business has declined. This decline has been offset to some extent by the availability of 'retail' media services worldwide, such as those of the BBC, CNN, and other newspapers and broadcasters that command independent worldwide news-gathering networks, although the strongest of these are principally American or British.

Thus another outstanding feature is the gathering importance of the Internet for the largest news agencies. These are the most able to benefit from the advantages that the internet affords them in terms of cost reduction, speed of news-gathering and dissemination, and access to 'wholesale' news services for mass markets.

NATIONAL NEWS AGENCIES

National news agencies are often the largest domestic news-gathering organizations, connecting central and peripheral media in a network with the national agency at its centre, collecting news from the different provinces, compiling a service of national and regional news for national dissemination. Some national agencies were originally established directly by or with the aid of the global agencies, and many were junior partners in a global network of news exchange in which the global agencies were dominant.

The global agencies typically supply their international news services to national agencies. Directly, or indirectly through national agencies, national media take international news from the global agencies (which are often the sole first-hand news sources for such news), and their news priorities are influenced by the global agencies. Globalization presents a somewhat different source of threat to the role of the traditional news agency. Media members of a national news agency cooperative increasingly find themselves subsumed within larger international corporations that have little sensitivity or respect for local news markets, needs or customs, and have a strong interest in cost reduction and profit maximization. The result may be pressure to reduce staff and to lower rates, or even to develop separate agencies whose sole mission is to serve the news needs of their owner corporation. This may be particularly dangerous in markets that are characterized by a high degree of concentration. In these cases, a small number of corporations control both the media and the national news agency which serves them: if one of these corporations withdraws from the cooperative then it seriously undermines the agency's claim to be 'national'. and its ability to sustain a viable concern. Many national agencies in Europe have experienced competition that emerges from within their memberships, although to date most such efforts have been repulsed or contained by incumbent national agencies. Such competition may sometimes take the form of regional challenges to centrally dictated news agendas.

National news agencies that have or have had strong ties to their respective national governments, among them the agencies of Central and Eastern Europe, face a somewhat different range of problems. Just as dependence on government for subsidy or for custom is itself a problem for agencies that are dependent on such funding, equally so, and for different reasons, are reductions in government subsidy or custom, a worldwide tread in the wake of processes of deregulation and political transition. These same processes simultaneously open the doors to competition from the global agencies that establish national or financial news services for local markets.

Evolution of Indian News Agencies

When India became independent, the Associated Press of India a subsidiary of Reuters, dominated the news agency scene to an extent where it could insist that no subscriber of API take any other news agency service. That was the Power which the API used to force the Free Press News Agency out of business. The Free Press News Agency, like the United Press of India, was formed by Indian nationalists who were dissatisfied at the meagre coverage given by API to the national struggle for independence. API could do nothing in that direction because of its connection with Reuters and the Government patronage that it enjoyed from the beginning. The UPI, which did not have teleprinters in a year after independence, never posed a challenge to API.

Soon after independence, the proprietors of Indian newspapers wanted API to be turned into a cooperative effort of Indian newspapers. Reuters was not prepared in the beginning to transfer its assets to Indian hands, but was forced to do so because of the stern attitude taken by Sardar Vallabh Bhai Patel, who was the Home Minister and also held the Information and Broadcasting portfolio. In 1948, the new company, Press Trust of India, began its operations. The same year the UPI, which till then had depended on Press Telegrams, acquired teleprinters. The news agency however, could not survive for long and collapsed in 1958. By now, it was realised that there was need for at least two news agencies 'each competing with the other and also acting as a corrective to the other'. Eight newspaper proprietors therefore came together and founded the United News of India (UNI) in 1961.

All these, namely, API, PTI, FPA, UPI and then UNI were English language news agencies. Indian language newspapers subscribed to their service, translated and edited the copy and published it in their respective languages. The concept of an Indian language news agency was still a distant dream. It was K.C. Roy who established the API . To S.S. Apte goes the credit for setting up the first Indian language news agency-Hindustan Samachar. In the beginning, its operations were limited to distribution of news through Devanagari telegrams. With the introduction of Devanagari teleprinters, however, it began supplying news to its Hindi and Marathi newspapers subscribers through teleprinters. The second Indian language news agency, Samachar Bharati, was founded in 1966. Several State Governments contributed to its share capital and, at one time, held more than 50 per cent of its shares.

Formation of Samachar

After the declaration for the national emergency in 1975, all the four agencies- PTI, UNI, Hindustan Samachar and Samachar Bharati- were merged into one agency which was named Samachar. The formation of Samachar meant higher pay packets for the employees and the prospect of a wider coverage for the newspapers. The process of integration was still underway when in the Lok Sabha election of 1977, the Janata Party was returned to power. Its leaders were committed to the dismantling of the monolithic Samachar. Though a committe appointed by the Janata Government recommended that there should be two agencies, the Government decided to restore the status quo as existed before Samachar was formed. All four news agencies thus began operating as separate units from 1978 onwards.

Subsequent events lead one to question the wisdom of this decision. Introduction of higher pay scale had imposed a heavy financial burden on the agencies. The Government agreed at the time of the break-up of Samachar to bear the burden of the extra expenditure for a few year. After this period, the agencies were expected to absorb it themselves. While PTI and UNI were able to do so, Hindustan Samachar and Samachar Bharati could not. Within a few years, they were in a worse plight than even before and their operations came to a standstill.

PRESS TRUST OF INDIA (PTI)

The father of Indian news agency journalism, K.C. Roy who founded the Associated Press of India (API), the forerunner of the PTI, first decided to have an Indian news agency. The Associated Press of India was acquired by Reuters in 1915 and was established as a limited company in 1946. In 1948 Indian Press formed the Press Trust of India; a co-operative, non-profit making news trust. PTI concluded an agreement with Reuters in September 1948, under which it took over the interest of API entirely, under commitments of approximately £ 60,000 to be repaid over a number of years. Simultaneously, PTI became a partner in Reuters Trust buying 12,500 of Reuters 90,000 ordinary shares. For the first three years PTI paid £ 30,000 as its contribution towards the general expenses in the collection and distribution of news. Functioning for three years as a partner of Reuters, PTI annulled the partnership in 1953.

PTI being a non-profit making co-operative, no dividends and no material benefits accrue to the shareholders except the services of the agency. The small newspapers being larger in number, it is difficult for bigger newspapers to control the agency. The newspapers being both the subscribers and owners of the agencies there is a tendency in their part to pay less for the services but demand a full and satisfactory service. They decide what the rates should be.

This aberration has been corrected to a certain extent due to strong pressure from employees' Union and the subscription is raised from time to time. It may sound strange that the newspapers which were using 60 to 70 percent of news supplied by news agencies did not pay even two to three percent of their revenue to the agencies. As a result modernisation was taking place at slower pace.

Earlier growth

The agency was registered in 1948 but began its operations in February, 1949. The teleprinter lines extended to 30,000 km throughout the country. These teleprinter lines had almost doubled to 55,000 km by 1975 indicating the continuous growth of the service. It had 30 bureaux in 1949 which were more than doubled by 1975 to 70 so that a number of cities and towns of India had been covered by the agency which had besides many stringers working as its correspondents in other district towns. The teleprinter links which numbered 1,150 in 1970 rose to 1,200 by 1974-75. By 1971 its revenue had risen to Rs. 1.52 crores, further rising to 1.90 crores by 1975. The number of subscribers had risen to 201 by that year.

During the fifties and sixties, a period of political stability and growth in different spheres of life, the name PTI became familiar to the people all over the country. In the world outside, PTI also made a name for itself as a major agency. The Reuters service which it continued to provide to the Indian subscribers was no longer an exclusive affair. PTI had exchange arrangements with a number of international and national news agencies and their news messages also became available to the Indian newspapers. Among them were such international agencies as the AFP, Agence France Presse of France; United Press International (UPI) of the United States; Antara of Indonesia; BSS of Bangladesh; Bernama of Malaysia; Novosty of the former Soviet Union; the former ADN of East Germany; and the Polish, Cuban, Yugoslav and Rumanian news agencies.

The first Press Commission, which reported in 1954, had recommended that PTI should become a public corporation with the shareholding newspapers holding a quarter of its share capital although its main concern was that the agency should become an unbiased and comprehensive news service. The corporation fortunately did not materialize but the agency amended its Articles of Association, providing for eminent public men, not connected with newspapers, being nominated to its board of director. The number of such directors is generally four and among those who have held the position are jurists like Nani Palkhivala, H.R. Khanna, former Chief Justice of India like M.Patanjali Sastri and J.C. Shah, and former Finance Minister C.D. Deshmukh.

PTI's earning capacity, however, remained unequal to its needs. The subscription by the newspapers, many of which were its shareholders, and, therefore, controlled agency's fortunes, did not rise in proportion to its expenses of news gathering. The subscription of the national broadcasting network of All India Radio, AIR was a sizable one but not considered adequate to the services provided by the agency to the network for whom news came next only to music as one of its major programme components. The national bulletins of AIR, emanating from Delhi relayed by a number of stations, covering national, regional and world news, had increased substantially. So had the regional news bulletins compiled and broadcast from the respective stations and largely covering news of the states concerned. PTI felt that the payment made to it for services rendered was insufficient and while the number of radio licenses grew fast and the network expanded the receipts of the agency did not rise proportionately.

Present scenario*

PTI has the largest national news network. Its subscribers include 450 newspapers in India and scores abroad. All major TV/radio channels in India and several abroad, including BBC in London, receive the PTI service. Overall the agency has some 2,800 subscribers. With a staff of over 1,600 including 400 journalists, PTI has over 100 bureaus across the country and foreign correspondents in major cities of the world including Beijing. Cairo, Dhaka, Islamabad, Kathmandu, London, Moscow, New York and Washington. In addition, about 300 stringers contribute to the news file at home while 35 part-time correspondents bring news from the rest of the world. The news services are provided at speeds of upto 1,200 bits second (about 1400 words per minute) by satellite, data channel and ticker lines.

PTI also distributes news and photo services to subscribers in USA, UK, UAE and Australia. It has arrangements with the Associated Press (AP) and Agence France Presse (AFP) for distribution of their news in India, and with the Associated Press for its Photo Service and International commercial information.

PTI exchanges news with nearly 100 news agencies of the world as part of bilateral and multilateral arrangements, including Non-Aligned News Agencies Pool and the Organisation of Asia-Pacific News-Agencies.

PTI and its Subsidiary Services

Over the year, PTI has developed its news service, modernized and computerized its operations in a gradual manner, introduced new services for the newspapers like a daily photo service of eight pictures a day. It

---

* Source: www.pti India.com.

includes photos from India as well as countries abroad. For this task, it has arrangements with the photo service of Associated Press of America. There are about 200 subscribers for it.

Stockscan is one of the two television services of PTI for commercial subscribers (or any one else) which brings them the share market rates from five principal stock exchanges., those in Bombay, Madras, Kolkata, Delhi and Ahmedabad, on a TV monitor while the bulls and bears fight it out in the bourses. The other TV service is News scan on TV monitors which adorn the desks of senior staff of dailies and the lobbies of hotels and the concourses of airports where the curious can scan through the headlines the changing Indian and World scene. While the Stockscan has as many as 656 subscribers the Newsscan has considerably less 270.

PTI Features service providing article written by subject specialists and journalists on a variety of subjects of Indian interest, both in English and Hindi, and of the Data India service which it has taken over from the Press Institute of India. More significant is the Hindi service of the agency. Bhasha, launched in 1986, four years after the Hindi service of the rival agency was set in motion, the Univarta. The agency has several bureaux in the Hindi speaking states and strives to make original stories available to the Hindi dailies besides stories translated from its English counterpart. If there are any special stories in the Bhasha service they are rendered into English for the subscribers of PTI, although such instances are not many. There are a few newspapers which subscribe to both PTI and its Hindi counterpart and there is a rebate for them as an incentive.

PTI was the first news organization in India to have TV service of its own, from supplying TV news clips to the national network. PTI TV has contributed significantly to the emerging TV scene in India. Started in 1986, PTI TV has done a number of relevant social and educational programmes on rural development as well as the ever interesting phenomenon of making money.

UNITED NEWS OF INDIA (UNI)

The United News of India was born from the ashes of the defunct United Press of India (UPI) on March 21, 1961 after UPI closed down. The teleprinters against which an advance was made by the Government of West Bengal were taken over by the Government, but the big newspapers in Calcutta, Madras and Delhi decided to have another news agency so that the spirit of competition gets better performance out of PTI and newspapers would have chance of qualitative choice. Funds came from newspapers and UNI got the teleprinter facilities of the old UPI. The United News of India was registered on November 10, 1959. The subscriber capital was Rs. 10 lakhs divided into 10,000 equity shares of Rs. 100 each.

The first Press Commission also stressed the need for India having a second news agency. It spoke of necessity and desirability for "at least two news agencies," each competing with each other and also acting as a corrective to the other." S.C. Bhatt in his book *Indian Press Since 1955* emphasized, the news agencies must be free and independent of any government or other control and interference in the collection and dissemination of news. It is equally important that there should be competition so that one agency spurs the other to act fast, be first with the news and not be subject to pressures of any kind. Competition should also mean that each agency would check the facts thoroughly before sending out the news to its subscribers, or 'creeding' it as the news agency and newspaper jargon goes. Competition means competition in being accurate and truthful too. Since the economic viability of a news agency is an extremely difficult proposition, the nation will have to do for a long time with two agencies only, although the Press Commission's report envisaged more than two. A single agency, in any case, is inclined to be a monopoly and more susceptible to external pressures.

Earlier growth

UNI began its operations in an extremely modest fashion from a room in the IENS, now INS (Indian Newspaper Society) building in Delhi but soon spread its wings all over the country. From just 13 subscribers in the first year of its operations in 1961 it grew to serve 50 newspapers and others by 1964, 109 by 1967 and as many as 223 as it completed the first decade of its work in 1971. By that time it was operating from 43 centres and had 249 teleprinters of its own. Its revenue was also growing fast but not soon enough to meet its needs. By 1971 it had gone up to Rs. 54.31 lakhs further increasing to Rs. 87.14 lakhs in 1975 when its staff strength was also 697, including 139 journalists.

Present Scenario*

UNI has more than 1000 subscribers catering to more than 100 centres in India and abroad including radio, TV, newspapers, websites, Government

* Source: www.uniindia.com and Jalali:, Chief Bureau, UNI, Shimla.

offices, private and Public sectors. It has more than 325 staff journalists and 250 stringers around the country. In addition, UNI has many foreign correspondents in major cities of the world including Washington, London, Dubai, Colombo, Kathmandu, Islamabad, Dhaka, Singapore, Sydney, New York, Moscow and Vancouver. It's communication network stretches over 90,000 km. in India and abroad and 750 takes are transmitted on wire everyday. 54 centres have been computerized and the rest will be in the next few months, besides installment of V-set for news gathering in a few months. Press releases from corporate and other organizations can be posted in the press release sections of their website.

UNI has collaboration with Reuters, DPA and UPI besides news exchange agreements with XINHUA (China), UNB (Bangladesh), Gulf News Agencies (Bahrain), WAM (UAE), KUNA (Kuwait), ONA (OMAN) and QUA (Quatar).

UNI's expansion programmes included the setting up of its Hindi service, Univarta, from May Day in 1982, which incidentally absorbed many journalists rendered unemployed by the near cessation of the operations of the two Indian agencies- Hindustan Samachar and Samachar Bharati. The modernisation programmes focused on the use of computers which were first employed in covering the election results in 1980 and 1984 and later in the transmission of news. The speed of transmission is 255 words a minute in the computerised centres and 55 elsewhere.

UNI's news agency service is subscribed by 313 newspapers in English and Univarta has 219 subscribers. There are 208 non-subscribers to the two services taken together. There are besides 22 subscribers to UNI's Urdu computerised service, a unique feature in as much as the newspapers are spared the tedious task of translating the stories from English into Urdu.

UNI had thus the distinction of being the first agency to start a Hindi wing and then a special service in Urdu. The agency has a large number of other services, including photo service, for which it has international connections with the AFP. A Unifin, a specialised service for banking, financial commercial organisations and Unistock, a service for stock exchanges and stock brokers.

The TV wing of the news agency provides news, features, clips and documentaries for Doordarshan and other organizations, yet another specialized service run by the agency is Uniscan—a news service fed into TV sets. The UNI has a number of mailer services, the oldest of them being backgrounders. Backgrounders come out weekly in both English and Hindi which has been widely used by fellow journalists, researchers and writers on current affairs. It was the first agency to have a full time science correspondent, an Agricultural service and a general features service. The response from the newspapers indicated that the service of the second news agency was well appreciated.

UNI also provides news service to subscribers in Gulf countries, besides Singapore and Mauritius. It has full time or part-time correspondents in several world capitals and news exchange arrangements, apart from AP, UPI, Reuters and DPA, with several national news agencies like IPS in Rome, and Tass-Star of Russia.

ASIAN NEWS INTERNATIONAL

ANI grew out of India's greatest documentary film production company, Asian Films. ANI was launched in the year 1975 by Mr. Prem Prakesh, South Asia's pioneering TV Journalist, cameraman honoured by the Queen of England for his contribution to the growth of TV News Industry in India and the United Kingdom. Today ANI is among the best professionally managed corporate media entities of the world.

ANI* is present all over South Asia. It has over fifty camera crews and journalists dotting the entire region that encompasses over a billion people in Afghanistan, Pakistan, India, Nepal, Bangladesh, Sri Lanka, Bhutan, Maldives and Burma. When it comes to covering South Asia, ANI goes across the globe to bring news of and from South Asia wherever it takes place. It also facilitates coverage in a remote area in a South Asia where you cannot afford to bring your own TV crew. Subscribers of ANI TV News service get this facility at a discounted rate. ZEE TV, SUN TV, RAJ TV, BBC, CNN, NBC, NHK, NRK and many others are availing this facility.

ANI's TV subscribers everyday receive twelve to fifteen video news clips, seven days a week, 365 days a year. This service supplies well edited stories with natural quality audio to meet the editorial needs of the clients spread all over the globe. Each story is ninety to one hundred and twenty seconds. The great newspaper of South Asia, radio networks and TV stations—all subscribe to the ANI wire that delivers nearly 20,000 words a day covering South Asia. The service is cost effective as claimed by ANI. It is delivered via E-mail or the traditional methods of teleprinters now turned online.

Most TV stations subscribe to ANI wire service as back-up data to the TV News moves some 16,000 to 20,000 words every day or some forty news items.

* Asian News International, 69, Vandana II Tolstoy Marg, New Delhi.

ANI Text News like its TV News companions offers breaking stories on politics, social issues, science, business and entertainment. In today's business conscious global economy it offers commodity price well as frequent news analysis of major events in India and overseas.

The hallmark of ANI News service is it's flexibility. It enables newspapers to request a unique tailor-made package, made to their editorial needs. Once the parameters are laid ANI seeks to meet those keep the subscriber happy.

To provide a global view ANI has News Exchange arrangement with several other News Agencies. ANI is a member of the OANA the Organization of Asia and Pacific News Agencies. ANI also has it's correspondents and representatives based in such strategic locations as Dubai, London, Washington, Tokyo among others. South Asia is it's home and every country in the region is well covered.

ANI service is delivered with speed, round the clock to specific requirements of the subscribers wither through teleprinter, on-line, fax or Email.

News Agency Style

Most of the news agencies have developed their own style which has been codified in the form of a 'Style Book'. The Non-aligned news Agencies Pool brought out a Style Book based on principles which are of universal relevance in news collection, processing and dissemination. Some of the salient points forming the style book are summarized below:

Lead of a News Story

The opening paragraph or lead of a news story should be short and crisp, so as to catch attention and direct the reader's interest to the body of the story. It should not be cluttered with details that can wait until later in the copy. If a reader has to look over a sentence a second time to understand it, then that sentence has no place in news agency copy. It certainly will not make the lead.

Basically a news story must answer the three W's What? When? And Where? As a rule the answers to these should find place in the opening paragraph.

Simplicity

A news copy should be written in simple and familiar language understood by the average reader. Simple, direct sentences are more effective than long, involved ones. The simple style enables all levels of the population, the rustic villagers as much as the urban elite, to grasp the contents of a news item. Further, where news reports required to be translated, especially for multi-language societies as in India, it makes the task of translation easier and speedier.

Unfamiliar words and jargon (expressions peculiar to various fields of special knowledge) should be avoided as far as possible. The choice of words should be simple and elegant. When not avoidable, as in a quotation, the unfamiliar words should be explained in simpler language.

Active Voice

The active voice is generally more effective in a news copy. "The Government today announced the appointment of a committee to study and report on." Has a better flow than: The appointment of a committee to study and report on........... was announced by the Government today."

Similarly, "India and Yugoslavia today singed an agreement providing for....." reads much better than "an agreement between India and Yugoslavia, providing for..... was singed here today."

However, in certain circumstances the passive voice is useful, especially where the deed is more important than the doer. Thus "A general strike has been called for tomorrow by.....to protest against......." Is more pointed than "The ....has called a general strike for tomorrow in protest against.........".

Identification

All persons named in a copy should be properly identified. Where the subject of a copy has multiple identifications, that is if he or she can be identified in more ways than one, the most pertinent among them – as a rule the office or position of consequence he or she currently holds – should be mentioned in the first instance, the others being suitably mentioned in later parts of the copy. Where the subject does not hold any office currently, he or she would have to be identified by the former office.

Objectivity and Use of Proper Language

Carrying only one version and ignoring others in the coverage of a controversial matter amounts to taking sides. Objectivity demands that both sides or all the points of view in a controversy are fairly presented.

A news writer should avoid reference to points about which he himself is not sure. If such a point has to be introduced, the copy should clarify that it is unconfirmed.

Similarly in view of the requirement of strict objectivity, no adjective or any other expression that smacks of bias, involves a value judgment or any snide or sarcastic observations, can be allowed in a news agency copy. An exception is when such an expression is a part of a quotation, and that too, if it is material to the story and has no defamatory implication.

Similarly, an agency can neither justify nor criticize any action by anyone, whether in authority or otherwise, since that constitutes a value judgment. For instance, it is not permissible to say, "The police had to open fire..." or ". Was forced to open fire" . The correct way is to say, "The police opened fire," which is a factual narration. However, if an official or a political leader states that the police had to open fire, that may be stated as attributed to them.

Sourcing

A news agency has to be very particular about the sources of the facts in its reports. There are certain types of stories where no source is required as, for instance, proceedings of legislatures and courts, or meetings and conferences.

In all other cases, a news agency report requires to be authenticated with a proper source, since the agency itself does not accept any responsibility for the statement issued or facts offered by any person. By dropping mention of the source, the agency would be needlessly accepting responsibility for views or information which may be open to question.

Takes

Each story should be split into parts, or takes, consisting of around 125 words each, and in any case not more than 150. The takes, except the first, should be numbered by the slug. Those at the receiving end are then able to connect the story as also to check on missing parts. Short takes facilitate the speedy clearance of a large number of stories coming in from various points around the globe. They also prove invaluable when repetitions are needed after long breakdowns.

All items should be serially numbered, so that at the receiving end items missed can be noticed.

The Manager and Chief Editor of the United News of India, the late G.. Mirchandani, offered the following tips to the newsroom staff on reporting accidents, communal incidents and crime.

REPORTING ACCIDENTS

Report with utmost caution the accidents involving defence establishments. Quote a competent authority. In other cases, quote a police, railway or district official or head of the establishment or service.

Mention the time and place of the occurrence and give the announced cause of the accident. In describing an accident, show respect to the dead. Avoid glory details, and do not give the names of those killed unless announced authoritatively. Legal complications may arise if you'kill' a person who is alive.

Describe accurately the nature of the accident: whether it was a crash, collision, sinking, house collapse, derailment, capsizing, skidding off, belly-landing, cloud burst or landslip.

Do not give your own assessment of the damage, loss or suffering caused by an accident. All such information should be attributed to competent persons

Be objective. Do not exaggerate.

Reporting Communal Incidents

The greatest care should be exercised in reporting communal clashes. Do not identify communities involved in a clash, nor should you refer to them as the majority or minority community. Generalized allegations and accusations of being anti-social or anti-national should not be made against an individual or a community. Do not give any facts or figures without verification. If their publication is likely to arouse communal passions, they should not be reported.

The source from which estimates of damage or casualty figures are obtained must be indicated. If unconfirmed figures must be filed because confirmed figures are unavailable or not forthcoming, indicate that your figures are unconfirmed, or are from a non-official source which must be identified.

News of incidents involving loss of life, lawlessness and arson should be reported strictly in an objective manner and attributed to a competent authority.

Do not say a temple, mosque or church was set afire, refer to it as a place of worship. Similarly, use the term holy book for the Gita, the Koran or the Bible.

REPORTING CRIMES

In reporting crimes such as murder, suicide, arson, sabotage and the like, information regarding the persons involved, the motive or cause should be attributed to a source. Do not say a person was arrested unless confirmed by the police. A person may be detained, held for questioning or may co-operate with an investigation without having been formally arrested. While reporting the arrest of an individual, give the charge against him.

In the eyes of the law a person is presumed to be innocent until he is found guilty by a court. Therefore, avoid describing a suspect or an accused as a culprit (which implies guilt) call him an alleged assailant or alleged spy. Do not give names of minors involved in crime. Attribute to the police all information provided by them.

Refrain from making conjectures about the manner in which a crime was committed, nor should you comment, draw conclusions or support of discount a particular theory.

These guidelines from the veteran journalist, who spent a lifetime in the service of the profession, would be equally valid for newspaper reporters. The brief salient points, extracted and summarized from the style book of the Non-aligned News Agencies Pool, 1985 would also help in appreciating the finer nuances of reporting for a news agency.

COPY DISTRIBUTION

Agency copy enters the newspaper as part of the daily news input. The standard practice is to give each story numbered catch lines, and a dateline to show place of origin. A story might be followed by Adds, i.e later material – and may be eventually a New Lead.

The more important running stories are transmitted under the following codes:

Flash	:	The first brief indication of the story – may be half a dozen words.
Rush	:	The first actual details available – may be a coupe of paragraphs.

Snap	:	Short messages giving brief details as they become available.
Rush full	:	The first full account based on the details so far available
Full	:	The full authoritative version.

Changing Trends and Challenges*

Though the advancement of technology and communication revolution has facilitated the working of the news agencies but it has also thrown up new challenges. The time factor and invasion of visual media has posed a big challenge to the wire news agencies.

Computers, satellites, CD-Roms and internet and a stunning array of new information technology has changed the media scene beyond recognition and 'online' is name of the game today.

The cultural invasion from the skies in already here and the information in the World Wide Web is only a mouse click away. There is 'no' tomorrow and the key word is 'now', information on demand anytime and anywhere.

The Indian scene is like the bullock cart co-existing with nuclear technology and the people in remote villages of India feeling the impact of TV and other mass-media- changing life styles spurring consumerism and raising expectations. The internet, satellite and e-mail have already penetrated into the media and the news agencies are on fast track to catch up with the technology.

The PTI has already computerised its operations, the old electro-mechanic systems are being replaced by new computerized equipment and techniques. From morse system to satellite system appears to be a long journey but all these developments have taken place in just ten years.

The teleprinters have gone and the news is supplied on computer terminals through satellites. The old teleprinter mechanics and operators are no longer required and the man at the desk has to manage everything. The time gap in gathering information and its dissemination has been drastically cut but the problem of absorbing the surplus staff has not been solved.

The introduction of Fax has helped the correspondents working at remote places to send their news immediately while the e-mail has made photo transmission so simple that the monopoly of photo agencies is over.

* Excerpts taken from the lecture delivered by P.C. Lohumi, Chief Bureau, PTI at Shimla in the Refreshner course of Journalism organized by Himachal Pradesh University, Shimla in July 2001.

The news agencies have also started their photo services and the initial cost of operation through Photo-Fax system has been reduced to ten percent through E-Mail.

Since the news agencies are still not quite wired up, they are trying to leapfrog through a new mass communication technology networking computers through satellite to the user as Fax, e-mail, mobile and internet has made the world a global village.

This revolution has brought a significant change in the viewing and reading habits of the people and entertainment seems to be emerged as king—and news, information and education are taking a back seat. Even the media like Doordarshan has forgotten its public service role.

The CNN coverage of Gulf war made all other media irrelevant as the people felt that they are fighting the war in their drawing rooms. We are afraid of entry of foreign media, but the fact is it has already entered through 'internet'. With a new generation of computer kids surfing the nets; the old war of foreign media has entered the cyberspace. The issue is broadly the same as was few years ago when the satellite TV appeared first on Indian origin a few years ago.

A piquant situation has been created with defenders of Indian culture and values calling for a check on invasions from the skies on the one hand and 'windows to the world' opening much wider on the other.

The problem with the internet is that it allows anyone with a telephone and modem to peep into any window and the governments can do very little to stop it.

As the information technology breaches the national barriers, the practitioners of new journalism—print, electronic or online need to address these questions and evolve a whole new code of ethics that sees responsible limits to freedom of media without trying to regulate or control it.

When we talk of entry of foreign media in reference to news agencies, it implies that no foreign news agency can directly supply news to the subscribers in India.

All the foreign agencies are providing news to the subscribers in India through bilateral arrangement with PTI or UNI. The PTI has news exchange arrangement with Reuters, AFP, TASS and about 100 small news agencies and there is a safe-guard that the undesirable news which is not in the national interest are not allowed to reach the subscribers.

Earlier the PTI has an arrangement with Reuters for supplying its commercial service but it was terminated a few years ago, causing a loss of Rs. five crore per annum to PTI.

How iong the Government will be able to remote the entry of foreign media is a matter of debate but the day direct entry of foreign media is allowed it will have a telling effect on Indian news agencies. The two major agencies are trying hard to expand the resource base but competing with foreign news agencies like AP, Reuter and AFP equipped with latest technology and superb information gathering and dissemination network, looks not only difficult but impossible. The future challenges and resource crunch may force the agencies to merge and pool their resource in the present scenario where corporate mergers are becoming the order of the day to fight competition.

The news agencies in India and other Asian countries are aware of these challenges and the emerging scenario and the main news agencies in the 'Organization of Asia Pacific News Agencies' (OAMA) came together to launch a unique international computer based service called "Asia Pulse" in February 1996 to enable the interested countries around the world to seize opportunities.

The PTI along with AAP of Australia, 'Antara' of Indonesia, 'Nikkei' of Japan and some other news agencies became equal partners in Asia Pulse which was registered in Singapore.

The PTI also joined the Asianet another enterprise promoted by OAMA which enabled the corporate and other organization around the world to have their press releases distributed in more countries in the Asia-Pacific region and the international companies are increasingly using this service.

Feature Syndicates/Agencies

Feature Syndicates/Agencies supply articles, features, photographs, comic strips, cartoons etc. on payment to newspapers and periodicals. The publicist may also avail of its service for placement of features in the newspapers and periodicals.

How the Syndicates work

A former syndicate editor, W. H. Thomas, wrote, "Of all the outlets available as a market for creative talent, none is so little understood or so ill defined as the newspaper syndicate, that insular and elusive shadow–organization whish exercise so much power within the various communication media". It is true that little is written about syndicate organizations, altogether even the largest of them are modest in size and complexity. But in spite of this, the lack of publicity and the variations among the syndicates, we can still make some generalizations about their working.

Syndicates coordinate many people and tasks, including contracts between the creators of syndicated material and the syndicate itself and contracts between the syndicate and subscribing newspapers. They also handle the flow of money from the newspaper to the syndicate and the payment of royalties to the writers and artists. A production staff prepares material for distribution to various media outlets. Additionally, syndicates promote and market their products through personal contacts, advertising and other means. To acquire material, syndicates maintain regular contacts with writers, designers, artists and others. Free-lance writers and artists also send material to syndicates regularly.

The syndicates usually offer a newspaper a contract for a variety of materials for a specified time at a specified cost. They charge less to the papers with small circulation. Some syndicates financially attractive packages, but most often newspapers buy material from several syndicates. Sometimes there is vigorous competition for a feature.

Thus syndicates are multifaceted organizations that link a wide variety of creative energies to potential outlets. Syndication can be carried out by large organizations or by the self-syndication efforts of a writer or artist. Syndicates are brokers, but they can also be quite creative. Some syndicates are responding to the communication revolution and making substantial changes. Most of the syndicates are privately held companies. Their size and scope is something of a mystery. One way to measure the reach of a syndicate is by the number of newspapers or magazines it serves.

The King Feature Syndicate which is owned by Hearst claims to have the greatest array of comic strips for the Sunday papers. This syndicate also has feature columnist who cover astrology, automobiles, books, bridge, politics, gossip, consumer advice, human relations, music, religion, TV, and other topics.

Some leading newspapers abroad have their own syndicated services offering to other publications right to the material published therein. Several Indian newspapers make use of the services provided by newspapers such as *The Guardian, The Observer* and the *Telegraph.* The two leading Indian news agencies – PTI and UNI also offer background material and features. This meets the requirement of the newspapers for write-ups on different specialist subjects.

The columns of Khushwant Singh, Kuldeep Nayyar, Tavleen Singh and many other well known senior journalists are translated into several Indian regional languages and published by newspapers all over the country. For a syndicated columnist it is important that he has a name and that his credibility is established.

Exercises

1. How does a news agency story differ from a story covered by a newspaper reporter? Clip any two news stories from any national daily and compare it with the wire copy.
2. Discuss in brief the origin of global news agencies.
3. How 'Samachar' was formed?
4. Write brief history of Press Trust of India.
5. To what extent PTI is successful in providing subsidiary services.
6. Discuss the origin of United News of India.
7. Do you think Asian News International (ANI) is among the best professionally managed corporate media entities? Elaborate your answer with suitable examples.
8. What are the points you will keep in mind while writing for wire copy?
9. Describe the challenges a wire news agency is facing today.
10. What is the relationship between global news services and the newspapers you read and the newscasts you hear?
11. What is the relationship between syndicates and the newspapers you read?

ANNEXURES

ANNEXURE I

Code of Practice for Journalists Adopted by Editors' Guild of India August 20, 2002

Why A Code?

Journalists resist any kind of "code" for their profession as something repugnant to the freedom of expression. But a good code imposes no fetters. It may only have some pitfalls discovered by those who have gone before, so that those who follow may anticipate and avoid them. That way useful guidelines will emerge and freedom will grow without running into aberrations. It may not be a mere coincidence that journalism has progressed most in those countries which also have evolved such codes more diligently. That is why it has been named Code of Practice, not Code of Conduct.

Journals are records of change. It will be odd if they were to show reluctance to record the changes that take place in their own field. Journalists must take note of changes and profit from precedents, and in doing so they must sift the more relevant and useful from the less relevant because no code can be universal or ever-lasting. All occupations profit from past experience for avoiding wrong practices which might have crept in, before these become settled habits. But journalism needs to do so more often and more diligently because its practice is a record of hourly change put together in a hurry. Mistakes are best seen from a distance from the rush of events. A code is an index of what is seen in this way to be desirable or otherwise. It makes a recurrence of past mistakes less likely and expands the scope for error-free innovation in the future.

That is why the code suggested by some members of the Editors Guild of India has drawn liberally from an existing code prepared by Britain's Society of Editors, while at the same time members of the Guild have been equally liberal in modifying the British code in the light of India's own experience. Much of the draft code suggested by them is addressed to media workers in the field and on the desk. That is where the rush of work makes the habit of correct judgement a more useful aid to both speed and safety.

But it is also addressed to editors, upon whom rests the responsibility of inculcating these habits in their colleagues in circumstances which have special angularities in India.

Among all countries which cherish freedom of the press, India has the maximum overlap because two entities which are often, though not always correctly, regarded as adversaries: the government of the day and the media. The overlap is extensive, sometimes troublesome, for such media whose owners and managers have interests which lie in ambivalent proximity to the political powers of the day. The interaction between them does not always make life easy for the editors of such media. Therefore, in addition to formulating a code of practice an organisation like the Editors Guild should help to promote such institutions as can shield the editor from the inclement effects of such interaction. Faithful observance of a good code, formulated and monitored by an organisation like the Guild can certainly help improve the climate.

All the foregoing considerations apply as much to the electronic as to the print media.

Credentials of the Media

The fact that the media are guided by a self-imposed code strengthens their credentials for demanding protection of their right to receive and impart information.

They would be strengthened further if the media eschewed more scrupulously any actions which would even remotely suggest that in exercising the right to receive and impart information they were beholden to special interests and groups for perks and favours and were thereby allowing their judgement to be swayed.

Particularly relevant in this respect are such favours as invitations for foreign visits and travel, whether from governments, industrial and commercial organisations, or other centres of power and patronage.

It might be difficult to forego these entirely, because in that case the less affluent among the media might not be able to provide even unbiased coverage of many events.

But three kinds of precautions should be taken:

First, the better-off media should set an example in providing self-supporting coverage. Second, where there is a choice between accepting offers of such facilities or denying suitable coverage to the audience, the media concerned should acknowledge that such facilities have been offered and accepted. Third, the offer should be made directly to the editor, leaving it to him to decide whom he deputes for the coverage to keep it free from extraneous considerations.

Editor's Domain

As the ultimate custodian of the personality of what he edits, the editors rightly gets all the blame and credit but four aspects of his role stand out the most. The hardest to define, but nevertheless essential, is that the publication must maintain and promote high standards of good taste. The publication may also aim at entertaining its customers in addition to reforming them. The more the mainstream media shift towards the kind of "entertainment" which was once the stock in trade of "glossies", the less they will be able to claim privileges in the name of the freedom of the press.

The other three aspects of the role of the editor are easier to explain.

Maintaining the credibility of the publication: Whatever its professed beliefs, stance or role, the publication can maintain them only to the extent it sustains its credibility by presenting facts honestly and commenting on them fairly, without any bias. But intentional mis-statement of facts and biased comments are not the only enemies of credibility. Sensationalism is another, because it distorts the perspective and meaning of what is reported. It may gain attention and popularity one day, but practised over a period of time it undermines the public's confidence in the editorial judgement of the publication.

Accuracy: Respect for accuracy is a better prop of popularity than sensationalism. It also serves better the people's right to know. That right implies that the people must be given the facts first, unmixed with comment and value judgement. There must be a place for the latter as well, but separately from the narration of facts, preferably in the space clearly set aside for comment, but at least separated from the facts in the news even if it has to be within the same space. Reliable facts should take precedence over conjectures and implied comment in the presentation of news. That only enhances the editor's capacity and his obligation to resist suppression of facts, along with his peers and organisations such as the Editors Guild. One part of this obligation is to resist laws requiring disclosure of sources except where a clearly higher cause intervenes.

But it is also a part of the editor's obligations to ensure that firstly, he lends his full weight to the functioning of peer organisations by actively participating in them; secondly, he publishes fairly and fully any proceedings of organisations which relate to any inquiry into his own or his publication's conduct; thirdly, he publishes correction of incorrect reports and apologises where an apology is called for; and fourthly, no member of his staff allows personal interests or any favours done to him to colour his work for the publication.

More than that, it is also the *editor's obligation to inculcate respect for all such obligations* in the minds of the staff of the publication. Much of the work of the staff has to be done at a time when the editor is not readily accessible for consultation, and they have to fall back on their own judgement. Therfore, its own standards must harmonise with those of the editor and must be as finely honed as his. One way of promoting this harmony is that the editor makes it a standard practice to discuss with the staff the rights and wrongs of his own and their decisions in specific cases.

These considerations, important at all times, are all the more so at times of internal or international conflict, particularly in a country like India which is situated in a sensitive neighbourhood and is the arena of many competing interests, domestic and external, of competing ideas about the rights of society and the individual, and the rights relating to gender, class, caste, religion and community.

Staff's Domain

Particularly important in this respect is the role of the chief sub-editor and his colleagues on the desk, a role which has unfortunately tended to fade, more so when the field staff is glorified by the personal by-line in the print media and the face on the screen in the electronic media. But the importance of the role of the chief sub-editor has only increased on account of these factors. All matter for publication passes through the hands of the subs. On the one hand, they are less exposed to the rush of events and pressures in the field and contact with interested persuaders, and on the other, they have, or should have, the time and resources to check data with references. Therefore, unless their own judgement fails them, given the time they have for thought, they can better insure the publication against errors. They are the safety net that catches mistakes which may slip through the hurried hands of the field staff.

Not only the subs but all members of the staff must take care of certain things. Among them, the following stand out, either because these are important or because these are more frequently encountered.

1. Verify facts and weed out inaccuracies from field reports with the help of an adequate, reference library which the publication must maintain. Conjecture should not be allowed to masquerade as fact.
2. Segregate facts from direct or implied comments thereon and put the facts in the space meant for facts. Confine comment to the space meant for comment, or identify it as comment, even if it has to be accommodated alongside the facts.
3. Measure the right to publish against the relevant "public interest" before according supremacy to the former.
4. Weed out unsubstantiated allegations or innuendoes which are not essential to the story, or retain them only after fully measuring their defamatory potential.
5. Give fair opportunity to the aggrieved party to reply or contradict, within reasonable limits.
6. Where apology is called for, offer it readily, frankly, and with dignity.
7. Should proceedings for defamation follow, cover them fairly, with due regard for the law.
8. Avoid undue publicity to the personal affairs of personalities if public interest is not clearly at stake. But if it is, pursue the matter with diligence and without fear but always with due regard for decency and good taste. Avoid harassing and intimidating sources.
9. Avoid exaggerating the story for the sake of heightening interest in it. Pushed beyond a point, exaggeration distorts facts. In the long run, objectivity sells better than sensationalism.
10. Allegations against actions of public servants in the performance of their duties should be double checked because rules of service often deny them the right to reply, with official material to back them. But where exposure is well founded it should be bold but not boastful or premature.
11. Suppression of facts under pressure is dereliction of duty.
12. Statements and facts received on non-attributable basis must not be attributed.
13. But anonymity should not be allowed to become a cloak for the source to dish out falsehood or calumny, while the right to protect the source should be exercised to the full limit of the law. Journalists should caution one another against sources which mislead under the garb of anonymity.

14. Scenes of personal grief are a delicate matter to handle. They should never be shown blatantly in the name of "human interest". Human rights are as important, and privacy of personal feelings counts among them.
15. The journalist's right to information an be used as a powerful instrument for personal gain. It should never be.
16. In writing about religions controversies, all creeds and communities must be shown equal respect. All parties to such and other controversies deserve equally fair reporting.
17. In reporting crime, particularly crimes of sex, and more so crimes involving children, utmost care must be taken to see that the report itself does not become a punishment that may blast a life without warrant. The alleged criminal and the victim, and the witnesses, must be identified with utmost care, with no implications of colour or race. Only on the strongest grounds of public interest should any of these considerations be diluted.
18. "Cheque book journalism" and paying for information, are equal to wages of sin. They should be resorted to only in extreme limits of public interest and when no other means of obtaining the necessary information are available. Even so, the payment must be disclosed in any relevant legal manner, and it should never be offered to those involved in a related legal matter. Do not mix financial journalism with playing the market.
19. Information should not be obtained through the use of clandestine listening (and photographing) devices or by intercepting private telephone conversations. Or through misrepresentation or subterfuge, except when justified only in the public interest and only when information cannot be obtained by any other means.
20. Journalists must not accept favours for themselves or for any member of their families from persons and institutions whose activities they are reporting or commenting upon.
21. Journalists should not seek or accept such favours or out of turn allotment of accommodation or land at subsidised rates, or similar privileges.
22. Where cases involving professional actions of journalists are filed at far off places away from the professional location of the journalist concerned, the management should provide legal protection so that the threat of such harassment is not used merely to scare the media away, from exposing unsavoury actions of powerful people. Otherwise, such cases can become a form of punishment without proof of guilt.

ANNEXURE II

Trends in Indian Journalism

Press Council's Guide to Journalistic Ethics

The Press Council of India has been established to preserve the freedom of the press and to maintain and improve the standards of newspapers and news agencies. The Council is enjoined to 'build up' a code of conduct for newspapers, news agencies and journalists in accordance with high professional standards. A compendium of broad principles evolved by the Press Council through its adjudications/principles was first published in 1983-84. In October 1992, the Council published an updated but succinct compilation of the principles of journalistic ethics sorted out from the adjudications of the Council and the guidelines issued by it in their wake. (The *Guide to Journalistic Ethics* was further revised and updated in 1995 by the then Chairman, Mr. Justice P.B. Sawant.) Below are excerpts from the *1992 guidelines:*

(1) *Accuracy and Fairness:* The fundamental objective of journalism, declares the *Guide,* is to serve the people with news, views, comments and information on matters of public interest, in a fair, accurate, unbiased, sober and decent manner. Publication of inaccurate, baseless, graceless, misleading or distorted material should be avoided.
All sides of the core issue or subject should be reported.

(1a) Verification and checking of news before publication is necessary where its publication and the comments based thereon can create complications, such as:

(i) where it is likely to incite communal passions
(ii) where it is of a slanderous nature.

(1b) However, failure to observe strictly this rule as to pre-publication verification would not necessarily amount to a breach of journalistic ethics on the part of the editor.

(i) where the impugned news item was merely a statement made by a responsible political leader of the ruling party at a press conference or a public statement of a recognised leader, or

(ii) where the impugned news items was based on the report of an accredited correspondent.

Provided in either case it was in respect to a matter of public concern.

(1c) Unjustified rumours and surmises should not be set forth as facts.

(2) Journalists should judge no one unheard.

(3) *Cautions against Defamatory Writings:* Newspapers should not publish anything which is *per se* defamatory or libellous against any individual or organisation unless after due care and checking they have sufficient reason to believe that it is true and its publication will be for public good.

(4) *Pre-publication Verification of Reports Necessary:* Whenever a newspaper receives a report or article containing defamatory or derogatory imputations or comments against a public figure, public servant or public organisation, touching his/her or its public conduct or character in so far as it appears in that conduct, the editor should, before publishing it, check with due care and attention, its factual accuracy—apart from other authentic sources, with the person on the organisation concerned to elicit his/her or its version, comments or reaction and publish the same. If the person or the organisation, likely to be affected by that report/article, refuses to give his/her counter-version or reaction, despite sincere efforts made by the editor, a footnote to that effect should be published along with the report or the article. If from the counter-version give by the person or organisation concerned, the editor'd mind is left rocking with doubt in regard to the veracity of any part of the report/article, he should omit from publication that part and publish the rest with consequential amendment, provided the editor is satisfied that the remainder is substantially accurate and its publication will be for public benefit. If such doubt permeates the whole of the report/article, the prudent course for him is not to publish it at all.

(4b) This salutary rule of journalistic ethics and fairness follow as a necessary corollary from two basic principles: the first is a fundamental canon of natural justice, that no one should be condemned unheard. The second is that freedom of the press is not merely a right of the publishers and editors but also of the readers'/

people's right to know all sides of an issue of public interest. The editor, therefore, cannot refuse to publish the reply or rejoinder merely on the ground that in his opinion the story published in the newspaper was true. That is an issue to be left to the judgement of the readers.

(5) *Privacy:* Instruction or invasion on the privacy of individuals is not permissible unless outweighed by genuine overriding public interest, not being a prurient or morbid curiosity.
Explanation: Things concerning a person's home, family, religion, health, sexuality, personal life and private affairs are covered by the concept of privacy excepting where any of these impinge upon the public or public interest.

Victims of Sex Crimes—Caution against Publication of Names or Pictures

(6) While reporting crimes involving rape or molestation of women, of sexual assault on children, or raising doubts and questions touching the chastity, personal character and privacy of women, the names, photographs of the victims or other particulars leading to their identity should not be published. While such publication serves no legitimate public purpose, it may bring social opprobrium to the victims and social embarrassment to their relations, family, friends, community, religious order or the institution to which they belong.

(7) Newspapers to eschew suggestive guilt by association. They should not name or identify the family or relatives or associates of a person convicted or accused of a crime, when they are totally innocent and a reference to them is not relevant to the matter reported.

(8) *Corrections:* When any factual error or mistake is detected or confirmed, the newspaper should publish the correction promptly with due prominence and with apology or expression of regret in a case of serious lapse.

(9a) *Right of Reply:* The newspaper should promptly publish at the instance of the person feeling aggrieved/or concerned by the impugned publication, a contradiction/reply/rejoiner sent to the editor in the form of a letter or note the editor has a discretion either to publish it in full or publish its abridged and edited version, particularly when it is inordinately long. But the remainder should be an effective reply to the allegations. However, the editor is not entitled to alter, omit or refuse to publish important portions of the reply/rejoinder which effectively deal with the material allegations in the news item. If the editor doubts the truth or factual accuracy of the contradiction/reply/rejoinder, even then, it is his/her duty to publish it, with liberty to add separately at the end, an editorial comment doubting its veracity, but only when this doubt is reasonably founded on unimpeachable documentary or other evidential material in his/her possession. The editor should not, in a cavalier fashion, without the application of mind, append such note, as: 'we stand by our story'. It must be remembered that the liberty to append an editorial comment to a rejoinder or reply is not absolute right. It is a concession which has to be availed of sparingly with due discretion and caution in appropriate cases.

(9b) However, where the reply/contradiction or rejoinder is being published in compliance with the direction of the Press Council, it is permissible to append a brief editorial note to that effect.

(10) *Letters to the Editor:* An editor who decides to open his columns for letters on a controversial subject is not obliged to publish all the letters received in regard to that subject. He is entitled to select and publish only some of them either in entirety or the gist thereof. However, in exercising this discretion he must make an honest endeavour to ensure that what is published is not one-sided but represents a fair balance between the views for and against with respect to the principal issue in controversy. In the event of rejoinder upon rejoinder being sent by two parties on a controversial subject, the editor has the discretion to decide at which stage to close the continuing column.

(11) *Conjecture, Comment and Fact:* Newspapers should not pass on or elevate conjecture, speculation or comment as a statement of fact. All these categories should be distinctly stated.

Paramount Interests of State, Society and Rights of Individuals not to be jeopardised.

(12) Newspapers should, as a matter of self-regulation, exercise due restraint and caution in presenting any news, comment or information which is likely to jeopardise, endanger or harm the paramount interests of the state and society, or the rights of individuals, for the protection of which reasonable restrictions may be imposed by law on the right to freedom of speech and expression under Clause (2) of Article 19 of the Constitution of India.

(13) *Newspapers may Expose Misuse of Diplomatic Immunity:* The media should make every possible effort to build bridges of cooperation, friendly relations and in developing better understanding between India and foreign states. At the same time, it is the duty of a newspaper to expose if any diplomat is trying to misuse or take undue advantage of the diplomatic immunities.

(14) *Covering Communal Disputes/Clashes:* News, views or comments relating to communal or religious disputes/clashes should be published after proper verification of facts, and presented with due caution and restraint in a manner which is conducive to the reaction of an atmosphere congenial to communal harmony, amity and peace. Sensational, provocative and alarming headlines are to be avoided. Acts of communal violence or vandalism should be reported in a manner as may not undermine the people's confidence in the law and order machinery of the state. Giving community-wise figures of the victims of communal riot, or writing to inflame passions, aggravate the tensions, or accentuate the strained relations between the communities/religious groups concerned, or which has a potential to exacerbate the trouble, should be avoided.

Headings should not be sensational/provocative and must justify the matter printed under them.

(15) In general, and particularly, in the context of communal disputes or clashes between them.

(a) Provocative and sensational headlines should be avoided.
(b) Headings must reflect and justify the matter printed under
(c) Headings containing allegations made in statements should either identify the body or the source making it or at least carry quotation marks.

(16) *Plagiarism:* Using or passing off the writings or ideas of another as one's own, without crediting the source is an offence against the ethics of journalism.

(17) *Recording Interviews and Phone Conversations:* Journalists should not tape-record anyone's conversation without that person's knowledge or consent, except where the recording is necessary to protect the journalist in a legal action, or for other compelling good reasons.

(18a) *Obscenity and Vulgarity to be Eschewed:* Newspapers/journalists should not publish anything which is obscene, vulgar or offensive to public good taste.

(b) Newspapers should not publish an advertisement containing that which is unlawful or illegal, or is contrary to good taste or to journalistic ethics or proprieties.

(c) Newspapers should not display advertisements which are vulgar or which, through a picture of a woman in nude of bad posture, provoke the lecherous attention of males as if she herself was a commercial commodity for sale.

(d) While publishing the tape-recorded statement of another, the editor should delete obscene or filthy epithets offensive to good public taste, with which the person stating might have punctuated the tenor or tone or his/her answers.

(19) *Glorifying Violence to be Eschewed:* Newspapers/journalists should avoid presenting acts of violence, armed robberies and terrorist activities in a manner that glorifies their acts or death in the eyes of the public.

(20) *Glorification/Encouragement of Social Evils to be Eschewed:* Newspapers should not allow their columns to be misused for writings which have a tendency to encourage or glorify social evils like Sati Pratha.

(21a) *Caution in Criticising Judicial Acts:* Excepting where the court sits *in camera* or directs otherwise, it is open to a newspaper to report pending judicial proceedings, in a fair, accurate and reasonable manner. But it should not publish anyting

(i) which, in its direct and immediate effect, creates a substantial risk of obstructing, impeding or prejudicing seriously the due administration of justice.

or

(ii) is in the nature of a running commentary or debate, or records the paper's own findings, conjectures, reflections or comments on issues, sub-judice, and which may amount to arrogation to the newspaper, the functions of the court.

or

(iii) regarding the personal character of the accused standing trial on a charge of committing a crime.

(b) Newspapers should not as a matter of caution, publish or comment on evidence collected as a result of investigative journalism, when, after the accused is arrested and charged, the court become seized of the case; nor should they reveal, comment on confession allegedly made by the accused.

(c) While newspapers may, in the public interest, make reasonable criticism of a judicial act of the judgment of a court for public good they should not cast scurrilous aspersions on, or impute improper motives or personal bias to the judge; nor should they scandalise the court or the judiciary as a whole; or make personal allegations of lack of ability or integrity against a judge.

(d) Newspapers should, as a matter of caution, avoid unfair and unwarranted criticism which, attributes to a judge extraneous consideration for performing an act in due course of his/her judicial functions, even if such criticism does not strictly amount to culpable contempt of court.

(22) *Newspapers should avoid Cross Commercialism:* While newspapers are entitled to ensure, improve or strengthen their financial viability by all legitimate means, they should not engage themselves through the print media, in mass commercialism or unseemly, cut-throat competition with their rivals, for earning ever more profits for their proprietors, in a manner which is repugnant to high professional standards and good taste, and tends to pull downwards the primary role of the free press as an essential institution of democracy to a secondary, subservient place.

(23) *Photographs of Dead Bodies of Victims of Crimes/Accidents:* Photojournalism is an important part of the print media. While intrusion through photography into personal grief, likely to hurt sentiments or arouse communal passions, should be avoided, publication of photographs serving the larger public interest cannot be termed unethical or in bad taste.

In the Indian environment, publication of the photographs of the dead bodies of the victims of accidents or natural calamity may not be *per se* wrong unless objected to by near relations of the deceased.

(24a) *Caste, Religion or Community Disclosures to be Generally Avoided:* In general, the identification of a person belonging to a scheduled caste or depressed class, with reference to his caste or by use of the word harijan should be avoided, particularly when in the context it conveys a sense or attributes a conduct or practice derogatory to that caste.

(b) It is not desirable for a journalist to describe a person accused of an offence by mentioning his caste when the caste does not have anything to do with the offence or the crime and plays no part either in the identification of any accused or proceeding, if there be any.

(c) Except when it becomes relevant and material, it is not proper and desirable to mention the caste, religion or community of an assailant or victim in a news item. Mention of caste, creed, religion, or community usually serves no useful purpose, but may at times have the unfortunate effect of creating ill-feeling among communities and individuals.

(25a) *Editor's Responsibility for all matter published in the Newspaper:* The editor shall assume responsibility for all matter, including advertisements, published in the newspaper. If responsibility is disclaimed, this shall be explicitly stated beforehand.

(b) Unconfirmed news shall be identified and treated as such.

(26) *Confidence to be Respected:* If information is received from a confidential source, the confidence should be respected. The journalists cannot be compelled by the Press Council to disclose such source; but it shall not be regarded as a breach of journalistic ethics if the source is voluntarily disclose in proceedings before the Council by the journalist who considers it necessary to repel effectively a charge against him/her. This rule, requiring a newspaper not to publish matters disclosed to it in confidence, is not applicable where—

(a) consent of the source is subsequently obtained.

(b) that editor clarifies by way of an appropriate footnote that since the publication of certain matters were in the public interest, the information in question was being published although it had been made 'off the record'.

27. *Dummy Advertisements:* Publication of dummy advertisements that have neither been paid for, nor authorised by advertisers, constitute breach of journalistic ethics.

ANNEXURE III

SPJ Code of Ethics

Preamble

Members of the Society of Professional Journalists believe that public enlightenment is the forerunner of justice and the foundation of democracy. The duty of the journalist is to further those ends of seeking truth and providing a fair and comprehensive account of events and issues. Conscientious journalists from all media and specialities strive to serve the public with thoroughness and honesty. Professional integrity is the cornerstone of a journalists credibility. Members of the Society share a dedication to ethical behaviour and adopt this code to declare the Society's principles and standards of practice.

Seek Truth and Report It

Journalists should be honest, fair and courageous in gathering, reporting and interpreting information.

Journalists should:

— Test the accuracy of information from all sources and exercise care to avoid inadvertent error. Deliberate distortion is never permissible.
— Diligently seek out subjects of news stories to give them the opportunity to respond to allegations of wrongdoing.
— Identify sources, whenever feasible. The public is entitled to as much information as possible on sources' reliability.
— Always question sources' motives before promising anonymity. Clarify conditions attached to any promise made in exchange for information. Keep promises.
— Make certain that headlines, news teasers and promotional material, photos, video, audio, graphics, sound bites and quotations do not misrepresent.
— They should not oversimplify or highlight incidents out of context.

- Never distort the content of news photos or video. Image enhancement for technical clarity is always permissible. Label montages and photo illustrations.
- Avoid misleading re-enactments or staged news events. If re-enactment is necessary to tell a story, label it.
- Avoid undercover or other surreptitious methods of gathering information except when traditional open methods will not yield information vital to the public. Use of such methods should be explained as part of the story.
- Never plagiarise.
- Tell the story of the diversity and magnitude of the human experience boldly, even when it is unpopular to do so.
- Examine their own cultural values and avoid imposing those values on others.
- Avoid stereotyping by race, gender, age, religion, ethnicity, geography, sexual orientation, disability, physical appearance or social status.
- Support the open exchange of views, even views they find repugnant.
- Give voice to the voiceless; official and unofficial sources of information can be equally valid.
- Distinguish between advocacy and news reporting. Analysis and commentary should be labelled and not misrepresent fact or context.
- Distinguish news from advertising and shun hybrids that blur the lines between the two.
- Recognise a special obligation to ensure that the public's business is conducted in the open and that government records are open to inspection.

Minimise Harm

Ethical journalists treat sources, subjects and colleagues as human beings deserving of respect.

Journalists should:

- Show compassion for those who may be affected adversely by news coverage. Use special sensitivity when dealing with children and inexperienced sources or subjects.
- Be sensitive when seeking or using interviews or photographs of those affected by tragedy or grief.

— Recognise that gathering and reporting information may cause harm or discomfort. Pursuit of the news is not a licence for arrogance.
— Recognise that private people have a greater right to control information about themselves than do public officials and others who seek power, influence or attention. Only an overriding public need can justify intrusion into anyone's privacy.
— Show good taste. Avoid pandering to lurid curiosity.
— Be cautious about identifying juvenile suspects or victims of sex crimes.
— Be judicious about naming criminal suspects before the formal filing of charges.
— Balance a criminal suspect's fair trial rights with the public's right to be informed.

Act Independently

Journalists should be free of obligation to any interest other than the public's right to know.

Journalists should:

— Avoid conflicts of interest, real or perceived.
— Remain free of association and activities that may compromise integrity or damage credibility.
— Refuse gifts, favours, fees, free travel and special treatment, and shun secondary employment, political involvement, public office and service in community organisations if they compromise journalistic integrity.
— Disclose unavoidable conflicts.
— Be vigilant and courageous about holding those with power accountable.
— Deny favoured treatment to advertisers and special interests and resist their pressure to influence news coverage.
— Be wary of sources offering information for favours or money, avoid bidding for news.

Be Accountable

Journalists are accountable to their readers, listeners, viewers and each other.

Journalists should:

- Clarify and explain news coverage and invite dialogue with the public over journalistic conduct.
- Encourage the public to voice grievances against the news media.
- Admit mistakes and correct them promptly.
- Expose unethical practices of journalists and the news media.
- Abide by the same high standards to which they hold others.

Sigma Delta Chi's first code of ethics was borrowed from the American Society of Newspaper Editors in 1926. In 1973, Sigma Delta wrote its own code, which was revised in 1984 and 1987. The present version of the Code of Society of Professional Journalists was adopted in September 1996.

Checklist for Improving Media Credibility

The American Society of Newspaper Editors (ASNE) interviewed 3,000 American and ran 16 focus groups to find ways to improve public trust in journalism. The ASNE's study came up with six areas in which journalists should concentrate to improve news media credibility.

1. *Inaccuracies:* Factual, grammatical and spelling errors undermine a story and its report's credibility.
2. *Sensationalism:* Sensational stories are often chased and overcovered because they are exciting, but they are not important.
3. *Objectivity:* Journalists should remove the perception of bias in their reporting—what stories are covered and how they are covered. Bias is defined as not being open-minded and neutral about the facts, having an agenda and shaping the news to report it, or showing favouritism to particular social or political group.
4. *Freedom from Manipulation of the Press:* The public believes the press can be manipulated by powerful people, organisations and advertisers to put a desired angle on stories. A big criticism is that newspapers are trying to make a profit instead of serving in the public interest.
5. *Name Sources:* Using anonymous sources lowers the credibility of a news story. Many people would not run the story at all if a source declined to go "on the record". Furthermore, journalists should tell the public why an anonymous source is used.
6. *Corrections:* Admitting errors and running corrections help credibility, not hurt it.

Source: Ravindran.

ANNEXURE IV

Guidelines for the State Governments and the Media in Relation to Communal Disturbances 1991

(i) The State Government should take upon themselves the responsibility of keeping a close watch on the communal writings that might spark off tension, destruction and death, and bring them to the notice of the Council;

(ii) The government may have occasion to take action against erring papers or editors. But it must do so within the bounds of law. If newsmen are arrested, or search and seizure operations become necessary, it would be healthy convention if such developments could be reported to the Press Council within 24 to 48 hours followed by a detailed note within a week;

(iii) Under no circumstances must have authorities resort to vindictive measures like cut in advertisements, cancellation of accreditation, cut in newsprint quota and other facilities;

(iv) Provocative and sensational headlines should be avoided by the Press;

(v) Headings must reflect and justify and matter printed under them;

(vi) Figures of casualties given in headlines should preferably be on the lower side in case of doubt about their exactness and where the numbers reported by various sources differ widely;

(vii) headings containing allegations made in statements should either identify the person/body making the allegation or, at least, should carry quotation marks;

(viii) News reports should be devoid of comments and value judgement;

(ix) presentation of news should not be motivated or guided by partisan feelings, nor should it appear to be so;

(x) language employed in writing the news should be temperate and such as may foster feelings or amity among communities and groups;

(xi) Corrections should be promptly published with due prominence and regrets expressed in serious cases; and

(xii) It will help a great deal if in-service training is given to journalists for inculcation of all these principles.

Guidelines to the Press on Ram Janambhoomi-Babri Masjid Dispute (21-22 Jan., 1993)

Guidelines for guarding against the commission of the following journalistic improprieties and unethicalities:

1. Distortion or exaggeration of facts or incidents in relation to communal matters or giving currency to unverified rumours, suspicions or inferences as if they were facts and base their comments on them.
2. Employment of intemperate of unrestrained language in the presentation of news or views, even as a piece of literary flourish or for the purpose of rhetoric or emphasis.
3. Encouraging or condoning violence even in the face of provocation as a means of obtaining redress of grievance whether the same be genuine or not.
4. While it is the legitimate function of the Press to draw attention to the genuine and legitimate grievances of any community with a view to having the same redressed by all peaceful, legal and legitimate means, it is improper and breach of journalistic ethics to invent grievances, or to exaggerate real grievances, as these tend to promote communal ill-feeling and accentuate discord.
5. Scurrilous and untrue attacks on communities, or individuals, particularly when this is accompanied by charges attributing misconduct to them as due to their being members of a particular community or caste.
6. Falsely giving a communal colour to incidents which might occur in which members of different communities happen to be involved.
7. Emphasizing matters that are apt to produce communal hatred or ill-will, or fostering feelings of distrust between communities.
8. Publishing alarming news which are in substance untrue or make provocative comments on such news or even otherwise calculated to embitter relations between different communities or regional or linguistic groups.
9. Exaggerating actual happenings to achieve sensationalism and publication of news which adversely affect communal harmony with banner headlines or distinctive types.
10. Making disrespectful, derogatory or insulting remarks on or reference to the different religions or faiths or their founders.

ANNEXURE V

Guidelines for Financial Journalists

1. The Press Council of India has counselled reporters/financial journalists/newspaper establishments to refrain from receiving any gifts/grants/concessions/facilities, etc., either in cash or kind, which are likely to compromise free and unbiased reporting on financial matters.
2. The Council in its Report has observed that the financial journalists today enjoy considerable influence over readers' minds and, therefore, they owe it to them to present a balanced and objective view of the financial dealings, status and prospects of a company. It observed that some companies are given excessive news coverage in the newspapers/magazines because they have issued advertisements to that print media. Sometimes, adverse reports are published of those companies which do not give advertisements to the newspapers or magazines. Again, when a media is not happy with any company/management for whatever reason, the negative aspects of the company are highlighted, while in the reverse situation, no negative aspects are brought to light. Some companies are also known to given gifts, loans, discounts, preferential shares, etc., to certain financial journalists to receive favourable and positive reports of the companies. At the same time, there is no mechanism for investors' education or for raising public opinion against such unhealthy practices.
3. The council feeling concerned over the malpractice in the Corporate Sector and after holding detailed deliberations and discussions with the representatives of financial institutions and journalists, has recommended the guidelines enumerated below for observance by the financial journalists:

(1) The financial journalists should not accept gifts, loans, trips, discounts, preferential shares or other considerations which compromise or are likely to compromise his position.

(2) It should be mentioned prominently in the report about any company that the report is based on information given by the company or the financial sponsors of the company.

(3) When the trips are sponsored for visiting establishments of a company, the author of the report who has availed of the trip must state invariably that the visit was sponsored by the company concerned and that it had also extended the hospitality as the case may be.

(4) No matter related to the company should be published without verifying the facts from the company and the source of such report should also be disclosed.

(5) A reporter who exposes a scam or brings out a report for promotion of a good project, should be encouraged and awarded.

(6) A journalist who has financial interests such as share holdings, stock holdings, etc., in a company, should not report on that company.

(7) The journalist should not use for his own benefit or for the benefit of his relations and friends, information received by him in advance for publication.

(8) No newspaper owner, editor or anybody connected with a newspaper should use his relations with the newspaper to promote his other business interests.

(9) Whenever there is an indictment of a particular advertising agency or advertiser by the Advertising Council of India, the newspaper in which the advertisement was published must publish the news of indictment prominently.

ANNEXURE VI

International Code of Ethics : Principles of Professional Values

International and regional organizations of working journalists, representing altogether 400,000 working journalists in all parts of the world, have held since 1978 consultative meetings under the auspices of UNESCO.

The second consultative meeting (Mexico City, 1980) expressed its support to the UNESCO Declaration on Fundamental Principles concerning the contribution of the Mass Media to strengthening Peace and International Understanding, to the promotion of Human Rights and to countering Racialism, Apartheid and incitement to War. Moreover, the meeting adopted the "Mexico Declaration" with a set of principles which represent common grounds of existing national and regional codes of journalistic ethics as well as relevant provisions contained in various international instruments of a legal nature.

The fourth consultative meeting (Prague and Paris, 1983) noted the lasting value of the UNESCO Declaration in which it is stated *inter alia* that "the exercise of freedom of opinion, expression and information, recognized as an integral part of human rights and fundamental freedoms, is a vital factor in the strengthening of peace and international understanding". Furthermore, the meeting recognized the important role which information and communication play in the contemporary world, both in national and international spheres, with a growing social responsibility being placed upon the mass media and journalists.

On this basis the following principles of professional ethics in journalism were prepared as an international common ground and as a source of inspiration for national and regional codes of ethics. This set of principles is intended to be promoted autonomously by each professional organization through ways and means most adequate to its members.

Principle I : People's Right to True Information

Peoples and individuals have the right to acquire an objective picture of reality by means of accurate and comprehensive information as well as to express themselves freely through the various media of culture and communication.

Principle II: The Journalist's Dedication to Objective Reality

The foremost task of the journalist is to serve the right to true and authentic information through an honest dedication to objective reality whereby facts are reported conscientiously in their proper context, pointing out their essential connections and without causing distortions, with due deployment of the creative capacity of the journalist, so that the public is provided with adequate material to facilitate the formation of an accurate and comprehensive picture of the world in which the origin, nature and essence of events, processes and states of affairs are understood as objectively as possible.

Principle III: The Journalist's social Responsibility

Information in journalism is understood as social good and not as commodity which means that the journalist shares responsibility for the information transmitted and is thus accountable not only to those controlling the media but ultimately to the public at large, including various social interests. The journalist's social responsibility requires that he or she will act under all circumstances in conformity with a personal ethical consciousness.

Principle IV: The Journalist's professional Integrity

The social role of the journalist demands that the profession maintain high standards of integrity, including the journalist' right to refrain from working against his or her conviction or from disclosing sources of information as well as the right to participate in the decision-making of the medium in which he or she is employed. The integrity of the profession does not permit the journalist to accept any form of bribe or the promotion of any private interest contrary to the general welfare. Likewise it belongs to professional ethics to respect intellectual property and in particular to refrain from plagiarism.

Principle V: Public Access and Participation

The nature of the profession demands that the journalist promotes access by the public to information and participation of the public in the media, including the right of correction or rectification and the right of reply.

Principle VI: Respect for Privacy and Human Dignity

An integral part of the professional standards of the journalist is respect for the right of the individual to privacy and human dignity, in conformity with provisions of international and national law concerning protection of the rights and the reputation of others and prohibiting libel, calumny, slander and defamation.

Principle VII: Respect for Public Interest

The professional standards of the journalist prescribe due respect for the national community, its democratic institutions and public morals.

Principle VIII: Respect for Universal Values and Diversity of Cultures

A true journalist stands for the universal values of humanism, above all peace, democracy, human rights, social progress and national liberation, while respecting the distinctive character, value and dignity of each culture, as well as the right of each people freely to choose and develop its political, social, economic and cultural systems. Thus the journalist participates actively in the social transformation towards democratic betterment of society and contributes through dialogue to a climate of confidence in international relations conductive to peace and justice everywhere, to détente, disarmament and national development. It belongs to the ethics of the profession that the journalist be aware of relevant provisions contained in international conventions, declarations and resolutions.

Principle IX: Elimination of War and Other Great Evils Confronting Humanity

The ethical commitment to the universal values of humanism calls for the journalist to abstain from any justification for, or incitement to, wars of aggression and the arms race, especially in nuclear weapons, and all other forms of violence, hatred or discrimination, especially racialism and apartheid, oppression by tyrannic regimes, colonialism and neo-colonialism, as well as other great evils which afflict humanity, such as poverty, malnutrition and diseases. By doing so, the journalist can help eliminate ignorance and misunderstanding among peoples, make nationals of a country sensitive to the needs and desires of others, ensure the respect for the rights and dignity of all nations, all peoples and all individuals without distinction of race, sex, language, nationality, religion or philosophical conviction.

Principle X : Promotion of a New World Information and Communication Order

The journalist operates in the contemporary world within the framework of a movement towards new international relations in general and a new information order in particular. This new order, understood as an integral part of the New International Economic Order, is aimed at the decolonization and democratization of the field of information and communication, both nationally and internationally, on the basis of peaceful co-existence among peoples and with full respect for their cultural identity. The journalist has a special obligation to promote the process of democratization of international relations in the field of information, particularly safeguarding and fostering peaceful and friendly relations among States and peoples.

Paris: 20th, November 1983.

Source: Communication Ethics: A south Asian perspective.

ANNEXURE VII

Broadcast Code Governing All India Radio

Broadcasts on All India Radio by individuals shall not violate Broadcasting Code, which prohibits the following:

1. Criticism of friendly country.
2. Attack on religion or communities.
3. Anything obscene or defamatory.
4. Incitement of violence or anything against maintenance of law and order.
5. Anything amounting to contempt of court.
6. Aspersions against the integrity of the President. Governors and Judiciary.
7. Attack on a political party by name.
8. Hostile criticism of any State or the Center.
9. Anything showing disrespect to the Constitution or advocating changes in the Constitution by violence. But advocating changes in the constitutional way should not be debarred.

Footnote

(i) If a Station Director finds that the above Code has not been respected in any particular or particulars by an intending broadcaster he will draw the latter's attention to the passages objected to. If intending broadcaster refuses to accept the Station Director's suggestions and modify his script accordingly, the Station Director will be justified in refusing his or her broadcast.

(ii) Cases of unresolved differences of opinion between a Minister of a State Government and the Station Director about the interpretation of the Code, with regard to a talk to be broadcast by the former will be referred to the Minister of Information and Broadcasting, Government of India. Who will decide finally whether or not any change in the text of the talk is necessary in order to avoid violation of the Code.

ANNEXURE VIII

National Integration Council Code

In June 1962, the National Integration Council (NIC) drafted a Code of Conduct for the media which goes beyond the traditional responsibilities of the press. Accordingly, the press should:

- take all active steps to develop a feeling of unity, solidarity and cohesion in the hearts of the people and should create a sense of common citizenship and a feeling of loyalty to the nation;
- subordinate group loyalties based on caste, community, religion, region or language to national interest;
- condone no move of any person, party or group to divide the country or to create tension between its peoples;
- condemn unreserved incitement to violence or advocacy of violence as a means of settling conflicts;
- withhold publication of unverified news, which would tend to create discord, and refrain from giving prominent display to such news; and
- Highlight all activities whether of the State or of the public which promote the progress of the nation and the unity of the country.

ANNEXURE IX

The Times of India Group's Code of Ethics

October, 1996

1. Journalists of The Times of India Group should desist from accepting gifts, favours, concessional benefits such as loans, discounts, preferential shares and the sort from corporate bodies or other entities that they deal within their professional capacity. Though nothing of value should be accepted, a commonsensical approach can be adopted towards accepting, say, a modest box of sweets, inexpensive pens, diaries, calendars and such other tokens of courtesy.
2. All invitations for sponsored trips should come to the Editor for nominating a representative of the newspaper. Under no circumstances should the individual journalist accept such an invitation on his own. The name of the host inviting agency and the fact that the trip was sponsored by it should be mentioned at the conclusion of subsequent articles. Given the sensitive nature of political journalism, no hospitality from an individual politician or party should be accepted. In order to preserve its independence, The Times Group would not like its journalists to accept the hospitality of governmental or non-governmental institutions in India. In cases where for convenience in covering a story the transportation provided by the government, a private company or other institution needs to be used, the company will pay an amount equal to the ordinary commercial cost of similar facilities.
3. Every journalist should ensure that professional objectivity is not influenced by personal likes, dislikes, friendships and ideologies. Journalists should refrain from being members of political organizations. Involvement in political activities, community affairs, demonstrations and social causes that could cause a conflict of interest with the discharge of professional duties should be avoided. Any situation of a potential conflict

of interest (such as covering the activities of a club/organization of which one is a member) should be brought to the attention of the Editor by the journalist concerned.

4. Reports which might be damaging to an individual or organization should not be carried without every effort being made to contact the affected party and obtain his or its views. In case no comment is available, the effort made to speak to the affected party should be reflected in the report.
5. A journalist should not use the normal requirement of protecting the confidentiality of his sources as a cover to write unsubstantiated or sensational reports. The journalist concerned must be armed with enough information and argument to satisfy the Editor about the authenticity of his report, should the occasion for any doubt or question arise. While a journalist should make every effort to ensure objectivity and accuracy, the newspaper should publish corrections and acknowledge errors.
6. A journalist who holds shares in a particular company must inform his head of department/editor before writing a story related to the company. Insider trading by a journalist on the basis of privileged information is a gross violation of professional ethics.
7. Journalists of The Times of India Group should not acquire flats/house/land at concessional rates courtesy any government quota. In case, there are any who have already acquired such property out of such a quota, they should declare to the company the acquisition along with the price paid. Accredited journalists occupying government accommodation on rent should conform to the newly announced guidelines of the Press Council of India in this regard: payment of a monthly licence fee to the government plus the house rent allowance given by the employer, declaration to the government on March 31 every year of details regarding salary, property acquired, etc.; vacation of accommodation on expiry of allotment, etc. Information on all these aspects should be declared to the Editor.
8. An advisory committee of staff journalists selected by the Editor will be set up to inquire into complaints of misdemeanour or bias against any journalist. The committee may call upon the journalist in question to submit a list of his assets or a record of his investments or any relevant documents, should the need arise. The committee's recommendations will be carefully considered by the Editor before taking action.

ANNEXURE X

Financial Express Code of Conduct

October, 1996

1. **Gifts:** No FE journalist will accept any gift at press conferences or at any other gathering. This ban excludes routine items like cheap plastic folders and pens. In case a reporter feels that in certain circumstances NOT accepting a gift is embarrassing, the matter should be immediately reported to the Editor/ Executive Editor and the gift article obtained will be suitably gifted to charity, or a generally agreed worthy cause. FE journalists should honour this code both in letter and spirit.
2. **Share Investments:** No FE journalists will dabble in share investments of a short and term/speculative nature. By this we mean that it is okay to invest/buy shares, but no one should play the market for short periods like a week or two without taking deliveries. This requirement is very particularly relevant to corporate reporters and those managing the investment section.
3. **Insider Information:** Corporate and market reporters may routinely come to learn about corporate developments of a price sensitive nature. This information, if not used in the paper, should not be disclosed to ANYONE OUTSIDE, especially market sources and brokers, or used for personal profits.
4. **Disclosure:** Journalists involved in market stories, or who are reporting on anything that would affect share prices in general will have to disclose their shareholdings to the Editor/Executive Editor. We expect FE journalists to disclose holdings in any company, wherever the values of their investments exceed Rs. 10,000/- in market value. In the case of those making market recommendations, writers will have to make the following disclosure at the bottom of each article: "Neither the author nor their close relatives have direct or indirect investments in the above company's shares." Or alternatively: 'The author has a

small/substantial investment in the above-mentioned share, and his views may, to that extent, be influenced by it.' The idea is to improve the paper's credibility with the reading public. (Here small means investments below Rs. 25,000/- in market value; substantial would be anything above that).

5. **Junkets:** Financial Express may accept junkets/free hospitality from companies both within and outside the country provided it makes editorial sense. All such junkets will have to be cleared by the Editor/Executive Editor. All invitations will be addressed to the FE Editor, and the Editor/FE reserves the right to send anybody for the trip. If the invitation is specifically directed to any one person, the Editor/FE reserves the right to decline it.
6. **Balanced Reporting:** FE is a corporate newspaper; what we write affects people's business. Whenever we write about a company, and especially if it involves adverse references to a company, we must make every effort to contact the company/ its spokesmen for their point of view. And, where necessary, we must give the companies enough time to respond. It is not right to call up someone at eight in the night and demand an immediate reply to a complex set of allegations. This is not fair reporting.

ALL FE JOURNALISTS WILL BE COVERED BY THIS CODE. VIOLATIONS OF THIS WILL BE TAKEN SERIOUSLY AND DEALT WITH ACCORDINGLY, EITHER THROUGH CENSURE OR IN EXTREME CASES, OUTRIGHT DISMISSALS.

ANNXURE XI

Workshop Resolution on Media Regulations for the News Times

Bangkok, Thailand, April 15-17, 1998

The arrival of the newer services such as the Internet, digital and interactive TV, as a result of convergence has opened a wide debate about how media should be regulated. This workshop on "Media Regulations for the New Times", organized by AMIC, has considered the current state of that discussion in several Asian countries and has formulated the following recommendations.

The crucial role of media in fostering democratic structures and development of the Asian region, leads us to reiterate that the newer services should be considered as an important opportunity for the development of the media and any action which stimulates access to the new technologies should be encouraged. A characteristic of Asia, being a diversity of languages and cultures, the rich possibilities offered by these technologies should be harnessed to enrich these cultures.

If regulation is considered to be necessary, it should conform to the fundamental principles of freedom of speech and the rule of law. When regulation is enacted full accountability of the implementation and enforcement of those regulations must be established.

Freedom of information should be an essential aspect of the relationship between governments, media and the citizens. New technologies, such as the WWW can allow public information more widely and at a lower cost, therefore we recommend that governments desist of perceiving these technologies as a threat but instead treat them as powerful tools of good governance.

While the newer technologies may offer an increased range of services, pluralism remains essential. It must inform the ownership of media and greater diversity of content.

The fast pace of technological developments throw up a complex gamut of regulatory challenges to society. This can be addressed by self regulation which would therefore be considered as the preferred model of regulation.

Although convergence is taking place, we recognize that there is still a need for tailoring regulation to the particular requirements of different media. We, therefore, recommend the following:

Print Media

Acknowledging that the right to publish is an aspect freedom of speech and as such a fundamental right for every citizen, we recommend that:

- A simple procedure of registration should be sufficient for the press.
- Self-regulatory mechanisms should be in place such Press Councils to deal with complaints against unfair practices of the Press.
- Press Councils and similar bodies should have sufficient powers and resources to enable efficient enforcement of their decisions.
- Given the public service nature of the press, efforts should ensure the effective representation of diverse sections of the community in the press and similar Councils.
- Legislation should be enacted to ensure maximum transparency to avoid abuse of ownership and control.
- Wherever there is an attempt to devalue the independence and the role of the editor and the editorial staff by any means, efforts should by made to monitor and discourage such practices by Press Councils and other bodies.
- Monitoring of the Press coverage by media watch groups is crucial to ensure fairness about the patterns and priorities of such coverage.
- Efforts should be made to encourage and promote grassroots and specialized journalism.

Radio and TV

Given the crucial importance to these media in reaching the poor and the illiterate, and their transitional impact we propose that measures be taken to:

- expand audience choices;
- enhance open competition and transparency in the licensing process;

- strengthen professionalism and ethical standards in broadcasting;
- promote greater regional co-operation in the sector;
- build regional consensus on content regulation;
- Encourage technologies, which facilitate a more efficient use of scarce resources such as the broadcast spectrum.

The Internet

In formulating an Internet policy, governments should set clear priorities, which should be as follows:

- Laws and policies should facilitate and encourage the development of the technological infrastructure and institutions related to the Internet.
- Attempts should be made to promote local hosting of information. Steps should be taken to develop national and regional networks of high bandwidth; to train programmers and users and to encourage the spread of local languages on the Net alongside English.
- A holistic and flexible approach towards regulation must be developed based on a mature understanding of the issues involved in a rapidly changing environment.
- Efforts should be made to clear obstacles to e-commerce given the importance of trade and commercial communications in the global market.

(AMIC Conference-1998)

ANNEXURE XII

Model Advertisement Policy Guide

Under the statute passed by the Parliament in 1978, the Press Council of India is enjoined upon to preserve the freedom of the Press and to maintain and improve the standards of newspapers and news agencies in India. This is further supported by clause (e) of section 13(1) of the Press Council Act, whereby the Council is required to "keep under review and development likely to restrict the supply and dissemination of news of public interest and importance". There have been a number of occasions where the Press Council has been called upon to look into the complaints of improper or arbitrary denial of advertisement by various authorities, severely affecting the economic viability of newspapers, particularly of those in the smaller category.

In disposing of these complaints, the Council has often observed that governmental authorities should not single out a newspaper for discriminatory treatment in the matter of release of advertisements on account of its critical writings. Release of advertisements should be done not on an ad hoc basis but on the basis of a notified policy formulated on some rationale criteria. Political consideration should not weigh in the issue. Distribution of advertisements should be equitable as far as possible but smaller newspapers which subsist on government advertisement revenue need special consideration of the governmental authorities. While advertisements cannot be claimed by newspaper as a matter of right, they are neither a grant to be released at the whim and discretion of the controlling authority.

Against this background, the Press Council of India has considered the question of formulating basic elements of what may be an advertisement policy for the Central and State Governments to adopt. These model guidelines propose broad principles of uniform applicability governing the release of advertisement by Central and State Government. Union Territory, administration vis-a-vis their distribution, rate fixation and payment and canalisation.

Criteria

(1) Newspapers registered with the office of the Registrar of Newspapers for India shall be eligible for inclusion in the approved list for release of advertisements.

(2) Advertisements shall be issued only to such newspapers as have been included in the approved list of Central/State Government for release of advertisements. For preparing the approved list, there should be a committee with due representatives of officials as well as non-officials from among media personalities. For the purpose of selecting the newspapers for release of advertisements of different kinds, the authorities should be guided by the following criteria:

(a) Newspapers will be considered as being eligible for advertisement if it has had regular and uninterrupted publication for four months.

(b) A newspaper seeking advertisement should fulfil the requisite qualification already prescribed by State and Central Government in regard to periodicity and regularity of publication, size of the publication, printing arrangements, editorial and managerial set-up.

(c) The circulation of a newspaper has a bearing on the extent of advertisement released. The sources from which authenticated circulation figures could be obtained are:

(i) The Registrar of Newspapers for India;
(ii) Audit Bureau of Circulation; and
(iii) Chartered Accountant, certifying annual circulation statement.

The figures obtained through anyone of these sources should be acceptable for determining the circulation of a newspaper to be enlisted and no other party should question the certificate issued by either of the three above.

(d) Payment of bills by the government should be made within a period of 45 to 60 days of the publication of the advertisement. The payment could be made at reasonable prevalent commercial rate, less 20% commission in view of the bulk value of release.

(e) It will be desirable that small newspapers having regional content are given some weightage.

(f) Suitable weightage may also be given to language newspaper/periodicals published from remote areas, such as North-East, tribal belts and hilly region and small paper run by linguistic groups.

(g) As far as possible, organs of political parties should not be unduly patronized by the governmental authorities.

General

A list of newspapers eligible for empanelment should be made a public document available on request. The list should be periodically sent to the Press Council of India, the RNI and also to the recognized newspaper associations.

All disputes regarding inclusion/non-inclusion/removal from the approved list for release of advertisements should be referred to an independent body which may consist of representatives of the government and disinterested members of Press from socio-journalistic fields. Alternatively, dispute could be referred to a body created on the pattern of Press and Registration Appellate Board, which may consist of the Chairman of the Press Council of India and four other members.

These guidelines are not exhaustive because of the limited nature of the issue involved. They have been prepared with the object to eliminate any possibility of discrimination, which may directly or indirectly affect the freedom of the press.

Press Council of India; 16th Annual Report
94-31 March 1995)

ANNEXURE XIII

Foreign news agencies operating in India are as follows:

Organization	*Address*	*Tel*	*Fax*
A.F.P. (Agence France presse)	410, Surya Kiran Building 19, Kasturba Gandhi Marg, New Delhi 110001	+91-11-3712963/ 3712973	91-11-331 11 05
A.N.S.A. (Italian News Agency)	C/o Beniamino Natale, 74, West New Friends Colony, New Delhi-65	+91-11 6844674/ 6800194	+91-11 6847358
A.P. (Associated Press of America)	6-B, Jor Bagh, New Delhi-110003	4628506	4616870
AP-DOWJones News Services	6, Jor Bagh Lane, New Delhi.	4628506/ 4616603	4616870
Cable News Network	F-162, Malcha Marg, Chanakyapuri, New Delhi- 110021	3014326	3017063
Depth News Asia	C/o Prakash Chandra F-25, Press Enclave Saket, New Delhi-17	668393	
D.P.A (German Press Agency)	C/o M G Srinath 27, Samachar Apts., Mayur Vihar, Phase-1 New Delhi - 110091	4617792	4635772
E.F.E. Spanish News Agency	C/o Isabel Calleja Solera D3/9, Vasant Vihar New Delhi-110057	6111785	6111786
Gemini News Service	C/o DK Joshi 201, Kaka Nagar, New Delhi-110003	4616393	
Inter Press Service Third World News Agency	49 (FF), Defence Colony Market New Delhi-110024	4634154	4624725

Organization	*Address*	*Tel*	*Fax*
Iraqi News Agency	C/o Smt. Manorama Dewan A-19, Gulmohar Park New Delhi-110049	667885	
Itar-Tass News Agency	A-10/6, Vasant Vihar New Delhi - 110057	672351	6886232
Korean Central News Agency	C/o Yu Hung Ryol, E-338, Greater Kailash-1 New Delhi	644007	
Knight-Ridder Financial News	C/o T.S.K. Lingam, C-4-C, 14/98,Janakpuri, New Delhi - 110058	4694337	
Jiji Press Japan	C/o Masashi Okuyama B-87, Greater Kailash-1, New Delhi		
Kyodo News Service	PTI Bldg., R. No. 5, 1st Floor, New Delhi-110001	3711954	3718756
Reuters	C/o N. Madhavan B-14-C, DDA Flats, (SFS-1), East of Kailash New Delhi - 110065	3012024	3014043
Syrian Arab News	C/o Dr. Waiel Shiekh Hassan Awaad, F-7/12, Vasant Vihar, New Delhi-110057		
US News & World Report	C/o Brahma Chellaney, A-14/10, Vasant Vihar New Delhi-110057	6877700	
United Press International	Ambassador Hotel Room No. 202, Sujan Singh Park New Delhi	4621991	4634152
Xinhua News Agency	C/o Mr Li Jiasheng 50-D, Shanti Path, Chanakyapuri, New Delhi-110021	670552	

ANNEXURE XIV

Sr. No.	Institution	Courses offered
1	Himachal Pradesh University, Shimla (H.P.)	1. B.J.M.C 2. Master of Mass Communication
2	Panjab University, Chandigarh	1. PG Diploma in Journalism & Mass communication 2. MMC
3	Guru Nanak Dev University, Amritsar at its Regional Centre, Jalandhar (Punjab)	1. PG Diploma in Journalism & Mass Communication 2. MJMC
4	Panjabi Unviersity, Patiala (Punjab)	1. PG Diploma in Journalism & Mass Communication 2. MJMC
5	Maharishi Dayanand University, Rohtak, Haryana	1. BJMC 2. MJMC
6.	Guru Jambheshwar University, Hisar (Haryana)	1. MMC
7.	Kurukshetra University, Kurukshetra (Haryana)	1. PG Diploma in Journalism 2. MMC
8.	Sirsa University, Sirsa, (Haryana)	1. MMC
9.	Rajasthan University, Jaipur (Rajasthan)	1. BJMC 2. Ph.D
10.	Aligarh Muslim University, Aligarh	1. MJMC
11.	Jamia Milia Islamia University, New Delhi	1. MA (Journalism)
12.	Bangalore University, Bangalore (Karnataka)	1. MS (Communication) 2. M.Sc (Electronic Media)
13.	University of Mysore, Manasgangotri, Mysore (Karnataka)	1. MA (Journalism)
14.	Mangalore University Manglagangotri, Mangalore (D.K)	1. MA (Journalism)

Sr. No.	*Institution*	*Courses offered*
15.	Karnataka University, Dharward (Karnataka)	1. MA (Journalism)
16.	University of Madras, Chennai	1. MA (Journalism) 2. M.Sc. (Electronic Media) 3. M.Phil
17.	Sri Padmavati Mahila University, Tirupati	1. MA (Journalism)
18.	Osmania University, Hyderabad (A.P)	1. MA (Journalism)
19.	Calicut University, Calicut (Kererla)	1. MA (Journalism)
20.	MAHE (Manipal Academy of Higher Education), Manipal (Karnataka)	1. MS (Communication)
21.	IIJNM, Indian Institute of Journalism & New Media, Bangalore	1. PG diploma in Journalism 2. PG diploma in Electronic Media 3. PG diploma in New Media
22.	COMMITS (Convergence of Mass Media and Information Technologies) Bangalore	1. MS (Communication)
23.	VBS Purvanchal University, Jaunpur (UP)	1. BA (Journalism and Mass Communication) 2. MMC
24.	CCS Meerut University Meerut (UP)	1. MJMC
25.	Awadh University, Faizabad (UP)	1. MJMC
26.	MG Kashi Vidyapeeth, Varanasi	1. BJ 2. MJ
27.	BHU (Banaras Hindu University), Varanasi	1. BJ 2. MJ
28.	Lucknow University, Lucknow (UP)	1. BA in Electronic Media 2. MJMC 3. Ph.D
29.	Mahatma Gandhi Kashi Vidyapith, Varanasi (UP)	1. Master of Mass Communication 2. BA (Mass Communication and Video Production) 3. PG Diploma in Media Writing 4. PG Diploma in Public Relations
30.	Madan Mohan Malviya Hindi Patrakarita Sansthan, MG Kashi Vidyapith (Varanasi)	1. MJ 2. Ph.D

Sr. No.	*Institution*	*Courses offered*
31.	Allahabad University, Allahabad (UP)	1. BJMC
32.	Assam University, Silchar	1. MA (Journalism)
33.	Berhampur University, Berhampur (Orissa)	1. MMC 2. Ph.D
34.	Tejpur University, Tejpur (Assam)	1. MA (Mass Communication)
35.	G.B. Pant University of Agriculture and Technology Pantnagar	1. MA (Agricultural Communication in Science and Extensions) 2. Ph.D
36.	Delhi College of Arts and Commerce, University of Delhi, Delhi	1. BA (Journalism)
37.	Hemwati Nandan Bahuguna Garhwal University, Srinagar, Garhwal (UP)	1. BJMC 2. MJMC 3. Ph. D
38.	Guwahati University, Guwahati (Assam)	1. BJMC
39.	IIMC (Indian Institute of Mass Communication) New Delhi	1. PG Diploma in English Journalism 2. PG Diploma in Advertising and Public Relations 3. PG Diploma in News Agencies 4. PG Diploma in Electronic Media 5. PG Diploma in Hindi Journalism
40.	Madurai Kamraj University, Madurai (Tamil Nadu)	1. MA (Mass communication)
41.	Nagpur University, Nagpur	1. BJMC
42.	Nagarajuna University, Nagarajuna (AP)	1. MA (Mass Communication)
43.	Ranchi University, Ranchi (Bihar)	1. BJMC
44.	Rani Durgawati Vishwavidyalaya, Jabalpur (Rajasthan)	1. MA (Mass Communication)
45.	Saurashtra University, Rajkot	1. PG Diploma in Journalism 2. MA (Mass Communication)
46	Shivaji University, Kolhapur, (Maharashtra)	1. BJMC 2. MJMC
47.	South Gujarat University, Surat	1. PG Diploma in Journalism

Sr. No.	Institution	Courses offered
48.	Sri Krishna Devaraya University, Anantpur (AP)	1. PG Diploma in Journalism
49.	University of Burdwan, Burdwan, (West Bengal)	1. PG Diploma in Journalism
50.	University of Kerala Thiruvanthapuram	1. MJMC
51.	Pune University, Pune	1. BJMC 2. MCMS (Master of Communica-tion Studies)
52.	Xavier University of Communication, Bombay	1. Diploma in Journalism in Development Communication 2. Diploma in PR 3. Diploma in Advertising & Marketing 4. Diploma in Film/ Video Production
53.	Manipur University, Imphal, Manipur	1. BA (Journalism)
54.	Rabindra Bharati University, Kolkata	1. MA (Mass Communication)
55.	Dr. B.S. Ambedkar, Marathawada University, Aurangabad	1. BJ 2. MJMC
56.	University of Mumbai, Mumbai	1. BJ 2. MCJ
57.	Andhra University, Vishakhapatnam (AP)	1. BJMC 2. MJMC
58.	Alagappa University, Alagappa Karaikudi (Kerela)	1. BJ (Sports Journalism)
59.	Bharathiyar University-Coimbatore (Tamil Nadu)	1. MA (Mass Communication)
60.	Mysore Vishwavidhyalaya Karya Saudha Crawford Mysore	1. BA (Jorunalism) 2. MA (Communication)
61.	MICA (Mudra Institute of Communication, Ahmedabad	1. PG Diploma in Communication
62.	YMCA, New Delhi	1. PG Diploma in Journalism
63.	Agra University, Agra (UP)	1. Diploma in Mass Media
64.	Bhavnagar University, Bhavnagar, Gujarat	1. Diploma in Journalism
65.	Manonmaniam Sundaranai University, Tirunelveli	1. Diploma in Journalism
66.	Srinagar University, Srinagar (J & K)	1. BJMC

Sr. No.	Institution	Courses offered
67.	Bharathidasan University, Tiruchirapalli (Tamil Nadu)	1. Diploma in Journalism
68.	Makhan Lal Chaturvedi Rashtriaya Vishwavidyalaya Bhopal (MP)	1. Master of Journalism 2. BA (Mass Communication) (Three Years) 3. PG Diploma in Video Production 4. MA (Advertising & Public Relations) 5. MA (Mass Communication) 6. Bachelor of Journalism(One Year) 7. PG Diploma in Media 8. Bachelor of Journalism(Three Years) 9. M.Sc. (Electronic Media) 10. M.Sc.(Electronic Media Informatics) 11. M.A. (Marketing and Management Communication) 12. MA (Audio-Visual Communica-tions) 13. M.A.(Broadcast Journalsim)
69.	Symbiosis Institute of Journalism and Mass Communication, Pune	1. MA (Mass Communication)
70.	Kuvempu University, Shankaraghata Shimoga, Distt. Karnataka	1. MJMC
71.	Devi Ahilya Vishwavidyalaya, Indore	1. BA (Mass Communication) 2. BJMC 3. MJMC 4. Ph.D
72.	University of Hyderabad, Hyderabad (AP)	1. MA (Mass Communication) 2. Ph.D
73.	Potti Sreeramulu Telgu University, OU Campus Hyderabad (AP)	1. BJ 2. MJ & MC
74.	IGNOU (Indira Gandhi National Open University) New Delhi	1. PG Diploma in Journalism and Mass Communication
75.	University of Baroda , Vadodara (Maharashtra)	1. MA (Mass Communication)
76.	Guru Ghasidas University, Bilaspur (Chhattisgarh)	1. BJMC 2. MJMC
77.	PSG College of Arts and Science Coimbatore (Tamil Nadu)	1. BJMC 2. MJMC
78.	Amity School of Communication, New Delhi	1. BA (Mass Communication)

Sr. No.	Institution	Courses offered
79.	Manorama School of Communication Kottayam (Kerela)	1. PG Diploma in Print Journalism
80.	Asian College of Journalism, Chennai	1. PG Course in Journalism with specialization in Print Broadcast and New Media
81.	CSJM University Kalyanpur, Kanpur (UP)	1. PG Diploma in Journalism and Mass Communication 2. MJMC
82.	M.J.P. Rohilkhand University, Bareilly	1. PG Diploma in Journalism and Mass Communication

GLOSSARY

Absolute privilege. The right of legislators, judges and government executives to speak without threat of libel when acting in their official capacities.

Absolutism. The ethical philosophy that there is a fixed set of principles or laws from which there is not deviation. To the absolutist journalist the end never justifies the means.

Actual malice Reckless disregard of the truth. It is a condition in libel cases.

Ad Abbreviation for advertisement.

Add Addition to a story already written, or in process of being written.

Advance In press association parlance, a story transmitted some time prior to its intended use. For instance, a story transmitted to newspapers on Monday or Tuesday, but intended for use on the following Sunday. Also, frequently, any story written a head for later use. Also a story written before an event.

Advertising department. The department of the newspaper responsible for advertisements. Most advertising departments have classified and display ad sections.

Agate Type 51/2 points high (often used in classified ads).

Agate line The unity of measurement for advertising; 14 agate lines equal one inch.

Anecdotal lead. A newspaper story beginning that uses humour or an interesting incident.

Angle The approach or perspective from which a news fact or event is viewed, or the emphasis chosen for a story. See **slant.**

Antinomianism. The ethical philosophy that recognizes no rules. An antinomies journalist judges very ethical situation on its own merits. Unlike the situation ethicist, the antinomies does not use love of neighbour as an absolute.

AP The Associated Press, a worldwide news-gathering cooperative owned by its subscribers.

Arraignment. A court proceeding at which a defendant is informed of the charge. At the proceeding, the defendant is asked to enter a plea, and bail may be set.

Art Pictures or other graphic illustration for print media

Asne The American Society of Newspaper Editors.

Assignment Any duty given to a reporter, usually a story to cover or write.

Attribution The source of a news story or of a fact within a story. To attribute is to indicate the source of a story or fact and thus give the information authenticity.

B.F. or **b.f.** the abbreviations for boldface (dark) type.

Background Anything added to or inserted in a news story to explain earlier actions or events; facts intended to refresh the reader's memory about earlier actions or events.

Backgrounder A news story that explains the background or origins of an issue or situation. It may be mere explanation or it may be somewhat interpretive. Sometimes called a *situationer.*

Banner the main headline on page one.

Beat (a) a timely news story acquired ahead of the competition; (b) a regular place or subject assigned to a reporter for gathering stories.

Bleed (page) To print an illustration so that it goes to the very edge of the page on one or more sides, without a border or margin.

Blind lead A lead in which a person is identified but not named until the second or third paragraph.

Body The main part of a news story after the lead. Sometimes called the *development.*

Body type The small type in which a news story (excluding heads and display lines) is printed. Usually 8 point (9 lines to an inch) or 9 point (8 to an inch)

Boil, boil down Shorten or condense copy.

Box To put a rule around a news story or picture. Any story that is enclosed in a rule.

Breaking news Unexpected, unplanned occurrences, for example, a plane crash. A story that must be covered quickly and without any advance preparation.

Bridge A transitional device for carrying the reader from the lead into the body of the story or from one part of a story to another. The bridge can be a word, a sentence or several sentences.

Brief A short news story, usually two or three paragraphs long. Newspapers often collect related short news stories under a single head, for instance, Business Briefs.

Bright A light, usually humorous or entertaining story used to lighten the newspaper and contrast with serious news.

Brightened A story, usually short, that is humorous or pleasing to the reader. It is also called a "bright."

Business paper A periodical devoted to a particular industry, trade, occupation, profession, etc.

By-line the reporter's name at the start of a story. In some situations, the author's name appears at the end.

Bureau A news-gathering office maintained by a newspaper at other than its central location.

Business department The newspaper department that handles bulling, accounting and related functions.

Canned copy (a) Publicity material; (b) Material from a syndicate.

Caps Capital letters.

Caption A headline over a photograph.

Chain A number of newspapers that are owned by one company.

Circulation The number of copies sold to people who subscribe to or otherwise purchase a newspaper or magazine.

Circulation The number of newspaper or magazine issues distributed each day or during a publication's normal distribution period.

Circulation department The department responsible for distribution of the newspaper.

City editor The individual (also known as the metropolitan, or metro, editor) in charge of the city desk, which coordinates local news-gathering operations. At some papers the desk also handles regional and state news done by its own reporters.

Civil law Statutes under which an individual or group can take action against another individual or group.

Classified advertising All-text advertising positioned in a newspaper or magazine according to categories such as employment, real estate, matrimonial public notices, appointments etc.

Classified display advertising Classified advertising that includes illustrations, borders, and other visual elements as a way of setting ads apart from all-tax ads.

Clips Stories clipped from your own or competing newspapers.

Closed-ended question A direct question designed to draw a specific response; for example, "do you watch TV?"

Composing Assembling of types or metallic characters and symbols by hand or by machines into lines of definite measurement.

Compositor The craftsman who assembles types prior to printing either by hand or by keyboard.

Comprehensive layout The finished model of a print ad.

Computer-generated imagery (CGI) A general term for visuals created on a computer system.

Computer personalization The tailoring of a message to specific individuals by printing letters or other promotional pieces by computer, using names, addresses, special phrases or other information based on data appearing in computer records.

Computerized Text rendered in digital form is recorded on a magnetic medium (tape or disk) and run through a computer.

Conditional privilege The right to report on the three branches of government if the report is full, fair and accurate, and the reporter does not seriously doubt the truth of the material.

Continuity The pattern of message repetition used in a media schedule.

Continuity scheduling A message schedule in which ads run consistently over a long period without gaps.

Contract rate A discounted ad rate based on a contract that states how many ads or how much space will be purchased during a given period.

Controlled circulation. The number of magazine or newspaper copies distributed free by mail to selected audiences or to the public through store and sidewalk racks.

Copy A story or article.

Copy Anything written for publication. A news story.

Copy desk The desk at which final editing of stories is done, headlines are written and pages are designed.

Copy editor A person who checks, polishes and corrects stories written by reporters. Usually copy editors write headlines for those stories, and sometimes they decide how to arrange stories and pictures on a page.

Copy-editing marks Symbols used to indicate corrections or changes in news copy. Copy-editing marks are always made at the place a change is desired, as distinct from *proofreader's makes,* which are made in the margin of a proof. Proofreader's marks should never be used on proof.

Copy fitting The process of making sure that copy will fit the space allotted for it.

Copyright The exclusive right to print or reproduce material during the life of the copyright owner and for 50 years after.

Correspondent A reporter who delivers his copy to his editor by wire, fax or e-mail.

Cover To keep abreast of significant developments on a beat or to report on a specific event. The reporter covering the police beat may be assigned to cover a murder.

CPU Central Processing Unit: the core of a computer, containing the processor and main memory, which reads and interprets the instructions from a computer programmer.

Credit line The name of the photographer who took a picture as it appears with or near the cutlines.

Criminal law Statutes under which a grand jury or an officer of the court can take action against an individual.

Crop To edit or delete portions of a photograph to increase interest or change proportions.

Crop To edit or delete portions of a photograph to increase interest or change proportions.

Cub A beginning reporter.

Cursor A rectangle of light on a video display terminal that indicates the writer's or editor's position within the text of a story. Changes in text are made with the keyboard and appear on the screen where the cursor is located.

Cut To eliminate all but the most important facts, those without which there would be no story or an incomplete one at best.

Cut and paste The process of cutting up manuscript, proof, illustration, etc, and pasting or affixing the cut up material in a new arrangement.

Cutlines The explanatory material beneath a photograph.

Data bank A collection of information (data), usually held in a computer store.

Data base A computerized information bank, usually accessible only on a subscription basis.

Data processing (1) An unpainted blank version of a paper often in miniature, used for page planning. (2) The systematic performance of operations upon data such as handling, merging, sorting and computing, synonymous with information processing.

Dateline The words preceding news stories that indicate the place and, sometimes, the date of origin.

Deadline The latest time at which a story can be accepted.

Delayed-identification lead Opening paragraph of a story in which the "who" is identified by occupation, city, office or any means other than by name.

Delete Take out, remove from copy. Primarily a proofreading term.

Demographics The collection of external, objective variables such as income, age, and occupation that describe a population.

Desktop publishing The process of using personal computers and specialized software to create camera-ready pages.

Developing story One in which newsworthy events occur over several days or weeks.

Direct quote A speaker's exact words, a verbatim report enclosed in quotation marks. Sometimes slightly edited to improve syntax or correct grammar.

Directory The index of stories within a video display terminal system.

Display advertising Print advertising that consists of headline and body copy, illustrations, and other visual elements that set the message apart from editorial material.

Display copy Copy in headlines, in logos, and everywhere else except the body; generally refers to larger sizes of type in an ad.

Documentary In-depth coverage of an issue or event, especially in broadcasting.

Dope story A story of speculation, prediction, comment, or background.

Down style An editing pattern calling for a minimum of capital letters.

Dummy A chart or pattern showing how a page is to be composed. See makeup.

Dupe or duplicate A carbon copy.

Ear The upper corners of a news page (usually page 1)

Ed & Pub Abbreviation for Editor & Publisher, weekly news magazine of the newspaper industry.

Edition One version of a newspaper. Some papers have one edition per day or per week; some have many. Not to be confused with **issue,** which usually refers to all editions under a single date.

Editor The top-ranking individual in the news department of a newspaper, also known as the "editor in chief." The term may refer as well to those at any level who edit copy.

Editorial department The news department of a newspaper, responsible for all content of the newspaper except advertising. At some papers this term refers to the department responsible for the editorial page only.

Editorial policies Guidelines followed by a media organization with regard to certain public issues or political positions.

Editorialize To include the opinions of the writer in a news story.

Editorial page editor The individual incharge of the editorial page and, at larger newspapers, the op-ed (opposite editorial) page.

Electronic compositor Computer that allows a user to arrange text easily on screen before it is electronically type set.

Electronic media Radio, television, and other means of communicating through electronics.

Em Unit of typographical measurement (one-sixth of an inch, or 12 points)

Embargo The stipulated time before which a story should not be published. Generally used in public relations handouts.

End mark A symbol, usually #, sometimes 30, typed at the end of a story to indicate that the story is complete.

Fair comment and criticism Opinion delivered on the performance of anyone in the public eye. Such opinion is legally protected if reporters do not misstate any of the facts upon which they base their comments or criticism, and it is not malicious.

Feature (1) The main news angle or news peg of a story. A special point or twist to a story. (2) A type of news story, sometimes called a *news feature*. It is usually not breaking news but a story closely related to the news. Features are often interpretive, give background, play up human interest and convey the colour of an event. (3) Non-news matter, for example, syndicated columns, comics, cartoons, horoscopes and so on, that appears regularly in the newspaper. (4) To give something prominence in a story; to emphasize something.

Featurize To play up an unusual angle or interesting point of a story rather than to rely on a bare recitation of five W's, the usual straight news approach, which might not make the best use of odd, unusual or interesting elements of a story.

Felonies Serious crimes punishable by death or imprisonment.

Field experiment A research technique in which the reporter deliberately takes some action in order to observe the effects. For example, a perfectly tuned automobile could be taken to several repair shops to find out if the mechanics would invent problems that required fixing.

File To send a story to the home office, usually by wire; to put stories on news service wires.

Filler Material used to fill space or time

Five Ws The basic questions that news stories must answer: who, what, when, where, why and how.

Flag The printed title of a newspaper on page 1. See **logo.**

Flash Brief news bulletin of great urgency (more emphatic than **bulletin**), taking precedence over all other matter.

Folio Page number

Follow Sometimes *folo*. A story that follows another, giving new facts or bringing the story up to date. Also a second-day story.

Format The pattern or structural outline of a newscast.

Fotog short for photographer.

Front-end system The electronic equipment—VDTs, computers, hard copy printers and peripheral equipment - on which the newsroom staff writes, edits and prepares the news for publication. Front-end systems have replaced the traditional composing room. Copy goes from the news writer's VDT to a computer, then back to an editor and from there to a phototypesetter.

Future book An editor's calendar of future meetings, programs and news events that must be covered. Editors keep a future book as one means of managing the coverage of the news.

Futures file A collection, filed according to date, of newspaper clippings, letters, notes and other information to remind editors of stories to assign.

FYI For your information. Frequently used to indicate that the material so marked is for background rather than for inclusion in a news story.

Galley A metal tray for storing or carrying type.

Graf A shortened form of paragraph, as in, "Give me two grafs on that fire."

Graphics (1) Illustrations/text which enhance a programs. A creative field using computers and other means. (2) Words and figures used on television screens, often specially drawn, as titles, illustration of statistics, etc.

Gravure printing A method of printing in which printing area is below the non printing area. It is reverse to letterpress printing.

Guild The Newspaper Guild, the union for newsmen and other newspaper employees.

Handout Prepared news matter offered by news sources or special interests to aid reporters or to gain publicity.

Hard copy Any copy on paper, either original copy prepared by a news writer or a printout from the newsroom computer.

Hard news Coverage of the actions of government or business; or the reporting of an event, such as a crime, an accident or a speech. The time element often is important.

Head Short for headline.

Head, headline Display type above a printed news story, or the concise summary of news stories in some news broadcasts.

Hold Do not release without permission.

Hole A gap in a news story. A hole in a story means that something essential to clarity or completeness is missing.

Hot type The process of producing a newspaper by mechanical means. The traditional system of newspaper production supplanted by computers, photo composition and offset printing. In the hot-type process, type is cast, using molten lead, type metal. The heart of the hot-type production system was the licensing machine: the Linotype, Intertype and Ludlow that set type a line at a time. Hot type also implies letterpress printing.

Human-interest story A piece valued more for its emotional impact or oddity than for its importance.

Hypothesis In investigative reporting the statement a reporter expects to be able to prove, as in, "The mayor took a bribe from that massage parlour." In an experiment the statement of what a researcher hopes to find.

Identification Facts used to identify a person, building, place or organization. The facts, for example, the age, street address, title or descriptive matter, that distinguish one person from another.

Immediate-identification lead The opening paragraph of a story in which the "who" is reported by name.

Indictment A document issued by a grand jury that certifies there is sufficient evidence against a person accused of a crime to warrant holding that person for trial.

Indirect quote Not verbatim but rather a slightly edited or paraphrased version of a speaker's words. Indirect quotes are not enclosed in quotation marks. An indirect quote represents what a reporter tells us someone said. See also *Direct quote, Partial quote* and *Paraphrase.*

Insert To add matter within the body of a story already written. Copy written to be inserted is called an *insert.*

Internet Globally interconnected telecommunication and computer network systems which allow for diverse forms of interactivity and data interchange. The internet is making rapid headway even in developing countries like India.

Inverted pyramid The organization of a news story in which information is arranged in descending order of importance.

Investigative reporting The pursuit of information that has been concealed, such as evidence of wrongdoing.

Investigative reporting (or) journalism) A style of reporting that emphasizes the careful assembly of facts in order to gain the inside story and expose wrongdoing.

Italics Type designed to slope to the right (thus: *italics*)

Itemizing lead A lead that lists the several points a story will cover. Sometimes called a 1-2-3-4 *lead.*

Jargon The technical or characteristic terminology used by persons of a given industry.

Jazz journalism A form of *yellow journalism* that persisted into the twentieth century. It was characterized by the *tabloid* format and the extensive use of dramatic photographs.

Journalism The trade, technique or profession of reporting news for the public by various means. Hence, newspaper journalism, broadcast journalism, magazine journalism and so on.

Journalism reviews Critical publications whose major interest is study and analysis of the press.

Jump To continue a story from one page to another; as a noun, the continued matter.

Kicker 1. A short story, usually humorous, used to close a newscast. **2**. A subordinated phrase preceding or following the main deck of a headline.

Kill To destroy copy or type that is not to be used, "Kill" is a final order to prevent copy from being used.

Layout The completed page drawing, or dummy.

Lead The first paragraph or first several paragraphs of a newspaper story (sometimes spelled "lede"); also, the story given the best display on Page One; also, a tip.

Lead-in An introduction to a filmed or recorded excerpt from a news source or from another reporter.

Lead story The major story displayed at the top of Page One.

Letterpress printing A method of printing which uses metal type that contacts or "presses" the paper directly. In this method printing area is above the non printing area.

Libel Damage to a person's reputation caused by a false written statement that brings the person into hatred, contempt or ridicule, or injures his or her business or occupational pursuit.

Linecaster A device used in hot-metal composition to set type.

Linkage machine A machine for moulding line of type from hot metal.

Lithography A printing method in which an image is applied to a stone or metal plate, then washed with an acid solution. Ink is then applied to the surface, adhering to the image portion only.

Localize Emphasize the local angle in a story.

Logotype or **logo** The newspaper's name plate or flag.

Makeup The arrangement of body matter, headlines, and illustrations on a page.

Managing editor The news executive who co-ordinates operations in the news department and usually hires news staff members.

Masthead The statement, usually on the editorial page, listing the newspaper's name, publisher, principle officers, editorial executives, and related information. Note: The term often is misused in referring to the flag on the front page.

Media Plural of medium, referring to means of communicating: newspapers, magazines, radio and TV stations, books, films, cassettes, etc.

Memo A written memorandum. Never give oral messages or instructions. Always write (i.e., no oral memos) or type a memo.

Misdemeanors Minor criminal offenses, including most traffic violations, which usually result in a fine or brief confinement in a local jail.

More An instruction typed at the bottom of a page of copy to indicate that the story is not complete and that another page or pages follows.

Morgue The newspaper library, where published stories, photographs and resource material are stored for reference.

Multiple-elements lead The opening paragraph of a story that reports two or more newsworthy elements.

Must Designating copy that must appear in a specific edition of a newspaper or broadcast.

Nameplate The newspaper's name or flag on the front page.

Network (1) National or regional organization distributing radio or television program's for a substantial part of each broadcast day to stations for simultaneous broadcasting, generally by interconnection facilities. (2) An organization composed of interconnecting broadcasting stations that cuts costs by airing the same program's.

New media technologies The large-scale technical developments in communication systems and their cultural consequences. The term is also used to refer to cable, satellite, digital and other computer based media in the current phase.

News conference An interview session, also called a "press conference," in which someone submits to questions from reporters.

News editor The supervisor of the copy desk. At some newspapers this title is used for the person in charge of local news-gathering operations.

News hole The number of columns of space available for news in a newspaper. The space not devoted to advertising. The space available to a particular editor, for example, a sports editor, for use in that day's paper.

News peg The significant or interesting point on which a reporter hangs a story. The angle, feature or twist to a story that makes it interesting or important.

News perspective A set of criteria used by news personnel in deciding whether and how to present a news item. They take into account a story's commercial value (that is, its likely effect on their rating), their limited resources, the availability of alternatives, the audience and their competitors' practices.

News release An item, also called a "handout," that is sent out by a group or individual seeking publicity.

News room The place where reporters and editors work.

News value How important or interesting a story is.

Newspaper A publication that regularly prints and distributes news of general interest to a broad audience, or of more specialized interest to some category of people. There are dozens of types of newspapers published by various groups for a variety of purposes.

Newsprint A soft, rough paper made from wood pulp and used in printing newspapers. Waste at the end of newsprint rolls is cut into 8½-by-11 sheets to be used for copy paper.

No-news lead A lead empty to information, for example, the lead that begins "City Council met last night." The council met, but what did it accomplish?

Non probability sample A sample in which you cannot determine the chances of any member of the population being selected.

Not for attribution Information that may not be ascribed to its source.

Obituary An obit, a story about a death. An obit reports facts about a death, funeral arrangements, a list of surviving relatives and at least a brief biography.

OCR Optical Character Recognition. The process in which reporters write their stories on electric typewriters and a device called an optical character reader translates the typed material into electrical impulses for processing.

Off the record Information given to reporters that is not for publication.

Offset printing A photographic-oriented method of printing in which a thin metal plate transfers the image to a rubber-covered roller which in turn transfers the image to paper.

Ombudsman A readers' representative who serves as a sort of middleman between the newspaper staff and the public.

On-line editing High quality process employing sophistication computer-assisted vision/sound editing processing equipment.

Open-ended question One that permits the respondent some latitude in the answer; for example, "How did you get involved in politics?"

Overset Copy set in type but not used because of space limitations.

Pad To add superfluous matter to a story. A padded story has more words or details than necessary. A frequent order from the copy desk is "take the padding out of this" or "take the fat out of this."

Page proof A page-size piece of paper with all the elements—type, photos and illustrations-positioned in their proper places.

Pagination Page makeup is sometimes referred to as pagination in computer terminology.

Paid circulation The number of newspaper or magazine copies purchased through subscriptions and at stores and newsstands.

Paragraph An arbitrary division of written copy, usually from one to three or four sentences. Newspaper paragraphs tend to be shorter than those in other published work, primarily because newspaper columns are narrower than book columns and other columns.

Participant observation A research technique in which the reporter joins in the activity he or she wants to write about.

Partisan paper A newspaper published or controlled by a political party or interest group and presenting its point of view more or less exclusively.

Paste-up A layout of proofs and art to be photographed for offset printing.

Payola Money or gifts given in the expectation of favours from journalists.

Personal computer (1) A low cost, portable computer with software oriented towards, easy, single user applications. (2) A general purpose single user microcomputer designed to be operated by one person at a time. Personal computers range from cheap domestic or hobby machines with limited memory, programmer storage on cassette tape, and an ordinary TV as the display device, to extremely sophisticated machines with powerful processors, large capacity disk storage, high resolution colourgraphics, systems and many other options.

Photo editor The individual who advises editors on the use of photographs in the newspaper. The photo editor also may supervise the photography department.

Photocomposition machine High-speed, computerized device that translates electronic impulses into images and words.

Pica 12-point type; approximately 1/6 inch; a unit of measurement used instead of inches by printers.

Pictorial journalism Reporting the news or other significant events through photographs.

Plagiarism The use of any part of another's writing and passing it off as your own.

Play up To emphasize a certain angle or fact in a news story. To give a story prominence by placing it on the front page.

Point A measurement of type; 1/72 inch.

Poll The measurement of opinion by questioning members of some small group chosen at random so as to be representative of the entire group. A poll is also referred to as a "survey" or "public opinion poll."

Popular press Newspapers that are prepared for and distributed to people in all levels of society, especially those in the middle and lower levels. They give less emphasis to intellectual content than to entertainment.

Population In scientific language the whole group being studied.

Precision journalism The technique of a gathering data - facts or opinion - by quantitative methods. A good example is the measuring of public opinion by survey, that is, polling of a carefully selected sample of the public.

Precision journalism A form of reporting that makes extensive use of the methods of social science, such as pools, surveys and statistical analysis.

Preliminary hearing A court hearing held to determine whether there is probable cause that a defendant committed a crime and whether the defendant should be bound over for grand jury action or trial in a higher court.

Press The machine that prints the newspaper. Also a synonym for journalism, as in the phrase "freedom of the press." Sometimes used to denote print journalism, as distinguished from broadcast journalism.

Press box The section of a stadium or arena set aside for reporters.

Press release A news story prepared by a public relations practitioner for use by newspapers or wire services. See also *Handout.*

Probability sample A sample in which every member of the population has a known (but not necessarily equal) chance of being included.

Production department The department of the newspaper that transforms the work of the news and advertising departments into the finished product. The composing room and pressroom are key sections of this department.

Profile A story intended to reveal the personality or character of an institution or person.

Proof an impression of type taken for comparison with the original copy to determine whether there are typographical (i.e. printer's) mistakes.

Proof Reader A person (used a printer) who reads proof to correct typographical errors.

Public figure A person who has assumed a role of prominence in the affairs of society and who has persuasive power and influence in a community or who has thrust himself or herself to the forefront of a public controversy. Courts have given journalists more latitude in reporting on public figures.

Public Relations Society of America An organization for people in public relations.

Publicity Promotional matter presented as news.

Publisher The principal owner or representative of the owners of a newspaper.

Pulitzer Prize The most prestigious of journalism awards. It was established by Joseph Pulitzer and is administered by Columbia University.

Punch To emphasize a word, a story, or an idea in a newscast.

Qualitative research Research that looks for in-depth answers that cannot be easily translated into quantitative statistics.

Quantitative research Research that tries to translated responses into statistical results.

Query A correspondent's inquiry as to whether he should cover a particular story.

Questionnaire A list of questions that respondents read and answer, a list of questions that telephone or in-person interviewers read to respondents, or a computer program that presents questions to someone sitting at the keyboard.

Randomization The mathematical process used to assure that every member of a population being studied has an equal chance of being chosen for questioning or observation.

Readership The total number of people who read a print vehicle.

Release A story provided to news media for use at a stated time.

Release date The time when a story issued in advance can be published or broadcast the media operate under a "gentlemen's agreement" hot to jump dates set by story sources.

Reporter A person whose job it is to gather and write the news for a publication or a broadcast outlet.

Retrieval Recovery of materials from a computer or other information storage facility.

Reverse White on a black background; this technique helps create emphasis.

Rewrite To write a story again. It also means to take information over the telephone from a reporter in the field and mould it into a story.

Roman Vertical (in contrast to *italic*) type.

ROP Short for "run of press," meaning a story or ad runs in all editions.

Rough layout Early version of a print ad.

Roundup A story including a number of related events. After a storm, for example, a reporter might do a roundup of accidents, power outages and other consequences of the storm.

Round-up A story that pulls together various aspects of a newsworthy event. For example, a weekend round-up of auto accidents provided for Monday issues of newspapers by the wire services. A round-up assembles a number of stories of a similar nature under one lead. Another typical round-up is the weather round-up.

Rule A metal strip that separates columns or makes borders.

Sample A portion of a group, or population, chosen for study as representative of the entire group.

Sampling error The allowance that must be made in any survey for the possibility that the sample questioned may not be exactly like all other members of the population.

Scanner The popular term for an optical character reader.

Scenic lead A lead that concentrates on a description of an environment.

Schedule (a) The list of reporter's assignment; (b) The editor's log of completed stories.

Second-cycle story A second version of a story already published, also called a "second-day" story. It usually has new information or a new angle.

Secondary readership The number of people other than the original purchaser or subscriber who read the same copy of a print vehicle

Series Two or more stories on the same or related subjects, published on a predetermined schedule.

Shield laws Legislation giving journalists the right to protect the identity of sources.

Shirt tail To add secondary matter to the end of a story. Also anything added in this way.

Sidebar A secondary story intended to be run with a major story on the same topic. A story about a disaster, for example, may have a sidebar that teils what happened to a single victim.

Silk-screen printing A stencil process in which ink is forced through the pores of a fabric screen bearing a reverse image of the design to be printed.

Situation ethics The philosophy that recognizes that a set of rules can be broken when circumstances dictate that the community will be served better by it. For example, a journalist who believes it normally unethical to deceive a news source may be willing to conceal his or her identity to infiltrate a group operating illegally.

Skyline The headline at the very top of page one.

Slant To make a story biased toward a particular viewpoint.

Slug (a) The one or two words that a reporter uses to identify a specific story; (b) A line of lead type used in letterpress printing.

Small caps (1) An alphabet of small capital letters. Usually the height of the font's normal x-height. (2) Capital letters that are smaller than the regular or full capitals of a font.

Sniff The preliminary phase of an investigation.

Soft lead A lead that uses a quote, anecdote or other literary device to attract the reader.

Sources People or places from which a reporter gets information. The term often is used to describe persons, as opposed to documents.

Spot news A timely report of an event that is unfolding at the moment.

Spot news News printed or broadcast as soon as possible after it becomes available.

Stereotype 1. A bromide, cliche, hackneyed expression or news concept. 2. A metal printing plate cast from a matrix moulded from type or other raised surface.

Stet Retain the text of copy that has been crossed out (used by copyreaders and proofreaders) or remain as it is.

Still A single-exposure photograph, as distinguished from moving pictures.

Storage Placing news or other information in a facility such as a computer or a library for possible later use. See **retrieval.**

Story The term most journalists use for a newspaper article. Another synonym is "piece," as in, "I saw your piece on the mayor." A very long story may be called a takeout or a blockbuster.

Straight news News written straightforwardly for informative purposes, as distinguished from human-interest or feature news.

Streamer A large headline covering a newspaper's entire width; also called a banner.

Stringer A correspondent paid on a piecework basis-by the number of stories he provides or their length.

Stylebook A booklet or list of rules stating a newspaper's preference, when there are choices, of spelling, punctuation, capitalization, abbreviations, and use of numerals.

Sub heads Headings or titles for sections within a chapter or article. Sub heads are usually set in type different from that of the text.

Summary lead The first paragraph of a news story in which the writer presents a synopsis of two or more actions rather than focusing on any one of them.

Superscript In mathematics or tabular material, a small numeral, letter, fraction or symbol that prints partly above the x-height.

Suspended interest A type of news story in which the main point or outcome is withheld until the end of the story rather than being summarized at the beginning.

Syndicate (a) A company that distributes editorial material (columns, cartoons, puzzles, features, etc.) to newspapers; (b) Ordinarily competing journalists who pool information gathered from their beats.

Syndicated programming Programming distributed directly to the stations, not through a network, although it may have first appeared on a network.

Tabloid A newspaper page half the size of a broadsheet.

Take One part of a running story being set in sections to the printers.

Teletext Electronic news delivery system in which the viewer uses a computer to select information from a broad spectrum of electronic pages that can be viewer on a TV screen.

Thirty or "30" A designation used to mark the end of a newspaper story.

Tie-back The sentence or sentences relating a story to events covered in a previous story. Used in follow-up or continuing stories or in parts of a series of stories. Also, the technique of referring to the opening in the ending of the story.

Time Copy stories that can be held and used when needed.

Tip A fragment of information that may lead to a story; also called a "lead."

Transition A word, phrase, sentence or paragraph that moves the reader from one thought to the next and shows the relationship between them.

Trim To cut or condense copy, See boil.

TTS Teletypesetter, a system used to produce coded paper tape that is read by an automated typesetter to produce type.

Type A single metal letter or character. Type family: Various forms of the same type face (roman, bold, italics, condensed, etc.). Type size: of type calculated in points which refers to the height of printed character. Type face: type style of font or set of characters in a certain style and given a special name.

Type families Collections of related type styles, such as the Universe family.

Typeface The basic design of type, such as letters that are elegant or casual, that have a classic or modern feel, and so on.

Typesetting The process of setting typefaces and arranging letters and words on the page.

Typographical error An error made by the compositor also called printers error.

Unity A design state that occurs when all the pieces work together to form a cohesive whole.

Universal desk A copy desk that edits material for all editorial departments of a newspaper.

Update To bring a story up to date or to make it more timely. Sometimes news stories are updated from edition to edition as new information becomes available.

UPI United Press International, a worldwide news-gathering organization that is privately owned.

Variable In an experiment, one of the elements being observed. The independent variable is what is thought to be a cause; the dependent variable is the effect of that cause.

VDT Video Display Terminal or Visual Display Terminal, a computer-assisted device with television-like display and attached keyboard for writing stories and headlines and editing copy.

Video prompter A mechanical or electronic device that projects the copy next to the television camera lens so that a newscaster can read it while appearing to look straight into the lens.

Videotex Electronic news delivery system in which the viewer interacts with the computer in selecting the exact content choice desired.

VOA Voice of America

Weekly A newspaper that publishes only one day a week. Many are produced in small communities or rural areas, others appear in suburban sections of large cities. There are many different types.

White space An uninterrupted expanse of a single colour, including black or white.

Wire service An organization that gathers news, stores, prepares them in a convenient form, and sends them (by wire or other rapid means) to newspapers and broadcasting stations around the country that pay for the service.

Word processor A text editing unit designed for preparation, storage and dissemination of text initiated on typewriter like devices.

Wrong Font or W.F. Wrong font or size of type; used on proofs to indicate printer's errors.

X height The distance between the base line and the mean line of a type. A type character without ascender or descender.

Yellow Journalism A late nineteenth-century type of newspaper publishing that placed profit above truthfulness and significance, emphasizing sensationalism. Human interest and reader appeal at the expense of public responsibility.

Zone A section of a publication that is changed (in regard to ads or news) to meet the interests of various geographical areas.

BIBLIOGRAPHY

A Manual for News Agency Reporters, New Delhi: Indian Institute of Mass Communication, 1978.

Aggarwal, Vir Bala and V.S. Gupta, *Handbook of Journalism and Mass Communication*, New Delhi: Concept Publishing Company, 2001.

Aggarwal, Vir Bala, *Media and Society: Challenges and Opportunities* (ed), New Delhi: Concept Publishing Company, 2002.

Aiyar R R, *Quest for News,* Macmillian Company of India Limited, Madras, 1979.

Alan, B. Albarran and David H. Goff, *Understanding the Web* (ed) New Delhi: Surjeet Publications, 2004.

Alexander Louis, *Beyond the Facts: A guide to the Art of Feature Writing*, 2nd ed, New Delhi: Surjeet Publications, 2004.

Alteschull, J.H., *Agents of Power: The Role of the News Media in Human Affairs*. New York: Longman, 1984.

Arant, D., Anderson, J., *Special Report: Online Ethics 2000*, available at http://www.elon.edu/andersj/summary.html, 2000.

Arora, S. *Interactive Options in Online Journalism—A Content Analysis of Indian English Newspapers.* Thesis Submitted to Punjab Agricultural University, p. 2, 2002.

Bacon, W., "What is a Journalist in a University?" In T. Flew, J. Sternberg and C. Hippocrates (eds), *Media Wars,* Brisbane: Key Center for Culture and Policy, 1999, pp.79-91

Beyond Those Headlines, New Delhi: The Media Foundation, 1996.

Black, J., Steele, B. and Barney, R. (eds), *Doing Ethics in Journalism,* 3rd edn. Boston, MA: Allyn & Bacon, 1997.

Bliss, Edward, Jr. and John M. Patterson, *Writing News for Broadcast*, 2nd ed. New York: Columbia University Press, 1978.

Brady, J., The Craft of Interviewing. Cincinnati, OH: *Writer's Digest*, 1977.

Breeen, M. (ed.), *Journalism: Theory and Practice,* Sydney: Macleay Press, 1999.

Brenard Rubin, *Questioning Media Ethics*, (ed.), New York Prager, 1978.

Brian S. Brooks et al, *News Reporting and Writing*, New York: St Martin's Press, 1988.

Bringhurst, Robert, *The Elements of Typographic Style*, 2nd ed. Point Roberts, Wash: Harltey & Marks, 1996.

British Council, *A Manual of Human Rights Reporting in India*, Press and People, New Delhi: 2001. York: St. Martin's Press, 1988.

Brooks, Brian. S. *et al. News, Reporting and Editing*, New

Bruce, D. Itule and Douglas, A. Anderson, *News Writing and Reporting for Today's Media,* New York: Mc Graw Hill Inc. 1994.

Byrd, Joann, Online Journalism Ethics: A New Frontier Questions Greatly outnumber the answers in exploring the ethical issues and values of the new media, *The American Editor, The American Society of Newspaper Editors,* November 1996, pp. 6- 7. http://www.asne.org/kiosk/editor/november/byrd.htm.

C.B. Rau, Media Under Microscope, *The Hindu,* September 18, 2001.

Carter III, Hodding; Is civic journalism an answer?; October Public Journalism Conference at the University of South Carolina in Columbia; hyperlink *"http://www.asne.org/" http://www.asne.org/,* 1998

Case, T., *Public Journalism Denounced,* Editor & Publisher, November 12, 1994.

Chomsky, N. and Herman, E., *Manufacturing Consent,* New York: Pantheon Books, 1988.

Collins, Tracy, Who Stole the News? *Design,* Spring, 1997, pp 6-8.

Conradc C. Fink, *Sports Writing,* New Delhi: Surjeet Publications, 2004.

Dagson, Jones, Eight Graphic Lies (and how to fix them), *Design* Spring, 1998, pp.10-12.

Dair, Carl, *Design with Type,* Toronto: University of Toronto Press, 1982.

Darylr, Moen, *Newspaper Layout and Design,* 4th ed. New Delhi: Surjeet Publications, 2004.

Dueze, M. Journalism and the Net : *Thinking About Global Standards.* p. 3 (Online Available).

Editors of the Harvard Post, *How to Produce a Small Newspaper,* Port Washington, N.Y: Harvard Common Press, 1983.

Edward, Bliss, Jr. and James, C. Hoyt, *Writing News for Broadcast,* New York: Columbia University Press, 1994.

Elliot, D., *Responsible Journalism,* Beverly Hills, CA: Sage, 1986.

Ettema, James S., Glasser, Theodore Lewis, *Custodians of Conscience: Investigative Journalism and Public Virtue,* Columbia University Press, 1988.

Evans, Harold, *Newspaper Design, book five,* New York: Rinehart and Winston, 1973.

Fang, Irving E., *Television News, Radio News,* 3rd revised ed., Champlin, Minn: Rada press, 1980.

Finberg, Howard I., and Bruce D. Itule, *Visual Editing: A Graphic guide for Journalists,* Calif: Wadsworth, 1990.

Fink, Conrad C., *Media Ethics,* Boston: Allyn & Bacon, 1995.

Fon F. Smith and Loraine M. O' Connell, *Editing Today,* 2nd ed., New Delhi: Surjeet Publications, 2004.

Frank Barton, *The Newsroom,* Bonn: Friedrick-Ebert-Stiftung, 1992.

Future of Print Media, New Delhi: Press Council of India, 2001.

Geoffrey Harris and David Spark, *Practical Newspaper Reporting,* London: Focal press, 1997.

George A. Hough, *News Writing,* New Delhi: Kanishka, 1998.

George, T.J.S, *Editing: A Handbook for Journalists,* New Delhi: Indian Institute of Mass Communication, 1989.

Gordon, A. David, and John Michael Kittross, *Contro-versies in Media Ethics,* 2nd ed., New York: Longman, 1999.

Graig, James, *Designing with Type,* New York: Watson – Guptill, 1981.

Gupta, V.S, *Handbook of Reporting and Communication Skills,* New Delhi: Concept Publishing Company, 2003.

Gupta, V.S. and Vir Bala Aggarwal, *Media Policy and Nation Building,* New Delhi: Concept Publishing Company, 1996.

Harrower, Tim, *The Newspaper Designer's Handbook,* 4th ed. Dubuque, Iowa: William C. Brown, 1998.

Hart, Jack and Janis Johnson, *A Clash Between the Public's Right to Know and a Family's Need for Privacy,* The Quill, May 1979.pp 19-24.

Hodgson, F.W, *Modern Newspaper Practice,* London: Focal Press, 1996.

Hodgson, F.W., *New Sub-Editing,* 3rd edn. Oxford: Butterworth-Heinemann. Review, 20 (1), 1998, 77-90.

James M. Neal and Suzanne, S. Brown, *Newswriting and Reporting*, Iowa: The Iowa state University Press, 2000.

Joseph, M.K., *Outline of Reporting*, New Delhi: Anmol Publications, 1997.

Judith M. Buddenbaum, *Reporting News about Religion, An Introduction for Journalists*, New Delhi, Surjeet Publications, 2004.

Kamath, M.V., *Professional Journalism*, New Delhi: Vikas Publishing House, 1980.

Kamath, M.V., *The Journalist's Handbook*, New Delhi: Vikas Publishing House, 1983.

Kamath, M V, *Professional Journalism,* Vikas Publishing House, New Delhi, 2000.

Katiyar, A. Value-addition is the key. Vidura, Vol. 34(No. 4), p. 17, 1998.

Katz, J., The Future is the Net, *Media Studies Journal*, vol 13, no 2, Spring, 1999.

Koch, T., *Journalism for the 21st Century,* New York: Praeger Publications, 1991.

Lasica J.D. A Scorecard for net news ethics. (Online available) hyperlink *"http://www.ojr.org/ojr/lasica/1017775272.php" http:// www.ojr.org/ojr/lasica/1017775272.php* (2002).

Leslie, Larry Z., *Mass Communication Ethics: Decision Making in Postmodern Culture,* Boston: Houghton Mifflin, 2000.

Lynette Sheridan Burns, *Understanding Journalism*, New Delhi: Vistaar Publications, 2002.

Manasfield, Matt, *Details on the New design*, Wordsmith, 1997, pp 9-10.

McManus, J., *Market-Driven Journalism: Let the Citizen Beware,* Thousand Oaks, CA: Sage, 1994.

Mencher, M., *News Reporting &Writing*, New York: W C Brown, 1991.

Mencher, Melvin, *Basic News Writing*, New Delhi: UBS, 1989.

Merritt, D., *Public Journalism: A Movement Toward Fundamental Cultural Change*, Wichita Eagle, p.17, October 30, 1994.

Metzler, Ken, *Creative Interviewing*, Englewood Cliffs, N.J.: Prentice Hall, 1977.

Michael Kunezik, *Concept of Journalism*, Bonn: Friedrick-Ebert-Stiftring, 1986.

Michael Norton and Purba Dutt, *Getting Started in Communication*, New Delhi: Sage Publications, 2003.

Nielsen, Jakob, *Differences Between Print Design and Web Design*, http://www.useit.com/alertbox/990124.html, 1999.

Palvik, V.J. *The future of online journalism.* Columbia University, USA (online available) http://www.cjr.org. 2000.

Parthasarathy, Rangaswami, *Here is the News: Reporting for the Media*, New Delhi: Sterling Publishers, 1994.

Patterson, Philip, and Lee Wilkins, *Media Ethics: Issues and Cases*, 3rd ed., Boston: McGraw-Hill, 1998.

Pavlik, J, Journalism Ethics and New Media, *Media Ethics*, 9 (2), 1992: pp 1-3.

Pew Center for Civic Journalism; hyperlink *"http://www.pewcenter.org " http://www.pewcenter.org.*

Phillips, D., *Evaluating Press Coverage*, Kogan page, 1992.

Powers, Jack, *Writing for Interactive Media,* Electronic Pages, 1995.

Ravindranath, P.K. *Press Laws and Ethics of Journalism,* New Delhi: Authors Press, 2004.

Rambo, David C., Obits: *Newspapers' Eternal Draw for Readers, Presstime,* November 1983, pp. 30–32.

Rehe, Rolfe, *Typography and Design for Newspapers*, Carmel, Ind: Design esearch International, 1985.

Rheingold H. The virtual Community (Online Available) *http://www.rheingold.com/howard.html,* 1993.

Robert M. Knight, *The Craft of Clarity: A Journalistic Approach to Good Writing*, New Delhi: Surjeet Publication, 2004.

Rose, Louis J., *How to Investigate Your Friends and Enemies*, St. Louis: Albion Press, 1981.

Rosen J. and Merritt, D., *Public Journalism: Theory and Practice, Kettering Foundation paper,* 1994.

Rosen, Jay. Public Journalism: First Principles. In Jay Rosen and Davis Merritt Jr., *Public Journalism: Theory and Practice.* Dayton, Ohio: Kettering Foundation, 1994.

Rucker, Frank W., and Herbert L. Williams, *Newspaper Organization and Management*, 5th ed. Ames, Iowa: Iowa State Unviersity Press, 1978.

Sanford, Bruce, *Synopsis of the Law of Libel and the Right of Privacy*, New York: World Almanac Publications: 1984.

Schaffer, Jan; hyperlink "http://www.american pressinstitute.org/" http://www.americanpressinstitute. org/, 2001.

Sethi, Patanjali, *Professional Journalism*, New Delhi: Orient Longman, 1977.

Sharma, G. *Impact of Online Journalism on Print Media.* Thesis Submitted to Punjab Agricultural University, p. 6, 2001.

Sharma, Jitendra Kumar, *Ethics of Journalism in Transition*, New Delhi: Authors Press, 2002.

Sheridan, L., *Some First Impressions,* in Staff News, John Fairfax & Sons Pty Ltd, Sydney, 1977.

Siebert, Fred S., Theodore Peterson and Wilbur Schramm. *Four Theories of the Press.* Urbana: University of Illinois Press, 1963.

Singh, S. Nihal, *Your Slip is Showing*, Indian Press Today, New Delhi: UBS Publishers, 1992

Sissors, Jack Z., Do youthful college-educated readers prefer contemporary newspaper designs? *Journalism Quarterly* 51: 1974, pp307-13.

Smith, Ron E., *Groping for Ethics in Journalism*, 4th ed., Ames, Iowa: Iowa State University Press, 1999.

Splichal, S. and Sparks, C., *Journalists for the 21st Century,* Norwood, NJ: Ablex Publications, 1994.

Steele, Bob; The Ethics of Civic Journalism: Independence as the Guide; *http://www.poynter.org/*

Stein M.L. and Susan F. Paterno, *The Newswriter's Handbook: An Introduction to Journalism*, New Delhi: Surjeet Publications, 2004.

Stephen G. Bloom. *Inside the Writer's Mind: Writing Narrative Journalism*, New Delhi: Surjeet Publications, 2004.

Stephens, M. and Lanson, G., *Writing and Reporting the News,* Orlando FL: Holt, Reinhardt& Winston Inc, 1986.

Tapsall, S. and Varley, C. , *Journalism: Theory in Practice,* Sydney: Oxford University Press, 2001.

Thapar, S. *Online Journalism—Strengths and Weaknesses.* National Conference on Media and Society, Himachal Pradesh University, Shimla, p. 2, 2000.

Thomas, R., *Learning News Writing: A Process Intervention in a Product Setting*, unpublished Master of Arts thesis. The University of Auckland, 1999.

Tony Silvia, *Global News: Perspective on the Information Age* (ed), New Delhi: Surjeet Publications, 2004.

Ullmann, John, and Steve Honeyman, editors, *The Reporter's Hand Book,* New York: St Martin's Press, 1983.

Ullaman and Honeyman, *The Reporter's Handbook – An Investigative Guide to Documents and Techniques,* Martins Press, New York, 1983.

Volkmer, I. Universalism and Particularism: The Problem of Cultural Sovereignty and Global Program Flow. 4(Online Available) http://www.ksg.havard.edu/rip/G/liconf/volkmer.html 1998.
http://www.onlinejournalism5-markdeuze.html 1998.
www.ojr.org/internet site—Online
www.newslink.org/ajrtoc/htm (Internet site—American Journalism Review Newslink, *Editor and Publisher Media Information Database).*

Walter Fox, *Writing the News: A Guide for Print Journalists*, 3rd ed., New Delhi: Surjeet Publications, 2004.

White, T et al, *News Writing, Reporting and Production,* Macmillian Publishing Company, New York, 1984.

Williams, Paul, *Investigative Reporting and Editing*, Englewood Cliffs, N.J. Prentice Hall, 1978.

Wolfe, T., *The New Journalism,* London: Pan Books, 1975.

INDEX